A Study of Buddhism in Arakan

Ashon Nyanuttara

ISBN: 0615940447
ISBN 13: 9780615940441

Library of Congress Control Number: 2013923282
Oo Thein Maung, Wheaton, IL

Ratanattaya Vandanā

Saṁbuddamatulaṁ Suddaṁ, Dhammaṁ Sanghaṁ Anuttaraṁ.
Namassitvā Pavakkhāmi, Rakkhaṅgadesasāsanaṁ.

To my parents, brothers, sisters, friends and *dāyakās*
for their kindness and unfailing support

ACKNOWLEDGEMENTS

First and foremost, I am thankful to Prof. Jeannine Hill Fletcher, Professor of Theology, Fordham University, Bronx, NY for her insight remarks on my book appearing as the preface in the book. And my debt of learning goes to my research supervisors, Dr. Wasantha Priyadarshana and Ven. Dr. Khammai Dhammasami for their kind concern, guidance and advice in my studies. My thanks are also due to Senior Prof. *Sumanapala* Galmangoda, Director of the Postgraduate Institute of Pali and Buddhist Studies (University of Kelaniya), Sri Lanka and all the academic and non-academic staff for their restless support and understanding that they have always provided to me throughout my studies at the institute.

Secondly, I would like to express my utmost gratitude to my late preceptor Baddanta Vannasāmi Mahāthera of Sri Mangala Mro Oo Monastery, Rathedaung, Rakhaing State, Myanmar for his kind permission given to me to be a novice monk (*sāmaṇera*) in 2000 March and his kind guidance and initiation to me into the world of Theravāda Buddhist learning. I am also grateful to all the Venerable teachers (*Ācariyas*) who taught me Pāḷi in different Pāḷi learning institutions in Myanmar especially to Ven. Paññā of Sāsanajotipāla Pāḷi Learning Monastery of Rathedaung.

A big thanks to my parents: U Thar Tun Aung and Daw Hla Saw Nyo, brothers and sisters, especially my brothers U Oo Than Hlaing and Maung Than Nyunt, all their love will always be remembered with gratitude. They have unceasingly bestowed upon me all the material necessities and moral support for my education and livelihood in the *Buddhasāsana* as a monk.

Here, it is not possible to leave Venerable Dr. Nāyaka of New York, U.S. to say thanks for his kind support to me when I arrived in Sri Lanka in 2006 January. To him I owe my deepest gratitude. My sincere appreciation also goes to Venerable Dr. Vicitta, Jayamaṅgala Buddha Vihāra, Singapore who encouraged and helped me to be in Sri Lanka for my further studies.

Thirdly, I wish to express my sincere gratefulness to the Most Venerable Alodawpyei Sayadaw Baddanta Ariyavaṃsa (Aggamahāpaṇḍita) for his kind help in the course of my Ph.D. studies. Additionally, all my financial supporters (*Dāyakas*), especially U Mya Han + Daw Khin Sabay Kyi and family (Yangon), U Maw Si Lwin + Daw Muyar Khin and family (Singapore) and Min Banyar San + Ma Thet Thet Shwe and family (Singapore) who have been kind enough to provide critical supports in the long time it took to bring out my studies. Without their kind and generous support, the present studies would have only been in my dream. It is to the aforementioned individuals that I dedicate this work as a small token from their unceasing bestowed upon me. I believe they will probably be happier than I to see my educational accomplishment.

Furthermore, my friend and so often, the driving force behind my work, Aung Myo Oo has encouraged me in my delay working on the studies in Sri Lanka. To him I am so grateful. His encouragement will always be remembered with appreciation. I also wish to thank my junior Ven. Raṭṭhasāra and Ven. Buddhavamsa for their help, patience and understanding me throughout in my studies.

In addition, there are many people remaining to thank, great and small, some of whom cannot be named for giving me the opportunity to widen my academic horizons. The study for this work could not have been done without the knowledge kindly imparted to me by my teachers and professors, as well as all the scholars on Rakhaing Studies, especially Rakhaing scholars. To them I offer my respect. Notably, among those the Late Rakhaing Researcher U Shwe Zan with whom I had a valuable discussion on my studies, to him I offer my deepest gratitude.

Last, but by no means the least, I am so grateful to Mr. Oo Thein Maung for all his help, patience in the endeavor of publishing this book.

PREFACE

We live in a globalized age, where information can race from one side of the globe to the other in an instant. This access to information brings into our awareness peoples, places and histories so readily that we, in the West, have become interested in an unparalleled way in the lives and histories of those peoples so geographically distant yet now accessible at our fingertips. Not unlike earlier ages where advances in travel brought new awareness and saw the demands for new scholarship, these advances in technology increase the demand for information from scholars equipped to provide a thorough context for our understanding.

But, our globalized age brings not only the movement of information; it also facilitates the movement of people through systems of travel in a way unlike any other in history. The interest in a history from the other side of the globe is also an interest in the story of our neighbors. What is the heritage they bring with them as they travel also through these networks that make our world a single place? Here, it is not only the story of the past, but also the continued influence on the present particularly in light of the culture and religion our neighbors bring with them.

This portrait of an age of easy access to information raises the question of *who* is the producer of this information, this knowledge about people and their history. Is the history presented the story of the people as they would present it, or the story told by those outside this history with their own interests in mind?

The history of Buddhism in the Arakan State is the promised new information Ven. Ashon Nyanuttara offers to his English-speaking audience. What is so important about this contribution lies precisely in the limits of the English-speaking world to access histories not filtered through Western scholars. That is, what we have in the West as information about Buddhism in the Arakan State has always come to us through the lens of Westerners. Thus, the history that has heretofore been available has been the history written by 'outsiders', by Westerners telling the story of a land and a Buddhism not their own. What Ven. Ashon Nyanuttara offers, then, is a history 'from within' drawing on Western and native Arakan scholars, and presenting this uniquely for an English-speaking audience.

The reader will be invited to learn about the distinctive history of Buddhism in this close neighbor to India. With its geographical proximity to the land of Buddhism's origin, the potential for a rich and ancient history is in evidence. While the initial presence of Buddhism through a visit of the Buddha himself to Rakhaing remains at the status of legend (not unlike the initial presence of Christianity in India with the apostle Thomas), Ven. Ashon Nyanuttara presents the inscriptions and archeological evidence that demonstrates Buddhism's ancient roots in the Arakan State. Geographically set apart, the compact area of Rakhaing afforded a distinct development of Buddhism in this place, and, as Ven. Ashon Nyanuttara demonstrates, served as site for significant events in the history of Buddhism more broadly. Through this comprehensive and detailed study, Ashon establishes Rakhaing as an area rich in Buddhist history, art and culture.

In being introduced to the history by Ven. Ashon Nyanuttara the Western reader learns both important dimensions of Arakan history *and* an insiders view of what is important in the Arakan culture. Thus, the reader learns from both the history about the place and the historiography (that is, the methods by which the history is constructed). By listening closely to what is emphasized in this study, the attentive reader leans also about which elements of a vast, rich and complex history are especially important to inhabitants of this land. The study, then, is not only informative about the past but gives the reader insight into the qualities and characteristics most valued in the culture as drawn out of the history by Ven. Ashon Nyanuttara.

PREFACE

For the English-speaking reader, this history is both fascinating and invaluable as it offers a window into a world rich in its history and intimately shaped by one of the great and growing religious traditions of the world. Ven. Ashon Nyanuttara's study adds to the understanding of Buddhism as a complex tradition, to knowledge about the Arakan State and its history, and to the awareness of the distinctive history of a particular land and its people as part of the shared story of our globalized world.

Jeannine Hill Fletcher
Professor of Theology,
Fordham University, Bronx NY

TABLE OF CONTENTS

Ratanattaya Vandanā iii
Dedication v
Acknowledgements vii
Preface xi
Abbreviations xix
Abstract xxi

Chapter One: Introduction 1
- 1.1. Sources 5
  - 1.1.1. Literary Sources 5
    - (a) Pāḷi Works 5
      - (i) Pali Scriptures 5
      - (ii) Pāḷi Chronicles 6
      - (iii) Pāḷi Commentaries 7
    - (b) Local Chronicles 7
    - (c) Miscellaneous Works on different languages 11
  - 1.1.2. Archeological Sources 13
    - (a) Inscriptions 13
    - (b) Numismatics 16
    - (c) Monuments and artifacts 18
- 1.2. Objectives 18
- 1.3. Structure and Style 21
- 1.4. Definitions of the Terms 24

Chapter Two: Periodisation of Rakhaing History 29
- Preface 29
- 2.1. Types of Eras Used in Arakan History 30
  - 2.1.1. Cancellation of Dates and Eras 31
  - 2.1.2. Significances of Mahā Era 36

2.2. Religious Era and Kawzā Era: Cancellation of Mahā Era 148 by Ajātasattu and Candasūriya · · · 37
2.3. The Conversion Factor · · · 39
2.4. Cancellation Dates · · · 40
2.4.1. Supporting Evidences of Mrauk Oo Period · · · 41
2.4.2. Supporting Evidences of Dhaññavatī Period · · · 42
2.4.3. Records made by Dr. Forchhammer · · · 46
2.4.4. Indirect or special proofs of Vesālī dating against Phayre's recordings · · · 47
2.5. Comparison of Three Consolidated Datings of Vesālī · · · 51
Summary · · · 54

Chapter Three: The Background of Rakhaing · · · 57
3.1. The Geographical Background: Part of Majjhimadesa? · · · 58
3.2. Flora and Fauna · · · 63
3.3. Emergence of Ancient Rakhaing: the Heredity · · · 63
3.4. Why the Name Rakhaing? · · · 74
3.5. The Inhabitants of Rakhaing and their Languages · · · 75
3.6. Ancient Capitals and their Early Communications and Durations · · · 78
3.6.1. The Capitals · · · 78
3.6.2. The Communications · · · 85
3.6.3. The Durations · · · 89
3.6.3.1. Dhaññavatī · · · 89
3.6.3.2. Vesālī · · · 92
Remarks · · · 94

Chapter Four: Introduction of Buddhism in Rakhaing Land: Legend and History · · · 97
Introduction · · · 97
4.1. Religious conditions: Pre-Buddhist Aryanization of Rakhaing · · · 100
4.2. Buddhism · · · 103

4.2.1. Buddhism as a Religion 104
4.2.2. Religion of the Lay-devotees 106
4.2.3. The History of Buddhism (5th – 4th century B.C.) .. 107
4.3. The Tradition of Gotama the Buddha's Visit to *Dhaññavatī* and the Earliest Evidences of the Presence of Buddhism in Ancient Rakhaing 108
4.4. Tradition of Image Worship in Buddhist Rakhaing 122
4.5. The *Mahāmuni* Image and its Traditions 126
4.6. *Sutthubimba Sutta* (Discourse of Image of the Buddha) ... 133
4.6.1. General Introduction 133
4.6.2. Text and Translation 137
4.7. Developments of Indian Buddhism 147
4.8. Asoka Mission 148
Summary 153

Chapter Five: The Developments of Buddhism in Rakhaing 157
5.1. *Vesālī* Period 157
5.1.1. Epigraphic Sources of Buddhist *Vesālī* 161
5.1.1.1. Quotation Inscriptions 163
5.1.1.2. Eulogy Inscription (*Ānandacandra* Inscription) 171
5.1.1.3. Donation and Royal Inscriptions 193
5.1.2. Archaeological Sources of Buddhist *Vesālī* 205
5.1.2.1. *Stūpa*s 207
5.1.2.2. Images 212
5.1.2.3. Miniature Bronze *Zetis* 217
5.1.2.4. Copper-Plate Land Grant 218
5.1.2.5. Bronze Bells 220
5.1.2.6. Bronze Lamps 222
5.1.3. Fourth Buddhist Council in *Vesālī* of Rakhaing .. 223
5.1.4. Patterns of Buddhist Developments in *Vesālī* Period 230

5.2. A Brief Account of Buddhism in Lay-mro Period 233
  5.2.1. Pañcā city 235
  5.2.2. First Purein city 236
  5.2.3. Second Purein city 236
  5.2.4. Naranjara Taungoo city 237
  5.2.5. Launggret city 237
5.3. A Brief Account of Buddhism in Mrauk Oo Period 238
  5.3.1. Political History 238
  5.3.2. Buddhist Culture 241
Remarks 245

Chapter Six: Arakan Buddhist Relationships with Sri Lanka 247
Introduction 247
6.1. Sources 251
6.2. Pāḷi: The Identity of Thera Tradition and Tool of Communication 255
6.3. Unknown in the Sri Lankan Sources 257
6.4. Sri Lankan Buddhist Revivals in the 16th and 17th Centuries by Arakanese Saṅgha 264
6.5. Religious and Cultural Syncretism 276
Resume 280

Chapter Seven: Concluding Reflections 281

Appendixes 287
Appendix I: Maps 287
Appendix II: Tables 307
Appendix III: Plates 321

Selected Bibliography 397
Index 415

ABBREVIATIONS

B.C.	Before Christ
BCC	Buddhist Cultural Centre, Colombo
B.E.	*Burmese Era*
A.D.	Anno Domini
BPS	Buddhist Publication Society, Kandy
ASB	Report of the Superintendent, Archeological Survey, Burma: Report on Archeological Work in Burma
BSOAS	Bulletin of School of Oriental and African Studies
cont.	*continued*
C.E.	Common Era (Christian Era)
CJHSS	Ceylon Journal of Historical and Social Sciences
Ch.	Chapter
Chs.	Chapters
DPPN	*Dictionary of Pali Proper Names*
CSCD	Satthasanghayana CD ROM
EI	*Epigraphia Indica*
etc.	*et cetera*
Ed.	*Edition or edited*
F.	*Fahrenheit*
ft.	*feet*
ibid.	*Ibidem* (the same)
JAAS	*Journal of Asian and African Studies, Tokyo*
JASB	Journal of Asiatic Society of Bengal
JBRS	Journal of Burma Research Society
ICES	International Centre for Ethnic Studies, Colombo
JRASCB	Journal of Royal Asiatic Society, Ceylon Branch
JRASSL	Journal of Royal Asiatic Society of Sri Lanka
JRASC	Journal of Royal Asiatic Society of Ceylon
Lt. Gen.	*Lieutenant General*

n.d.	no date
No.	Number
op. cit.	*opere citato (*in the work cited)
p.	page
pp.	pages
PEAL	Publishers of Eminent Arakan Literature, Rangoon
Pl.	Plate
Pt.	Part
PTS	Pali Text Society, London
Prof.	*Professor*
q.v.	quod vide (used to direct a reader to another part of a text for further information
R.E.	Rakhaing Era
SEAMEO	Southeast Asian Ministers of Education Organization
sq.	*square*
SLJHSS	Sri Lanka Journal of Historical and Social Sciences
Skr.	*Sanskrit*
SOAS	School of Oriental and African Studies
Trans.	*Translation or translated*
UCR	University of Ceylon Review
URL	**U***niform* **R***esource* **L***ocator, the* address of a World Wide Web page
VOC	*Vereenigde Oost-Indische Compagnie (*East India Company)
V.	*Verse (Gatha)*
Vs.	*Verses*
Vol.	Volume
Vols.	Volumes
Ven.	*Venerable*
viz.	*videlicet (namely)*
WPD	*Working People's Daily*
yrs.	years

A STUDY OF BUDDHISM IN ARAKAN (RAKHAING)

Despite the fact that many researches in Rakhaing Studies has been dominant focusing on political, cultural and archeological issues, this study is an attempt to elucidate the general feature of the history and culture of Buddhism on the inhabitants of Rakhaing frontier land with major attention on Buddhism in Dhaññavatī and Vesālī periods and its Buddhist relationships with Sri Lanka on the basis of the historical dates available focousing local chronicles and epigraphic sources how Buddhist developments taken place in ancient Rakhaing from the period in which the local account of the Buddha's visit to Rakhaing i. e. 6th B.C. to the Burmese conquest in 1784 broadly .

This study comprises of seven chapters. Firstly, in the introduction which forms chapter one, a critical study of the sources, both primary and secondary, is made using them to highlight the importance of Buddhist Rakhaing history in Southeast Asia; in addition to the previous studies by various scholars who have had little access to the original sources, this thesis makes use of the original sources much of it not available to scholars before this. In the second chapter, the periodisation of the Rakhaing history is critically discussed. The third chapter deals with the geographical and ethnic backgrounds to the development of the earliest Rakhaing. It is followed by the feature of religious milieu of the pre-Buddhist Rakhaing. Different Buddhist traditions especially introductions of Buddhism and the tradition of Mah muni Buddha Image are discussed therein. A general introduction and annotated translation of the *Satthubimba Sutta* is also presented. And how Buddhism was introduced into the land is critically examined. Furthermore, in the following chapter, developments of Buddhism in Rakhaing throughout centuries especially in Ves l period are discussed. A special account on the Buddhist relationship between Rakhaing and Ceylon has been discussed in the chapter six. The final chapter reflects on the Buddhist history and culture of Rakhaing which thus emerges, examining in details the rationale behind the developments of the concept of the Buddhist tradition in the land.

CHAPTER 1

INTRODUCTION

Rakhaing has long been a transit land where South Asia and Southeast Asia meet for the development of political, economic, and religio-cultural institutions in the area, and the inhabitants of Rakhaing have been shaped by these developments accordingly, especially by Buddhism. The Rakhaing people possess rich Buddhist traditions in the eastern bank of Bay of Bengal and in the westernmost strip of Southeast Asia.

The Rakhaing people had a long history of self-rule until the Burmese conquest in 1784. There were numerous chronicles written throughout its long history. Many chronicles, however, have been lost due mainly to the considerable long years, Rakhaing's location in the wet tropical zone, no proper maintenance, and past brutal and bitter wars with foreign countries. In addition, until recently, students of Rakhaing history did not focus their attention sufficiently on Buddhist influences on the Rakhaing people because there were few Buddhist historical records directly dealing with these people. Some historians also had difficulty getting access to the original languages of the people. Unlike in Ceylon, where there have been recorded histories like

Dīpavaṁsa, Mahāvaṁsa, Cūlavaṁsa, and so on from the ancient times to the present era, in Rakhaing we had only a few records written on palm leaves that were in the possession of the Rakhaing people or foreigners who occupied the land and may have taken away many ancient manuscripts. In the late 1900s, what records were left were committed into printing under the heading of different *Rāzawons,*[1] mostly by local learned monks and lay people.

Although the majority of researchers on the history of Rakhaing cannot determine the exact dates of the beginning of the royal lineage in the land, they accept that there has been a Buddhist *Candra Dynasty* since about the fourth century AD based primarily on the excavated stone inscriptions, copper plate inscriptions, coins, and cultural artifacts known to us so far. According to the *Ānandacandra Inscriptions,* although we know that there was another dynasty before the Candra Dynasty, we need more archaeological evidence for a complete picture of this dynasty. The archaeological evidence currently available has brought to light a cluster of some definite features of the past Rakhaing to reconstruct Rakhaing history. This, however, mainly deals with the political and religious history of the land. References to other aspects of history such as Buddhist cultural effects on the people are still very meager. Despite the many researches in Rakhaing studies[2] by compe-

1 *Lit.* "king lineage" (most of the Asia Chronicles are written only on kings and their works, which is why those are called Rājavaṅsa in Pāḷi)

2 Pamela Gutman, "Ancient Arakan: With Special Reference to Its Cultural History between the fifth and eleventh Centuries" (PhD thesis, Australian National University, 1976); Jacques Leider, "Le royaume d'Arakan, Birmanie. Son histoire politique entre le début du XVe et la fin du XVIIe siècle" (PhD thesis, Institut Nationale des Langues et Civilisations Orientales, Paris, 1998); Michael W. Charney, "Where Jambudipa and Islamdom Converged: Religious Change and the Emergence of Buddhist Communalism in Early Modern Arakan (Fifteenth to Nineteenth Centuries)" (PhD thesis, The University of Michigan, 1999); Stephan Egbert Arie van Galen, "Arakan and Bengal: The Rise and Decline of the Mrauk Oo Kingdom (Burma) from the Fifteenth to the Seventeenth Century AD" (PhD thesis, Leiden University, 2008); Ashin Sri Okkantha, "History of Buddhism in Arakan" (PhD dissertation, University of Calcutta, 1990).

tent non-Arakanese scholars, no one (except Okkantha) has yet written in any European language a fairly continuous Buddhist cultural history of the land, whereby the rise and progress of the monarchy and of the religious monuments and Buddhist secular and cultural sketches might be traced, and Rakhaing's Buddhist relations with foreign lands, such as Ceylon, explained.

In the earlier works, the full history of early and modern Rakhaing has been described and explained in a more connected form. But there still remain blanks to be filled in the Buddhist cultural history of Rakhaing. For instance, why did Buddhism become a major religion of the people despite the fact that other preexisting belief systems like Brahmanism still prevailed when Buddhism entered into Rakhaing? Although the inhabitants of Rakhaing practiced Brahmanism and other belief systems, their kings as the heads of the state were influenced by the dynamic values of Buddhism because Rakhaing was easily assessable by land and sea routes from the birthplace of Buddhism. Therefore, what circumstances caused the ordinary inhabitants of Rakhaing to adopt Buddhism? To what extent did Buddhism affect them? What role did Buddhism play in instilling the religious identity and cultural values in the inhabitants of Rakhaing Land? When the *Buddhasāsana* entered Rakhaing, what vicissitudes Buddhism had to go through, and what type of Buddhism prevailed throughout the centuries are still hot topics among the researchers of Buddhist studies in Rakhaing. In addition, why was the use of Sanskrit so significant in the history of Buddhism in the Vesālī period in the Rakhaing coastal strip? The purpose of this study is to elucidate the general effect of the history and culture of Buddhism on the inhabitants of Rakhaing frontier land with a focus on Buddhism in the Dhaññavatī and Vesālī periods and Rakhaing Buddhist relationships with Sri Lanka on the basis of the historical dates available. The period from the local account of the Buddha's visit to Rakhaing Land in the sixth century BC to the

Burmese conquest in 1784 is broadly discussed. Until the numerous undeciphered lithic records and bronze and stone images are studied carefully and a careful and systematic periodization of Rakhaing history is made in order to adjust the chronological misconception initially made by Phayre[3] and followed by his nonnative successors, this analysis will remain incomplete.

Additionally, this study explores the Rakhaing's Buddhist relationships with Sri Lanka in the light of local accounts together with the existing secondary literature, and it attempts to give a fairly overall picture of Buddhist intercourses between the two countries. This study especially attempts to correct some mistaken names of Rakhaing and to supplement some missing points in the writings of earlier scholars in this field.

Briefly, this study tries to answer the following questions:

(a) Rakhaing kings had to make alterations or cancellations of then-existing eras in Rakhaing history. Why was that necessary?

(b) When scholars of Southeast Asian history do researches on Burma, why do they mostly neglect to acknowledge the earliest accounts of the presence of Buddhism in Rakhaing and its influence on the people, even though Rakhaing culture is older and more advanced than that of Burma?

(c) How has the geographical position of the Rakhaing frontier affected its cultural developments, especially Buddhism?

(d) Why were the traditions of the introduction of Buddhism and the Mahāmuni Buddha Image so powerful to the

3 Sir Arthur P. Phayre, *History of Burma: Including Burma Proper, Pegu, Taungu, Tenasserim, and Arakan*, 1967 ed. (London: Susil Gupta, 1883). *N.B.* Sir Arthur P. Phayre (1812–1885) was the first commissioner of British Burma (1862–1867). In 1846 he was appointed assistant to the commissioner of the Province of Tenasserim, Burma, and in 1849 he was made commissioner of Arakan. After the Second Anglo-Burmese War in 1852, he became commissioner of Pegu. In 1862 Sir Arthur P. Phayre was made first chief commissioner for the entire province of British Burma. He left Burma in 1867.

Rakhaing people? And what is the significance of the *Satthubimba Sutta*?

(e) What type of Buddhist ascendency flourished in Rakhaing: Theravāda or Mahāyāna? And what vicissitudes did Buddhism go through in the religious history of Rakhaing?

(f) Why did the Sangāyanā (Buddhist council) in Vesālī and Pañcā, cities of Rakhaing, have to take place?

(g) Why did Buddhist Rakhaing have to make a number of contacts with his[4] counterpart, Buddhist Sri Lanka, and vice versa in the history of Buddhism in Rakhaing, and what were their impacts on the people?

1.1 Sources

The sources basic to our present study are divided into two categories: literary and archeological.

1.1.1 Literary Sources

The literary sources on which this work is based may generally be divided into three groups: (a) Pāḷi works, (b) local chronicles, and (c) miscellaneous works on different languages.

(a) Pāḷi Works

The Pāḷi works may chronologically be divided into three parts: **(i) Pāḷi Scripture**: In arguing the different features of Buddhist life, predominately that of the *Sangha*, as discovered by the Pāḷi commentaries and other sources, the aid of the scriptures, both the *Dhamma* and the *Vinaya*, is sought wherever necessary to trace their historical development. Researching either Buddhist doctrinal aspects or the

4 The Arakan people metaphorically called their land "Father Arakan"; it is not exemplified with mother. This adoption was to those of France, Germany, Iran, Afghanistan, Korea, and Vietnam. *State Gazetteer (History Section)* p. 50.

Buddhist religio-cultural milieu is impossible without the Pāḷi scriptures as the earliest and most authentic body. **(ii) Pāḷi Chronicles**: There are chronicles composed in Pāḷi, first in Ceylon and then in Burma. In Ceylon, the well-known ones are *Dīpavaṁsa, Mahāvaṁsa,* and *Cūlavaṁsa,* which have attracted the attention of the commentators who wrote *tīka* such as *Mahāvaṁsaṭīka.* Among the Pāḷi chronicles produced by the Burmans, *Sāsanavaṁsa* is the best known. Here it is thought that no further clarification on those chronicles is needed, because a number of attempts on the textual exercises of those treatises have already been made by Geiger,[5] Law,[6] Malalasekera,[7] and others. Those works are mainly concerned with the religious history of Ceylon and Burma, and very little of Rakhaing (i.e., Arakan, as it is known to the world outside the present Myanmar) has been written or indeed mentioned. A number of studies on Ceylonese relationships not only with Burma but also with Rakhaing have been carried out by scholars using those Pāḷi chronicles. However, so far, the big picture with regard to religious connections with Rakhaing Land remains sketchy. Further research on the Arakanese Buddhist contacts with Ceylon using present available sources, especially the Rakhaing chronicles, is long overdue, and therefore the present research intends

---

5 *The Mahāvamsa or the Great Chronicle of Ceylon,* trans. William Geiger, assisted by Mabel Haynes Bode, with an addendum by G. Mendis (Colombo 1950, 1st ed. 1912); *Culavamsa, Being the More Recent Part of the Mahāvamsa,* chaps. 37–72, trans. William Geiger, and from the German into English by C. Mabel Rickmers (née Duff) (Colombo 1953), chaps. 73–101 for PTS.

6 *Dipavamsa,* trans. BC Law in *The Historical Journal,* vol. 7, no. 4, Colombo, 1958; Paññasāmi, Ven. *The History of the Buddha' s Religion (Sāsanavaṁsa),* trans. Bimala Churn Law, Delhi: Sri Satguru Publications, 1986.

7 G. P. Malalasekera, "The Pāḷi Literature of Ceylon" 1st pub. in 1928 by Royal Asiatic Society of Great Britain and Ireland; repub. by BPS, Kandy, Sri Lanka, 1994.

to mainly fulfill this task. **(iii) Pāḷi Commentaries**: For the reconstruction of the religious history of *Rakkha-maṇḍala* (Arakan), the Pāḷi commentaries, mainly by *Buddhaghosa* at the *Mahāvihāra* at *Anurādhapūra* in the fifth century, are a reliable and fertile source of material. It is worth mentioning here that *Samantapāsādika*, a commentary on *Vinaya*, contains information regarding Indian Buddhist contacts with ancient Rakhaing Land in the reign of the Indian emperor Asoka of the Maurya dynasty. Here again, however, no additional elucidation of those commentaries is needed, because these areas have already been much explored.

(b) Local Chronicles

The chief authorities that I have followed in this study are local chronicles. These are divided into two types: Rakhaing and Burmese. It is a failure that most non-Arakanese/Burmese scholars have only partially consulted or touched on those chronicles and have not listened to them, which is why they could not see the real nature of Rakhaing. There are many hidden things in the local chronicles which we should know of. But the subject of it that has captured the hearts of Rakhaing people throughout the centuries has not received a proper attention it deserves. This is due to difficulty on the part of scholars in getting access to the sources in the original languages.

Chronicles and local legends also serve as primary sources. Although these have appeared at later dates, they are still useful because they usually contain data on both Buddhist practices and indigenous beliefs.

According to *The Rakhaing State Gazetteer Part I History Section* published by the Rakhaing State People's Council in 1984, there were forty-eight Rakhaing chronicles, but only a few of them are now available. We know[8] that a few chronicles[9] exist as the palm-leaf manuscripts. Apart from them, *Rakhaing Razawon Theik Kyan* (New Arakanese Chronicle) by Ven. Candamalālaṅkāra,[10] *Dhaññavatī Razawon Theik* (New Dhaññavatī Chronicle) by Ven. Ñāṇa of Rathedaung,[11] and *Rakkha Maṇḍala Rakhaing Razawon* (Rakkhamaṇḍala Rakhaing Chronicle) by Aung Tha Oo[12] are important for the present study, even though those chronicles are mainly written based on former chronicles, such as *Rakhaing Razawon* by Nga Mae, *Rakhaing Arei-daw-poun* by Ven. Kavisāra, *Dhaññavatī Razawon Theik* (New Dhaññavatī Chronicle) by Ven. Paṇḍi, and various other Rakhaing and Burman chronicles. However, *Rakhaing Razawon Theik Kyan* (New Arakanese Chronicle) in two volumes by Ven. Candamalālaṅkāra is much more reliable and gives a correct chronology for the study of

8 Michael W. Charney, "Living Bibliography of Burma Studies: The Primary Sources," *SOAS*, London, 2002.

9 Shin Kavisara, "Rakhaing Arei-taw-poun" [palm-leaf manuscript number 136913] 1839 [copy of 1787 original], National Library, Ministry of Culture, Yangon, Union of Myanmar; "Rakhaing Murn Raza-krì Arei-taw Sadan" [palm-leaf manuscript, number 1632], AMs, n.d. National Library, Ministry of Culture, Yangon, Union of Myanmar.; Mae, Nga; "Rakhaing Razawon" [palm-leaf manuscript, number 3465a][circa 1840], Oriental and India Office Collection, British Library, London; "Rakhaing Razawon" [palm-leaf manuscript, number 95], 1791, Museum of the Asiatic Society of Bengal, Calcutta, India; "Rakhaing Razawon-ngei," MS Orient, 3413, British Library, London; Sithugammani-thinkyan, "Rakhaing Razawon" [palm-leaf manuscript, number 2297], National Library, Ministry of Culture, Yangon, Union of Myanmar; Ù. No, "Mahā-mrat-muni Thamaing." [palm-leaf manuscript, number 40206] 1745, Universities Central Library, Yangon, Union of Myanmar.

10 Ven Candamalālaṅkāra, *Rakhaing Razawon Theik Kyan* (New Arakan Chronicle vols. 1 and 2 in Burmese), 1st pub. Hanthavadi Press, Rangoon, 1931, reprinted by Publishers of Eminent Arakan Literature (PEAL), Rangoon, November 1997.

11 Ven Ñāṇa, *Dhaññavatī Razawon Theik* (New Dhaññavatī Chronicle), vols. 1 and 2, 1st pub. Hanthavadi Press, Rangoon. (1954), reprinted by PEAL, Rangoon, July 1996.

12 Aung Tha Oo, *Rakkha Maṇḍala Arakan Razawon* (Rakkhamaṇḍala Arakan Chronicle), Mraratana Press, Rangoon, 1955.

Buddhist Rakhaing history. *Rakhaing Razawon Theik Kyan* (New Rakhaing Chronicle) by Ven. Candamalālaṅkāra is regarded as secondary source material.[13] Even though the presently available *Razawons* were written in the late 1900s and were based on former chronicles, such as Nga Mae's *Rakhaing Razawon,* we consult them extensively for this study.

Almost all these chronicles of Rakhaing—like other Indian culture–influenced Southeast Asian chronicles mentioned from *Mahāsammata,* the very first legendary king of the world—record a list of Rakhaing kings starting around 3000 BC. The ancestors of these kings were *Sākiya Clan* from the *Majjhimadesa* of India. Moreover, those chronicles equally claim that the *Buddhasāsana* (dispensation of the Buddha) still flourishing at the present in Rakhaing Land was planted by the Buddha himself during his visit to *Dhaññavatīrattha*[14] from the *Majjhimadesa* of India. *Theravāda Buddhasāsana* in the reign of King Sūriyacakka in the third Dhaññavatī period (580 BC–AD 326) was planted by the missionary *Thera*s, one of the nine groups sent after the third Buddhist synod held in the Indian city of *Pātaliputta* during the reign of *Emperor Siri Dhammāsoka.* Right after the third Dhaññavatī period, that *Sāsana* successively thrived through the Vesālī, Lay-mro, and Mrauk-Oo periods until now. However, such claims would most likely be treated as legends in the writing of Asian history, because legends are the beginning of history; in other words, they help reconstruct some definite picture of the past, which otherwise would not be possible.

---

13 Michael Walter Charney, "The Bibliography of Burma (Myanmar) Research: The Secondary Literature" (2004 Revision), *SOAS,* p. 44.

14 *Lit.* Grain Blessed Land (classic name for Ancient Arakan in the reign of King Candasūriya, a contemporary of the Buddha Gotama).

Here, it is worth mentioning an abstract from *History of Burma: Including Burma Proper, Pegu, Taungu, Tenasserim, and Arakan*, by Lt. Gen. Sir Arthur P. Phayre, the earliest non-Arakanese scholar on Southeast Asian history to recognize the importance of local chronicles (*Rāzawons*):

> The chronicles of Burma are well supplemented by ancient stone inscriptions, generally those which record the building of Pagodas, and include historical events connected therewith. The inscriptions upon bells cast for religious purposes and suspended in the precincts of monasteries and pagodas, in many instances furnish important historical information. Each principle pagoda has also a 'Thamaing' which purports to give the history of the founder of the building, and of its subsequent benefactors. Such documents include notices of secular events.[15]

As for the Burmese chronicles, *Man-Nan-Mahā-Yazawin-Daw-Gyi*[16] and U Kala's *Mahā-Yazawin-Daw-Gyi*[17]are of great value as parallel sources for a political or cultural history of any part of Southeast Asia. In 1829, King Bagyidaw (AD 1819–1837) appointed scholars, monks, and lay people to compile the *former chronicle*, covering Burmese history until 1821. Among those compilers, Minister Scholar Dhamma Thein-gyan, disrobed Maung-daung Sayadaw, was the head of the compilation committee. The chronicle is called *Man-Nan-Yazawin* because

---

15 Phayre (1883), pp. *viii* and *ix*.

16 *Hman-nan Mahā Yazawin-daw-gyi*, 8th ed. (in 3 volumes), Thiha Yadana Sarpay, Yangon (2008 reprint). *The Glass Palace Chronicle of the Kings of Burma*, trans. Pe Maung Tin and G. H. Luce (Rangoon, Burma: Rangoon University Press, January 1960).

17 U Kalà, *Mahā-ya-zawin-gyì*, ed. Hsaya U Khin Soe (Rangoon: Hantha-waddy Press, 1961).

it was compiled in the vanguard of the glass palace. A successor king, Mindon Min, appointed a committee of Burmese scholars from 1867 to 1869 to create the *Dutiya Mahā Yazawin Dawgyi* (The Second Great Royal Chronicle). *Man-Nan-Yazawin* was based on U Kala's *Yazawin*, which was written in 1724 and covered Burmese history until 1711.[18] For this study, however, those Burmese chronicles are less useful in the findings of religious and cultural development in ancient Rakhaing.

(c) Miscellaneous Works on Different Languages

In this group, many Sinhalese works, such as the *Nikayasangaraha*, *Sulurajavaliya*, *Pujavaliya*, *Rajavaliya*, *Rajaratnakaya*, and especially the *Curnika Pota* palm-leaf manuscript, contain valuable historical information for exploring the relationships between *Rakkhangadesha*, as Rakhaing was called by the *Sinhalese*, and *Thein Kho Kywan*, as Ceylon was and still is called by the Rakhaing people.

Outstanding Rakhaing works composed in the Vesāli period (AD 327–818) are many. Some of them are described briefly here. (i) *Medha Paññā Mawgwan Lankā* by Poet Medha Paññā, a minister of the Vesālī Kingdom in the early eighth century AD. (ii) *Thein-Kan-me-dwon Ratu* by Poet Suvannadevi Saw Prai Nyo, queen of Crowned Prince Singhacandra (in the reign of King Sricandra of Vesāḷī, AD 665–701). (iii) *Byee Thone-Se-Thone-Lone Hledaw Than* (*lit.* Thirty-Three Consonants Boat Songs) by Chief Minister Dhamma-zeyah during the reign of King Culacandra (AD 733–769), son of King Singhacandra. Later Rakhaing works such as *Chandra Bwae* (eighth century AD), *Rakhaing Murm Tha Mee E-chum* (fifteenth century AD), and *Okkar Byan Ratu* (seventeenth century AD) were written

18 Patricia Herbert, Anthony Milner, and Southeast Asia Library Group. *South-East Asia* (University of Hawaii Press, 1989), pp. 5–21.

by noted courtiers.[19] *Ratu, Bwae,* and *E-chum* are lyrical poems and are meant to be sung. Their subjects deal with a historical background that injects a sense of patriotism in the listener. There is also a book of well-known legal precedents called *Mahā Paññā Kyaw Shouk Htoon* that was written in the sixteenth century AD. In reality, Rakhaing's royal and lyrical writing were in the Sanskrit and Pāḷi languages up to the Vesālī period. But in AD 677, the practice of using Sanskrit and Pāḷi was stopped, and writers started to use the Rakhaing language and Rakhaing scripts (*Rakkhavaṇṇa*), closely related to those of Aryan and Aryo-Dravidian languages. We find no trace of the Mongolian language in the Rakhaing language. The concept of Mongoliod domination over Rakhaing, therefore, is an absurdity. All these works are used as the foundation sources for the present study, especially for evidence to show how eras were altered or canceled throughout Rakhaing history, in collaboration with the archeological sources.

The Rakhaing State People's Council published *The Arakan State Gazetteer* (in five volumes *viz.* Historical Section, Political Section, Economical Section, Social Section, and Cultural Section) in Burmese in 1984. The present study has frequently consulted Vol. 1 (Historical Section) and Vol. 5 (Cultural Section) of the *State Gazetteer.* The Burmese Socialist Programme Party (formed by General Ne Win and the only political party between 1974 and 1988) published *Cultural and Traditional Customs of Nationalities: Rakhaing* in Burmese in January 1976. It gives a great help for this study as well. We are fortunate to have at our disposal materials that were not available to those previous scholars who worked on the ancient Buddhist culture of Rakhaing; any lack of consultation

19 Tun Shwe Khine, *Rakhaing Sar-so-daw-myah (The Arakanese Poets)* (Rangoon: Saikthay-daw Sarpay, 1991, Burmese).

with those materials would render any reading of Rakhaing history unsatisfactory.

The Journals of Burma Research Society, especially San Shwe Bu's works on Rakhaing studies between the 1910s and 1920s[20] and a number of works by Prof. San Tha Aung and Tun Shwe Khine, also give massive support for this study.

In the later 1990s, many writings on Rakhaing, such as local magazines, journals, and periodicals, were published mostly by *Rakhaing Thar-Gree Sarpay* (Publishers of Eminent Arakanese Literature) in Rangoon. Among those, contributions made by Ven. Cakkinda, a local monk, are greatly useful for this study. In addition, this study has received great assistance from U Shwe Zan, a local Arakanese historian who I interviewed about the chronology and Buddhist culture of ancient Rakhaing history.

1.1.2. Archeological Sources

Archeological sources, equally important as the literary sources for the present study, are broadly divided into three groups: inscriptions, coinage, and monuments and artifacts.

(a) Inscriptions

As having flourished the Buddhasāsana along the history of Rakhaing, in doing of meritorious works, building pagodas, cetiyas, monasteries, scripture libraries, and so on, many inscriptions of donation records were made by kings, royal families and notable citizens of Rakhaing. Such inscriptions are still found in the present day, usually in the vicinities of ancient pagodas and ruins across Rakhaing Land. As those inscriptions are legitimate records, they are essential for all researchers to reconstruct history.

---

20 San Shwe Bu, *Research Papers on Old Arakan* (Yangon: republished by PEAL, 1998.)

The inscriptions found in Rakhaing can be categorized into four types: (i) stone slab inscriptions, (ii) rock inscriptions, (iii) pillar inscriptions, and (iv) image inscriptions (usually inscribed at the back of an image).

Because they include some discourse of the Buddha and chronological dates of kings, those inscriptions are valuable evidence in adjusting the dates of kings' ascents to the throne of Rakhaing. Moreover, they also show the evolution of scripts in Rakhaing. Thus far, Rakhaing culture had been immensely shaped by Buddhist culture.

The Rakhaing inscriptions are a recognized source of trustworthy information for the reconstruction of the social and religious history of Rakhaing, and they are extensively used here in depicting the Rakhaing background. With the help of stone and metal inscriptions, a number of rediscoveries have already been carried out both by local and foreign scholars.[21] But, unfortunately, few of them have been critically studied in the advancement of the academic milieu; in other words, much hard evidence is still being neglected for use in academic research. Notably, the earliest work as an archeological report was done by Forchhammer in 1892, the first head of the Burma Archeological Survey in the ruins of Arakan.[22]

Although the people of Rakhaing claim a history that began in 3325 BC, archaeological evidence has been found

21 "Vesālī Coins" in Sittwe and Mrauk Oo Archeological Museum; "The Ānanda Chandra Inscriptions" (729 AD) at Shit Thaung Temple Mrauk Oo; E. H. Johnston, "Some Sanskrit Inscriptions of Arakan," *BSOAS* XI (1944) 357–385; E. C. Sircar, *Inscriptions of the Chandras of Arakan*, vol. 23, 1957, pp. 103–109, and plates opp. pp. 108–9; Gutman (1976); Gutman (2001); San Tha Aung, *Arakanese Coins* (1979); San Tha Aung, *The Buddhist Art* (1979); San Tha Aung, *Arakanese Scripts* (1974); San Tha Aung, *Anandacandra Eighth Century Rakhaing King* (1975).

22 Dr. E. Forchhammer, *Report on the Antiquities of Arakan* Superintendent, Government Printing and Stationary (Rangoon, 1892).

for a later period of the beginning of the Christian era, after the excavations of the Dhaññavatī City. Rakhaing was a sovereign, independent state from the earliest times up to the Burmese conquest in 1784. Many of its historical documents, however, were lost due to a number of reasons. Only a few primary sources for proper academic research have to be taken into account. Its fine history has been mostly forgotten by Southeast Asian historians. Fortunately, some Western scholars have studied Arakan history by using records of the earliest Western travelers, mainly focusing its political history; however, they paid little attention to the religious history of Rakhaing. And the early history of Rakhaing has been generally considered to be that of a province of eastern India, and perhaps due to this very fact, its study has been neglected by both Indian and Southeast Asian historians. This research therefore examines the dynamics of the religious history from the beginnings of urbanization until the rise of the Burma Empire, which subsequently dominated Arakanese culture. Those records belonging to the earliest era are very much concerned with archaeological and epigraphical accounts—prayer, merit sharing, and chronology of kingship—and most of them are very short donative inscriptions. Even the very short inscriptions of the early centuries contain valuable information, often casually in a word or a phrase on the right back of a Buddha statute, while the longer inscriptions of the later centuries directly offer a wealth of historical material. Ancient inscriptions of Rakhaing include documents, both government and private.

The stone inscriptions are in Sanskrit, Pāḷi, and Arakanese. The Ānandacandra Inscriptions, dating back to AD 729, originally from Vesāli and now preserved at *Shit Thaung Pagoda*, indicate adequate evidence for the earliest foundation of

Buddhism. Dr. Johnston's analysis[23] reveals a list of kings that he considered reliable beginning from the Candra dynasty. The western face inscription has seventy-two lines of text recorded in fifty-one verses describing the Ānandacandra's ancestral rulers. Each face recorded the name and ruling period of each king who was believed to have ruled over the land before Ānandacandra. Additionally, the Ānandacandra Inscriptions confirm the Rakhaing Buddhist relationship with Ceylon in the beginning of the eighth century AD, if not earlier. Archeology has shown that the establishment of so many stone pagodas and inscriptions, which have been totally neglected for centuries in different parts of Rakhaing, indicates popular favor of Buddhism. A few of these many Rakhaing inscriptions, except recently found evidence, have already been reexamined by Dr. Pamela Gutman in her work.[24]

(b) Numismatics

Arakanese coins are the precious archives of the people. Those coins made of gold or silver have been found throughout the years from all four *Vadīs*:[25] *Dhaññavadī, Rammāvadī, Meghavadī*, and *Dvārāvadī* of the state. Some are found through the erosion of mountains or river banks or through digging. Many times, a pot or bamboo tube has been found filled with coins. Where have those coins gone? Some have been maintained by the people who found them. Some have been bought and preserved in the archive collections. Some have been

23 Johnston (1944), pp. 357–385.

24 Gutman (1976)

25 Historically, the four *vadis* were used as the representation of the major regions of Arakan after the Burmese occupation in 1784. In the earlier *vadis*, Arakan had seven administrative provinces, including Moravadī, Jeyyavadī, and Sallāvadī.

bought by businesspeople who do not know the value of the antiques and sell them by high interest only for monetary benefits. Finally, some coins have been melted and made into ornaments by people who have no knowledge about the antique arts.

The Arakanese coins had been used since the fourth century AD as money or for the elucidation of the king's mandate to rule.[26] The coins may broadly be divided into two types: uninscribed and inscribed. Coins stamped around the fourth century AD have no script inscribed, but they have suspicious signs. Later coins mostly have both suspicious signs and scripts, each mentioning title of the king and his date.

These Arakanese coins are especially valuable to the study of Arakanese history. In fact, these coinages prove to be indispensable for those who delve into Arakan's past, as they confirm and supplement the evidence of the names of the inscriptions, and, to some extent, enhance our knowledge of the development of the script.[27]

For nearly a century between the 1800s and 1900s, the coins of Rakhaing were studied by many numismatic scholars.[28]

---

26 San Tha Aung, *Arakanese Coins,* (1979), p. 3.

27 Gutman (1976), p. 131 (italics are mine).

28 They may be explained chronologically as: (i) Latter, Thomas. "The Coins of Arakan: The Symbolic Coins of Arakan." *JASB,* Vol. XV (1846), (ii) Phayre, Arthur. "The Coins of Arakan: The Historical Coins" *JASB* (1846), (iii) Fryer, G. E. "Note on an Arakanese Coin." *JASB,* Vol. 41 (1872), (iv) Phayre, Arthur. "Coins of Arakan, of Pegu, and of Burma." *The International Numismata Orientalia Series,* London (1882), (v) Theobald, W. "On a Symbolic Coin of the Weithali Dynasty of Arakan" *JASB,* Vol. 61 (1892), (vi) "Early Coins of the Kings of Arakan" from Johnston (1944), (vii) McDowell, D. W. "Eight Coins of Arakan from Sylhet." *Numismatic Chronicle* XX (1960), (viii) Collis, M. S. in collaboration with San Shwe Bu. "Arakan's place in the civilization of the Bay: A study of coinage and foreign relations." *Burma Research Society, 50th Anniversary publication's No. 2,* Rangoon, 1960, (ix) Rustom, C. A. "Some Coins of Arakan." *Nation Supplement.* Rangoon. (Nov. 11, 1962), (x) Oo, Aung Tha. "History of Arakanese Coins." *Rakhing Tan Soung Magazine.* 1972, (xi) Chapter III *The Coins* from Pamela (1976), (xii) Aung, San Tha. "*Arakanese Coins*" 1979.

With fresh and important material coming to light, these commendable works may sometimes need to be revised and enlarged into the spectrum of the new evidence. Here in this connection, it is gratifying to report many newly found coins of Rakhaing with reference to this study. The works of E. H. Johnston, M. S. Collis and San Shwe Bu, Pamela Gutman, and San Tha Aung are used as references whenever possible in this study.

(c) Monuments and artifacts

Most of the ancient monuments and artifacts throughout the dynasties of Rakhaing history are Buddhist buildings (i.e., *cetis*), *stupas*, Buddha or *boddhistva* images, temples, *sīmās*, palace sites, *pitikat tikes*, monasteries, royal lakes, and so on. Many other remains are still unknown. I have been to famous pagodas and historical sites in Arakan State during my research as field studies.

With regard to Buddha images, Prof. San Tha Aung's *The Buddhist Art of Ancient Arakan (An Eastern Border State beyond Ancient India, east of Vanga and Samatata)*, Daw Saw Saw Sarpay (1979) and Dr. Pamela Gutman's *Burma's Lost Kingdoms—Splendours of Arakan* (2001), and many other local articles engraved in magazines and periodicals greatly assisted this study.

1.2. Objectives

This study explores how Buddhism influences the inhabitants of Rakhaing Land and how it functions within Buddhist culture. As mentioned earlier, while the dominant focus of Rakhaing studies for the past few centuries has been on political and archeological issues, this study concentrates on religious sketches, particularly those of Buddhists that produced them, and why and how these sketches and practices shaped Buddhists in Rakhaing.

From a variety of perspectives, including historical, literary, epigraphic, archeological, social, and cultural, this study explores the issues that have proven important and definitive for identifying what is has meant, individually and socially, to be Buddhist in this particular region. The study also focuses on historical annals and stone inscriptions to describe how Buddhist developments took place in ancient Rakhaing.

Furthermore, the miscalculation of Rakhaing chronology by Phayre[29] deprives Rakhaing of its real position in world history in general and in Buddhist history in particular. As a result, all successive historians who follow him, especially Westerners such as Gutman,[30] Charney,[31] and many others, have misled us regarding the list of kingships in Rakhaing Land. Therefore, this study argues the incompleteness of those otherwise praiseworthy previous works with the help of the sources now available, especially the Rakhaing literary sources.

Though by no means claiming to be comprehensive, the study nonetheless intends to give a more complete history of Buddhism in Rakhaing throughout the centuries, because all scholars have so far focused only on the socio-political and religio-cultural history of the land. Specifically, this research aims to focus only on Buddhist history of Rakhaing Land before the eleventh century AD as revealed especially by the epigraphic sources, thus contributing to the understanding of the history of Rakhaing in particular and of Theravāda Buddhism in general.

---

29 It should be noted that Phayre was somewhat of a pioneer in the British school of Arakanese history, publishing two important early accounts, "An Account of Arakan" and "On the History of Arakan" in the *Journal of the Royal Asiatic Society of Bengal* in the 1840s.

30 Gutman (1976).

31 Charney (1999).

Although Charney[32] has examined Buddhism in Rakhaing very well in his presentation, there is still much work to be done, because he has only focused on ethnonyms of early modern Rakhaing Buddhists and Muslim immigrants. Dr. Gutman's excellent work[33] on the cultural history of Rakhaing covering the fifth through the eleventh centuries has brought to light a cluster of its culture in that period. However, aside from the fact that her definition of the chronology of Buddhist Rakhaing is contrary to the position generally taken by local historians because she has followed Phayre's miscalculation, she also thinks that ancient Buddhism in Rakhaing was Mahāyānistic. This study argues differently from Gutman's assertion. Besides, this presentation covers some of the remaining phases like before the fifth century and after the eleventh century of Rakhaing culture, especially Buddhism in general, which has not been dealt with previously.

Concerning the debate over when Rakhaing established a Buddhist relation with Ceylon and vice versa, a separate chapter plans to present a new date different from the fourteenth-century date that recent Sri Lanka scholars have suggested. With regard to this, the Colombo Museum *Curnika Pota,* the British Museum *Rakkhangasasana Curnikava, Mahāvamsa,* and many other Sri Lankan local accounts give some information about the three missions made to the land of Rakhaing. Additionally, the Buddhist connection between the two has been the subject of

32 Michael W. Charney, "*Buddhism in Arakan: Theories and Historiography of the Religious Basis of Ethnonyms.*" In: Arakan History Conference, 2005, Bangkok. (Submitted)

33 Gutman (1976).

several scholarly studies by Jayatilaka,[34] Fernando,[35] Wagenaar,[36] Bandu de Silva,[37] Mudiyanse,[38] and others. As mentioned above, they have done some good work on the link between the two countries. It is worth noting, however, that according to local accounts, Rakhaing has sent a number of Buddhist missions to Ceylon since the second century AD.

1.3. Structure and Style

The study comprises seven chapters. First, in the introduction, which forms chapter 1, a critical study of the primary and secondary sources is made, using them to highlight the importance of Buddhist Rakhaing history in Southeast Asia. In addition to the previous studies by various scholars who have had little access to the original sources, this study makes use of the original sources, many of which were not available to scholars before this. In the second chapter, the periodization of Rakhaing history is critically discussed. The third chapter deals with the geographical and ethnic backgrounds to the earliest development of Rakhaing. This chapter is followed by a description of the religious milieu of pre-Buddhist Rakhaing. Different Buddhist traditions, especially introductions of Buddhism and the tradition of Mahāmuni Buddha Image, are

34 Jayatilaka. "Sinhalese Embassies to Arakan," *JRASCB*, vol. 35 (1940): 1–6.

35 P. E. Fernando, "The Rakhanga—Sannas-Curnikava and the Date of the Arrival of Arakanese Monks in Ceylon," *UCR*, vol. 17.1–2 (1959): 41–46.

36 Lodewijk Wagenaar, "Looking for Monks from Arakan, a Chapter of the Kadyan-Dutch Relations in the Eighteenth Century," *JRASSL*, vol. 48 (2003): 91–110.

37 Bandu De Silva, "A Study on Trincomalee in the Sixteenth and Seventeenth Centuries with Special Reference to Relations with Arakan as Revealed by Portuguese Sources," *JRASSL* (New Series), vol. 52 (2006): 175–208.

38 Nandasena Mudiyanse, "Cultural Missions to Arakan (Rakkhanga-Desa)," *JRASC* (New Series), vol. 15 (1971): 26–35.

discussed therein. A general introduction and annotated translation of the *Satthubimba Sutta* is also presented, and how Buddhism was introduced into the land is critically examined. Furthermore, in the following chapter, developments of Buddhism in Rakhaing throughout the centuries, especially in the Vesālī period, are discussed. Chapter 6 discusses a special account of the Buddhist relationship between Rakhaing and Ceylon. The final chapter reflects on the Buddhist history and culture of Rakhaing that thus emerges, examining in detail the rationale behind the developments of the concept of the Buddhist tradition in the land.

According to Antoine Prost,[39] historical writings are of three types: narratives, sketches, and commentaries. Wickramasinghe[40] enlightens more:

> The first type, the narratives, can be characteristics by a clear trajectory of a topic in time. The plan of the book, if not its titles is mainly chronological. In its minimal form it starts from one element, goes on to another later in time, and explains how one went from one to the other although chronological order may not always be respected. The narratives can embrace very long periods such as a reign, a century or a millennium. But on the whole it is adapted to an explanation of changes (why has something happened?). It involves researching causes and intentions. In Sri Lankan studies a good example of a narrative would be Walpola Rahula's *History of Buddhism in Ceylon: the Anuradhapura Period, 3rd Century BC–10th Century AD.*[41]

39 Lucien Febre, cited in Antoine Prost, *Douze Lecons sur l'Histoire,* Paris (1996): 239–241.

40 Nira Wichramasinghe, *History Writing: New Trends and Methodologies*, (Colombo: ICES, 2001), pp. 5–6.

41 Walpola Rahula, "History of Buddhism in Ceylon: the Anuradhapura Period, 3rd Century BC–10th Century AD" (PhD dissertation, Colombo, 1996).

The second type, the sketch, is the mode of historical expose that brings out coherent features. Essentially it answers the question: what were things like? The sketch as a mode of historical writing is less focoused on changes than on what conveys unity. It is usually chosen for works on a particular society or a social group at a given time. For example, Marc Bloch's *Feudal Society* or Kumari Jayawardena's *Nobodies to Somebody. The Rise of the Colonial Bourgeoisie in Sri Lanka.*[42] Cultural history too sometimes needs sketches in order to give an idea of the mental world at a given time.

The third type, the commentary, is the rarest mode of historical writing. It starts off from the various interpretations that have been proposed by historians or contemporaries. It is in fact an essay that analyses other texts seen in context. Francois Furet's *Interpreting the French Revolution*[43] is one example.

The style of the current research has mostly been of the first type, the narrative, but many sketches, comments, and analyses will also be included, because very few academic studies[44] on religious history in Rakhaing have been done. This research basically hopes, as mentioned above, to contribute to what has already been written in those theses and to present a more comprehensive picture. This research, therefore, incorporates not only narratives but sketches and commentaries as well; that is, it is tri-style mixed.

---

42 Marc Bloch, *Feudal Society*, vols. 1 and 2 (London: 1961); Kumari Jayawardena, *Nobodies to Somebody: The Rise of the Colonial Bourgeoisie in Sri Lanka* (Colombo: 2000).

43 Francois Furet, *Interpreting the French Revolution* (Cambridge: 1981).

44 Okkantha (1990), Gutman (1976), Charney (1999).

1.4. Definitions of the Terms

In conducting research on Buddhism in Arakan State (i.e., Rakhaing Land), one immediately confronts the two terms "Arakan State" and Buddhism. Because these two terms have been used in different contexts, their meanings are varied and nuanced. With this come misunderstanding and misinterpretation due to the fact that these terms are rarely defined when they are used. For the purpose of this study, we shall try to narrow the meanings of these terms as they are used herein.

"Arakan State"

The term "Arakan State" is a relatively modern political or administrative term as one of the fourteen states and divisions that constitute the Republic of the Union of Myanmar (formerly Burma). It was born as a state along with the new constitution of the Socialist Republic of the Union of Myanmar in 1974.

Regarding the name of the state, Dr. Pamela Gutman writes:

> Arakan was discovered and forgotten by the rest of the world as its power rose and fell. In the first century AD the Alexandrian geographer Ptolemy knew it as Argyre, the land of silver, which was visited by merchants from southern India. Chinese Buddhist pilgrims of the seventh century knew it and the area of east Bengal within its cultural sphere as A-li-ki-lo or Harikela. The Burmese inscriptions of Pagan and Ava from the twelfth to fifteenth centuries refer to the Country as Rakhaing, the Tibetan historians Rakhan, and the Sri Lankan chronicles Rakhanga. Portuguese explorers from the fifteenth century call it Rachani and Aracan, and were followed in this by the later Dutch and English traders. The spelling "Arakan" became standard in the eighteenth century.[45]

45 Gutman (2001), p. 4 (italicizations by me for emphasis.)

INTRODUCTION

There was no such entity as “Arakan State” until a very recent effort to define the region, mainly as an administrative unit within the Union of Myanmar (Burma). However, this definition is meaningful only for the government of Myanmar and essentially meaningless to its people until the insurgency settles down among the nationalities of the present so-called Union of Myanmar. In this study, we define Arakan or Rakhaing as an independent, sovereign land or country. We will also use the native term “Rakhaing” to represent not only Arakan State but also the majority of the people (i.e., Rakhaing) that lived before and are now living therein throughout this study. The area covered by the term may include places like the twelve Bengal cities (modern Chittagong area), lower Burma (i.e., Pegu), and Syriam (present Than Lyan), for some time in history governed by kings of Arakan.

The term is commonly used differently among scholars, even those from the same field. Gutman and van Galen use simply “Arakan.” Leider, however, prefers Arakan with an adjective “frontier,” while Charney uses “Arakan littoral.”

Geographically, Arakan State is in the westernmost coastal part of Burma in Southeast Asia, and its northern part is the immediate frontier with mideastern India. Southeast Asia is usually divided into two regions: mainland and archipelago. This study prefers Arakan more to be a frontier land between South Asia and Southeast Asia or an immediate land of the far-east Indian peninsula. The main difficulty here lies with the application of the term to regional cultural studies. There is an attempt to divide Southeast Asia into two parts, using its different cultures as the guiding principle. The first consists of the modern countries of Burma, Thailand, Laos, Cambodia, and the insular region; the second consists of Vietnam.

For want of an adequate principle to delineate the area of Arakan State, we shall rely on our own. Since this work proposes to examine mostly ancient Buddhism in the area, we shall use Buddhism itself as the norm to limit the area. We shall deal only with the region where Buddhist culture is present. This area includes mostly the northern part of present Arakan State (i.e., the Kaladan-Laymro Valley), which is now regarded as "Sittway Plain," with some additional reference to the other areas influenced by the ancient city-states, namely, parts of Bengal and lower Burma as stated above. However, there is one pitfall. The political boundaries of the present era cannot be used, for in that earlier time, the ancient civilizations of Arakan were yet to be designated as Arakan State or Rakhaing State.

"Inhabitants"

Inhabitants generally refer to the diversity of people living in "Arakan State" as stated above. Of them, it especially refers to the majority "Buddhist Rakhaings." Throughout the study, Rakhaing refers to the people and Rakhaing Land to their country.

"Buddhism"

The use of the term "Buddhism" gives rise to another set of problems since it is a cultural as well as a religious term. Any attempt to define it must take into consideration its historical context. This study is primarily concerned with the impact and importation of Buddhism into Rakhaing, but in order to study the process of its acculturation, an understanding of its Indian cultural roots is essential. Brahmanism, later known as Hinduism, cannot be neglected, nor can indigenous beliefs be disregarded. The spread of Indian cultures as a whole has been referred to as "Indianization," a term that is also problematic.

Even if we limit our scope to "Buddhism" or even "Buddhism in the Rakhaing State," we do not find ourselves in an easier position. Buddhism has a long and complex history. It comprises not only the Theravāda school but also numerous other schools. These schools have been grouped and designated under various names in different periods, and most difficult of all, there is certainly no single principle to differentiate among them.

Even though the title of this study uses the term "Buddhism," it will not deal exclusively with this particular Buddhism, but rather the ascendancy of Buddhism as substantiated by scholars will be taken as a culminating point or temporal limit for the study. This investigation will focus on Buddhism's effects on the people of Arakan as a whole, with particular emphasis on culture.

"History"

The word "history" is used here in the broadest sense of the term, avoiding any theorized definition or interpretation. The periods in which the inhabitants of Arakan went through with Buddhism, whether the periods are traditional or mythical, are included because the local chronicles write about it and the possibility of the periods can be imagined rationally. Only the periods in the history of Arakan from the earliest times, that is, the fifth century BC, until the end of Arakanese rule in 1784 will be examined. This particular time span can be roughly divided into four great periods: Dhaññavatī, Vesālī, Lay-mro, and Mrauk Oo. Some regard Dhaññavatī as legendary or just a myth. This study will only elucidate some facts on the existence of Buddhism in those great periods, especially in the Vesālī period and its Buddhist culture.

"Culture"

The word "culture" is also used here in the broadest sense of the term, avoiding any theorized definition or interpretation. Here it will mean that predominately the culture of Rakhaing has been a Buddhist phenomenon. It cannot be denied that Indian civilization helped shape Rakhaing culture, but it is incorrect to regard the region as "Indian." The people of Rakhaing, especially those who call themselves Buddhists, are recognized as the creators of the Rakhaing culture.

CHAPTER 2

PERIODIZATION OF RAKHAING HISTORY[46]

Preface

Periodization is inevitable and, if not explicit, almost always implicit in historical discourse. However, cutting up time is no easy task. It is a highly subjective act in historiography and embodies within it emphasis on a particular approach to history or a specific interpretation. Every time one makes incisions across the flow of time in history and decides that suitable segments have been separated, one soon finds that there are so many elements irregularly protruding from the separated segments and across the marked-out incisions. They may tend to suggest that the separations into periods had not been made appropriately, perhaps not at the correct and exact places where the incisions should have been.

46 This chapter is largely indebted to and dependent on U Shwe Zan, *Wethali: The Land of Historic Finds* (Rangoon: Hlaing Kyi Phyu Dhamma Vira Publishing House and e-library, November 2010), pp. 5–59.

Historical study often focuses on events and developments that occur in particular blocks of time. Historians name these periods of time in order to allow "organizing ideas and classificatory generalizations" to be used by historians.[47]

As is further pointed out by John Tosh, "The names given to a period can vary with geographical location, as can the dates of the start and end of a particular period. Centuries and decades are commonly used periods, and the time they represent depends on the dating system used. Most periods are constructed retrospectively and so reflect value judgments made about the past. The way periods are constructed and the names given to them can affect the way they are viewed and studied."[48]

By far one of the most important epigraphical sources for the periodization of Rakhaing history is the Ānandacandra Inscription, which is supported by much epigraphic, archeological, and numismatic evidence from the fourth century AD onward. All will be used and consulted for this study. As for literary sources, Ven. Candamālālaṅkāra's *Dhaññavatī Rāzawon Theik* and local poems written during the Vesāli, Lay-mro, and Mrauk Oo periods, including the periods in which the Burmese and British were present, give a huge help to the study. The aforementioned primary data and secondary sources have also been consulted.

2.1 Types of Eras Used in Arakan History

There are so many essential points to be remembered in Rakhaing history that most non-Arakanese/Burmese scholars disregarded in their writings, so that the chronology of it almost completely went wrong.

47 Arthur Marwick, *The Nature of History* (The Macmillian Press Ltd., 1970), p. 169.

48 John Tosh, *The Pursuit of History* (Pearson Education Ltd., 2006), pp. 168–169.

Based on Rakhaing chronicles and epigraphical data, we have learned that the people of Rakhaing have been using different types of eras for dating. They are namely:

(a) King Kusa Era,
(b) Añjana Era or Mahā Era,
(c) Religious or Sāsana Era, and
(d) Kawzā Era.

Four instances of cancellation or alteration have been observed in early periodizations of Dhaññavatī and Vesālī. The first cancellation took place during King Kan Rāzā Gree's reign, the second and third cancellations in the reign of King Candasūriya, and the fourth and last cancellation in the Vesālī period.

2.1.1. Cancellation of Dates and Eras

In the first cancellation of the King Kusa Era (Kutha Murn), the year 8645 was placed to year 2 by King Añjana[49] in India as well as by Rālamāru in Rakhaing, starting a new era of Añjana or Mahā. In the second cancellation of King Añjana or Mahā Era, the year 148 was set to year 1 by King Ajātasattu of Magadha as well as by King Candasūriya of Dhaññavatī, which started a new religious era by starting year 1 on the date of the Buddha's Parinibbāna. Moreover, King Candasūriya not only started a religious era but also simultaneously started a new Kawzā Era.[50] Third, King Sūriyacitta, the sixteenth in the line after King Candasūriya, altered the Kawzā year 609 to year 2. Fourth and lastly, King Siricandra, the thirty-second king after King Candasūriya or the ninth king after King Dvencandra, renamed the Kawzā year 560 to year 0 and started a fresh era afterward.

---

49 Grandfather of the Buddha.

50 *Medha Paññā MawKun Laṅkā.*

We have learned from Sir Arthur P. Phayre's writing that he seemed to ignore such cancellations and also neglected some essential points in the recordings of Rakhaing history.[51] Moreover, the most unthinkable and unacceptable dating done by Phayre is that he dared to end the BC dates without any reason just after Rālamāyu's cancellation date and started a new Christian year, AD 15. From that same starting point of the Mahā Era, he also recorded the date of King Candasūriya as AD 146.[52] He continued the dating of the successive kings with the same trend, and the end of the third Dhaññavatī became AD 788.[53] At the same time, this ending date became a starting date of the Vesālī. From this point, Phayre started to mention the Rakhaing Era as 150. That means he tried to equate the conversion dates of the two eras by using the conversion factor 638 wrongly. If we count backward from this point, it is sure to reach Candasūriya's reign and coincide with the accession date of the same king in AD 146. If we proceed further backward, it will definitely reach the starting Christian Era AD 15, at the same point of King Rālamāru's cancellation date, which is also the starting date of Mahā. In fact, this sort of conversion method applying in the circulations can be done only after the last cancellation date (i.e., 560 Kawzā) in the Vesālī period. That is also the reason why the ending date of Vesālī became AD 1018, which is two hundred years away from its actual ending date, AD 818.

First of all, let us show one of the supporting pieces of evidence of inscription records engraved Rakhaing Kawzā Era

51 Phayre (1883).

52 Chronological Table of the Kings of Arakan by Phayre (1883); See appendix 2, table 5.

53 Comparative Dates of Vesāli provided by *New Rakhaing Chronicle* by Ven. Candamalalankara.

belonging to the Vesālī period. It is a metal vase with an inscription mentioning a land grant in the Harikela Kingdom, which is now displayed at the National Museum of Bangladesh in Dhaka.[54] It is interesting to note that Rakhaing Kawzā Era dating was engraved as an era of priority among the varieties of eras in existence at that time, and two persons by the name of Kulacandra and Ratnacandra are mentioned in the lists of donors. They are supposed to be the descendants of Candra kings of Rakhaing Vesālī. The Rakhaing Kawzā Era engraved on the vase is 77 RE, which coincides with the reign of King Singhacandra of Arakan during the Vesālī period recorded in the Rakhaing chronicles.

Based on that event, it seems that dating with the Rakhaing Kawzā Era indicates faithfulness to their fatherland as well as Rakhaing culture and their strong Buddhist belief. This remarkable inscription is dated to some years after the final cancellation of 560 RE by King Siricandra. In other words, it was inscribed some years before the ending date of the Vesālī or the start of the Lay-mro period. We cannot count this date by Phayre's recording of the Vesālī period or we cannot say it was during the reign of King Sūriyaketu of the third Dhaññavatī period. That would let us entirely impossible to calculate the period. These discrepancies provide strong supporting evidence that the Rakhaing chroniclers' dating is more reliable than Phayre's recording.

After reviewing all the records of Phayre, it is crystal clear that Sir Arthur P. Phayre had never encountered the records of Vesālī mentioned in the inscription of the Ānandacandra

54 Vasent Chowdhury, *India Museum* (Town Press). "The picture of metal vase" Instead of any other method of dating practiced there at Vanga and Samatata only establishes how prevalent the Arakani (Arakan) cultural penetration was in the Harikela territory at that point of time. (See app. 3, pl. 57.)

Pillar. In the inscription, Dvencandra started to rule Vesālī in the year AD 370, the date of Dr. Sircar's tentative assignment, which is six years from the Rakhaing scholar's date. King Ānandacandra engraved this record in the ninth year of his reign, on which Dr. Sircar's tentative date is AD 729.[55]

From our analytical study of the Rakhaing chronicles, many verses like *Thein Kan Min Dwon Ratu* of Poet Saw Prai Nyo, *Tha Swa Lay Poem* of the Lay-mro period, Adu Murn Nyo's *Rakhaing Murn Tha Me E-chum* (lullaby), and U San Hla's *Mahāmuni Ni Gone Rwa Verses,* and dynastic records inscribed in the stone pillar, we can conclude that there had been more kings who ruled Vesālī for some extra years, which means King Ānandacandra still continued to rule ten years more. After engraving his inscription on the pillar, before his death, Cūlacandra succeeded to the Vesālī throne for thirty-six years after the death of his brother, Ānandacandra. Afterward, Amratu reigned for seven years, Pe Phru for seventeen years, for less than one year by an unknown king, and Nga Murn Nga Tone, son of Cūlacandra and Candādevī, for twenty-four years successively.[56] That means there were ninety-five more years left before the end of Vesālī after King Ānandacandra.

Therefore, the total lifespan of Vesālī becomes 454 years;[57] in other words, the ending date of the dynasty is AD 824. But, the starting date of Vesālī is AD 364, and the ending date is AD 818, which results in a six-year difference between the

55 See appendix 4, Table 4, "Comparative Dates Between Chronicles and Inscription Sides of Vesālī Period."

56 *Ibid.*

57 In contrast to Phayre's counting of 230 years.

two records.[58] Moreover, U Nyunt Han of the Archaeology Department of the Ministry Culture conducted an excavation process during 1981 and 1984 that suggested that Vesālī also existed between the fourth and ninth centuries.[59]

There is more evidence of inscription records engraved with Kawzā or Rakhaing Era dates from the Lay-mro period. Likewise, Kawzā or Rakhaing Era dates such as 180, 290, 451, 452, 480, 488, 573, 612, 657, 692, 718, 759, 783, and 792[60] coincide with the exact reigns of Khetta Thurn, Murn Reng Phru, Murn Bon Than, and Murn Pati of the Pañcā period; Kawlia and Datha Rāzā of the Parein period; Kanbā Long Nge of the Narañjarā Taungoo period; and Alo Mar Pru, Murn Htee, Nan Kyar (younger), and Murn Saw Mon Narameikhla of the Lounggret period, respectively, as mentioned by the Rakhaing scholars.[61]

When reading Phayre's recordings as mentioned in the list, it can be noticed that the dates do not agree with the inscription records mentioned in the Rakhaing chronicles' recordings. These sorts of things have occurred because of unfair adjustments of the Lay-mro period done by the British scholar. Hence, we may assuredly claim that Phayre's recording of the appropriate periods with adjusted Kawzā or Raking Era dates as well as corresponding Christian dates are neither acceptable nor authentic.

Yet again, the two recordings of the Rakhaing chronicles and Phayre seem to be different in many ways due to their two

---

58 U Nyant Han, "Reports on the Excavations of Old Vesālī," *Rakhaing Magazine*, no. 17 (1995), pp. 97–101.

59 U Shwe Zan, "Dilemma of Vesālī Era and the Answer," *Rakhaing Thahaya Magazine*, no. 4 (1997).

60 List of inscription records engraved with Kawzā or RE dating in the Lay-mro period.

61 See appendix 1, tables 2 and 3.

contradicting concepts. We have, therefore, found many discrepancies between the two recordings, especially in Christian Era dating.

2.1.2. Significances of the Mahā Era

Some remarkable occasions to be remembered during the Mahā Era are:[62]

Fig. 1

	Mahā	(Kaliyug)	(Vikram Sambat)
1. Buddha's birth	68	624 BC	578 BC
2. Buddha's renunciation	97	595 BC	543 BC
3. Accession of Candasūriya	97	595 BC	543 BC
4. Buddha's enlightenment	103	589 BC	537 BC
5. Buddha's visit to Dhaññavatī	123	569 BC	517 BC
6. Buddha's Parinibbāna	148(1)	544 BC	492 BC
7. King Candasūriya's death	149(2)	543 BC	491 BC

Present year Kawzā Era of 1374 is the year 560 RE has been counted as the year 1, in other words, which is the total length between the postcancellation date and present date. But the final cancellation date of the Rakhaing chronicles and Phayre do not coincide with each other. The Rakhaing chronicles' date is 560 RE of King Siricandra of the Vesālī period, whereas Phayre's cancellation date is AD 638 (AD 638+10) of King Sūriyarenu's reign in the third Dhaññavatī period.[63]

62 U Shwe Zan, "Pre-Arakan Daññavadī," *Myat Panthazun, Arakan Women Magazine* (2002). pp. 29–40.

63 U Shwe Zan and U Maung Kyaw. *Ancient History of Arakan (Daññavadī Period).*

Phayre overlooked or most probably neglected the first cancellation date of King Rālamāru's reign in King Kusa Era 8645, which is the year corresponding to 638 BC.[64] The Mahā Era started from year 2 at that point, which is the beginning of the most important era, whereby events such as when Gotama the Buddha was born, renounced the world, attained enlightenment, and passed into Nibbāna, were recorded. According to *Medha Paññā Maw-gwan Laṅkā* and *Records of Dhaññavatī*, King Candasūriya ascended the throne, met Gotama the Buddha, cast the Mahāmuni Image and other bronze images, and passed away in the same era. The British scholar failed to mention those facts and figures, which are the most important to a Buddhist country like Rakhaing.

2.2. Religious Era and Kawzā Era: Cancellation of Mahā Era 148 by Ajātasattu and Candasūriya

According to ancient Buddhist records like *Mahāvamsa, Cūlavamsa*, and *Glass Palace Chronicle* (1992 ed.), Ajātasattu of Magadha and Candasūriya of Dhaññavatī[65] on the same day

---

64 Clarifications: 638 BC coincides with the cancellation date of 8645 king Kusa Era and was made 2 Mahā Era, the Buddha attained Nibbana 148 Mahā Era = 492 BC = 1 RE Mahā (148 + 492 = 640) = AD 1 AD = 1 RE + 492 = 493 Arakan scholars Mahā 2 = (Ralamaru's first cancellation) = 638 BC.

65 King Ajatasattu of Magadha was a contemporary of King Candasūriya of the third Dhaññavatī.

king Sri Dhammāsoka of Maryura's		king Sūriyacakka of third Dhaññavatī's	
Accession date 218 RE	274 BC	Accession date 214 RE	278 BC
Buddha's death Mahā 1	218 RE (+)	Buddha's death Mahā 1	214 RE (+)
		492 BC	492 BC
Lifespan of the Buddha	80	(+)	Lifespan of the Buddha
80 (+)			
(i.e., Buddha's birth)	572 BC	Buddha's birth	572 BC

Reference: Zan, U Shwe. and U Maung Kyaw. *History of Ancient Arakan (Dhaññavatī Period)*, pp. 157–166.; Hla, U San. *Mahāmuni Nigone Rwa Verse Reference to Doe Wai's History.*

cancelled the Mahā Era 148 after the Buddha's Parinibbāna. The new eras of Sāsana and Kawzā started after that. The corresponding Christian years of the Buddha's birth and his Parinibbāna are in the seventh century BC and the sixth century BC respectively. The Religious Era and the Kawzā Era have been used in the Rakhaing chronicles up to today.

The Sāsana or Religious Era has been used without break since the date of Buddha's Parinibbāna. There were, however, two more alterations or cancellations in the Kawzā Era made by King Sūriyacittra, the sixteenth in the line of Candasūriya and Siricandra of Vesālī, the thirty-second king after Candasūriya. The last cancellation date is in 560 Kawzā Era; from that date, a fresh Kawzā date was started in AD 638 as proved in the following. The present Kawzā became 1374, which is the length of years counted between the cancellation date of King Siricandra and the present date.

The three types of eras being used at present in Burmese or Arakanese calendars are:

1. Sāsana (Religious) Era 2556
2. Kawzā Era 1374
3. Christian Era AD 2012

Fig. 2

Kawzā era	Christian era	Conversion factor
1374	AD 2012	(-) 638
Vice Versa		
Christian era	Kawzā era	Conversion factor
AD 2012	(-) 1374	(+) 638
Religious era	Buddha's Parinibbāna	Christian era
2556	(-) 544 BC (Kaliyug)	(+) AD 2012

In fact, these are establishing facts in the recordings of the Rakhaing chronicles. Without the knowledge of the above mentioned particulars, it will be very difficult to get correct and authentic records of the Rakhaing chronicles.

Moreover, Christian Era dating was introduced only by British scholars in the nineteenth century. The British came to Rakhaing Land after the country had experienced forty years of Burmese rule from 1784 to 1824. Hence, they could not form a correct idea of Rakhaing Kingdom from antiquity. They could only form a superficial idea of Rakhaing having seen its ancient monuments.

2.3. The Conversion Factor

Two different concepts of last cancellation dates and corresponding Christian Eras become the conversion factor for both sides.

(A) Rakhaing chronicles' counting in reverse order starting from the present day to the postcancellation date in King Siricandra's reign of Vesālī:

1. AD 2008 to 1948 (Independence Day) = 60 years
2. AD 1948 to 1824 (British occupation) = 124 years
3. AD 1824 to 1784 (Burmese rule) = 40 years
4. AD 1784 to 1430 (Mrauk Oo period) = 354 years
5. AD 1430 to 818 (Lay-mro period) = 612 years
6. AD 818 to 638 (Postcancellation date of Siricandra and ending date of King Ngaton or starting date of King Khetta Thurn) = 180 years

Total Years = 1370 years

(B) Phayre's counting in reverse order starting from the present day to Sūriyarenu of the third Dhaññavatī period:

1. AD 2008 to 1948 (Independence Day) = 60 years
2. AD 1948 to 1824 (British occupation) = 124 years

3. AD 1824 to 1784 (Burmese rule) = 40 years
4. AD 1784 to 1430 (Mrauk Oo period) = 380 years
5. AD 1430 to 1401 (Lay-mro period) = 386 years
6. AD 1401 to 818 (Vesālī period) = 230 years
7. AD 788 to 638 (up to King Sūriyarenu's reign of the third Dhaññavatī) = 150 years

Total years = 1370 years

Rakhaing Chroniclers Phayre Difference

1. Mrauk Oo period	354 years	380 years	-26 years
2. Lay-mro period	612 years	386 years	+ 2 2 6 years
3. Vesālī period[66]	180 years	230 years	-50 years
4. Dhaññavatī period	150 years	-150 years	

Balanced

If we countercheck the difference between the two groups, we will definitely get a balanced sheet as shown above. It is, therefore, unjustified to allege that Phayre's periodization and dating of the Rakhaing chronicles is inauthentic, as it is only an unadjusted and makeshift documentation of recordings, which should be kept aside from the ancient historical records.

2.4. Cancellation Dates

According to the Rakhaing chronicles, Siricandra of Vesālī and Popa Saw Rahan of Bagan were the contemporary kings who took the last cancellation of Kawzā 560 in Rakhaing and Burma respectively. But, in contrast to the Rakhaing chronicles' concept, Phayre equates Popa Saw Rahan with Sūriyarenu of the third Dhaññavatī[67] instead of Siricandra of the Vesālī. It has also occurred because

66 Between the postcancellation date and the ending date of the Vesālī period.

67 A. M. B. Irwin, *The Burmese and Arakanese Calendar,* (Rangoon: Hanthawaddy Press, 1909), p. 92.

of adjustments made by Phayre especially in the Lay-mro, Vesālī, and third Dhaññavatī periods. It is very much doubtful to say that the motive of Phayre is the standing positions of Bagan and Vesālī periods.

2.4.1. Supporting Evidence of the Mrauk Oo Period

So far we have already verified the periods of Vesālī and Lay-mro. To complete the whole records of the Rakhaing chronicles, it is better to continue to show more supporting evidence of the rest of the periods of Rakhaing. We can show at least two types of inscription records belonging to the Mrauk Oo period. One is a record inscribed in stone slabs engraved with Rakhaing Kawzā dates, and the other is coins engraved with Rakhaing Kawzā dates on both sides, which is presumably the accession date of a king who is believed to have ruled Mrauk Oo in this particular date. Certain powerful kings occasionally issued coins more than once in some special occasions during their reigns. Here, we prefer to present the records of Mrauk Oo coins issued by successive kings of three periods. Out of the collections of Mrauk Oo coins, we can show at least twenty-nine types of coins engraved with Rakhaing Kawzā Era starting from the founder King Narameikhala, an alternate name of Murn Saw Mon, up to the ending King Samatta Rāzā, also called Aggo Puñña Zaw, covering thus all of the Mrauk Oo period. If we sum up the years between the coins of successive kings throughout the three periods, we will get 354, which agrees with the total span of the Mrauk Oo period as recorded by the Rakhaing chroniclers. But the total length of the Mrauk Oo period as recorded by Phayre is 380 years. It has been also shown that there are certain discrepancies in the recordings including even the Mrauk Oo period.

2.4.2. Supporting Evidence of the Dhaññavatī Period

Up to now, we have clarified the Vesālī period of the Rakhaing chronicles. It is essential to continue to clarify the remaining Dhaññavatī period, out of which the range starting from Rālamaryu's reign, the twenty-fourth in line of Kan Rāzā Gree dynasty, down to Sūriyaketu's reign, the last king of Candasūriya dynasty and father of Mahā Taicandra, the founding king of the Vesālī period, are the most important to be clarified. Why and how? The following are some of the reasons why it has to be shown.

If we go back about three millennia, deep into the ancient history of the land, we may notice some occasions, out of which two events in the early part of the third Dhaññavatī (i.e., in the sixth to fourth centuries BC) are the greatest and most interesting of all regarding the development of Buddhism in Rakhaing.

From the ancient Rakhaing historical point of view, Rakhaing King Rālamaryu, twenty-fourth in the line of Kan Rāzā Gree, altered the ancient King Kusa Era 8645 to 2 as mentioned above, and what is more, the resulting era happened to be called the Mahā Era (*Mi Ba San Zi*).[68] In that era, as already mentioned above, Gotama the Buddha was born in the year 68 (624 BC). According to Vikram Sambat, the Buddha renounced the world in the year 97 Mahā (595 BC), attained enlightenment in 103 Mahā (589 BC), and passed into Nibbāna in 148 Mahā (544 BC).

Moreover, we have further learned that Candasūriya, the founder of the third Dhaññavatī, was also born in the year 72 Mahā (620 BC), ascended to the Rakhaing throne in the year

68 See U San Tha Aung, *Arakanese Coins*; Ibid.; U Shwe Zan, "Mrauk Oo Period Coins or History Foretold by Coins," *Rakhing Magazine*, vol. 24 (Sittway).

97 Mahā (595 BC), and passed away in 149 Mahā (543 BC). In other words, Gotama the Buddha and King Candasūriya were contemporary to each other in the Mahā Era (seventh century to sixth century BC).

Furthermore, we have also learned that Gotama the Buddha is said to have visited Dhaññavatī and preached to King Candasūriya and his subjects in 123 Mahā (569 BC). And King Candasūriya was allowed to cast a famous bronze image of Mahāmuni in that time.

As we all know, for forty-five years, the Buddha and his disciples traveled from place to place, preaching to people of all spheres of life, and the greatest kings of the time favored the Teacher and his disciples. The local chronicles attest that those events happened during King Candasūriya's reign.

Yet again, after a lapse of nearly three hundred years, another important and impressive event occurred. This time, it happened during the reign of King Sūriyacakka, a religious king, a great-great-great grandson of King Candasūriya, the founder of the third Dhaññavatī dynasty, the original donor of the famous Mahāmuni Image, and the foremost Buddhist king and believer of Buddhasāsana.

King Sūriyacakka ruled Rakhaing Kingdom of the third Dhaññavatī from 214 to 258 Sāsana Era or 278 to 234 BC with the chief Queen Rūpitā.[69] King Sūriyacakka was a contemporary of King Asoka of Pātaliputta of ancient India. King Asoka descended the Maurya throne in 218–255 Sāsana Era or 282–252 BC, only different four years from the accession date of King Sūriyacakka of Rakhaing.[70]

---

69 *Medhapaññā Mowgwan Laṅkā*, passage 3.

70

Sri Dhammāsoka Reign	= 218-258 RE	282-252 BC
Sūriyacakka Reign	= 214-258 RE	272-234 BC

King Asoka, conqueror of the Mauryan dynasty in India, is in world social history reputedly described as courageous, wise, and honorable. The king sponsored the Third Buddhist Council led by Thera Moggaliputtatissa and five hundred senior monks in 235 Sāsana Era. The Buddhist Synod lasted from June to February in 235 Sāsana Era (257 BC) with senior monks.[71]

Just after the end of the third synod, the Mauryan Emperor sent religious missions to nine regions with some of Gotama the Buddha's relics, which were secretly kept by Ajātasattu, the king who sponsored the First Buddhist Council and simultaneously cancelled Buddha's parinibbāna date of 148 Mahā Era and started a new Sāsana Era by year 1 as a new starting date, which can be equated with 544 BC.[72]

Among those Buddhist missionaries, a group of missionaries lead by Thera Mahādeva, together with four other senior monks, is said to have been assigned to go to *Mahinsakamaṇḍala*, Dhaññavatī City of ancient Rakhaing.[73] Here we have observed that the arrival date of this mission to Dhaññavatī is supposed to have coincided with the casting times of the Candamuni Buddha Image and four other images by the King Sūriyacakka. We have learned that the metals used in the casting of these images happened to be from the same stock of noble alloy (mixture of gold, silver, copper, iron, and lead) used in casting of the famous Mahāmuni Image. Out of these five images, only one, known by the auspicious title "Candamuni Image," is left today. This image is now resting

71 U Shwe Zan and U Maung Kyaw, *Ancient History of Arakan (Dhaññavatī Period)*, vol. 1, p.166; Ashin Tilokathāra, *Myat Mangalā Buddhist Questions and Answers* (May 1990), p. 26.

72 Ibid.

73 *Medhapaññā Mowgwan Laṅkā*, passage 3.

magnificently on top of a hillock in the precinct of Bandulla Monastery in Mrauk Oo, the last capital of Rakhaing.[74]

Moreover, the Buddhist mission, together with the king and people, built *stūpas,* cetiyas, and pagodas enshrined with Buddha's relics, ranging from Selāgīri Kyauktaw Hill to U Rait Taung Hill of Ponnagyun.[75]

Those are, in fact, the pagodas erected as predicted or foretold by Gotama the Buddha to Ānanda when the Buddha visited Dhaññavatī in 123 Mahā or 569 BC.[76] To support these great occasions as mentioned above, we have discovered inscription records in the Pāḷi language with Brahmi scripts. The first one is called Taung Bouk Gree Brahmi Inscription (rock inscription)[77] and describes the aerial visit of Gotama the Buddha with his five hundred disciples to Dhaññavatī. The inscription also reveals information about their landing on the Selāgīri Hill in the east of Kissapanadī (now Kaladan River). That is the supporting evidence of Gotama the Buddha's visit to Dhaññavatī.

The other one is the Fat Monk Stone Image Inscription inscribing *Saccakaparibbājaka(ji)na* in Brahmi script at the back of the artifact.[78] This is one of the Buddha's incidents with Saccaka ascetic. In fact, an incident in Buddha's life story is one of the indications of the flourishing time of Buddhism in Rakhaing Land where we have collected the artifacts.

---

74 Kyaw Zaw Hla, *Candamuni Image.*

75 U Shwe Zan, "Pre-History: Dhaññavatī Period," *Myat Pan Thazin Magazine* (Rangoon: Rakhing Women Association), pp. 9–12; U Sein Nyo Tun, *The History of Rakhapura as Foretold by Guatama Buddha.*

76 Ibid.

77 U Shwe Zan, *Dhaññavatī Period.*

78 Ibid.

2.4.3. Records Made by Dr. Forchhammer

Dr. Forchhammer, a renowned German archaeologist, in his work entitled "Mahāmuni Image," also stated the importance of a palm-leaf manuscript by the name of *Sappadānapakārana* recording the legend about Gotama the Buddha's visit to Dhaññavatī with his five hundred disciples by aerial journey. While sojourning in Dhaññavatī during the Candasūriya's reign, the Blessed One complied with the king's request for permission to cast an image, Mahamuni, the exactness to the great Teacher.[79]

We have understood that those former two inscriptions are supposed to be engraved with similar language and scripts used in the Asokan period of India, where Theravāda Buddhism has flourished to the full blossom. It shows that King Suriyacakka's reign in Rakhaing and King Asokan's period in India were contemporary to each other and existed within a millennium before Christian dates.

Recently, we have discovered an eighteen-inch copper image of excellent workmanship with Bumiphassa and Dhammacakka mudras on which the date 520 RE and the name of the donor King Sūriyakula have been inscribed at the back of the image.[80] The famous *Ye dhammā* verse in Pāḷi with Brahmi script has also been inscribed at the front of the pedestal. In the Rakhaing chronicles, we have read that Sūriyakula is the fourteenth king, the one that reigned before Sūriyacittra, the king who ordered the third cancellation of Kawzā Era 609

---

79 Forchhammer (1892); U Shwe Zan, *The Golden Mrauk Oo: an Ancient Capital of Arakan*. Yangon: U Shwe Zan (Patron, Rakhaing Thahaya Assocition), Second Edition, 1997.

80 Zan, U Shwe. "Pre-History: Dhaññavatī Period." *Yangon: Myat Pan Thazin Magazine*, Rakhaing Women Association, 2002.

(AD 116/AD 79) in this period. Without doubt, it is also evidence that Rakhaing was the place where Buddhism flourished well.

In fact, those happenings and findings are really remarkable records and supportive evidence of the flourishing time of Theravāda Buddhism before the Christian Era in both Mauryan India and Rakhaing Dhaññavatī. Phayre's concept of dating in AD era starting from Rālamaryu is in sharp contrast to the Rakhaing chronicles, which is entirely unacceptable.

To confirm the actual positions of the respective period and dating, see the Comparative Statement of Dates of Rakhaing Chronicles, Phayre and Dr. Sircar's Tentative Assignment (tables provided in appendix 2).

2.4.4. Indirect or Special Proofs of Vesālī Dating against Phayre's Recordings

There are two types of recordings in the Vesālī period: chronicles and inscriptions. Firstly, let us brief the possession of inscribed Vesālī coins and artifacts, which belong to the same period and inscribed with the names of donor kings or queens in chronological order as listed below.

Fig. 3

Coins[81]	Artifacts[82]
1. Suriya coins	1. Yaksa General Panāda inscription of Mahāmuni Shrine
2. Rājacandra coin	2. Copper plate land grant of Bhuticandra,
3. Devacandra coin	3. Dedicatory inscription of Nīticandra.
4. Yajanacandra coin	4. Dedicatory inscription of Vīracandra.
5. Candrabandhu coin	5. A ring belonging to Nīticandra.
6. Bhūmicandra coin	6. Inscription of Dhammavijaya (land grant)
7. Bhūticandra coin	7. Ānandacandra Inscription Pillar (Shitthaung pillar)
8. Nīticandra coin	8. Dhammavijaya inscription
9. Vīracandra coin	
10. Priticandra coin	
11. Prithivicandra coin	
12. Dhriticandra coin	
13. Dharmmaraja coin	

81 U Shwe Zan, *Wethali: The Land of Historic Finds. Ibid.* p. 17 abstracting from Sandamuni Bhikku, U. *Origin and Development of Arakanese (Rakhing) Script* Volume I. PhD (Arts) Thesis, Calcutta, University Kolkata, 2003, Plates VIIIa-VIIIb, XVI, XIX, XXX.

82 *Ibid.*, Chapter IV. p.138, Paleography of Coin legend: Vesālī Period. (Vol: II Pl. XLVI to Pl. LVIII); Zan, U Shwe. *The Golden Mrauk Oo: an ancient Capital of Rakhine.* Yangon, 1997, p.55, Coins struck by Rajasondra and Varieties of other coins found in Khayine village. Text by U Sandaumi Bhikkhu, Vol: 1 SN 17 (Vol. II PIXIX), SN 36 (Vol. II xxxVIIa, xxxVIIb), SN 37(Vol: II Plts. xxx 1xa, xxx1xb)

14. Dharmavijaya coin
15. Dharmmacandra coin
16. Ānandacandra coin
17. Sula Mahā Raza coin

On the contrary, we have not collected any artifacts or coins of Vesālī kings belonging to the chronicle. It shows that there existed no two Vesālī but only single Vesālī recording in two different versions: namely, one named with traditional alternate names of kings (chronicle version) and other with ancient nicknames of kings (inscription version). Nevertheless, it is very fortunate to say that we are able to select certain common kings with alternate names out of those two versions of recordings. Those kings are, in fact, the most remarkable ones among the rulers belonging to the Vesālī period. They are listed in figure 4.

Fig. 4

Inscription side	Chronicle side	Remarks
1. Dvencandra	1. Taingcandra (See V 19, 20, 31)[83] of Ānandacandra Inscription (Second Vesālī period)	Founder king
2. Rājacandra	2. Rāzacandra	Second in line of the Vesālī period
3. Kālacandra	3. Kālacandra	Third in line of the Vesālī period

83 Zan, U Shwe. *Some Justifications about Vesālī: a single Rakhine Dynasty existing between Fourth and* Ninth *century*. Yangon: Myat Pan Tha Zin Magazine, Arakan Women Association. p. 206 and p. 212; Zan, U Shwe. and U Maung Kyaw. "*Study of Ancient Arakan History-Vesālī Kyauk Hlay Gar Period*" Vol: II, Parts 1 and 2.(Unpublished)

4. Dharmasura	4. Dharmarājā Synonymous with Dhammavijaya (coin found)
5. Dharmavijaya	5. Siricandra Patron of Buddhist synod and the last king, who cancelled the Kawzā Era 560 and started a fresh Kawzā Era
6. Dhammacandra	6. Singhacandra Husband of Queen Suvannadevi
7. Ānandacandra	7. Thūlacandra[84] Saw Prai Nyo and father of Ānanda Chandra and Cūlacandra
8. Sulacandra	8. Sulacandra The king who was drowned in Nagries Bay after returning from the Tagaung expedition

Moreover, with the help of table 1 provided in appendix 2, we can equate the two records of each with only few differences of years, which is rather negligible difference of figurers.

84 Hla U San. "*Mahāmuni Ni-gone-rwa Poem (Establishing City and Palace Section)*" Passage 2. Paragraph 3, Mentioning of : *Htula Chandra, known another as Ananda, Epithets of the King* (ထုလစန္ဒြ တွင်ပြားတစ်ဖြာ အာနန္ဒာဟု သညာနာမံ့ဘွဲ့အဘိဓာန်ရင်မှာ); *born as Chadra, later Ānanda* (စန္ဒရားဇာတ အာနန္ဒာလျှင်)

2.5. Comparison of Three Consolidated Datings of Vesālī

Fig. 5

Different Datings	Starting Date	Ending Date	Span
1. Chronicle Dating	AD 327	AD 818	491 yrs.
2. Inscription Dating[85]	AD 370	AD 824	454 yrs.
3. Phayre's Dating	AD 788	AD 1018	230 yrs.

By reviewing the above comparisons of dating methods, we may claim with certainty that we cannot definitely equate either Phayre's starting/ending dates or their spans with inscription side dating of Vesālī. Unquestionably, it is another proof of Phayre's unacceptable and unreliable recording of respective period and dating of Rakhaing Chronicles. In fact, these sorts of discrepancies happened because of unfair and unreasonable adjustments of reigns by only whims and fancies of the British scholar. After all, these things are said to be unjustified recordings of Phayre by making so many puzzles to the actual and authentic recording of the Rakhaing Chronicles.

In conclusion, we have noticed that the whole length of Rakhaing historical periods prepared by Phayre is 695/621 years shorter than the one counted by Rakhaing Chronicles. It shows Phayre was a person who adjusted or rearranged the reigns of each king as well as the length of each period to shorten the whole lifespan of Rakhaing Chronicles starting from Mārayu down to Sammatarāzā, the last king of Rakhaing Kingdom.

85 Dr. Sircar's *Tentative Assignment,* table 2 Comparative Dates between Chronicle and Inscription side Vesālī period. Chorological Tables of the kings of Arakan Dynasty of Vesālī by Sir Arthur P. Phayre's *History of Burma* (1883),"*Chronological Table of the Kings of Arakan, Dynasty of Dhannavati*" See appendix 2, table 5.

Phayre firstly measured the length of the first Dhaññavatī as it can be found in the chronicles' record as 1818 years: The Kyauk Padaung period of Kan Rāzā Gree, when the king settled there for 24 years before he occupied the Dhaññavatī City and from that place downward to Rālamaryu's reign, is measured as 824 years. The total sum of the three figures happened to be 2666 years. Phayre counted these numbers as BC dates, thus making the figures 2666 as 2666 BC as the founding date of first Dhaññavatī by King Mārayu. In the same way, the addition of total length between King Kan Rāzā Gree and the twenty-fourth king Rālamaryu is 1842. After deduction of 1842 years from 2666 years, the result is 824 years. Phayre again marked the addition of 824 + one year = 825 as the founding date 825 BC of second Dhaññavatī by Kan Rāzā Gree.

This downward trend in Rālamaryu's reign would become the turning point of BC dates into AD dates. Rālamaryu dating became AD 15, and consequently, the accession date of Candasūriya became AD 146. If we proceed further downward, the date of Sūriyarenu, the nineteenth king of the third Dhaññavatī, became AD 638, which Phayre counted as the contemporary date of conversion factor 638 of Bagan. From that point of Sūriyarenu, the Christian Era 638 became the conversion factor of Phayre's recording of the Rakhaing chronicles, and from that date downward, the British scholar counted the Christian Era in to Rakhaing Kawzā Era. By this way of calculation, the ending date of the third Dhaññavatī and starting date of the Vesālī are counted as AD 788. If we proceed further downward, the ending date of the Vesālī and starting date of the Lay-mro period would become AD 1018. Surprisingly, Phayre failed to count the Rakhaing Era or Kawzā Era from Sūriyarenu down to Sūriyaketu, the last king of the third Dhaññavatī.

Since there is no Kawzā Era to be counted, Phayre's using figure of the king's reign by adding the conversion factor 638 to get the Kawzā date is an improper, twisted, and turned way. Only in the case of the reign of Mahātaicandra, Phayre could show the Kawzā dates 150 RE[86] abruptly with an unreliable date in contrast to the actual date of 249[87] Kawzā Rakhaing date accepted by Rakhaing Chronicles.[88]

Due to the Phayre's wrong way of calculating dates, he counts the end of the third Dhaññavatī and the starting date of the Vesālī as the eighth century AD. Similarly, the ending date of the Vesālī and the starting date of the Lay-mro period are counted as the eleventh century AD with the result being at least two hundred years different from the Rakhaing chronicles. Moreover, the total length of the Vesālī counted by Phayre is 230 years instead of 454/491 years as given by Rakhaing chroniclers. The Lay-mro period was also counted by Phayre as 386 years instead of the actual length of 612 years.

By looking at table 4 of appendix 2, between the chronicle and the inscription with Dr. Sircar's tentative dating, the two sides can be compared,[89], whereas Phayre's recording and Dr. Sircar's tentative dating are not comparable because of unfair adjustments of reigns and periods made by the British scholar.

In conclusion, we can say that Phayre's dating is not authentic for scholars and history students of today in Rakhaing studies.

---

86 It seems the Kawzā date 150 RE, which was the same date mentioned in *Daññavadī Rāzawon Theik* by Bago Murn Kyaung Saradaw U Pandi. See, Vesālī Period of Daññavadī Rāzawon Theik by U Pandi, which was the exact copy of the Myanmar Kin Wun Min Gyi's palm-leaf manuscript, See p. 11 footnote of Myanmarsa Nunt Boung Kyan, Pt. I.

87 Ibid.

88 Abstracting from the Palm leave Manuscript, U San Hla's *Mahāmuni Ni-gone-rwa Poem* (Establishing City and Palace Section) rewritten in 1019 Rakhing Era, passage 2, "ကံ့သုံးဆံ့ဦ၊ ထီးဖွမ်ဂြာ၊ တစ်ခွင်တာတွင်၊ စွန္နီပြီးလမ်း၊ သကရာဇ်လျှင်၊ နှစ်ရာ့လေးဆယ့်ကိုးဝယ်တွင်" It seems to consult with *Rakhing Razawon* by Kin Won Minister's Manuscript and *New Dhaññavatī Razawon* by U Pandi.

89 *Ibid.*

Summary

Briefly, the important dates of eras to be remembered in Rakhaing chronicles are as follows.

1. The founding date of the first Dhaññavatī is 3325 BC.
2. The founder king of the first Dhaññavatī is Mārayu.
3. The founding date of the second Dhaññavatī is 1507 BC.
4. The founder king of the second Dhaññavatī is Kan Rāzā Gree or Kamma Rāzā.
5. The first cancellation date of the Mahā Era started in the seventh century BC after alteration of the ancient King Kusa Era 8645 to the year 2.
6. The founding date of the third Dhaññavatī is the sixth century BC.
7. The founder king of the third Dhaññavatī is King Candasūriya.
8. The second cancellation was made by King Candasūriya in the sixth century BC.
9. King Candasūriya's accession date is in the sixth century BC.
10. The new Sāsana Era started in the fifth or sixth century BC after the second cancellation of Mahā 148, one year before the death of King Candasūriya of the third Dhaññavatī.
11. The Kawzā Era started in the same date as above.
12. The third cancellation date took place in 609 Kawzā by the sixteenth King Sūriyacitra of Dhaññavatī (i.e., AD 79/116).
13. The last king of the third Dhaññavatī is in 249 RE or 856 Sāsana Era of the fourth century AD (AD 370) (AD 327) (AD 364) (Mentioned as any other possible year for the last king of the third Dhannavati.)
14. The founding date of the Vesālī is in the fourth century AD.
15. The founding king of the Vesālī is Mahā Taingcandra in the chronicles.
16. The founder king of the Vesālī (table 2) in the inscriptions is Dvencandra.
17. The final cancellation was made in 560 Kawzā in the Vesālī period by King Siricandra, and the corresponding date of the Christian

era was AD 638. A fresh Kawzā era started after the final cancellation date. Popa Saw Rahan was a contemporary king or counterpart king of Bagan, who cancelled Kawzā 560 in the Myanmar Era.

18. The ending date of the Vesālī is in the ninth century AD.
19. The last king of the Vesālī is Nga Murn Nga Ton, son of King Cūlacandra and Queen Candādevi.
20. The Lay-mro period started in the ninth century AD.
21. The founder king of the Lay-mro period (Pañcā) is Khetathin.
22. The founder king of the Parein period is Letya Murn Nan.
22. The founder king of the second Parein period is Datha Rāzā.
23. The founding date of Parein is in the twelfth century AD.
24. The founding date of Khreik is in the twelfth century AD.
25. The founder king is Murn Phone Sar.
26. The founding date of Sambwak is in the twelfth century AD.
27. The founder king of Sambwak is Danu Ru Paw.
28. The founding date of Narañjarā Taungoo is in the twelfth century AD.
29. The founder king of Narañjarā Taungoo is Myitzu Thin.
30. The founding date of Laung-gret is in the thirteenth century AD.
31. The founder king of Laung-gret is Alo Mar Phru.
32. The ending date of Laung-gret is in the fifteenth century AD.
33. The last king of Laung-gret and the Lay-mro period is Murn Saw Mon.
34. The founding date of Mrauk Oo is in the fifteenth century AD.
35. The founder king of Mrauk Oo period is Mong Saw Mon (or) Nara Meik Hla.
36. The ending king of the first Mrauk Oo is Mong Khaung Rāza.
37. The founder king of the second Mrauk Oo is Murn Bā Gree.
38. The founder king of the third Mrauk Oo is Narapadigree.
39. The last king of Mrauk Oo is Sammata Rāza (or) Aggo Puñña Zaw.
40. The ending date of Mrauk Oo or the last date of Arakan Kingdom is in Kawzā 1146 or AD 1784 or in the eighteenth century AD.

CHAPTER 3

THE BACKGROUND OF RAKHAING

This chapter is going to reveal, first of all, the geographical features of the land as the background of Rakhaing being the immediate southeast frontier of India (formerly Majjhimadesa)[90] for the transfusion of its religions and culture into the land by sea or by land. Secondly, the short description of its flora and fauna is followed. Then, it is followed by how the forefathers of Rakhaing came into the land, why it is called Rakhaing, and a critical examination of its languages, inhabitants, and ancient capitals as we know about those especially from Dr. Thin Kyi's article,[91] *The*

---

90 An area located in central India where the Buddha was born, was called the Middle Land (Majjhima Desa). It was so called because it was believed to be, by the people who lived there, the center of the earth. The whole area consists of a vast, flat, fertile plain through which flow two great Rivers, the Ganges and the Yamuna, and many smaller Rivers. (http://www.wisdomlib.org/definition/majjhima-desa/index.html)

91 Thin Kyi. "Arakanese Capitals: A Preliminary Survey of their Geographic Siting." *JBRS* LIII, ii (December, 1970): pp. 1–14. Hereafter this work will be abbreviated as *Thin Kyi: Arakanese Capitals*

State Gazetteer,[92] *Cultures and Traditional Customs of Nationalities: Rakhaing*[93] and other available literature in Arakanese, Burmese, and English.

3.1. The Geographical Background: Part of Majjhimadesa?

Particular geographical locations, such as continents, countries, and cities, can form the basis of historical study. Understanding why historic events took place is important. To do this, historians often turn to geography. Weather patterns, the water supply, and the landscape of a place all affect the lives of the people who live there. For example, to explain why the ancient Egyptians developed a successful civilization, studying the geography of Egypt is essential. Egyptian civilization was built on the banks of the Nile River, which flooded each year, depositing soil on its banks. The rich soil could help farmers grow enough crops to feed the people in the cities. That meant everyone did not have to farm, so some people could perform other jobs that helped develop the civilization.[94]

Tradition has it that Majjhimadesa ends at Rakhaing Roma Mountains. After sojourning in Dhaññavatī, Gotama the Buddha proceeded as far as Tan-Gyi-Taung, the east bank of the Irrawaddy River, where he predicted that the Sri Kettarā Kingdom would be formed in the opposite bank in the future. We have to assume that Majjhimadesa ends in the west bank of the Irrawady (Ayeyawady)

---

92 *The Arakan State Gazetteer [Vol. I (History Section) and Vol. V (Culture Section)]* published by The Arakan State People's Council (1984). Hereafter these works will be abbreviated respectively as *State Gazetteer (History)* and *State Gazetteer (Culture)*

93 *Cultural and Traditional Customs of Nationalities: Rakhaing*, published by The Burmese Socialist Programme Party, (1976 January). Hereafter this work will be abbreviated as *Rakhaing Cultural and Traditional Customs*

94 http://en.wikipedia.org/wiki/History#Philosophy_of_history

River. Once Dr. Than Tun[95] remarked that Gotama the Buddha had never been to outside Majjhmadesa. Though we may deem it correct, we should bear in mind that since the ancient times, Dhaññavatī was included in the Majjhimadesa. If this is so, we can accept with some confidence that the traditional belief of Gotama the Buddha's visit to Dhaññavatī could be possible.

In the local chronicles and historical annals, Arakan in the past was known as Suvaṇṇapura, Rāmasuvaṇṇapura, Ayujjhapura, Rakkhapura, Dhaññavatī, Mahāvihinka, and Mahinsakamanḍala. Arakan State (Rakhaing Land) is situated on the western coast of present Burma (Myanmar). It is bordered by Chin State in the north; Magway Region, Bago Region, and Ayeyarwady Region in the east; the Bay of Bengal to the west; and the Chittagong Division of Bangladesh to the northwest. It is located approximately between latitudes 17°15′ north and 21°17′ north and longitudes 92°11′ east and 94°55′ east.[96] The Arakan Mountains (Rakhaing Roma), which rise to 3,063 meters (10,049 ft.) at Victoria Peak, separate Rakhaing State from central Burma. Off the coast of Arakan State there are some fairly large islands such as Cheduba, Ramree, and Myingun. Rakhaing State has an area of 36,762 square kilometers (14,194 square miles) and its present capital is Sittwe (formerly Akyab).[97]

Dr. Daw Thin Kyi describes:

> Its latitudinal spread, though extensive, as far south as Cape Negrais and the Pagoda Point, however, is much narrower in depth except in the case of the present Akyab district, which is actually the centre or the nucleus of the kingdom and

95 Than Tun. "*Old Burma History (Kheit Haung Myanma Yazawin)*" Vol. 1. Maha Dagon, Yangon. (1964)

96 *State Gazetteer(History)* p.1

97 http://en.wikipedia.org/wiki/Rakhine_State

this is *(being also the area)* where the Arakanese capitals are *(have been)* situated. The east-west extension is even far less *(extensive)* than the north-south extension. At the northern end, form the kingdom's western limit *(the kingdom's western limit is formed;), (the distance)* from the Bay of Bengal to the eastline of the Arakan Yoma, the distance is about 100 miles but further south about the latitude of Sandoway, the distance *(it)* is only about 25 miles and far to the south the width narrows until at Pagoda Points it ends at the point. Again the north-south extension (latitudinal spread) is 360 miles as the crow files, but at the home base of the Arakanese, the Akyab district, the extension is only 60 miles or so. This will, therefore, emphasize the smallness of the home base occupied by the Arakanese people, a region between 5,000 to 6,000 sq. miles in area. (The area of Akyab district is 5,251 square miles.) The present area of the Arakan Division is 14,200 square miles. Adding the small strip to the south the area could not have been *(covered)* more than 15,000 square miles. This comprises the essential area of the kingdom of Arakan, although at the times of maximum extension of the area could be nearly twice this figure.[98]

It is important to note that Burman-occupied territory was demarcated from historical Arakan in the Randaboo Treaty, which was signed between two alien powers, the British colonial administration in India and the Burman expansionists, on February 24, 1826. The treaty bestowed upon the Burman kingdom some territory of present-day Arakan, plus the southernmost part of historical Arakan from the Kyauk-chwan River to Haigree (Haigyi) Island, Pagodas Point, and Cape Negrais, as well as the Northern Arakan Hills that are the Paletwa district today. The total area of the lost territory was 21,694 square miles.

98 *Thin Kyi, Arakanese Capitals* p.2

Moreover, when the southernmost portion of the Bessein (now Pathein) was partitioned during the British administration in 1853, the area of Arakan was further reduced to 18,945 square miles. Again after 1952, the Northern Arakan Hills of the Paletwa district were separated from Arakan and renamed the "Chin Hills" by the Burman-dominated government of postindependence Burma. The area of modern Arakan State, which borders with Chin State and Bangladesh in the north and Magwe Division in the east, and faces the Bay of Bengal in the west is 14,200 square miles.

According to the note by Colonel Albert Fytche[99] on August 23, 1867, in Rangoon, the land of Arakan was 18,630 square miles when Arakan and Tenasserim were annexed to the British territories from the Burmese power in 1826.

Regarding the land, rivers, and climate of Rakhaing,[100] first, the high ranges of Rakhaing Roma extend from the Chin Hills to Pagoda Point, forming a series of ridges and spurs reaching to the sea and enclosing narrow strips land in the Kyaukphyu and Sandoway Districts.

In Sittway District west of the main ranges, low ridges trend south-south-east a continuation of Chittagong Hills, separating the series of Rakhaing rivers: Naat, Mayu, Kaladan, and Laymro, which have built up narrow alluvial flood plains.

The second, in the main Kaladan-Laymro valley the hills often stand out at low ridges above the flood plain. The flood plains of

99 Albert Fytche, "Memorandum on the Comparative Progress of the Provinces now forming British Burma under British and Native Rule" p. 199, *Proceedings of the Royal Geographical Society of London*, Vol. 12, No. 3 (1867–1868), pp. 198–201, Published by: Blackwell Publishing on behalf of The Royal Geographical Society (with the Institute of British Geographers). Article Stable URL: http://www.jstor.org/stable/1798974

100 The help of Mg Tun Shwe's paper, "*Evolution of Rakhine Ancient Capitals: Geographical Appraisal*" Research Paper submitted for PhD, Yangon University, 2003–2004. p. 2, at this writing, it is most gratefully acknowledged. Hereafter this work will be abbreviated as *Tun Shwe: RAC Research.*

the Kaladan and Laymro Rivers have coalesced to form a single deltaic plain, with a few ridges rising above the plain like islands. The ridges, of early Tertiary age, were to supply the sandstone for the religious structures and early city walls at the urbanized capitals.

The rivers in Rakhaing are still tidal. The main river, Kaladan, is tidal up to almost Paletwa, about fifty miles from the ancient city, Dhaññavatī. It may have been possible to reach the oldest Rakhaing city just by sailing.

The building up of land by the big rivers like Kaladan and Laymro have been so gradual that early settlements were limited to northern part of the Sittway plain. Thus at the time of these early settlements the whole plain must have been crisscrossed by these tidal steams ringed with mangroves.

Even today in the southern portion, large areas of mangroves need extensive draining to alleviate flooding and drain salt water so that cultivation is possible. However, the agricultural base of Northern Rakhaing was capable of producing a surplus of rice, which may have been the reason why this land is known as Dhaññavatī (Grain-blessed) in ancient time, and why area was always the most important part of the kingdom. The ancient capitals of Rakhaing comprised agricultural based urban settlements.

The third, the climate is hot and tropical monsoon. The average annual temperature is about 78°F. Annual rainfall ranges from 160 inches to 220 inches. It is very suitable for continuous cultivations throughout the year. Besides, ancient Rakhaing capitals in order to shield against windy rainy weather used neat bricklaying and thickly applied cement.

All ancient Rakhaing capitals were situated in the alluvial area. The rivers are still tidal. Most of the streams on the alluvial plain are trial and salty water. The dominant problem for royal capitals was that of a regulated fresh-water supply. Thus all the Rakhaing capitals have a series of large storehouses centered around the palace sites as is evident even from the recent Google Earth photos.

3.2. Flora and Fauna[101]

The flora and fauna of Rakhaing consist of a kaleidoscopic collection. While the Rakhaing Region is covered with tropical rainforest, about one hundred species of mammals are found in Rakhaing Mountains. Famous white royal elephants were once found in the forest of northern hills near the ancient Rakhaing capitals.[102] Throughout Rakhaing history, many well-trained elephants served in royal elephants' military force. About three hundred species of birds dwell in the hills and forests. The great crocodile is also found in the tidal creeks.

3.3. Emergence of Ancient Rakhaing: the Heredity

Ancient Rakhaing entered into Rakhaing strip from the northeastern parts of India. Massive groups of Aryans and Mongoloids migrated into India and settled there. It is difficult to estimate the year of its happening accurately. Some scholars estimated that it occurred two thousand or more years BC.[103] Aryans settled in the central region of northern India (now Agra and Ude) and extended their settlements along the Gangetic plain and Bengal state.[104] At the time Mongoloids settled at the southern slopes of

101 *Tun Shwe: RAC Research.* p. 2

102 In recent past, a number of white elephants from Northern Rakhaing were captured and taken to serve as a Royal elephants in Burma Capitals: Yangon and Naypyidaw.

103 Latourette, K. S. *A Short History of the Far East,* New York: The Macmillan Company, 1957 (3rd Edition), p. 42.

104 Havell, E. B. *The History of Aryan Rule in India.* London: George G. and Co. Ltd., 1891. p. 34.

Himalayan range, which comprised Kamma Rupadesha Magadha, Gangetic plain, and Bengal.[105]

Aryans and Mongoloids cohabited there and may have been related each other. After Aryans and Mongoloids of blood relation, their offspring and ancestors entered into Rakhaing strip. Otherwise it would be difficult to think that the races mixed after they entered into the Rakhaing strip. If we look at it from the civilization viewpoint, civilization of Aryans was superior to those of Mongoloids, which would follow the path of Aryans. In ancient Rakhaing civilization we could trace the diffusion and permeation of Hindu faith and Sanskrit knowledge. The most antique Rakhaing epigraph with Sanskrit inscription had a strong influence on the Rakhaing civilization.

In Rakhaing Chronicles, Rakhaing people entered into Rakhaing strip from the central part of the Northern India (Magadhadesa).

Relating to these events various Rakhaing Chronicles recorded that the King Vāsudeva including his ten brothers from the central part of Northern India invaded the Rakhaing's Dvārāvatī and established the first Rakhaing Kingdom. When the enemies approached the kingdom, Dvārāvatī would be able to ascend upward to the sky. Then this city was first secured with iron hooks and conquered. Its name was *Than Twe* (hooked and attached with iron chain). In *Seinda Kyaw Thu U Aw*'s treatise on table of spelling rules (stanza 352) describes it. *Myaung Hla* township officer *U Chaint*, who served under the kings *Mindon* and *Thibaw* as an official in foreign affairs also wrote about it.[106] He wrote about Rakhaing history by referring to various treatises, according to which Kyeekan Shin's puzzle in lyric form relating to the Dvārāvadī and *Than Twe*

---

105 *Chatterjee,* Dr. *S. K. Kirat Janakriti.* Calcutta: ASB, 1951. p. 22.

106 *Kavilakhanā Dipanī.* Rangoon: Thudhammawadi Press, 1930. pp. 194–198

was answered by Kyeethe Sayadaw. Most scholars remarked that this story had been derived from a similar one known at the time of the Buddha.[107]

When the first group of migrants entered into the Rakhaing strip, they found an aboriginal tribe. They were known as Rakshas. In the Rakhaing chronicles, they were described as Rakkhish or Rakkhik. The terms Rakkhisha, Rakkhish, and Rakkhik are close to each other in pronunciation. The first group of migrants named that region as Rakkhik Land (Rakkhapura) mainly according the name of the aboriginal tribe. Thus, Rakkhapura and Rakhaing were accepted.[108]

These aboriginal Rakkhiks were conquered by the first group of migrants. So Ramree Saradaw Ven. Candamalalankara remarked that the land the Rakkhiks dwelt in was subdued and conquered and named Rakhaing by the first arrivers from Magadha. Stone Age implements were excavated in Rakhaing. They were used by Rakhaing Stone Age peoples. When the Aryans entered into the Rakhaing strip, they were likely to live together in peace. But the aboriginals were inscribed at the northern face of Ānandacandra Pillar as Arekādesh still survived there.

Rakhaing's cultural heritages were developed by Rakhaing kings and the Kaladan-Laymro Valley city states were formed since around 3000 BC until Mrauk Oo's fall exactly on January 5, AD 1785. On the January 10, the last Rakhaing king abdicated, and his dynasty was put to an end by the Burmese King Bodawphaya.

However, the efficient achievements in social and cultural aspects will never fade away in human history. More light should be

---

107 *Ibdi.* pp. 194–195

108 *Rakhaing Cultural and Traditional Customs* p. 35.; "*Sway Sone Kywa Htin Kyan,*" First Book, Sway Sone Kyaw Htin Pitakat Press, Rangoon (1289 BE)

shed on these achievements, and more accurate data and systematic arrangements of the sequence of events should be carried out. Thus conveying the authentic Rakhaing history is a responsibility of all Rakhaing people and others as well.

The dawn of civilization began at the place where Southeastern Europe, Asia Minor, the Caspian Sea, and the Black Sea meet. According to several studies, a lighter-skinned tribe dwelt there in about the seventh millennium BC.

The civilization of these was higher than those of others. They cultivated and raised poultry and vegetable crops. They invented wooden wheeled carts to commute here and there.

As they dwelt in tropic zone they had to move from the place of drought to the place of greener grass with their herds of cattle, flock of sheep together with poultry. Based on this fact, the historians called these tribes as nomadic. These nomadic tribes lived at the source and along the riverbank.

When the season constantly changed and became drier, cultivation and farming became harder. When their agricultural skill improved, their population increased in number. Therefore, they could not stay any longer there, and thus they moved to the southern part of the Middle East (now Iraq). They proceeded to the northwestern part of India.

Even if there was some ancient migration to India, this could have taken place some thousands of years before the date assigned to Mohenjo-Daro. As such, for all practical purposes we can treat them as the indigenous inhabitants of India.

Mohenjo-Daro and Harappa are far apart. It was sheer chance that led to the discovery of these ruins in these two places. There can be little doubt that there lie many such buried cities and other remains of the handiwork of ancient man in between these two areas. In fact, this civilization, as we find it, was highly developed and must have taken thousands of years to reach that stage.

There is a reason for believing that it spread to the Gangetic Valley.[109]

Sir John Marshall noted, "One thing that stays out clear and unmistakable both at Mohenjo-Daro and Harappa is the civilization hitherto revealed at these two places is not an incipient civilization, in our already age-old and stereotyped on Indian soil, with many millenniums of human endeavor behind it."[110]

From that it is clear that the formation of a civilized city took thousands of years. These two cities existed between 5000 and 2500 BC, and both of them suddenly collapsed.

Nehru further questioned, "What happened to the Indus Valley Civilization and how did it end? Some people (among them, Gordon Childe) say that there was a sudden end to it due to an unexplained catastrophe. But there is always an unexplained six or seven thousand years ago when the Indus Valley Civilization probably began."[111]

About seven thousand years ago, approximately 5000 BC, lighter-skinned Caucasian people migrated to the northwestern part of the Indian subcontinent group by group and permeated among the aborigines.

The Caucasians migrated into the Indian subcontinent through the dangerous mountain passes, such as Bolan, Khyber, Comal, and Zojila, and thence they settled at the source of Indus River.

To differentiate among them we use term "Aryan of Indo-Aryan" to those who dwelt there about 5000 BC and "Indo-European" to those who entered in about 200 BC. But in Indian

---

109 Nehru, Jawahalal. "*The Discovery of India*" (1st Edit. 1946), 1989 Edit. p. 74, p. 132.

110 Sir John Marshall, *Mohenjo-Daro and the Indus Civilization*, 3 vols., Asian Educational Services, Facsimile of 1931 ed. (March 1, 1996)

111 *Ibid.* Nehru (1989)

history, Dravidians intruded there four or five millennia BC, and formerly they were lighter skinned. Under the constant seasonal changes their skin became darker. Thousands of years elapsed, and they entered into the northwestern part of India (now Pakistan) and journeyed to the Indus River, where they drove out the Negroid race Dravidian to the southern part of the subcontinent. They occupied what the Dravidians had left.

The nomadic Aryans settled in the Indus Valley because of the favorable weather and geographical position. They established villages and cities along the riverbank. Then it was termed as *River Valley Civilization.*

Successive Aryan migrants proceeded to find new territories up to the source of Bramaputra River-basin. Then the Aryans entered the Rakhaing strip, spread to the area between Gissapanadī (now Kalandan River) and Añjananadī (now Lay-mro River) and thence spread throughout Dhaññavatī. These colonizers were known as Aryo-Dravidians.

The Aryan descendants, who entered there between 5000 and 4000 BC, established the cities, such as Rammāvatī, Dhaññavatī, and first Vesālī. Those who entered there about 2000 BC were not spread throughout Rakhaing. The people who accompanied with the King Kamma Raja from Kamma Rupan Manipur in 1470 BC seemed to be from the first group.

The Aryans migrated along the Indus River in 5000 BC and settled and built two famous cities by the name of Mohenjo-Daro and Harappa in more than 4000 BC.

When the archaeologists excavated these two sites, they discovered wells, thoroughfares, gardens, aqueducts, bathrooms, and concrete buildings. They also discovered the art and craft of jewelry making, statues, and other household appliances with artistic touches. They used metals, but they seemed to especially adore gold. Other relics of minor cities and villages were also excavated.

These two ancient cities could be compared with that of the city Eridu, which happened to be situated between the Euphrates and the Tigris (now Iraq) in antiquity. It would take a long time to build such a magnificent city. Beginning as a village tract, it then developed into a town, and hundreds and hundreds of years later, it would become a magnificent city. The findings of facts and evidence confirmed the existence of Indo-Aryans since 5000 BC.

Other scholars[112] summarized: Archaeology has discovered ancient ruins in the Indus Valley Civilization of the third and fourth millennium BC, which was fairly advanced with city walls, bathrooms, and elaborate drainage systems, and which seems to have had kingship culture of Mesopotamia.

"Remains of stone age man make it clear that stage of civilization was known in both north and south India. In the north this was followed by an age of copper. Then came iron."[113]

More than four thousand years BC, a race of longheaded, fair-skinned men entered India through one of the northwestern passes. Perhaps not long after the founding of Eridu about more 4000 years BC ago, these newcomers settled in the valley of the Indus River and built cities with fine, broad streets laid out systematically, as well as large buildings, sewer systems, and public bathing pavilions. They were amazingly modern.[114]

When the next wave of immigrants entered through the northwestern mountain passes, they found settlements and urbanization along the Indus River. Agriculture was flourishing, and canalization and irrigation systems were improved. Large and small boats

112 Latourette (1957), pp. 121–133; Southworth (1954), p. 47.

113 Latourette (1957), *op. cit.*

114 Southworth (1954), *op. cit.*, p. 47 *cont.*

piled up and down the river. They had already been commenced with the cities at the rim of the Persian Gulf.

In 2000 BC, the Indian subcontinent was prosperous, and existence of the people in 5000 BC was confirmed. When the Aryans entered the Rakhaing strip in 5000 to 4000 BC, they also encountered the Dravidians of Neolithic Age. There existed cannibalistic tribes like cave-dwellers Nga Saddan and his followers in 3280 BC, who destroyed first Vesālī. Like Aryans who fought against Dravidians when they migrated into India, they fought as well against Dravidians when they entered Rakhaing. But some of the aborigines dispersed and hid in the forest.

The Gupta Empire, which included Aryans and Dravidians, ruled along the Indus and Ganges rivers. This way the northern part of Indian subcontinent lasted from AD 300 to 535. Its military might have flourished throughout the whole India. But when the cruel and terrible Mongoloid horde invaded Indus river-basin, Gupta's backbone of military had been broken. These invaders were from the north-western part of China (now Mongolia). The Mongoloids conquered and occupied the Indus river basin, and they allied with the militant Rajput. The combined invading forces advanced through Gangetic plain and looted and devastated the cities.

During the reign of these barbaric Huns, most of the Hindu and Buddhistic heritage was totally destroyed. The Hun soldiers on horseback used the lighting swift strategy. But their strategy could not be used in marshy and mountainous region of Rakhaing. Therefore, they could not even invade and ravage the twelve regions of Rakhaing State. If the Han did, they would be on the way of no return. It would not be easy for them to cross secretly over Ganges, deltaic region of Bramaputra, Mayu, Naaf, and Gissapanadī. When most of India was overrun by Hans, Vesālī was ruled by successive kings such as Bhūmicandra (AD 438) and

Mahāvīra (AD 594–606). When U Tun Shwe Khine compared the inscription on the face the then silver coins and stone pillar, it confirmed that only the Candra dynasty including Bhūmicandra, Bhūticandra, Nīticandra, Vīracandra, Priticandra, and Paticandra ruled there. Thus, it is evident that the Rakhaing kings were not threatened by Huns. There were no chances of cohabitation. Four of the Vesālī kings did not appear to be Candras; they ruled there about twelve years. The power and authority of Huns gradually faded away, and Rakhaing was absolutely spared from Huns. Huns started to retreat their forces.

After reigning in Kyauk Hlay Gar about five years, King Pay Phru (AD 776–793) removed to Mrauk Oo realizing that Vesālī came to an end. After reigning there twelve years, the Chinese army advanced in AD 794, the king realized that he could not fight against those invaders and retreated to Thabeik Hill. Then the king passed away. Thereafter the prince and the old Candradevī took command and defended from Champwet which was only five miles and seven furlongs from the frontier in AD 794. They made stronghold at the east bank of Laymro River. There was a saying that "When the Chinese gave pressure, the Shan felt strain, and the Burma refuged to the west." Apparently, the Burmese forces occupied most of the region in Rakhaing. Sandoway was under the control of Mon. Peoples form Dhaññavatī, Vesālī, and Mrauk Oo fled and took refuge at Thabeik Hill after upturning the Champwet. Under these circumstances, the relatively superior Chinese army could not fight against Champwet and Thabiek Hill. They destroyed and looted only three big cities. They stayed there nearly a year, and later they faced famine and feared of Rakhaing people's retaliation fled into Burmese soil. They brought back several Rakhaing prisoners of war to the Sagain. They still occupied Shan hills when Bagan was no longer a kingdom when Pin Ya and

Sagain were at rise. The Chinese occupied most of the Shan hills for about one hundred years. Such a situation never occurred in Rakhaing Land.

The next wave of invasion of the Mongoloids and the Khan army occurred during the reign of kings Murn Phone Sar and Murn Htee. But they were destroyed and expelled at the border. To ascertain that mixing or blood relations did not occur between the Rakhaing, Chinese, and Mongols, their occupation in Rakhaing was very brief.

In AD 794 when Mongoloid Sung dynasty ruled the mainland China, the Chinese army invaded from the south-western part of Yunana into Bramaputra, Assam, and Burma by way of Irrawaddy River. They proceeded and spread through the land of Pyu, Thailand, Cambodia, Annam, and thence to Mekhong River-basin. They also tried to invade into Rakhaing. They took a foothold at the source of Añjananadī, thence to Gissapanadī river basin and approached Dhaññavatī, Vesālī, and Mrauk Oo. At that time King Pay Phru, who ruled over Mrauk Oo, Vesālī, and Kyauk Hlay Ga, realized that his own army was inferior to that of the Chinese. Therefore he departed from the place with his royal attendants and retreated to the Thabeik Hill situated at the west bank of Yoe Chaung (Yoe Creek).

At that time, Queen Candradevī and King Cūlacandra's nephew, Prince Candra Gupta, kept guarding the Thabeik Hills. King Cūlacandra and Queen Candradevī's son, Prince Ngaton, marched along with the massive strength of the Thet army and recruited the refugees from Dhaññavatī, Vesālī, and Mrauk Oo. Then the massive forces blocked the Sung army at the Añjananadī and Champawet. Then the stranded Sung army looted and destroyed the three Rakhaing cities and carted out most of the booty. They escaped through the southern war-free zone and entered into the Burman soil. It was in AD 797 that Sung army destroyed and devastated Dhaññavatī, Vesālī, and Mrauk Oo, which was a conquest that lasted about a year.

Some of the members of Sung army settled and inhabited at the northeastern part of Burma and were later called Shan. The inhabitants along the Mekong River, Thailand, Cambodia, and Annam were called Thai (Khmer) in AD 906. These records were described in the history of ancient Southeast Asia nations and Chinese history.

For the second time, the Sung with an intention expanded and colonized on other territories, migrated from Yannan. Their massive migration spread from Bramaputra to the Mekong River. It was the time of Lay-mro period when Rakhaing King Min Phon Sa (AD 1142–1149) ruled there, like the King Pay Phru, he defended and exterminated the oncoming aggressors at the source of Añjananadī and mountainous region thereby. The king's army not only exterminated the enemies in Rakhaing soil, they followed the escapists in Burman soil and Shan hills and exterminated them also. The Rakhaing army occupied some of the portions of Burman soil and Shan hills.

For the third and last time, when Kublai Khan's Mongol army and the Sung army invaded Bagan in AD 1284–1300, their forces entered and occupied the Añjananadī and Lay-mro regions in Rakhaing soil. In this way, the people living therein were dominated by Mongols. The Sung's aggression came to an end in Laung Krat period under the reign of King Min Htee in AD 1283–1389.

Apparently, though the Rakhaing was under the Mongol conquest, there was no trace of mixed blood with Mongoloids.

Tibeto-Mongoloids made difficult ascent up the Himalaya ranges and seeped into India, they lived only in Bhutan, Sikkin, Nepal, and Assam. They could reach only the west bank of the river Ganges and Bramaputra. They cohabited there but could not cross into Rakhaing.

When the Rakhaing kings rejoiced victory over the enemies, they used to bring back the prisoners of war. But these prisoners of war were forced to live at the eastern side of Rakhaing mountain range. For example, Thet prisoners of war were placed at the Thayet, and some of the prisoners of war were treated as servants in cities. Among them most of the Mongoloids were likely contained with other prisoners of war. According to the Rakhaing custom, none of the people could mix with any other race; therefore, the Mongoloids were marked as aliens.

Most of the Rakhaings who dwelt in modern-day Bangladesh never renounced their race, customs, or faith. Though the Rakhaings do not possess lighter skin as those of the original Aryans, it is because it depended on the nature of their occupation, habit of eating, and climatic condition. It could be likened to Jews in Ethiopia. Ethiopian Jew's skin was as black as Negroid race. The physical appearance thus happens within one to two thousand years.

3.4. Why the Name Rakhaing?

The exact origin of the word Rakhaing is unknown, though it is believed to be derived from the Pāḷi "Rakkha," meaning protector. Some accounts claim that the word may have been derived from Bilu, aborigines of the land, named Rakhsha in the local chronicles, a cannibal flesh eating ogres which used to live in the land times immemorial. Indo-Arayans migrated to Rakhaing from the northwest, while Tibeto-Burman peoples migrated from the Himalayas. The modern Rakhaing people are a blend of these people.

Local Arakanese scholars[115] try to explain the term Rakhaing by the linguistic background: etymologically, "Arakan" is a derivation from Pāḷi word "Ārakkha." The prefix "ā" means adjacent,

115 In the works by local historians and researchers such as: U Oo Thar Tun, U Aung Tha Oo, U San Tha Aung, U Shwe Zan, U Tun Shwe Khine and Ven. Cakkinda

surrounding; "rakkha (rakkhane-pāle)" means preserving, protecting, maintaining. To preserve what? "Silavaṃsaṃ rakkhatīti rakkho" that means people (rakkho) are those, who preserve their morality and stock or race. Which is why, Ārakkha means the people who not only maintain their morality and lineage, but preserve their surroundings as well. It had been named since the late fifteenth century onward by Westerners such as Portuguese, Dutch, Persia, English, etc. The word represents Rakhaing people and their littoral land between Rakhaing range and Bay of Bengal. Here Rakkha is not Yakkha. It is to be noted that Yakkha in Pāḷi means ogres, flesh eating uncivilized creatures. And Rakhaing can pronounce /r/ sound perfectly. Rakhaing (also derives from the Pāḷi word *Rakkha*; see earlier) call themselves Rakhaing. Rakhaing is known as Arakan to the West. Rakhaing is called Mug by Bangles because Rakhaing people are descendants of Magadha. Rakhaing Land is named Ārekhadesa in the famous Ānandacandra inscriptions and is known to Laṅka people as Rakkhaṅgadesa (Rakhaing-desa).

3.5. The Inhabitants of Rakhaing and Their Languages

The major nationality of the people living in the land is Rakhaing. Only the name Rakhaing is by all means accepted even though they are living in different provinces. The colonist English however caused dissension among the Rakhaings as Rakhaing-thar, Rambree-thar, Manaung-thar, Chaung-thar, Sandoway-thar etc. by making good use of an opportunity to note the little dialectical difference. Those ideologies are wrong to Rakhaings, and they never accept such dissention among themselves.[116]

As stated above, the Rakhaing people are an ethnic community native to the historic region of Arakkhadesa (present

116 *Rakhaing Cultural and Traditional Customs* p. 28

Arakan) in westernmost costal region of Southeast Asia. They speak Arakanese, which is an archaic language of the Burmese of the Tibeto-Burman group, thought its first form may be close to Magadhi Prakrit and Sanskrit languages, because they primarily belong to Indo-Arayan and Mongolian, and are closely related to Austro-Asiatic, Dravidian, Tibeto-Burman languages. As such, Rakhaings are a homogeneous but considerably diverse ethnic group with heterogeneous origins. Even though Arakanese is very much close to Burmese, the vocabulary and the usage are distance from each other. One of the differences in pronunciation between them is the sound */r/* (i.e., for an Arakanese */r/* is */r/*, whereas for Burmese it is */y/*). Practically, most of the Arakanese people can understand Burmese easily, but Burmese cannot, even though both are linguistically close.

Rakhaings are naturally good-natured people, sincere and open hearted by birth. They tried to be eugenics. They did not want to be of mixed blood. They have preserved their tradition and followed Buddhism. In *Ashon Nāginda's Record*, Rakhaings were defined as preservers of purity race and discipline (Vamsa and Sila). Rakhaing metaphorically call their land "Father Rakhaing," understanding it as in the maternal sense. It was adopted by people of France, Germany, Iran, Afghanistan, Korea, and Vietnam.[117]

Physical appearance of most of the Rakhaings' skin is darker with prominent eyelids and nose. The height is not unusual. Some of the researchers assumed that Rakhaings were Indo-Mongoloids. Researcher Griffith Taylor thought that Mongolians descended from Aryans.[118]

117 *State Gazetteer (History)* p. 50

118 *Ibdi.,* p. 49–50

Apart from Rakhaings, there have been other nationalities[119] called in different names due to communicative difficulty with each other some time ago, even though all are same genes. They are, namely: (a) Thet, (b) Daingnet, (c) Mro, and (d) Mrama.

Thets of Rakhaings have been living in the vicinity of Assam called Bo Murn Htaung, Thet Htaung, Pha Lan Htaung, and Mru Htaung. All of Thets, Bo Murns, Pha Lans, and Mrus are the same descendants like Rakhaings, and all are Buddhists.

Daingnets are so called because originally Daingtack (qualified in shielding) gradually became known as Daingdack, Daingnet. There are eight subraces in Daingnets. They are Buddhist.

Mro people have many different breeds. It is said by the old Mros that there have been about one hundred lineages or genealogies of Mro. However, only fifty-seven have been yet recorded. Only about thirty survive now. The name Mro is given by the Rakhaing, but they are known Khami by themselves.

---

119 Here, "Kalar" (mostly Muslim people) named by the Rakhaing peoples, among them presently so-called "Rohingya" is neither accepted as one of the brother nationalities of Rakhaings, nor counted as one of the indigenous peoples of Burma. Dr. Aye Chan's learned paper "*The Development of a Muslim Enclave in Arakan (Rakhine) State of Burma (Myanmar)*" SOAS Bulletin of Burma Research, Volume 3, Issue 2, Autumn 2005, p. 397, points out:

> In the early 1950s that a few Bengali Muslim intellectuals of the northwestern part of Arakan began to use the term "Rohingya" to call themselves. They were indeed the direct descendants of immigrants from the Chittagong District of East Bengal (present-day Bangladesh), who had migrated into Arakan after the province was ceded to British India under the terms of the Treaty of Yandabo, an event that concluded the First Anglo-Burmese War (1824–1826). Most of these migrants settled down in the Mayu Frontier Area, near what is now Burma's border with modern Bangladesh. Actually, they were called "Chittagonians" in the British colonial records.
>
> The Muslims in the Arakan State can be divided into four different groups, namely the Chittagonian Bengalis in the Mayu Frontier; the descendants of the Muslim Community of Arakan in the Mrauk-U period (1430–1784), presently living in the Mrauk-U and Kyauktaw townships; the descendants of Muslim mercenaries in Ramree Island known to the Arakanese as Kaman; and the Muslims from the Myedu area of Central Burma, left behind by the Burmese invaders in Sandoway District after the conquest of Arakan in 1784.

Bengali-speaking Mrama Gree are Buddhists. Tradition and customs are comparable with those of Rakhings. In ancient times, Mrama were called Baruva.

Thet, Daingnet, Mro, and Mrama have their respective dialects. Though their languages are different from Arakanese, they all are of the same language family, but dialectically differ. Thet has also their own; most of them can speak Arakanese. So can Mro and Chin as well. Thets speak a language similar to Bengali, and they are Buddhist. The Buddhist Daingnet also speak a language close to Bengalese. Mros are used to speak to each other by Mro language. It is a different language. They, however, differ in palatal and apical sounds from each other in accordance with their places. Among ten Khami words, at least two are common. Khami and Mro languages are familiar. They are living together. Islamists Ka Man peoples also speak like Rakhaing people Rambree Township.

The Burmese are using some Rakhaing vocabulary as their archaic (porāṇa) due to the fact that Arakanese and Burmese would have been the same in ancient time.

3.6. Ancient Capitals and Their Early Communications and Durations

3.6.1. The Capitals[120]

The early chronicles of Rakhaing usually begin with the descriptions of the events of Sakya (Sākiya) migration into Rakhaing. They were led by the princes of royal blood, who left their country especially in the direction to northern India, near Himalaya, for political reasons. They found a new city named Dhaññavatī on the bank of Gissapanadī (present

120 This section is largely dependent on Prof. Daw Thin Kyi's *Arakanese Capitals*, JBRS LIII (1970) and Mg Tun Shwe's *Evolution of Rakhine Ancient Capitals: Geographical Appraisal*. Research Paper submitted for PhD, Yangon University, 2003–2004.

Kaladan River). The city was the first urban settlement of Rakhaing.

Kan Thone Sunt

The fifty-five descendants of Mārayu reigned in this city; the last of them, King Murn Ngay Pyaw Hla Sethu, left Dhaññavatī and founded the city in 1508 BC.

Nila Pan Daung

Soon after the new city was built, the king was assassinated by three nobles, who collectively ruled for a year. The queen of the last king, Saw Site, then marched with her followers north and founded a new city, Nila Pan Daung.

Kyauk Pan Daung (1507–1483 BC)

At about this time Kan Raza Gree, who had been obliged to relinquish the kingdom of Tagaung to his younger brother, came to Northern Rakhaing and settled with his followers on a high mountain site called Kyauk Pan Daung. Kan Raza Gree joined the queen of the last Rakhaing king and married to her two daughters.

Second Dhaññavatī (1483–580 BC)

After twenty-four years Kan Raza Gree left Kyauk Pan Daung and rebuilt Dhaññavatī on the same site of the old city. The Rakhaing Chronicles relate that twenty-eight kings of Kan Raza Gree's descendants had reigned over the kingdom successively for nine hundred and twenty-seven years.

Third Dhaññavatī (580 BC–AD 326)

The dynasty founded by Kan Raza Gree comprised of twenty-eight kings. It was succeeded by the Suriya Dynasty, the first king of which being Candasuriya. The king founded a new city and built a palace on the site of old Dhaññavatī. According to the local chronicles, it was during the time that the Buddha is believed to have visited Rakhaing with his five hundred disciples. It was said, that the famous Mahāmuni Image was cast with his consent as a memento of his sojourn in the country. The Suriya Dynasty consisted of twenty-five kings who ruled the country for nine hundred and six years. The Suriya Dynasty was then succeeded by the dynasty of Candra.

Vesālī (AD 327–776)

The first king of the Candra Dynasty was Mahā Taicandra. He ascended the throne in AD 327. The tumult which arose at that time was due to the mysterious decline of fortune and influence of the old capital. The two chief queens had died, and the astrologers suggested that a change of site was necessary. The king, Mahā Taicandra, therefore, left the old capital, and rebuilt the old city of Vesālī, which he made his new capital. In that city, nine kings of this dynasty reigned in succession bearing the surname of Candra.

Mrauk Oo (AD 776–792)

The last king of the Candra dynasty was Cūlacandra who drowned in the sea. Thereafter, the reign was succeeded, or rather temporarily taken over, by a chief of the Mro tribes, Ah Mra Thu, and his nephew, Pay Phru. King Pay Phru built a new city, Mrauk Oo, was his birthplace and it was proclaimed as the capital, though Vesālī still existed as a city of the time. Then Shans from the Northern Roma invaded Rakhaing and occupied it for years. According to records, Ko Lo Fend (AD 749–779) also had overrun the upper region of the Irrawaddy, at about the same period. The country collapsed under the invasion of the Mongolians (Shans) and, although in unsettled conditions, Vesālī continued to flourish till AD 1018.

This is a very important period for Rakhaing history. It seems that the Mongols had intermarried freely with the native people who were then, most probably, Aryans (Indians). Because of this intermarriage, Rakhaing still retains some of the customs, manners, languages, cultures, and practices of the Indo-Mongoloids.

Tha Beik Taung (AD 793)

After the King Pay Phru had ruled for about seventeen years, a vigorous Tibeto-Burmese tribe came down from the upper Añjananadī (now Kaladan River) and occupied the city, Mrauk Oo. During this time the Mro King Pay Phru, being forced to abandon his capital, retired with his followers to the valley of Yo Chaung (Creek) and built a temporary city Tha Beik Taung.

Sambawet (AD 794–818)

When Cūlacandra, the last king of Candra Dynasty, died, he left an infant son. During the troubled days, the child prince was carefully hidden away by the loyal followers and was brought up in an obscure hilly region in the northern part of the country. It was in the Saing Durn Waterfall region which was invalidated by the Thet tribes. When he grew to manhood he brought together a considerable force of the hill tribes (Thets) to which the people of Rakhaing also joined in large as he came down to the plains. When the prince was twenty-three years old he was enthroned as a king. He built a new capital named Sambawet in AD 794. The prince was called by the Thets as Nga Ton Murn, meaning 'our king'. Hence the Rakhaing Chronicles have mentioned this king as such. Sambawet city lies six miles south-east from the old Vesālī. It was a small city situated on the bank of the Lay-mro River.

Pañcā (AD 818–1103)

King Nga Ton Murn was succeeded by Khetta Thurn. He was a descendant of a Candra king. His father was the nephew of Cūlacandra, the last king of Vesālī. Previously the king had been hidden for a long time in an obscured hilly region of upper Khrit River. After King Ketta Thurn had driven out all his enemies he abandoned Sambawet and built the new city of Pañcā situated on the Lay-mro River, which was about a few miles south from the old city. Fifteen kings ruled in that city for two hundred and eighty-five years, until AD 1103.

Parein (AD 1103–1123)

In the Pañcā dynasty, the last three kings were usurpers. Murn Bilu, the last king of the regular line, was assassinated by a noble who usurped the throne. His son, Murn Rai Baya, fled with his family to the country of Kyansitha at Bagan. For thirty-five years, the Rakhaing royal family remained there in exile. The queen of Murn Rai Baya gave birth to a son named Letya Murn Nan. When his father passed away, the reigning king of Bagan promised to help the young prince to regain the throne of Rakhaing.

According to the popular tradition, an army of a hundred thousand Phyus and a hundred thousand Talaings was sent by sea and land to Rakhaing. Letya Murn Nan ascended the Rakhaing throne in AD 1103 with the help of Phyus. He has been also known in the history as Phyu Ta Thein Murn (Lord of a hundred thousand Phyus). A Burmese inscription at a temple therein by Letya Murn Nan mentions about it.

On the advice of the astrologers, who said that the city of Pañcā had lost all its power and glory, and predicted that the country could not prosper if administered from that city, Letya Murn Nan left the old capital. He crossed the Lay-mro River and found a plain that was as flat as the surface of a big drum. There he built a temporary city named Laung Gret. Many people including a princess and animals died in that city. Letya Murn Nan then left Laung Gret and built the new city of Parein on the bank of Paungduk Chaung (Creek).

The Paungduk Creek is a boundary lines between Laung Gret and Parein. Parein (N 20°34′, E 93°14′) holds a much better position than other capitals. It faces the Lay-mro River and has at its back a ridge that runs parallel to the main ridge which is situated between the Kaladan and Lay-mro rivers.

It lies four miles southeast of Mrauk Oo. The seventh king of Parein Dynasty Dassa Rāzā (AD 1123–1139) reformed the city as Second Parein in AD 1123. The reign of the eight Parein kings lasted for thirty years until AD 1142.

Khrit (AD 1142–1154)

Murn Bone Sar, who succeeded his brother Ānandasiri, the last king of Parein dynasty, then built another capital Khrit in AD 1142 on the left bank of the Laymro River. It is now uninhabited. The king had to move up the river for security reasons when the dynasty was in decline. The area was just over thirty acres wide. It was surrounded by a narrow moat, which is now occupied by paddy fields. Each wall of the city measures only about twelve hundred feet.

The city was a very unhealthy place for habitations, and only three kings, including the last one, King Danurupo, managed to live there. They resided in the city only for twelve years.

Second Sambawet (AD 1154–1163)

After King Danurupo ascended the Khrit's throne and stayed there for three years, he left the Khrit city and reoccupied the old Sambawet in AD 1154. The king was assassinated by a noble named Calanka Bo in AD 1160. The usurper-king occupied the throne of second Sambawet for about one year. He was succeeded by Mañjuthurn, son of Danurūpo. King Mañjuthurn ruled this city only for two years.

Mrohaung Taung Ngu (AD 1163–1251)

After the Manjuthurn had stayed there for two years, he left the old city and built a new capital named Mrohaung Taung Hgu. He built this city on the east bank of Lay-mro River in AD 1163. It lies four miles east of Laung Gret City. Most of the city ground had been eroded by the Lay-mro River. Some ruins of a Buddha image, and palace site, a fort and a wall have recently been unearthed on the bank of the Lay-mro River. Altogether seventeen kings reigned in this capital for eighty-eight years. The capital is also called Narañjarā.

Laung Gret (AD 1251–1406)

The last king of Mrohaung Taung Ngu dynasty was Alomā Phru, who ruled only one year in that city. He did not like the old city. Once the astrologers said that the city had lost all its power and glory and that country could not prosper if administered from that city, King Alomā Phru set out to find a suitable place for a new city. He crossed the Lay-mro River, selected a site with the help of his ministers and astrologers, and built the new city of Laung Gret in AD 1251. An old saying states that it was so named (Laung Gret = Boat-fowl) because during the search for the site, a jungle fowl flew out of its cover and alighted on the prow of the royal barge, whereupon the king's advisers unanimously interpreted it as highly propitious. They advised the king to build the new city along the bank from which the fowl came. They said the city would have a long life and his successors would be great and powerful.

Today, Laung Gret is situated on an island in the river Lay-mro, being bounded by the Lay-mro on the east and the Paungduk Chaung on the west. There is a small ridge in the northeast corner against which the city was supposed to have been built. The eastern walls as well as two-thirds of the palace-site happened to be eroded by the River.

There is a resemblance in the layouts of Parein and Laung Gret. Both faced east on the Lay-mro. There is a considerable expanse of plains on the northern and southern side. Access either by land and water is convenient.

Laung Gret lays five miles southeast of the city of Mrauk Oo and was capital for a hundred and fifty-five years.

Mrauk Oo (AD 1430–1784)

The last king of Laung Gret, Murn Somon founded the city Mrauk Oo in AD 1430. The city is the biggest in size, as its walls were built up again and again whenever threatened from Hansāvatī (Bago) and the west Bengal. Taking advantage of the ridges, the city walls have been built by simply damming up the small streams between the ridges.

3.6.2. The Communications[121]

Most internal and external communications in ancient Rakhaing were conducted by water. The rivers in Rakhaing are tidal. It would have been possible not only for domestic but also international sailing ships as well to reach Dhaññavatī via the Tha-re-chaung, and Vesālī via Ran-chaung, both being the tributaries of the Kaladan River.

There are two land routes connected with India, one of which is the way from the Chittagong-Ramu coast and the other from the upper reaches of the Kaladan River following the mountain ridge. The first route is directly linked with Nālanda, lacking high mountains except plains, brooks, and rivers. The second route is ancient, and according to the Rakhaing historical records, members of the Sākiya (Sakya) dynastic clans from India and Tagaung of Burma came to Rakhaing by this route and founded city states there up on the high land. For example, Sākiya Ajjhuna Hermit somewhere around 3000 BC and Kan Raza Gree from Tagaung in the sixteenth century BC. Present nationalities in Rakhaing state such as Rakhaing, Thet (Sak), Mro, Dine Net, Khamwei,

121 More detailed accounts of this can be found in Daw Thin Kyi's *Arakanese Capitals*, JBRS LIII (1970) pp. 1–13 and Pamela Gutman's *Ancient Arakan* (1976) pp. 3–9.

Mrama, entered the valley this way.[122] In 1611, Portuguese Diplomat Reverend Sebastiao Manrique reached to Golden Mrauk Oo by the way of Ganges plains.[123] That was probably the most ancient route.

Connecting with the Tsang-Ko road between Szechuan and Assam, this route was in use from about the fourth century to the mid-seventh century AD. According to Chinese records, certain twenty monks used this route during Sri Gutta period.[124]

Recent excavations by the Bangladesh Archaeological Survey have unearthed a Buddhist complex at Ramkot, on the road known as the old Rakhaing Highway, two miles east from Rāmu. The archaeological excavation of Mainmati, a Buddhist center near Comilla in Bangladesh, has provided new evidence of Rakhaing's contacts with the northeast India, Ganges.

Contact with the East by land was easier. A number of routes over the Rakhaing Roma in the south are possible, although the best-known is over the Taung Gup pass, which connected the Rakhaing Vesālī with Sri Kettarā (Sri Ksetra). Further north the Ann pass has been a route to the cities of central Burma, connecting Ann with the Man Valley in Minbu District. The traditional route between the northern capitals of Rakhaing and the capitals of Pyu (Hanlin, Vishno, and Sri

---

122 Bu, U San Shwe. *A Brief Note on the Old Capitals of Arakan*, p. 3, 135; Tun Shwe Khine, *Ancient Arakanese Capitals*, pp.20–29.

123 Maurice Collis, *The Land of the Great Image*, pp. 180–190.

124 *Chinese Test Taisho 2066* Vol. LI, pp. 1–12.; G. C. Rigby, *History of Operation in Northern Arakan and Yawdewin Hill. 1886–1887, with a Description of the Country and Its Resources, Notes on the Tribes and Diary*. Superintendent, Government Print., Burma, 1897; Brown, G. E. Grant. *Northern Arakan Hill Tracts*. Supt., Govt. Print. and Staty., Burma, 1960. p. 2.

Ksetra) was the Bu Ywet Ma Nyo Road, which led to the Laymro Valley.[125]

During the first century AD, Hippalos discovered the local monsoon. There are two kinds of seasonal monsoon changes in the Bay of Bengal: the southwest monsoon occurring from May through October and the northeast monsoon blowing from November through April. These winds are dependable for those who travel in the Bay of Bengal and are of much help to the development of the Rakhaing region. They can be observed to fit in with the Rakhaing coast, India, and Sri Lanka. Contacts with the west via the Bay of Bengal were no doubt well-established by the beginning of the Christian era.

Coedes in details describes that the Bay of Bengal plays the most important place in the process of Indian cultural influences to Southeast Asia. But, it is worthy to note that he has never mentioned of Arakan in his celebrated work. As Indian emperors used to buy valuable items through Siberia at first, they used to import those items from Roma Empire by the closure of that route around 200 BC. When Roman Emperor Vespasian prohibited the gold trade beyond the Empire, in order for Indians to get gold and silver they turned over to the East. Indian people now thought of *Suvannabhumi* and *Suvannadipa* as the gold sources.[126]

As the Arakan coastal strip lies in the position closer to India, it is unknown to us when the first contact took place. It is however presented by Gutman that contact with the West via

125 Bu, U San Shwe. *Buywetmanyo Road,* ASB (1920–1921) pp. 39–40; Oo, U Sein Maung. *Old Sri Kettara City,* University Paññapadesā Journal. Vol. 3, Part 1, pp. 202–203; Shin, U Ba. *Old Vishnu City and Historical Outlook on It,* University Paññapadesā Journal. Vol. 3, Part 3, p. 200 cont.

126 Coedes, George. "*The Indianized States of Southeast Asia*" Edit. Walter F. Vella; Trans. Susan Brown Cowing, Honolulu, East-West Centre Press (1968)

the Bay of Bengal was no doubt well-established by the beginning of the Christian era.[127]

Pomponius Mela (c. AD 50) was the first to mention, that islands Chryse and Argyre (Gold and Silver) were beyond the Ganges.[128] Gutman further says, "However, after century the references are more specific. In the later half of first century, the anonymous author of the Periplus saw in South India some vessels "called Kalandiophonta, very large, which hoist sail for Chryse and the Ganges," implying a route passing across the Bay of Bengal and along the Rakhaing coast."[129]

In an interesting paper by Colonel Yule on the oldest records of the sea-route to China from Western Asia, the author identified the country, named "Argyre" in Ptolemy, as Arakan. Ptolemy, a well-known geographer, who sailed along the Rakhaing coast in the second century AD, mentioned a number of ports in Argyre (Silver Country) which might be Rakhaing because his list begins with the port of Barakaura, which can be identified as situated at the mouth of the river Naff the border between Bengal and Rakhaing. The name Arakan is supposed to be derived from the silver mines existing there at that time. This name may be a corruption of the native name Rakhaing, from which the modern European form Arakan is derived.[130]

Luce, quoting Ptolemy, who in turn was citing Pomponius Mela (circa 43) on the location of ancient Arakan, said:

---

127 Gutman (1976), p.7

128 Hall, D. G. E. "*History of South East Asia*" pp. 14–15.

129 Gutman (1976), p. 8, *op. cit.*

130 *Ibid.*

"Descending the coast south-eastward from the mouth of the Ganges, he names first the Airrhadoi (with the port Barakoura) [this was presumably in the Chittagong region]; then the country of Argyre["Silver Land" i.e., Arakan] with [the towns of] Sambra, Sada, Berabonna and Temala [which Gereni believed was cape Negrais]; then a Cape; then the cannibals of Besynga [thought to be in the region of the mouth of the Irrawaddy River, in the Sarabak Gulf [most likely to Gulf of Martaban].[131]

Archaeological evidence further corroborates the existence of a sea route from South India to Rakhaing's capitals from about the end of the fourth century.

3.6.3. The Durations

Under this section, we are going to elucidate the durations of the two ancient cities of Arakan: Dhaññavatī and Vesālī.

3.6.3.1. Dhaññavatī

As San Shwe Bu points out, Rakhaing historical records state systematically about ancient capitals and their founders, reason of moving capitals, the period of their reign, and calculating the calendar with charts starting from 3325 BC.[132]

The earliest capitals, such as Dhaññavatī of Vāsudeva and Bhaladeva, Vesālī, Nga-kwe-thurn-taung of Brahma Rāzā

131 G. H. Luce, *The Tan (AD 97–132) and the Ngai-Lao,* p. 232.

132 Bu, U San Shwe. "*Legend of the Early Aryan Settlement in Arakan*" JBRS. Vol. 11, Pt. II, 1921

were so ancient that it was difficult to trace back and almost legendary.[133]

The first in dynastic chart is King Mārayu. His father, prince, migrated into northern Rakhaing from Majjhimadesa of India. He married local tribe leader's daughter and had a son, who later became a king. He was brave and powerful. He attacked and occupied Vesālī to establish first Dhaññavatī.[134]

This story was stated in ancient version of song poem written by Minister Badu Murn Nyo in Mrauk Oo Era of King Ba Saw Phru (AD 1459–1482).[135]

That five-hundred-year-old song-like poem (E Churn) is known as *Rakhaing Princess E Churn*, and it is earlier and most comprehensive in Burmese Literature. Because of its involvement with Rakhaing history's remarkable characteristics, it is of great value for Rakhaing history researchers.

The first Dhaññavatī, lasting 1816 years for fifty-four kings, collapsed after that by rebellion. The survivor queens continued to build new capitals: Kan Thone Sunt and Nilar Pandaung. They were just temporary ones. In 1531 BC King Kan Raza Gree from upper Irrawaddy,

133 Oo, U Aung Tha. "*Rakhaing Dynasties*" Typeset p. 2.

134 Aung, San Tha. "*The Early History of the Kingdom of Arakan up to 1000 AD*"; Gutman (1979) p. 3; Khine, Tun Shwe. "*The History of Arakan Dynasty*" (1985) p. 186

135 Khine, Tun Shwe. "*Rakhaing Princess E Churn*" (1990) p. 33.

Tagaung City came down along the West Roma Mountain ranges and crossed it to build Kyauk Padaung City.[136]

After staying there for twenty-four years, he came southward to the more fertile economic center of the valley region, took up the queen of the Mārayu dynasty, and founded the second Dhaññavatī.[137]

The second Dhaññavatī endured twenty-eight kings lasting for 927 years. In 580 BC, famous King Candasuriya ascended to throne and established third Dhaññavatī and Suriya dynasty. Suriya dynasty was contemporary with King Bimbissāra (528–554 BC), Ajatasattu (554–527 BC) in Magadha region (now in Bihar State), India.[138]

The third dynasty had twenty-five kings and lasted for nine hundred years until AD 326, the year King Dvencandra moved to Vesālī. Most of those kings' names were either Canda or Suriya. Canda means moon, while Suriya denotes sun.

---

136 Ancient and strange city, yet fully evidential, can fairly be traced back. In present there is a plateau by the name of Kyauk Padaung near Me Chaung's origin by Same Town of Chin state. That is 8 miles long, 4500 feet high plateau. It has been stated in record by Captain G. C. Rigby that on the plateau there may have available water, pleasant, could be an old place settled by human, and have walls, lakes, and human cultivations. Rigby, Captain G. C. *History of Operations in Northern Arakan and Yawdwin Chin Hills* (1896) p. 97; Pandi, U. *Dhaññavatī Razawon Theik,* p. 41; Candamalālaṅkāra, Ven. *Rakhaing Razawon Theik Kyan,* p. 230.

137 *Rakhaing Cultures and Traditional Customs* p. 142. It is supposed that Kammaraza from Tagaung coming from Sakya clan and the local queen coming from Añjana were easily married, because they both were from noble good clan. U San Shwe Bu is of the opinion that anyway he ruled his people there as an independent local chief until he came down south to the plains with a large army and married the windowed queen from Kan-Thone-Sunt. According to the custom of those days, this marriage established his right to the throne of Arakan, and the people without question accepted him as their ruler. This is supposed to have been taken place in 825 BC.

138 U Aung Tha Oo, *Buddhasāsana and Rakhaing Land,* p. 3.

Based on observations from the geographical point of view, it seems that the old Dhaññavatī represented the third Dhaññavatī before Vesālī in Rakhaing history. It would be more objective to base the findings on knowledge acquired from systematic excavation by the Archaeological Department.

3.6.3.2. Vesālī

According to Dhaññavatī chronicle, Vesāli was founded in AD 152. However, according to the book "New Rakhaing History" by Ven. Candamālālaṅkāra, it was founded in AD 249.[139]

The Candra dynasty presumably started in the middle of the fourth century, as mentioned by U Aung Thaw, the director of the Department of Archaeology. [140] The first head director of the Archaeology Department of Burma, Dr. Forchhammer (followed by Sir Arthur Phayre), stated that new Vesālī was built in 152 BE. (AD 789).[141] Dr. Forchhammer and successive western historians carried through the facts. Western historians seemed that by adding 638 to BE in order to convert it to CE, following Rakhaing historical literature and historians' trend.

The fact that Vesālī was founded in AD 327 was unanimously supported by the Rakhaing national scholars and both "*Cultural and Traditional Customs of Nationalities: Rakhaing*" by Burmese Socialist Program Party and "*The*

139 Eras were counted after the cancellation of then the existing era 609 to 2 by Suriya Cittra.

140 Thaw, U Aung. "*Historical Sites in Burma*" p. 117

141 Forchhammer (1892) p. 8; Phayre (1883) p. 45.

State Gazetteer Vol. 1, History Section" by the Rakhaing State Peoples' Council.[142]

Professor E. H. Johnston and Indian Inscription Master D. C. Sircar studied this matter meticulously and deciphered the inscription of King Ānandacandra near Shitthoung temple relocated from old Vesālī by Murn Bā Gree of Mrauk Oo dynasty in the sixteenth century. Johnston estimated the Vesālī foundation period to AD 350 and Sircar to AD 370 by the dynastic chart. This has also been supported by U Myint Shwe.[143] It has been found that the estimation of Rakhaing scholars of the founding of Vesālī as AD 327 is very similar to that of Dr. Johnston and Dr. Sircar. According to aerial photos, the Vesālī City wall, design, and foundations are similar to those in Sri Kettara, Hanlin, Beikthano (Vishano) in Burma's Irrawaddy valley, Dvāravadī in Siam, and Angkor Wat in Cambodia.[144] They were contemporaries to each other, which scholars have proven already.

The excavation report of Vesālī further says that the symbol of auspiciousness *srivatsa* found in the coins of Vesālī is alike with those from Pyu capitals, Vishano,

142 Ven Candamālālaṅkāra, *Rakhaing Razawon Theik Kyan*; Pandi, U. *Dhaññavatī Razawon Theik*; U Aung Tha Oo, *Rakhaing Culture: Vesali Period* p. 27.; *State Gazetteer (History)*; *Rakhaing Cultural and Traditional Customs* p. 174

143 U Myint Shwe, *Ānandacandra's Sanskrit Inscription*, p.15; Johnston (1944) pp. 357–385; Sircar (1957) pp. 103–109.

144 E. Lee Sherman, *A History of Far Eastern Art* p. 235; U Ba Shin, "Old Vishnu City and Historical Outlook on It," *University Paññapadesā Journal, Vol. 3, Part 3,* Map. 1.

Hanlin, and Sri Kettarā, conveying the fact that there were communications among contemporary capitals.[145]

Many different opinions about the duration of Vesālī were discussed, and it was found that western historians' belief that it was founded in AD 788 is not correct. The most logical starting year is AD 370, based on Johnston, Sircar, and findings of modern Rakhaing historians.

The new discovery was objectively supported by findings during systematic excavation of Vesālī and report of Burmese Archaeological Department. It states: Excavated finds at the third season of excavation at Vesālī, show how archaeological excavations help to solve historical problems. Excavated finds from Vesālī indicate that Vesālī flourished between the fourth and eighth centuries AD.[146]

Remarks

To summarize what has been said up to here, we have embraced the natural boundaries of mountains Rakhaing Roma and sea Bay of Bengal protecting a compact area suited to dry and wet rice cultivation factors which led to the evolution of the urban settlement of ancient people in Rakhaing Kaladan-Laymro Valley and centralized organization, while both sea and land routes made direct contact with India possible.

From the viewpoint of historical development of Rakhaing, it is interesting to note that it has been an independent kingdom throughout its history. Besides, the Rakhaing people were able to control large

145 Min Nyunt Han, *Third Season of Excavation at Vesālī*, Part II. (1982), WPD Sep. 10, p. 5. "Coins bearing a *srivatsa* on one side and a couchant bull on the other have been frequently discovered inside the old city of Vesālī. As the *srivatsa* was considered an auspicious symbol used during Pyu period in Old Pyu capitals such as Vishano, Hanlin, Sri Kettarā, etc., scholars generally assume, that when Vesālī flourished in the western part of Burma, it reached the zenith of power and prosperity."

146 *Ibid.*

tracts of area along the sea-coasts to the east, west, and south, far beyond borders of the Fatherland. The Rakhaing Empire extended westward to Dacca and Tripūra for a long time and also conquered Bago. For a short time, Rakhaing held the lower part of Burma and even extended its influence to Martaban.

On one hand, the physical boundaries of Rakhaing determine the extent of control by a central authority. On the other hand, as will be shown in coming chapters, it was helpful in giving rise to a good opportunity for the growth of Buddhist religion and Indian-influenced culture, which should be seen not only as an introduction of Indian Buddhism itself, but as help of three ways of trade, missions, and pilgrimage.

Briefly, ancient Rakhaing's geographical background, its peoples and cities with their unique position on the eastern bank of the Bay of Bengal where South and Southeast Asia meet, with both land and sea routes to the east and west, resulted in the development of political and cultural traits, especially that of Buddhism and later in emergence of it as a "maritime kingdom" or a "cultural frontier" in the region.

CHAPTER 4

INTRODUCTION OF BUDDHISM IN RAKHAING LAND: LEGEND AND HISTORY

The Buddha had died in 543 BC. Altogether 2173 years had elapsed since then, and for that immense period the image of the Founder of the Religion had reminded on Sirigutta, the oldest, most mysterious, the most holy object in the world. The relics detailed to the disciplines on Selagiri had all been found and enshrined. Arakan was a sacred country; it was the heart of Buddhism; and he (king Thiri-thu-deamma) as its king, was the most notable Buddhist ruler in existence. Grave indeed was his responsibility. He had not only to maintain the state as the homeland of the Arakanese race, but as the one place on earth where an authentic shape of the Buddha was preserved, a possession of greater potency than The most precious relics.

(*The Land of Great Image* by Maurice Collis, p. 168)

Introduction

The Buddha established his *Sāsana* in ancient India in 563 BC. When the Buddha entered his final *prinibbāna* in about 483 BC, almost all the important states in north India seems to have been deeply influenced by the new teaching among many other contemporary religio-philosophical religions. *Buddhasāsana* and Buddhist culture travelled and spread to Ceylon, Burma, Siam, Indochina, Indonesia, far-north Asia, eastern Asia; Tibet, China, Koreas, and Japan beyond North India, not only due to the Buddha himself went here and there to preach the *Dhamma*, but also by the tireless efforts of the Buddhist missionaries: monarchs, *Bhikkhu Sanghās* after the *prinibbāna* of the Buddha. In such transfusion of Buddhism, each differs from another. Scholar Coedes who studied especially on the Indian cultural influences including Buddhism over to Southeast Asia, is of the opinion that Indianization of Southeast Asia was not happen at a particular time, by all alone, from a particular place, but it happened one group after another, stepping one by one like a serial events gradually during over long years.[147] What we are going to present now is how *Buddhasāsanā* entered into the land, which is by far the nearest place among all the Indian cultural, literary, and Buddhist influenced states by its geographical location. It is connected by land and sea with India. With regard to the study of and presenting this region, it might, however, be rational to take other historical evidence into account, in addition to the presently available sources, even though archaeological discovery has not yet been done fully over the ruins of the land.

Earlier writing of historians, particular those of pro-Indian or Indian historians, on the copious archeological and epigraphical material unearthed in Southeast Asia, based as they were on sentiments of nationalism, had eloquently spoken of colonization of Southeast Asia by the Indians, of far-flung kingdoms, of a Greater India and of

147 Coedes (1968)

cultural and religious invasion of Southeast Asia by Indian culture and religions. While this trend in history writing had its own utility in preindependence India, it has been hoped that a factual reassessment of those materials at this point of time, with special reference to recent discoveries, would help in greater and more objective understanding and interpretation of the nature, depth, and intensity of Indian influence on Southeast Asia. Hereunder is the elucidation which seeks to reassess some of the old archeological and epigraphical discoveries found in Rakhaing in collaboration with local chronicles and to introduce the recent findings.

Concerning how Buddhism reached into the Rakhaing Land and its later developments, one, first, has to study the geographical location between the birth place of Buddhist India and the Rakhaing strip, how communications took place between by sea or land, what historical features or circumstances of them were, and what the general characteristics of them had been.

About the land what we are going to study at the present has been fenced by the six-thousand-foot-high Rakhaing Romas (Mountains) in the east which lines from north to south, in the east beyond there had been ancient Pyu urbanized cities: *Vishnu, Hanlin, Sri Kettara.* To where by using the passages: Taung-gup, Ann and *Buywetmanyo,* the peoples from the strip could reached and *vice versa.*[148] The land had been in the northwest, Bengal, the Buddha's enlightened place Ganges Valley in northern India, and the central places of Early Buddhism such as *Varanasi* (Benares), *Bodh Gāya, Nālanda,* etc., in the south and west of the land, Bay of Bengal, in the west bank of the Bay, the places of then-Buddhist civilizations of South India such as *Andhara, Amaravati, Nāgajunakoṇḍa,* and *Laṅkā Dīpa.* Approximately, it is 525 miles from the

148 San Shwe Bu, "*Buywetmanyo Road*" ASB, 1920–21. pp. 39–40; Oo, Sein Maung. "*Old Sri Kettara City.*" University Paññapadesā Journal. Vol. 3, Pt. 1, pp. 202–203; Shin, U Ba. "*Old Vishnu City and Historical Outlook on It.*" University Paññapadesā Journal. Vol. 3, Pt. 3, p. 200 cont.

land to the *Bodh Gayā*, 500 miles to *Nālanda*, 850 miles to *Amaravatī*, and 1200 miles to Ceylon.

Observing the geographical location of the land as mentioned above briefly and in detail earlier in 3.6.2., there has been communications with the birth place of Buddhism and with later developed Buddhist cultural places, such as South India and Ceylon from times immemorial and memorial. The establishment of Buddhism in Rakhaing is proven not only by local literary evidence such as the Razawons, but by the archeological remains, which assigned to be the nearest periods of the actual happenings. First, we are going to elucidate religious conditions in Rakhaing before the arrival of Buddhism. It is followed in the second by the significance of Buddhism as an important fact. In the third and fourth, we will discuss about the Buddha's arrival to Rakhaing and casting of the Great Image (*Mahāmuni*) in the reign of King Candasuriya (620–543 BC), and in the fifth, the evolution of Buddhism in India after the Buddha's *paribibbāna* and before the third Buddhist council in *Pātaliputta*; in the sixth, Asoka's Buddhist Mission from *Pātaliputta* of Magadha Empire to Rakhaing as the second important event in the religious history of Rakhaing; finally, the general examination on the religious identity during the said periods in Rakhaing.

4.1. Religious Conditions: Pre-Buddhist Aryanization of Rakhaing

Religion is a spontaneous expression of the heart; it is based on feeling and faith, and every person, primitive or modern, is religious. The religious experience, however, varies from people to people, from age to age, and gives rise to widely different myths, superstitions, dogmas, and creeds.

It is found that the starting and earliest place having recorded in the local chronicles is *Dvārāvatī* (present Sandoway). This is not *Dvārāvatī* of Mon land between present Thahton and Menan

Valley founded around the sixth century AD said by researchers. *Dvārāvatī* of Rakhaing was founded by legendary ten brothers: *Vāsudeva, Bhaladeva,* etc., it is however not exactly known the fact that in what date or in what century it was found by them. Early local historians have mentioned merely very ancient time ago in normal tone. Whenever the ten bothers tried to occupy Dvārāvadī City, it was unsuccessful because the city went fly up to the sky. Finally they consulted with Hermit *Kannhādīpāyana* in order to catch the city. It is also found that Hermit *Ajjuna,* then-king of *Kapilavattu* in India, came down along the river Kicchapa and settled down under a bayan tree by the river, before the establishment of Dhaññavatī City in northern Rakhaing. By observing these facts, it is supposed that prehistoric people believed in and paid respect to hermits, sun-god, moon-god, guardian god of the city, of the forest, of the mountain, etc.[149]

It is said in the chronicles and by local historians that Aryan people, fathers of the existing Rakhaing people, had settled the land five thousand years ago, which is about twenty-eight hundred years (3000 BC) before the emergence of Gotama the Buddha. It is known by the light of literary historical evidences that the people inhabited in the land worshiped and loved by awe to many variety of gods such as natural gods before the arrival of *Buddhasāsana.* Even they had worshiped gods of different images and statutes as of thinking and ideas along the evolution of civilizations. For that, the Buddha himself practically says the following verse:

Bahuṁ ve saranaṁ yanti, pabbatāni vanāni ca
āramarukkhacetyāni manussā bhayatajjitā.

149 Bu, San Shwe. "*Legend of the Early Aryan Settlement of Arakan*" JBRS, (1921) Vol. II, part 2; Candamālālaṅkāra, Ven. "New Rakhaing Razawon" (1931) Vol. 1, p. 213; Oo, Aung Tha. "*Buddhasāsanā and the Land Rakhing*" (1974) p.1

Because of awe as danger, men go to many a refuge, to mountains and forests, to parks and gardens, and to sacred trees and shrines.[150]

Ancient people of Rakhaing like ancient Aryan people in India worshiped different *Brahmanical* gods such as sun, moon, Vishnu, Shiva, Nandi, Fire, Wind, Water, guardian of the town, of the city, of the land etc. before the advent of Gotama the Buddha like many other ancient peoples of the world. There is no doubt that the early kingdoms of Rakhaing were Brahmanical city states. Some Brahmanical deities were found in ancient cities. It was believed that the worshipers of Sun God derived from the family of the Sun, *Suriyavamsa*, or the worshipers of Moon God from the family of the Moon, *Candravamsa.* Aryans who lived in Babylonia around 2000 BC worshiped the Sun God. It was also in Rakkhapūra in the third Dhaññavatī period that King Candasuriya and his successors were called the Sun's generations (*Suriyavamsa*). The successive of previous period, before Vesāli Kyauk Hlay Gar period, King Mahā Taicandra (*Dvencandra* in the Inscription) and his successors were named the Moon's generations (*Candavamsa*). Such are of Aryan culture.

It is not that some researchers are of the opinion so as to the generations of Candra kings from India came and ruled in Vesālī Kyauk Hlay Gar City. In reality, it was King Dven Chandra, son of King Suriyaketu, the twenty-fifth king after Candasuriya, who left the third Dhaññavatī City to establish and rule the Vesālī Kyauk Haly Gar City. Seeing of the symbols of sun and moon inscribed in the coins is precisely the blotches of the *Suriyavamsa* and *Candavamsa.*

In accordance with the circumstances of the land and time, they worshiped and performed rituals to gods such as Vishnu, Shiva, Rain, Wind, Water Flood, Fire, etc. It is therefore said by researcher historians that such kinds of God worshiping religion

150 Verse No. 188, Buddhavagga, Dhammapada (*translation are mine*) [Unless otherwise indicated, all Pāḷi and Pāḷi Commentarial references mentioned in the dissertation are from the CSCD ROM).

has also been found in the lands of ancient China, Egypt, Syria, Babylonia, Greece, Roma, etc. However, Brahmanism might have been replaced by Buddhism when the kings and people became Buddhists. The spirit or god worship is still found especially in Southeast Asia at the present as a customary or traditional worship, even though people accept and practice any new religion, it is because practicing such religion (i.e., Brahmanism for a considerable long period).[151] And because beliefs ingrained in the minds of men from time immemorial cannot be eradicated at one stroke, something had to be offered in place of what they wanted to be abolished, and some old practices which were comparatively less objectionable had to be given the approval of the new creed. The veneration of statues of the Buddha and of *stūpas* was supposed to be adopted with a new interpretation as a means of honoring the memory of the Founder of the Faith. Festivals connected with the worship of *stūpas* and the statue of the Buddha weaned the people away from in great measure from older observances in which were certain features of a morally reprehensible nature.

4.2. Buddhism[152]

Buddhism, which was a younger contemporary of Jainism, struck a new keynote in Indian religious life—a via media between the rigorism of the *Jains* and the secularism of the sacrificial *Brāhmaṇas.* It advocated a moderate life for its recluses, and permitted them just enough food, clothing, and shelter to maintain their physical strength in order to be able to practice concentration of thoughts and to acquire knowledge. It chalked out a well-thought

151 *State Gazetteer (Culture)* p. 1.

152 This section is largely dependent on Nalinaksha Dutt's work incorporated in *History of Ceylon* Vol. 1, Part I, University of Peradeniya Sri Lanka, pp. 122–124.

out path known as the *aṭṭhaṅgikamagga*, or the Eightfold Path, which trained an adept morally, psychologically, and intellectually.

The monks and nuns were prescribed ten precepts, of which four were in agreement with those of the *Jainas*. The Buddhist householders were required to observe only five of them with option to increase them to eight temporarily. For the monks, the ten precepts were enlarged into 227 rules codified in the *Pātimokkha Sutta*, and likewise for the nuns, and elaborated further in the *Vinaya-piṭaka*. Apart from the observance of disciplinary rules, the monks and nuns were asked to practice meditations, divided into lower and higher categories, known as *jhānas* and *samāpattis*. These are dealt with analytically in the *Abhidhamma-piṭaka* and systematized by *Buddhaghosa* in the *Visuddimagga*.

Along with these practices, the monks and nuns, with a few exceptions, were required to pursue a program of studies for intellectual development (*paññā*). The main object of such studies was to comprehend the three cardinal tenets of Buddhism, viz., momentary impermanence (*khaṇika-anicca*), nonsubstantiality (*anattā*), and painfulness or suffering (*dukkha*) of all worldly objects and beings. This comprehension could take place by means of constantly observing the dynamic nature of worldly objects governed by the law of causation (*paṭiccasamuppāda*). The intellectual acquisition led to *Nibbāna*, usually known *paṭisaṅkhā-nirodha*. The Buddhist monks are graded according to their spiritual acquisitions.

4.2.1. Buddhism as a Religion

Being not too austere as Jainism, Buddhism offered a better scope for the development of its religious aspect. In its early stage, the monks and nuns were advised to refrain from worship of Buddha-images or *stūpas*, and were asked to concentrate on their self-exertion and progressing along the spiritual path, outlined above. They were prescribed monasticism, which was a complete departure from the traditional forms of Indian recluse-life. It necessitated a few ceremonial formalities, which might be regarded as the religious aspect of early Buddhism. These may be summed up briefly as follows:

(1) *Tisaraṇa* or the taking of refuge in the three *ratanas.* Every monk or nun or a householder must express his faith thrice in the Buddha, the Dhamma and the *Saṅgha* with set formulae.

(2) *Pañca-* or *dasa-sīla* or the administration and avowal of five or ten moral precepts. The administration is done formally by a senior monk to a junior monk or novice, or by a monk to a householder; for the former, the number of precepts is ten while for the latter is five.

(3) *Pabbajjā* and *upasaṁpadā* or the lower and higher forms of ordination. The former is meant for an entrant into the noviciate (*sāmaṇera*), while the latter is for a trained novice seeking admission into the *Saṅgha* as a full member, a *bikkhu.* These two ordinations are done ceremonially, for which is laid down a systematic procedure.

(4) *Uposatha* or the auspicious day of meeting of the monks. On every full-moon or new-moon day, the monks dwelling in a parish must assemble at a central monastery, declare their innocence of breach of all *pātimokkha* rules, or confess their breaches of rules, if any, and take absolution. If the breach be of a serious nature, the offending monk is excluded from the assembly and is placed under suspension or probation. In the assembly after the formal election of the president, the rules of the *pātimokkha* are recited by him, and all monks present, and the absentees by their proxies, have to say that they were all pure according to the rules. This ceremony is usually followed by a discourse or religious discussion, which could be listened to by the householders.

(5) *Vassāvāsa* or the Rainy Season Retreat. During the three months of rains, the monks are enjoined to stay at a fixed abode and not to move beyond the boundaries of a certain

limited area without very special and urgent reasons, for which again prior sanction of the *Saṅgha* was necessary.

(6) The Retreat is ended by a ceremony called *pavāraṇā*, which is similar to *uposatha* described above. In this ceremony, the monks or nuns are required to confess if there be any breach of the *pātimokkha* rules during the whole period of the Retreat. This ceremonial occasion is considered by the lay-devotees as very sacred for offering gifts of cloths, for making robes for the inmates of the *Saṅgha*. There is a special function called *kaṭhina* performed after *pavāraṇā*. In this ceremony, some monks are given special privileges for cutting and sewing the cloths into robes quickly, so that they may be distributed to the inmates of the *Saṅgha* before their dispersal.

4.2.2. Religion of the Lay-devotees

More latitude was given to the lay-devotees than the monks and nuns for expressing their devotion to their faith. These are as follows:

(1) To supply the monks and nuns with robes, food, beds, and medical requisites, which are said to ensure them long life and happiness in the next world;

(2) To construct monasteries for the residence of monks and nuns;

(3) To erect *stūpas* enshrining to the relics of the Buddha and of his saintly disciples and to worship them;

(4) To visit the four places: *Kapilavastu*, *Bodh Gayā*, *Sārnāth* and *Kusinārā* sanctified by the Buddha's birth, enlightenment, first preaching, and *Mahāparinibbāna*, respectively;

(5) To make and install Buddha images for worship;

(6) To take *tisaraṇa* and five precepts, and occasionally eight precepts for a short period;

(7) To attend *uposatha* assemblies;

(8) To offer cloths for robes at the *pavāraṇā* ceremony.

4.2.3. The History of Buddhism (Fifth to Fourth Century BC)

In the second century after the Buddha's demise, during the period of the *Sisunāga* dynasty (414–396 BC), the *Saṅgha* became divided into a number of sects, some affiliated to the orthodox section called *Theravāda,* while others to the unorthodox called *Mahāsaṅghika.* The latter had their main center in the *Āndhra* province, for which they were also called the *Andhakas.* They introduced substantial changes not only in the disciplinary rules, but also in the conception of the Buddha and in the *summum bonum.* They made some of the *Vinaya* rules lax, conceived of the Buddha as the highest conceivable being (*lokuttara*), whose apparitional form appeared in the world as Gotama Buddha, and that the *summum bonum* was not *Nibbāna* but *Buddhahood.* This new movement brought in its train the worship of Buddha images on a large scale. It laid more stress on *Jātaka* stories, and popularized the *pāramitā* cult, making the lay-devotees feel that they could, without embracing the recluse-life, derive the benefits of the religion. It is regarded as a forerunner of *Mahāyāna* Buddhism, which later swept over Northern India and Northeastern Asia. The orthodox sect, *Theravāda,* had also many subsects, one of which, the *Sabbatthivāda,* became very popular in Northern India, particularly at *Mathurā,* in *Gandhāra* and Kashmir, and also in Central Asia. Another subsect, the *Sammitīya,* became popular in Sind, as also in the western part of India. The *Theravāda,* which retained its stronghold in Central India and moved southward to the brothers of India, adhered to the orthodox principles and doctrines as found in the *Pāḷi Piṭakas.* The establishment of Buddhism in *Daññavadī* of ancient Rakhaing and its historical developments which led to a number of significant events will be dealt with in the next.

4.3. The Tradition of Gotama, the Buddha's Visit to Dhaññavatī, and the Earliest Evidences of the Presence of Buddhism in Ancient Rakhaing

> "The tradition is intimately connected with the religious history of Arakan and Burma in general; it is as old as Buddhism itself in that province. Nearly all pagodas within the confines of Dhaññavatī and..."[153]

The chronicles claim that the Buddha is said to have visited not only to Dhaññavatī of Rakhaing, but both lower and upper Burma as well.[154] Ceylon also makes the same claim. As books on history of the land usually begin with the arrival of Buddhism in the region, it is a kind of indigenous nature of writing Buddhist history of their own. The problem is not, perhaps, Buddhism's entry into the land itself, but rather how, when, by whom, from which part of India, and to what part of the region was Buddhism first introduced. The last question sometimes involves nationalistic pride concerning which country can claim to be the first to have become Buddhist among the Southeast Asia Buddhist world. For Rakhaing we have evidence beyond the chronicles to substantiate the chronicles' assertion, so the date can be verified. In fact, there is no such datable evidence even in the *Tripiṭaka*.

Regarding the chronicles and traditional claim of the Buddha's visit to Rakhaing, Prof. San Tha Aung commented, "According to the Arakanese historical annals and the *Selagiri* tradition, Buddhism was introduced into Arakan during the lifetime of the Buddha. The legend asserts that during the reign of *King Candasuriya*, the king of *Dhanyawadi* (Ancient Arakan) who

153 Forchhammer (1892) p. 2

154 "New Razawon" pp. 247–265, *op. cit.*

was a contemporary of the Buddha, Gotama the Buddha visited Arakan with five hundred disciples. On the *Selagiri* Mountain, which is opposite Kyauktaw town on the Kaladan River, the Buddha held a prophetic discourse."[155]

In Rakhaing, the archaeological explorations: first in 1882[156] in Dhaññavatī, second as the site observation of Dhaññavatī in April 1975 by a team,[157] studies[158] both in Dhaññavatī and Vesālī by Prof. Johnston, Prof. Sircar, Sir Arthur Phayre, U Myint Shwe, Min Nyunt Han and many others, laid bare the culture of an ancient people, who lived since some over three thousand years ago in the Kaladan and Lay-mro Valley: their culture similar, and in some aspects superior, to that of contemporary Pyu and Talaing. They used utensils of stone, lived on agricultural products, and utilized domesticated animals. Their religion had certain features that appear in later Hinduism. Their culture differs in some features from that of the neighboring Pyu in typography and religious phenomena, but most are relatively the same.

The discovery of the ruins at Mahāmuni Temple and Kyauk Taw Hill and vicinities of the ancient cities of Dhaññavatī and Vesālī came in the wake of the excavations of ancient inscriptions, Buddhist sculptors and *stūpas*, symbols, and religious artifacts,

155 San Tha Aung, (1979) "*Buddhist Art*" p.53.

156 *Ibid.*

157 It comprises the former Director General of the Department of Higher Education Prof. U San Tha Aung, Sanskrit Scholar U Myint Swe from Mandalay University, University Translation and Publishing Department Chief Editor U Tin Oo and Local Historians, notably including the then PhD candidate Pamela Gutman from Australian National University.

158 Johnston (1944) pp. 357–385; Sircar (1957) pp. 103–109; Phayre (1882) "*Coins of Arakan*"; Shwe, U Myint. "*Ānanda Chandra Sanskrit Inscription*" Literature and Social Science Journal, Union of Myanmar (1969) Vol. 2. No. 3; Min Nyunt Han, "*Third Season of Excavation at Vesālī*" WPD (Sep. 10, 1982).

which, according to the discoverers such as Dr. Forchhammer,[159] Prof. San Tha Aung,[160] U Aung Tha Oo,[161] etc., were inscribed in stone and mental, made with bronze, which might have been a rendezvous of the Buddhism in prehistoric days in Rakhaing, are the very presence of Buddhism.

Most of the Rakhaing Chronicles are used to talk about the event of the Lord Buddha's visit to the land. This event of the visit by the Buddha was also composed by a Rakhaing Poet Mra Doe Wei in AD 1757.[162]

The historic event has been narrated by Dr. Forchhammer, one of the earliest researchers on Rakhaing studies. He retold the story by using the *Sarvasthānaprakarna* (Pāḷi–*Sabbadānapakāraṇa*), an ancient Arakanese manuscript of great value. Here it will be appropriate to refer to two abstract narratives from his work:

> "Then Gotama, accompanied by Ānanda and 500 rahans, flew through the air and alighted on the summit of the Selagīri (the hill opposite Kyauk-taw). Here he held a discourse with his disciples and then addressed Ānanda thus: 'Ānanda, to the west of the Gacchabha river, which flows past this hill, there is a plain; here have I in former existences been born many times."[163]

---

159 *Ibid.* Forchhammer.

160 San Tha Aung, (1979) *The Buddhist Art*; San Tha Aung, *Alphabet used in Rakhaing in Sixth century and Before*, Tauk Tauk Win Press, Rangoon (Nov. 1974).

161 Aung Tha Oo, *Rakhaing Culture (Vesāli Period)*, Vol. 1, No. 1, Rangoon: Aung Ratana Press, Sep. 1966, Burmese.

162 U Shwe Zan, *Wethali: The Land of Historic Finds*, pp. 299–300; Aung Tha Oo, *Rakhing Cultural History and its View by Researchers* (1978 typeset copy) (reprint 1985); Goyamray Saw Won, *Rakhing State and Buddhasāsanā*, Tat Lam Literature, Printed by Siddhi Myiing, Yangon (Dec. 1994).

163 *Ibid.*, Forchhammer (1892) p. 2.

"Then the Blessed One addressed his disciples thus: "O Rahanas, my beloved sons! in the island of Jambūdīpa and among the 16 countries of Majjhimadesa the food offered to the priesthood consists of a mixture of maize, beans, corn, and millet. But in this country the food offered consists of various kinds of barley and rice; such food is eaten by the priests with relish; my presiding elder brothers (Kakusandha, Gonagamaṇa, and Kassapa, i.e., the three Buddhas who preceded Gotama) have called this country Dhaññavadī, and as the inhabitants have never suffered from famine, this region shall in all times to continue to be called Dhaññavadī (i.e., the grain-blessed)."[164]

An Arakanese scholar says concerning the reason why the Buddha paid a visit to Dhaññavatī in collaboration with the local chronicles, "The History of Rakkhapura as foretold by Gautama Buddha. Gautama (Buddha) visited Dhaññavatī with the object of leaving his Sāsanā as well as his image, for he foresaw that the Sāsanā would get lost in India after his passing to Nirvana. On arrival at Selāgīri Kyauk Taw Hill, Gautama Buddha related to Ānanda, the history of the Rakhaing Kingdom, in order that he may know in what kind of a country. He was leaving his Sāsana, as well as his image."[165]

He continues, "Some are of the opinion that Majjhima ends at the Arakan (Rakhaing) Romas. Since Gautama Buddha travelled as far as Tan-gyi Taung, on the west bank of the Irrawaddy River and from there predicted that Sri Kettarā Kingdom will be formed on the opposite bank, in the future. We have to assume that Mijjhima ends on the west bank of the Irrawaddy River and

164 *Ibid.*, Forchhammer (1892) p. 5.

165 Tun, U Sein Nyo. "*Review of the Most Ancient Rakhing History*" (1966 May).

the country to the east of the Irrawaddy is known as pacchandara, is a place where no Buddhas travel to. Hence Gautama Buddha was explaining to Ānanda, that he was still in Mijjhima."[166]

The conversion of the people of Rakhaing to Buddhism, with which the authentic history of the land begins, profoundly influenced the subsequent course of events therein, and has imparted to its culture its distinctive character. Historical records of the land are unanimously inserting that the acceptance of doctrines of the Buddha by the people of Rakhaing was the outcome of the enthusiasm display by the great Rakhaing King Candasuriya for the invitation of the Buddha from *Majjhimadesa.* Contemporary records do not throw such blaze of light on the personality of *Candasuriya* and the Buddha's arrival.

With reference to how Buddhism entered into ancient Rakhaing and the practice of Buddhism by the inhabitants, there are many pieces of evidence noted as the earliest ones. First of all,

166 Tun, U Sein Nyo. (1966 May). *op. cit.*

a fragmentary Taungbauk Gree Brahmi Inscription[167] mentioning the event of the visit of the Lord Buddha on the summit of Selāgīri (Kyauk Taw Hill) near Dhaññavatī city was discovered by U San Shwe Bu, the then Honorable Archaeological Officer for Arakan

---

167 Regarding this, here it will be appropriate to refer to the information footnoted by U Sandamuni Bhikkhu, in his work, "The Origin and Development of Arakanese Script" PhD Thesis, *Inscriptions belonging to Third Dhanyawaddy Age and to Wethali Age* (2007), the scholar argued why this inscription is not regarded as an evidence even though it is an eye-copy one. The footnote runs: "information regarding the Taungpaukkri Fragmentary Inscription can be had as early as 1974 when San Tha Aung's book "*Scripts of Rakhine Sixth Century and Before*" (in Burmese) was published. But, curiously enough, Pamela Gutman in her unpublished thesis did not take any notice of this was made of Aung's aforesaid book. See Gutman, P. "*Ancient Arakan*" PhD thesis (unpublished) 1976, p. 370. About one-and-a-half decades later in 1992 and Arakanese scholar referred to this inscription in his unpublished thesis, "*History of Buddhism in Arakan*" the eye-copy of the inscription, first mentioned in Burmese books published in 1974, is not, however, considered as evidence by Ashin Okkantha. See Ashin Sri Okkantha, "*History of Buddhism in Arakan*" (Unpublished PhD thesis), Calcutta University 1992, p. 41, n.1. We do not, however, see any reason why the eye-copy of the inscription cannot be accepted as evidence. In the support of our conviction, the following points may be stated:

(i) The eye-copy of the inscription was made long before its destruction during the Second World War by San Shwe Bu, an eminent Rakhaing Historic and U Tha Tun, one of the distinguished scholars of Rakhaing. If the eye-copy made by these two learned men of Rakhine cannot be taken as evidence; it then raises as grave doubt about the integrity of these two scholars. This is unfortunate.

(ii) Only an expert epigraphist can testify to the accuracy or otherwise in respect of writing the alphabet in the eye-copy of the inscription, though unfortunately, the original inscription is now lost.

(iii) A comparative study of the letters of the Taungpaukkri Fragmentary inscription with the Indian Brahmi inscriptions of the third and second centuries BC (Asokan Brahmi inscriptions as well as the one found at Maasthan in Bogra district Bangladesh) on the one hand and the Fat Monk image inscription found in Rakhaing on the other proves that quite a few letters of the Taungpuakkri inscription bear a close similarity with the alphabet of the above noted contemporary inscription from India as well as Rakhaing.

(iv) The claim in the book by Ashin Candamālālaṅkāra that "in the inscription of the history of Buddhism in Rakhine had been fixed in the period of the Buddha" (See Okkantha A. S., *ibid.*) may be contested, but what is certain is that paleographically, the inscription cannot be dated much earlier than the second century BC.

(v) For a fuller list of the alphabet and the problem relating to its gradual development a details discussion will be found in the following chapters.

and his student, U Oo Thar Tun (Rakhaing-Myanma Pandit) in April 1932. This is known as the Taungbauk Gree Inscription (see appendix 3) because it was found in the vicinity of Taungbauk Gree village. That they copied the inscription was written in *Pāḷi* with Brahmī scripts. There were altogether twenty-five lines of inscriptions, but only five were readable, inscribed on the naturally exposed surface of the rock. During World War II (1942–1943), this rock was exploded by mine and crushed to ruin. The style of writing and use of alphabets seem to be in the reign of King *Suriyacakka*, contemporary with Asoka Dynasty of India in the third century BC, because the alphabet */ka/* in the inscription has been inscribed as (+), the */na/* as (T). It coincided with the event when the king of *Pātaliputta* sent *Sarīradhātu* (body relics) of the Buddha to the king of Arakan.[168]

The five readable lines can be written in Romanized Paḷi as follows:

Athakho bhagavā bhikkhusanghaṁ pāsādam āruhāpetvā
Pañcapāsādasataparivuto Dhaññavatīratthaṁ
Ākāsamaggena cārikaṁcaramāno
Dhaññavatīmahānagarassa pacchimadisābhāge
Gacchapanadīyā pūrattimatire selāgīri pabbhatamuddhami(ni)
Orohitvā patiṭāti

The above Pāḷi may be translated briefly as follows:

Having thinking of visiting to, Lord Buddha with sorts of power and glory accompanied by his five hundred disciples by aerial way descended and took a rest on the top of the Kyauk Taw Hill

168 San Tha Aung, *Alphabets used in Rakhing Sixth Century and Before*, Tauk Tauk Win Press, Rangoon (1974 Nov). pp. 63–67; Oo, Aung Tha. "*Buddhasāsana and the Land of Rakhing.*" (3rd Nov, 1974) pp. 8–9; *Rakhing Cultural and Traditional Customs* (1976) p. 154; Oo, Aung Tha. "*Rakhing Cultural History and its View by Researchers*" (1978 typeset copy) (reprint 1985) pp. 21–23, (Some Part are found in the Silver Jubilee Magazine, Rakhing Thahaya Association Dec. 1987); *State Gazetteer (Culture)* (1984) pp. 59 and 146.

(*Selāgīri pabbhata*) situated on the eastern bank of *Gacchapanadī* in the west of the great city of Dhaññavatī.

Secondly, Prof. San Tha Aung has studied "the Fat Monk Image" of Arakan (see appendix 3), by referring to Gordon Luce's "Old Pagan," the existence of that image is a widespread and ancient type of image frequently found in ancient sites in Burma proper as well. He has further explained about the image that the backside of the back-slab has not been tampered with, and still possesses a line of inscription in the Brahmi script, which can be written in Pāḷi as *Saccakaparibajaka(ji)na.* The image is assigned by the paleographical consideration of the script to 200 or 100 BC or around the beginning of the Christian era.[169]

In Buddhist literature, it is found that *Saccakaparibajaka* was a wandering ascetic belonging to a religio-philosophy founded by *Nigantha Nataputta,* a contemporary of the Buddha. Dr. Malalasekera has noted that later Saccaka was mentioned as one of those who became a follower of the Buddha. By observing this Fat Monk Image provided by Prof. San Tha Aung, we can safely say that this is one of the earliest representations of the presence of Buddhism in the third Dhaññavatī period of ancient Rakhaing.

A number of sculptures were found in the vicinity of Kyauk Taw Hill.[170] First of all, somewhere from the eastern side of this hill, a stone relief sculpture in *Dhammacakkamudra*, now kept in the Mrauk Oo Museum, was found earlier in 1923. This relief sculpture (appendix 3) found on the Selagiri Hill representing the Buddha preaching Dhamma to the King Candasuriya, is suggested

169 Aung, San Tha. (1979) "Buddhist Art" pp.14–15.

170 Charles Duroiselle, "1924 Report of the Superintendent Archaeological Survey of Burma" (ASB) pl. Vand pp. 44–45, Arch. Neg. 2694 (1925–6); Tun Shwe Khine, *A Study of Buddhist Sculptures found in Rakhine old Dhanyawaddy city compared with in Indian old Buddhist Arts.* Ministry of Education, Myanmar Academy of Arts and Science, the 7th Research Conference. (27th Oct. 2008); U Shwe Zan, *The Golden Mrauk-U: An ancient Capital of Rakhine* (1997) pp.162–163

to be dated to earlier than the fifth century AD by Prof. San Tha Aung.[171] It portrays the belief that the Buddha actually visited their kingdom by the people lived in that century.

About this sculpture, Prof. San Tha Aung, remarks, "This scene represents neither the first Sermon nor the Miracle at Sarvasti. Instead it represents a local tradition which I have mentioned before as Selargiri tradition. In this tradition Buddha came to Arakan and stopped at the Selargiri hill. King Candasuriya of Dhayawadi, whose city was only five miles east of the hill, came to Selargiri hill to meet the Blessed One and invite him to his city. Buddha preached the dharmacakra sermon to king."[172]

Additionally, five more red sandstone slabs with the carvings were found close to the south of this Selagiri Hill in 1986 (see all in appendix 3). They are the same type as the single slab found earlier in 1923.

Carving of slab (1) represents a *Bhumiphassamudra* of the Buddha, meaning of Mara attacks and *Bodhisatta*'s Enlightenment.

Carving of slab (2) represents a *Karunāmudra* of the Buddha.

Carving of slab (3) depicts one of the scenes from the life story of the Buddha. The two deer at the Buddha's feet are the symbol of the deer park, and the two figures near them represent Upatissa, to be Ven. Sāriputta, who assimilated *ye dhammā* verse recited by Ven. Asajjhi, the youngest of the Buddha's five disciples from the historical picture which depicts all those five disciples in front of the Blessed One, in the style of *Dhammacakkamudra.*

Carving of slab (4) represents the Buddha's laying down on a couch spread between two Sala trees by Ven. Ānanda. He laid on his right side like a join with one leg placed on the other. The trees burst into blossoms although it was not the flowering season, and the spirits hovered round the bed. It is a *mudra* of *Mahāparinibbāna.*

171 San Tha Aung, "Buddhist Art" (1979) p.79.

172 "Buddhist Art" *op. cit.*, p.78.

The slab (5) carries the sculpture of a noble man whose head-dresses and decorations in the upper portion of the dress itself bear strong resemblance to the *Candasuriya* figure carved in the first slab. This sculpture may, therefore, be assumed as the figure of King Candasuriya of Dhaññavatī, who was the patron donor of Mahāmuni Image. The newly found slabs are now kept under the custody of the Mahamuni Trustee Committee.

Another notable example, a slab statue of *Senāpadi Panāda* with twelve lines inscribed on the back, was found in the second stage in the corner of northeastern of the *Mahāmuni* Mount by the National Archive and Research Department in later part of 1958 (see appendix 3). A readable line from it runs as *Yaskasenāpadipanāda* and is dated to either the fourth or fifth century AD by Prof. San Tha Aung.[173] A detailed study of it has first been done by Dr. Forchhammer, and after that, by Prof. San Tha Aung. In the *Dighanikāya* of the *Suttapiṭaka*[174] assigns that *Yaskasenāpadipanāda* is one of the twenty-eight guardians led by *Kuvera*, who are supposed to guard the Buddha surrounded by. It can, therefore, be said that the *Mahāmuni* Image had been on the *Siriguttamahāmuni* Mound since or before the fourth or fifth century AD or *Buddhasāsana* had been prevailed therein.[175]

Moreover, evidence such as the miniature *stūpas* dated to the earlier the fourth or fifth century AD has been found in different parts of Rakhaing (appendix 3). As pointed out by Prof. San Tha Aung that to Buddhist the word over, the *stūpa* is an emblem of Buddha's *parinibbāna*, for the *stūpa* is a monument erected over relics of the Buddha. And because Buddhists revere the relics of

173 "Buddhist Art" *op. cit.*, p.116.

174 Mahāsamaya Sutta, Mahāvagga Pāḷi, Digha Nikāya, CSCD.

175 Forchhammer (1892); "Buddhist Art" (1979), *op. cit.* p. 116.

the Blessed One, it naturally follows that the *stūpa* plays a leading role in Buddhist architecture. The miniature stone *stūpas* with the *ye dammā* verse inscribed on them have been found in Rakhaing. The inscribed *ye dhammā* verses on the *stūpas* are the very basis of Buddhism doctrinally. A details account of this can be found in Prof. San Tha Aung's work. As a result, the *Buddhasāsana* has been flourished in Rakhaing before the fourth or fifth century AD as the sun's rays and moon's light.

Additionally, there is also an important sign on a stone slab concerning the presence of the Buddhism in ancient Rakhaing. This slab is now near the *Ānandacandra* Inscriptions on Shitthaung Pagoda Hill in Mrauk Oo (see appendix 3) representing how the evolution of Buddhism in Rakhaing is shown. In one corner of it, engraving a clockwise white conch-shell, upper of it a lotus, *dhammacakka* symbol is placed above the lotus. That *dhammacakka* symbol is connected with the lotus. We have known that such kinds of symbols as Moriya Art were used by *Asokan* kings since and after the third century BC in India. Therefore this slab can be dated during later part of the third Dhaññavatī period or in the beginning of the Vesālī period.

Regarding this, for the very first, Dr. Forchhammer has made, "Close to the inscribed pillar lies a large stone slab, 12′ long, 4′2″ broad and 10–12″ thick; at the lower end is depicted, in relief, a conch, with the opening of the convolution to the right; a lotus flower grows out of the aperture; the tip of the petals touch the outer rim of the "*dhammacakka*," the "wheel of the law." The design (wrought, as already stated, by Hindus) appears to be emblematic of Brahmanism (the conch), which produced Buddhism (the lotus flower), the *dhammacakka*."[176]

176 Forchhammer (1892) p. 20.

There have been an another octagonal stone pillar, also opposite the Ānandacandra Inscription, 8′10″ high above ground; the circumference of the base measures 72″ (9″ to each side); the decorative designs near the top are in relief supposed to be a representation of spreading *Buddhasāsana* (*dhammacakka*) or showing of king's ruling legitimacy (*rājacakka*); the pillar contains no inscriptions; the shaft and base are roughly hewn.

About this, in a local magazine, an article reads, "A large stone slab, probably related the early phase of the Buddhistic introduction to Arakan, lies close the Ānandacandra Pillar at the Chitthaung Pagoda, Mrauk Oo. It, 8 feet 6 inches long, 2 feet 9 inches broad and 1 foot 3 inches thick, is depicted, in relief, a couch, a lotus flower and a *dhammacakka* symbol. Lotus flower represents the nativity and *dhammacakka* the wheel of the law representing the first sermon of the Lord Buddha and were widely used as the symbol of Buddhism in the preiconic worship in India. The symbolic worship faded away when the iconic worship emerged. It may be wrong, but may not lose the chance of presuming that these two symbols are the earliest evidence revealing the coming of Buddhism in Arakan."[177]

An inscription consists of three lines on the plinth of an image is found at the *Mahāmuni*, Kyauk Taw township. Although almost illegible, it is preserved enough to date paleographically. In the report for the year 1958–59, the director of archaeology of Burma says, "the plinth on the *Mahāmuni* Mound is supposed to be in scribed during the fifth and sixth centuries AD. So it is possible to assume that the *Mahāmuni* Image, later taken from Arakan to

177 Tha, Kyaw Zan. "*Buddhism in Arakan before Ye Dhamma.*" Rakhaing Tan Saung Mazagine, No. 16. (1980)

Mandalay by Bodawpaya, existed in the Gupta Period of the fifth and sixth centuries AD."[178]

Pamela Gutman, in her thesis, compares of this inscription with those of the inscriptions of the Kumara Gupta I, issued toward the middle of the fifth century AD, and concludes that this inscription may therefore by paleographically dated to the same period.[179]

According to these suppositions there may be a Buddhist center, *Mahāmuni*, sometime before the middle of the fifth century AD in Rakhaing. As it is possible to set up such center only after Buddhism become popular among people, Buddhism might have flourished before the setting up of *Mahāmuni*. Regarding this, Forchhammer's remark is, however, notable.

The religious zeal of *Anawratha* and *Narapadijayasuriya* again secured supremacy to Buddhism. But there are old Buddhist traditions among the Talaings and Arakanese traditions, which could not have originated with the southern Buddhist school, but the remnants of the old northern Buddhism, which reached Arakan from the Ganges. When India was mainly Buddhistic, they form a substratum cropping up here and there apparently without any connection, its center is the Mahāmuni pagoda, the most important remains of ancient Buddhism in Burma, antedating in this province both Brahmanism and the Buddhism of the Southern school.[180]

This inscription of the period depicts the religious condition of the age (the generosity and charity of some broad-hearted donors). For the first time, we get a list of ruling kings of early Rakhaing from this inscription. A few earlier kings and queens

178 Annual Report of the Superintendent, Archaeological Survey of Burma. 1958–1959, p. 25.

179 Gutman (1976), p. 118.

180 Forchhammer (1892) p.1.

are also known to have issued edicts with the object of making donations to religious establishments. All this testified to the vigorous and creative activities in preserving thoughts of enlightened section of Rakhaing for the benefit of posterity.

Bronze and copper images of the three rulers of the third Dhaññavatī period have been identified (see appendix 3). Those images were enshrined in Rakhaing Land up to the end of Mrauk Oo dated 1785, *viz.* (i) the Great Mahāmuni Bronze Buddha Image (now in Mandalay) donated by King Candasuriya dated Mahā Era 123 (542/7 BC), (ii) Shon Gyaw Muni Bronze Buddha Image (now in Shwe Taung, Bago) donated by King Candasuriya dated Mahā Era 123 (542/7 BC), (iii) Ran Aung Mrun Bronze Buddha Image (now in Zalun, Irrawaddy) donated by King Candasuriya dated Mahā Era 123 (542/7 BC), (iv) Candamuni Bronze Buddha Image (now at the Bandolla Monastery in Mrauk Oo) donated by King Suriyacakka dated 214 Kozā Era (278 BC), (v) Cakkrāmuni Copper Buddha Image (now nearby Lokananda Pagoda, Sittway) donated by King Suriyakula dated 520 Kozā Era (AD 23).[181]

A local account asserts that while the Buddha was in Dhaññavatī by the invitation of King Candasuriya, the casting of the Great Sage Image (*Mahāmuni*) was done. The king had been to *Sotāpanna* stage in spirituality, his wife and daughter entered to the *Buddhasāsana* as a *bhikkhunis* and attained the *Arahatships* later. And at the request of the king, the Buddha left Ven. Bākula Thera and others for the extensive missionary in the land. But we do not know anything concrete about it.[182]

As stated above that before the emergence of Buddhism in Rakhaing, through the time they used to worship sun-god, moon-god, fire-god, etc. (i.e., Brahmanism), as soon as Buddhism was

181 Thu Mrat (Mahā Aung Mray), *Mahāmuni and Remain Five Munis* (1995).

182 Goyamray Saw Won, *Rakhine State and Buddhasasana.*

therein the local inhabitants somehow first difficult to adapt the new religion in their used to religion, but not for so long they believed in the Buddha, his Dhamma, and his community (of monks and nuns) for the religion of their kings and royal family first adapted Buddhism directly from the Buddha in the reign of King Candasuriya in the half of the sixth century BC. And successive kings of Candasuriya might have brought this religion as their serious concern for the advancement of *Buddhasāsana.* But the ancient kings of Rakhaing have given the right to prayer to other contemporary religions as well. This statement, royal support of Buddhism and availability of other religions in Rakhaing, is firmly supported by all local chronicles of Rakhaing.

4.4. Tradition of Image Worship in Buddhist Rakhaing

The Buddhist tradition reveals that there were images and drawn portraits of the *Buddha,* displaying his contemporary likeness in existence, during his lifetime. The sublime teaching of the Buddha provides the complete supra-cosmic-psychology extant, which transcends the three illusory planes of being.

It has no place for the worship of icons and idols. His followers knew that form is not realistic. They offer flowers and burn incense and light a lamp, not to expect favors, or offer prayers to image of the Buddha. Thereby they pay homage to the Buddha in gratitude. The aim of the practitioner is to find which is beyond change. The correct perspective of the Buddha could be had through the idiom of the '*Dhamma.*' According to reliable sources, it is evident that the authentic shape of the *Buddha* has been preserved to-date. It was the habit of the Buddha to allow those assembled to receive his blessings, before walk into the cell for a brief respite, after premeridian repasts. When the Buddha was away on a mission, those followers who called to glimpse the Buddha for his blessings were visibly saddened. This situation came to the notice of king *Pasenadi* of *Kosala*, who sought the permission of the Buddha to have his likeness cast, so that people could still show their gratitude to the Buddha without feeling much about his absence.

The request of the king was granted by the Buddha. Thus, in the very lifetime of the Buddha, the first image of the *Buddha* was carved, with his permission, in white sandalwood, at the behest of King Pasenadi of *Kosala*. The Buddha examined the finished image and assented that it resembled him in mien. A complete account with more details of the making of the sandalwood image of the Buddha is in '*Kosala Bimbavaṇṇanā*.'

The illustrious *Fa-Hien* tells that, King Pasenadi of *Kosala*, who had known and revered the Buddha from his young manhood, until he and the Buddha were eighty, caused an image of the Buddha, to be carved in Sandalwood, and this was the first images of the Buddha, and became the specimen for all subsequent ones. *Fa-Hien* saw this image at Jetavana School in the fifth century AD. Puri, the present seaside resort of Orissa, was the ancient capital Odanthapuri of King *Brahmadaththa*, from where the Tooth Relic of the *Buddha*, was taken to king *Kittisirimegavaṇṇa* of Sri Lanka, by Prince Dhantha and Princess Hemamālā, for its protection.

Today this ancient site is full of Buddhist associations. Most of the noble monuments of the ancient Indian civilization were destroyed by the iconoclastic invaders in the eleventh and twelfth centuries. Buddhists were able to shift the sandalwood image of the Buddha to Puri for protection. Sir Edwin Arnold and Anagārika Dharmapāla identified this image, worshiped by Buddhists and Hindus alike in Puri, as the original sandalwood image of the Buddha, carved by king Pasenadi of Kosala, twenty-five hundred years ago. The temple of '*Jagannatha*' of Puri in Orissa was considered as one of the eighty Holy Places of worship in India, on the basis of Buddha's Relics. *Huen Tsiang* described about five *Cetiyas* where the Relics of the Buddha were preserved.

The Buddhists believed that, the Rib-Bone of the *Buddha*, still remain in the wooden image of '*Jagannatha*'. Indian scholars agree that, all the ancient cave temples of *Puri* in Orissa have been the work of the primitive Buddhists.

King Candasuriya of Rakhaing, on hearing about the fame and the sublime teaching of the Buddha, decided to visit central India, and pay homage to the Buddha. Knowing the good intension of the noble monarch, the Buddha, with his brethren visited Selagiri of Rakhaing, and showed six places in the vicinity to the disciples, where the *Bodhisatta* spent six of his previous existences.

On hearing of the presence of the Great Teacher in his kingdom, King Candasuriya arrived in Selagiri with alms and offerings. The Buddha instructed the king and his subjects in the five and eight precepts and about the ten great virtues a righteous monarch should observe. The king invited the Buddha and the disciples to his capital, Dhaññavatī, where the Buddha delivered sermons to the people for a week.

The pious king made a request to the Buddha seeking permission to cast his likeness, for them to pay homage thereafter. The wish was granted, and the Buddha rested under a banyan tree on Sirigutta Hill. The likeness of the Buddha cast by them was extraordinary. The king ordered his men to place the statue on a jeweled throne, in a shrine surmounted by a carved spire, built on the summit of the Sirigutta Hill.

"I shall pass into *Nibbāna* in my eightieth year, but you, instinct with my essence will live five-thousand years, which is the life-span of my teaching." The Buddha addressed the image thus, and took his departure, after delivering the final sermon to Arakanese people there. This image remained on the summit of the hill for twenty-four hundred years, before reaching Mandalay.

Rakhaing was invaded by Mongolians who destroyed the capital in AD 957. Arakanese people came back to power in AD 1060. and renovated the temple destroyed by the invaders.

The kings had a great veneration for it, and attempted to take it to Burma, on several occasions. Failing which, they often made pilgrimage to the shrine. Rakhaing became the land of the great image. Burma united under its *Alungphaya* dynasty in 1784, and it invaded and acquired Rakhaing during the reign of Bodaw Phaya. Burmese monarch took the great image of Sirigutta Hill, to his capital, *Amarapura* (now Mandalay) where it is installed at present.

The British acquired Burma in 1885. The original city built by King Candasuriya, walls of the Sirigutta Hill temple including its three courts, the reservoir, statues of the guarding angles, and many more others have been discovered by the British archaeologists. In the library of King Sirisudhamma, situated in the first court of the temple, near the west gate of the Sirigutta Hill, there were a number of ancient books on ola-leaf manuscripts.

The most ancient and notable was known as '*Sappadanapakarana*', which provides a details account of the Buddha's visit to Rakhaing, and casting of the image of the Buddha, and the erection of the temple premises on Sirigutta Hill by King Candasuriya to mark the visit of the Buddha Gotama, to his country.

This famous image, a bronze, ten feet high, represent the Buddha, legs folded left hand opened on the lap, the right touching the earth, with the tip of the finger, a symbolical gesture denoting compassion for all beings. This image was the blood, and life of the Arakanese people.

It is the object of fervent worship by millions of pilgrims monthly throughout the ages. It has been coated so thickly with gold-leaf each year, and its original slender and antique beauty (i.e., the true likeness of the Buddha), has been hidden from the world at present.

4.5. The Mahāmuni Image and Its Traditions

The Mahāmuni Image and its successive Buddha images by historic kings, queens, etc. of ancient Rakhaing not only possess their own concepts of tradition and traditional values, but have their own concepts of history and historical values proved by the present available literary and archaeological evidence to say the legitimacy of a particular values. This tradition seems to be a means to warmly keep Rakhaing so strong and alive in the history. This section is mainly based on local chronicle accounts. Some translations from them have to be retold, so that one can grasp the background of the image.

The strong feeling of religious identity of the Buddhist Arakanese has developed around the myth of the *Mahāmuni* statue. According to Dr. Pamela Gutman, an Australian scholar who did research on the early Rakhaing history, the *Mahāmuni* is a statue of the Buddha, probably *Mahāyānist*, and dating back to the fourth to sixth century AD.[183] For most Arakanese, though, it is an unshakeable article of faith that during the lifetime of Lord Buddha, King Candasuriya of Rakhaing invited the Buddha to his land. The Enlightened One flew through the air and descended on Mount Selagiri near the modern Kyauktaw village where King Candasuriya requested the favor of having a true to life copy made of the Buddha. The veneration of the *Mahāmuni* by the Arakanese and the importance of this paragon statue for the Arakanese monarchy for centuries are next only to the prestige and the status of the Tooth Relic of the Buddha in Sri Lanka.

The account of *Mahāmuni* tradition in English is retold by Dr. E. Forchhammer, referring an ancient manuscript, "*Sappadanapakarana*" of Rakhaing.[184] It is also evident that most

183 Gutman (1976), p. 326.

184 Forchhammer (1892), *op. cit.*

Arakanese literary sources mention this image and its tradition; in other words, all historical Rakhaing literature seems to center at *Mahāmuni* and its tradition.

Tradition has it that King Candasuriya knew that the Buddha, after residing there only a week, and returned to *Majjhimadesa*, the king felt anxiety and pleaded the Lord to allow to cast an image. The Buddha favored the king's wish and allowed to cast image on his destined to be deconstructed by unbelievers and king of *devas* would it before the destruction. The image in Dhaññavatī would last five thousand years. Hence, the Buddha allowed casting his own image.

As soon as the king got the allowance to cast the image he collected five kinds of metal[185] and put them into the gold container and offered to the Lord. When the image was casted it cracked three times. So the Buddha put seven fistful of warmth from his bosom into the crack. After that there was no crack in the image.

Additionally, after casting of the image, the king requested the Buddha to preach the fruits of making Buddha image. Thus, the Buddha is said to have preach a *Sutta* called "*Sutthubimba Sutta*." A general description of this *Sutta* and its translation are being discussed and presented below respectively.

In the famous verse of ancient Rakhaing, it describes about the *Mahāmuni* as well that when King *Candasuriya* constructed the pavilion, the *Brahma*, *Sakka*, and other spirits helped to finish it. It was the summer time in the month of Kason (April/ May). At the auspicious time when the celestial body *Visākha* was in proper position they began to cast the image. The Buddha managed to empower the image he inserted seven fistful of his body-warmth into the casting. The image was successfully executed on Thursday.[186]

185 of gold, silver, copper, iron, and tin.

186 Royal poet Medha Paññā who served under the King Siri Chandra of Vesālī Kyauk Haly Gar Period in AD 677, composed about the King Candasuriya who erased 148 Mahā Era without remainder.

Furthermore, here it will be appropriate to refer to the translation of the stanza 9 of the Poet Phadu Murn Nyo's "*Rakhaing Princess's Lullaby*" It reads, "While the Candasuriya reigned golden city Dhaññavatī he managed to cast the image of Lord Buddha under the very eyes of him, he collected and mixed five kinds of metal. When he casted the image, it was unsuccessful. Then, the Buddha exerted seven fistful of his body-warmth. Finally, the casting of image was successfully accomplished."[187]

In about AD 800, Rakhaing boat-song was composed by Dhamma Zeya. In his boat-song there was an expression about the event of how the King Candasuriya casted the image of Mahāmuni as well.[188]

Mahāmuni Shrine stands on a thirty-food-high hill north of the palace site of Dhaññavatī. Known as Sirigutta Hill, this was the original resting place of the *Mahāmuni* until the army led by the son of King Bodawpaya carried the image off to *Amarapūra* in 1785.[189]

For centuries, people regarded the *Mahāmuni* Image and the shrine with sacred devotion and religious awe, making a legend to grow the legend being that of the Great Teacher's arrival in

187 The ministerial poet Phadu Murn Nyo's "*Rakhaing Princess's Lullaby*" and Mya Doe Wai's "*Lyrical Verse of Rakhaing History*" and another ministerial poet Dhamma Zeya's "*Boat-song*" were the hard evidence of the existence of the king Candasuriya. In reality Rakhaing's royal and lyrical writing were used in Sanskrit and *Pāḷi* languages up to Vesālī period. But in AD 677, those were renounced and started to write with Rakhaing language and Rakhaing alphabets, closely related to those of Aryan and Aryo-Dravidian languages. We find no trace of Mongolian language in Rakhaing language. So the concept of the Mongoloids' domination over Rakhaing is an absurdity.

188 *State Gazetteer (Culture)*; San, Dhañña. "Rakkhamandaing,"; Khine, Tun Shwe. "Arakanese Poets"

189 Than Tun, "Paya Lanma—Lord's Highway, over the Yoma—Yakhine Range" *JAAS*, ILCAA, Tokyo University to Foreign Studies, XXV 1983, pp. 223–241; Than Tun, "Royal Orders of Burma" Vol. IV.

Rakhaing. The earliest literary record about the legend has been mentioned in *Sabbadānapakaraṇa*, an ancient palm-leaf manuscript of a great value as mentioned by Dr. Forchhammer.[190]

After casting *Mahāmuni*, King Candasuriya cast two other images from the same stock of noble metal. Afterward thirty-three smaller likeness of the *Mahāmuni* and countless *Mahāgyan* (lit. left or remain over) images were also cast by the king.

Starting from the time of the casting of the *Mahāmuni*, the *Mahāmuni* and Sirigutta Hill became the centerpiece of Rakhaings' faith. The image and the hill became an integrated institution. A magnificent shrine was built during *Suriyacitra*'s rule (AD 79–115). After the perfumed chamber with bricks and donated a ruby studded gold crown for the Image. During the rule of the son of *Dvencandra* a richly ornamented stone pedestal was installed. Besides, the shrine was roofed with brass sheets. After completion of the renovation works, the monks from Lankā Dīpa and other neighboring countries were invited to the inauguration ceremony.

Deva figures like *Yeksa General Panada*, some receiving sermons and others guarding the holy precincts, were erected around the shrine in about the fifth century AD. *Cūḷa Taicandra*, the last *Vesālī* monarch, dug ponds for the pilgrims at the western part and many times restored the shrine.

In time, the *Mahāmuni* became renowned and pilgrims form far off destinations like Ceylon and Indo China paid regular visits. The *Anandodhaya* monastery as stated in the *Ānandacandra* Inscriptions was probably situated on this holy ground.

At the end of the Vesālī period, King Anurudhā (Anawrahtā) of Pagan (AD 1044–1077) renovated the shrine and an elaborately ornamented graduated turret above the prayer hall was credited to him.

---

190 Forchhammer (1892), *op. cit.*

King *Asankhayā* (AD 1068–1076) of Pañcā city is also accredited for stone stair-case roofed with graduated turrets (the northern approach still preserves the old masonry) and also for restoration of the shrine.

In two abortive campaigns, Anawrahtā Murn Saw and Alungsithu from Pagan, attempted to carry off the Mahāmuni Image to their capital.

The year 1103 proved to be the worst hour in the history of *Mahāmuni,* since the Image was lost in hiding. Only when King Dassarājā came to the throne (AD 1123–1139) was the image discovered, and lesser kings and lords were given the responsibility for its upkeep. A highway was also constructed from his capital city of Parein to the *Mahāmuni.* He also took precautionary measures against any future safety of the shrine.

King Murn Saw Mon, the founding king of Golden Mrauk Oo, renovated the *Mahāmuni* simultaneously with that of his capital. His younger brother, Murn Khari, deposited the whole set of *tipiṭaka* brought from Sri Lanka in the *piṭaka* library he had built in the precincts of the shrine. From then on, the *Mahāmuni* and its environs up as the focal point of Buddhist learning. The Mrauk Oo kings their reign maintained the shrine as the most sacred nurturing ground of Rakhaing Buddhist faith. King *Sirisuriya* is reported to be built numerous monasteries and supported one thousand monks' ordinations every year.

To honor the soil of origin and the *Mahāmuni* Image, Maurice Collins, the famous British author of the twentieth century entitled his one of the outstanding publication as "*The Land of the Great Image.*"

King *Narādhipadi* had the *Yattarā* bell cast and placed in the platform of *Mahāmuni* Shrine in AD 1734 the magical formulas and numbered squares make it the rarest of its kind in the world. The bell inscriptions in *Pāḷi*, *Rakhaing*, and *Sanskrit* were used to ward off the work magical spells upon any invading troops. Details of the procedure were inscribed on the bell. This bell was lost in 1950 and never recovered when the building was ravaged by an earthquake in 1961. A detail discussion about *Yattarā* bell can be found in Dr. Forchhammer's famous work "*Arakan.*"

It is beyond doubt to say that Vesālī kings and people could enjoy the worshipping of those outstanding Buddha images throughout the Vesālī Age.

There is a new saying in the old capital that a visit to Mrauk Oo is not accomplished unless reached and paid homage to *Candamuni* Image. The original donor of the Image of more than two thousand three hundred years old was King *Suriyacakka*, sixth in the line of King *Candasuriya*, the founder of the third Dhaññavatī. This magnificent great Image is now resting majestically in the precinct of for more than a century old Bandhulla Monastery in the southern part of old city Mrauk Oo. The Image is now housed in a new consecrate structure with modern architectural design.

The first place of the *Candamuni* Image was at Taung Oo, a hillock to the north, not very far from Mrauk Oo. The Image was shifted by Murn Saw Mon and placed onto the hillock called Bābu. During the British annexation of Rakhaing, the image was hidden by a few Rakhaing patriots. First, it was put to rest under water for twelve years and then under a cement coating for nearly a century to stop the image from being taken by foreigners. The cement coating of the Phara was outstripped by the abbot of the monastery in 1987. To the surprise of everyone around, the real *Candamuni* Great Image is enshrined once again now in Bandolla Monastery.

This old monastery can also be claimed as a place of archaeological interest. We can witness many antiques of ancient periods, relics of *Arahats*, and various kinds of artifacts including Buddha's tooth relic replica presented from Ceylon.

The short accounts of *Cakkramuni* are as follows: the image is made of copper, height eighteen inches, right hand of the image is dropped over the knee, but it does not touch the ground. Left palm rests on its back and the eight pointed start rests on the palm. At the center of the star there exists a wheel that symbolizes the *dhammacakkra.* There are numerous minute images on its head and across the body. It is very rare and craftily executed. At the center of the forehead there is spiral mark. The name of the donor is ascribed as King Suriyakula (520 RE). If we examine this image from the point of view of iconography its style of execution is neither related with Mrauk Oo period nor with Laymro as well as Vesālī period. It resembles with that of Man Aung Mrun Muni of Zalun.

Its face seems to be smiling. The eyes are looking downward. Its posture is elegant and executed with the rule of Buddhist treatise. The prototype image done by Rakhaing can easily differentiate. The earlobes of image are dropped down, but they do not touch the image's shoulder. The two arms do not contact with the body, by observing such characteristics, the image was casted and molded by none other than Rakhaing artisans.

The *mudra* of this image is a combined posture. It was extraordinary and craftily executed. Combining postures are *bumiphassa* and *dhammacakkramudras.* The latter is symbolically expressed with an eight-pointed star that indicates the eight cardinal points—all the directions except above and below. It symbolizes that *dhamma* propagates and spread all round. It also denotes the eightfold path to *nibbāna*, the way out of suffering. This image is now rested with special shrine in the precinct of modern Lokānandā Pagoda at Akyab (present Sittway).

By examining Mahāmuni type images of the third Dhaññavatī period we can assume that the donors and peoples were deeply rooted in Buddhism.

4.6. *Sutthubimba Sutta* (Discourse of Image of the Buddha)

4.6.1. General Introduction

Largely unknown to the academic world of Buddhist studies on Buddhist vernacular texts in Southeast Asia, *Suttubimba Sutta* is traditionally believed by Rakhaing people to have been said by the Buddha himself to King Candasuriya and his subjects when he visited Dhaññavatī, an ancient Rakhaing capital.[191] With the historical tradition of the casting of the Mahāmuni Image, there has been a *Sutta* strangely attached to it. The *Satthubimba Sutta* belonging to none of the Pāḷi Canon, not to be found in any of the Pāḷi canonical works either. It however is the great valuable Sutta regarding the fruits of making or casting of Buddha image in the history of Buddhism in Arakan, which the famous archaeologist Dr. Forchhammer missed to take into account in his valuable contribution in the Rakhaing studies, even though he referred to the *Sappadānapakāraṇa*, an ancient Arakanese manuscript of great value. According to an interview made on December 26, 1984, to the local historian U Oo Thar Tun by the famous Venerable Nyanissara of Burma, the Sutta was named as *Sutthubimbapūjaniyanisesa Sutta* and was in the form of a palm leaf manuscript.[192] The present printed version of 1993 is supposed to have been copied from that manuscript in later sometimes.

191 Except an interesting work entitled, "Kosala-Bimba-Vaṇṇanā" by Richard F. Gombrich (1978), no other resemblance has ever, if any, been found.

192 "*Questions Concerning Emergence of Theravāda Buddhasāsana in Rakhaing Land*" Interview to U Oo Thar Tun (Rakhaing-Myanmar Pandit) by Ven. Nyanissara of Burma on December 26, 1984. Published by Executive Committee, Arakan National League for Democracy (Exile), Bangladesh. (2002 August). Republished by Research and Recording Dept., All Arakan Students' and Youths' Congress (AASYC), Mae Sot, Thailand. (2010 August).

The Sutta is a verse type comprises of thirty-nine verses excluding the introductory. The opening begins with the Sutta is addressed by the Buddha at the request of King Candasuriya. Technically the background of the request goes back to the Buddha's visitation to the Dhaññavatī City, and the appeal by the King Candasuriya to leave an image of the Buddha before he leaves to Sāvatthi with his five hundred disciples from the then-great Dhaññavatī City (*Dhaññavatīmahānagara*). In addition, the major question regarding the results of making or casting of a Buddha image or statue was asked. The remaining verses are the Buddha's reply on the advantages and fruits upon the subject questions made by the king. Although the theme of the discourse should be the consequences of doing Buddha image as suggested by the title, however, there are other details relating to how to make of it, which could be categorized under different elucidations. The Sutta is of utmost historical and cultural value, especially introduction to the study of Buddhism in ancient Rakhaing, and therefore, it has become a sourcebook for students of history of Buddhism in Rakhaing.

Before going to detail textual study of the Sutta, a serial of problems arises that if the Sutta be not in Pāḷi Canon, why it is called as a Sutta. Is it a fresh literary invention by a scholar in early days past? When, where, by whom, or how it first came down to us? Where it was first written, what kind of form a manuscript or an inscription before printing? In this work, I have attempt to trace in traditional and historical perspectives the themes found in the Sutta, which is subject to analysis in regard to its form and contents paying due attention to the deviations and the early teaching of the Buddha.

The antiquity of the Sutta traditionally goes back to the days of the Buddha. The colophon of the Sutta is attributed to the Buddha traditionally and supposed to be dated the same as the legendary Mahāmuni Image as the way how Sutta tradition goes back to its story as well. There are many discourses (*Suttas*) which were not said directly by the Buddha, attributed to him. For example, *Madhupindika Sutta* of the *Majjhima Nikāya* is actually said by Ven. Mahā Kaccana, but it is attributed to the Buddha. Thus far, this discourse is named as a Sutta even though it is not incorporated in the Pāḷi Canon. In Buddhism, the Sutta refers mostly to canonical scriptures, many of which are regarded as records of the oral teachings of Gotama the Buddha. The Pāḷi form of the word, Sutta is used exclusively to refer to the scriptures of the early Pāḷi Canon, the only texts recognized by Theravāda Buddhism as canonical.

According to the available information associated with Sutta with reference to the interview of U Oo Thar Tun, we have known that this Sutta is incorporated in, as a part of, *Sappadanapakarana*, an ancient Arakanese manuscript of great value as mentioned by Dr. E. Forchhammer, the first ever writer of mentioning the manuscript into English world. Thus, this has its antiquity, but the colophon of the Sutta is totally unknown to us. In 1993, the printed version of the Sutta came out by an effort of a local Buddhist monk named *Baddanta Sundara*. It mentions a little about the Sutta, "This Sutta is found not only in the ancient Arakanese manuscript *Sappadānapakāraṇa*, but also in the Rakhaing Razawon manuscript number from (*ka*) to (*ko*)[193] discovered in 1898. Being said about the fruit of making Buddha image, it is a *Sutta* of great value for all Buddhists."[194] How he has got the Sutta, *Baddanta Sundara*

193 Alphabetical order of marking plate number of manuscript in Rakhaing.

194 "Satthubimba Suttam" arranged by Baddanta Sundara, (in Burmese) Rangoon (1993), pp. 2–3.

reported that the Sutta had been received via U Oo Thar Tun and Ven. Cakkinda, a local writer about Rakhaing culture in late 1988.

As the Sutta is named as *Satthubimba Sutta* as for U Oo Thar Tun, *Sattubimba- pujaniyanisesa Sutta,* the name of it may be translated into English as just 'Buddha Image Discourse' or 'Discourse of the Fruits of Making Buddha Image.' *Buddharupa* in Pāḷi refers to statue or model of the Buddha and literally means form of the Awakened One. There is also another term *paṭimā* means likeness or image. Like mentioned above, *Satthubimba* represents the image or statue of the Buddha. All the terms may also be used in reference with images and paintings of the Buddha. The term *bimba* is Sanskrit origin means, "image or reflection, also referred to as the disk of brightness surrounding the sun or moon."

We do not find any direct reference of making and worshipping Buddha image, relic, etc. in Sutta Literature of Early Buddhism regarding the Sutta. However, we read certain information about division of relics finally enshrining with erection of eight cetiyas or monuments enshrining the relics of the Buddha in the *Mahaparinibbana Sutta* of the *Dīgha Nikāya.* The concept of Buddha image or statute may evolve from it. As early Buddhism bans on *Buddharūpa* (Buddha Image) is well known. An old disciple of the Buddha, Vakkali was eager to see the Buddha before he died. One day the Buddha came and said to him "O *Vakkali* why do you crave to see this body of impure matter, one who perceives Dhamma perceives me. One who perceives me perceives Dhamma" On different occasions through dialogues and sermons Buddha spoke against adoration of his *Rūpakāya* or *Buddharūpa.*

In the later third century BC, Buddhists may have exaggerated many types of the concept of paying respect the Buddha. In the Buddhist commentarial literature, one may find four types of veneration objects: *dhātucetiya* or *sarīrikacetiya* (the bodily relics of the Buddha), *dhammacetiya* (the teachings of the Buddha, [i.e., Pāḷi Canon or the bearer of Pāḷi Canon, which are Buddhist monks]), *pariobhogacetiya* (the personal articles used by the Buddha such as bowl, robe, etc.), and *udissakacetiya* (religious symbols such as the Buddha image or pagoda). Thus *buddharūpa* or *satthubimba* can be put under the category of *udissakacetiya.*

A comprehensive introduction and English translation of the Sutta is being presented below for the first time as far as academic study of this Sutta is concerned. Being a vernacular text as in Buddhist studies with reference to the study of Buddhism on the inhabitants of Rakhaing Land especially, the Sutta, here, deserves more than its broad introduction and English translation.

4.6.2 Text and Translation

Anusadhi

Connection

Anātho me tuvaṃ bante, desanatthāya cāriko
Tasmā tvaṃ ihatāya, dadāhi paṭibimbakaṃ.

"I will be destitute, lord, as (you) wander to preach (elsewhere), therefore, give (me) here an image ("reflection") of yours."

Dasabalo mārajino atulo saṃmāsaṃbuddho
So bhagavā Dhaññavatīraṭṭhaṃ candasuriyarājānaṃ
Ārambha imaṃ satthubimbaSuttaṃ kathesi.

"The perfectly self-enlightened One, of ten powers, conqueror of the Tempter,
He, the Exalted One, in the Dhaññavatī country, by the (influence of) King Candasuriya, (as a) beginning, preached this Discourse on the Buddha's Image (*SatthubimbaSuttaṃ*)."

1. *Devaloke*[195] *manusseca, aparā-para-cetanā*[196]
   Ācikkha me mahāvīra, sotumicchāmi taṃ gunaṃ

"In the world of gods and men, by the former and future intentions,
Explain to me, great hero; I wish to listen to that virtue (of making Buddha's image)."

2. *So tassa vacanaṃ sutvā, bhagavā etamabravī*
   Sādhu sādhu mahārāja, tamattaṃ pucchitaṃ tayā

"Having heard his words, He, the Exalted One, said this:
It is good, it is good, the matter asked by you, great king."

3. *Ye narā paṭimā karā, lekhakāca bimbā bahū*
   Mahāgune labhanti te, kathessāmi sunohi me.

"Whosoever makes a statue, or even draws many images, they receive a great quality, I will preach, listen to me."

---

195 In Indian religions, a *devaloka* is a plane of existence where gods and *devas* exist. The *devalokas* are usually described as places of eternal light and goodness, similar to the concept of heaven. Teachers of different Hindu denominations may call such homes of the gods by other names, including *svarga,* each differing in nonfundamental aspects. To Hindus, *devaloka* is a plane of blissful existence that can be reached as soon as one is sufficiently attuned to light and good. However, to become even better and to learn more, one must return to a life on Earth, until all the learning possibilities here have been exhausted. Then, any other lives become unnecessary, and liberation (*moksha*) is achieved. When that happens, the practitioner can even reach higher planes, such as *Vaikuntha* and *Sivaloka* (*Kailasa*), places of union with Vishnu and Shiva. In Buddhism, a *devaloka* is a dwelling place of the Buddhist devas. The worlds of the *devas* differ greatly from each other depending on the nature of their inhabitants in Buddhist cosmology. See http://en.wikipedia.org/wiki/Devaloka

196 cetanā: "volition," will, is one of the seven mental factors *(cetasika,* q.v.) inseparably bound up with all consciousness, namely sensorial or mental impression *(phassa),* feeling *(vedanā),* perception *(saññā),* volition *(cetanā),* concentration *(samādhi),* vitality *(jīvita),* advertence *(manasikāra).* Cf. Tab. II, III. With regard to kammical volition (i.e., wholesome or unwholesome kamma) it is said in A. VI, 13: "Volition is action (kamma), thus I say, o monks; for as soon as volition arises, one does the action, be it by body, speech, or mind." For details, s. *paṭiccasamuppāda* (10), kamma. See Buddhist Dictionary

4. *Micchādiṭṭhikaṭhānesu,*[197] *asaññā*[198] *arūpinoca*[199]
Saddhāvantā na jāyanti, bimbalekhassidam phalaṃ

"In the places of those of wrong view, unconscious and formless, (these) faithful ones will not arise, this is the fruit of a drawer of (Buddha's) image."

5. *Athavā asaññasattesu, arūpesu tathevaca*
Saddhāvantā na jāyanti, ye karā bimbamuttamaṃ

"Also, among *asaññasattā,*[200] as well as among the (brahmas) without form, (these) faithful ones do not arise, who would make the ultimate image."

6. *Paccantike*[201] *na jāyanti, majjhimevaca*[202] *jāyare*

197 Places where wrong views prevail.

198 asañña-satta: The "unconscious beings" are a class of heavenly beings in the fine-material world; s. *deva* (II). "There are, o monks, heavenly beings known as the unconscious ones. As soon, however, as in those beings consciousness arises, those beings will vanish from that world. Now, o monks, it may happen that one of those beings after vanishing from that world, may reappear in this world..." (D. 24). Further details, s. Kath., Yam. (Guide, pp. 68, 79, 96 ff.). See Buddhist Dictionary

199 The immaterial world *(arūpa-loka),* corresponding to the 4 immaterial absorptions. See Buddhist Dictionary

200 realm of nonconscious brahmās, See above.

201 Paccantrika (skr.) or paccantika (Pāḷi) actually means a place where it is far away from urban places; technically, it means a place where is no teaching of the Buddha.

202 The country of Central India that was the birthplace of Buddhism and the region of its early activities. See http://www.palikanon.com/english/pali_names/ma/majjhimadesa.htm

Micchādiṭṭhi[203] *na jayare, itthi-byañjana-paṇḍakā*[204]

"In places void of Buddha's teaching (these people) do not arise, (they) arise only in the Middle-Land, they do not arise (with) wrong view, (or even as) eunuchs of female marks."

7. *Kālakañcikanāmesu,*[205] *hīnesvasurakesuca*

Petaloke[206] *tiracchāne, na te gacchanti duggatiṃ*

"Among those called Kālakañcika and inferior titans, in the world of ghosts, in the animal realm (these people) do not go to the woeful states."

8. *Nijjhāmataṇhapetesu,*[207] *khuppipāsāhi pīḷitā*

Saddhāvantā na jāyanti, ye bimba lekhakā karā

"Among the ghosts of consuming thirst, torn by hunger and thirst, those faithful are not born, who drew (and) made the image."

---

203 *diṭṭhi* means view, belief, speculative opinion, insight. If not qualified by *sammā,* "right," it mostly refers to a wrong and evil view or opinion, and only in a few instances to a right view, understanding, or insight (e.g., *diṭṭhi-ppatta,* q.v.; *diṭṭhi-visuddhi,* purification of insight; *diṭṭhi-sampanna,* possessed of insight). Wrong or evil views *(diṭṭhi* or *micchā-diṭṭhi)* are declared as utterly rejectable for being a source of wrong and evil aspirations and conduct, and they are liable at times to lead man to the deepest abysses of depravity. See Buddhist Dictionary

204 Femininity; neither male nor female (*napuṅsakapaṇḍaka,* etc.)

205 Peta (ghost). See below.

206 (Sanskrit *preta):* lit. 'departed spirit', ghost; s. *loka.* See Buddhist Dictionary

207 *Nijjhāma* (Sk. *Nihksāma*) means burning away, wasting away, consuming, or consumed. *Nijjhāmataṇha* (adj.) of consuming thirst, very thirsty; *Nijjhāmataṇha* denoting a class of *Petas.* See Pāḷi -English Dictionary, TW Rhys Davids, William Stede

9. *Mahāavīcinamake,*[208] *tathā lokantaresuca*[209]
Nirayesu nuppajjanti, ye bimba lekhakā karā
"Among those named by great Avīci ("gapless hell"), as well as those at the end of the world, they are not born in hell, who drew (and) made the image."
10. *Taṃ kammaṃ kusalaṃkatvā, yāvajīvaṃ anussare*
Na jāyanti duggatiṃhī, avīciṃhī niraye tappe
"Having done that skillful action, remembering it throughout the life, they are not born in the woeful states, in the burning gapless hell."
11. *Yoyaṃ kalyāṇaṃ bimbañca, patthento tividhaṃ sukhaṃ*
Saṃsaritvāna saṃsāre, devasukhañca mānusaṃ
"He, also, by the good image, should wish threefold happiness, while wandering in the cycle of birth, the happiness divine and human."
12. *Okkantamattā ye dhīrā, taṃ kulaṃ ativaḍḍhanti*
Hiraññena suvaṇṇena, dhana dhaññena vaḍḍhati
"Those wise entered to whatever measure (of happiness), they increase that family very much, By unwrought gold of good color (and) by grain wealth increases."
13. *Puttena dāsi dāsena, hatthi-assa-rathenaca*
Pavaḍḍhati nuppajjhanti, ābādhā mātuyā dukkhaṃ
"In sons, female and male servants, elephants, horses, and vehicles, it increases, (and) the suffering of motherhood does not approach one."

---

208 Avīci is the name of one of the most frightful hells (*niraya*, q.v.). See DPPN, See also http://www.wisdomlib.org/definition/avici/index.html

209 A series of hells, each one being bound by three *cakkavālas*. See http://www.wisdomlib.org/definition/lokantaraniraya/index.html

14. *Devesu devarājāno, manussesu manurājā*
Catudīpe[210] *issaroca, buddhabimbassidaṃ phalaṃ*
"Divine king of gods, human king of men, ruler of the four islands, this is the fruit of (making) Buddha's image."
15. *Subhagā devarūpāca, jitāmitte arogino*
Samiddhā viriyā tesaṃ, buddhabimbassidaṃ phalaṃ
"Fortunate and of divine body, victorious among (their) friends, void of sickness, they are magnificent in effort, this is a fruit of (making) Buddha's image."
16. *Akilantāca te kāyā, sukhaṃ niccaṃ arogino*
Anto kucchi vasantānaṃ, koci rogo nuppajjati
"And their bodies are tireless, with steady health without sicknesses, In those living inside the womb, there does not arise any sickness."
17. *Jahetvā mānussaṃ dehaṃ, devaloke uppajjanti*
Vimānaṃ labhanti seṭṭhaṃ, ruciraṃva pabhassaraṃ
"Abandoning the human body, they are born in the world of gods, they receive an excellent mansion of the *Rucirā* ("brilliant") or *Pabhassarā* ("resplendent") gods."
18. *Ākiṇṇā devakaññehi, accharā kāmavaṇṇinī*
Saṭṭhitūriyasahassehi, pappotentā karontitā
"Among crowded divine women, celestial nymphs of colors of pleasure, among sixty thousand musical instruments, approached (and) playing."
19. *Maraṇakāle asammūḷhā, ujuṃ gacchanti sugatiṃ*
Paṇḍitā dānasūrāca, buddha bimbassidaṃ phalaṃ

210 One of the four Mahadipas, or great continents viz. Uttarakuru (northern), Aparagoyana (western), Jambudipa (southern right), Pubbavideha (eastern), which are included in the Cakkavala and are ruled by a Cakkavatti. They are grouped round Mount Sineru. See at http://www.wisdomlib.org/

"At the time of death, not bewildered, they go directly to happy states, wise and generous heroes, this is a fruit of (making) Buddha's image."

20. *Karitvā paṭimaṃ seṭṭhaṃ, likhitvāca yathārahaṃ*
Mahātejā sadā honti, vimalo suriyo yathā

"Having made an excellent statue, (or) drawing (it) as is proper, they are always of great glory, like the sun, unstained."

21. *Jaccandhajātiyāceva, andhabadhirajātiyā*
Mūgapakkhā na jāyanti, visuddhavacanā honti

"Of kind, who are blind since birth, of kind who are blind and deaf since birth, dumb or handicapped, they are not born, they are of pure speech."

22. *Kuṭṭhaṃ gaṇḍoca kilāso, kāso sāso pamārako*
Saddhāvantā na jāyanti, ye karā bimbamuttamaṃ

"(With) leprosy, swelling, eczema, cough, deadly asthma, the faithful are not born, who were making the noble image."

23. *Antarāya karā ye bimbaṃ, paccāmittā cupaddavā*
Pakkhamūgādyantarāyā, kāye tesaṃ na okaḍḍhaṃ

"To those who were making the image, danger, enemies and misfortune, dangers of (becoming) handicapped, dumb and so on, do not drag away their body."

24. *Dvekule*[211] *uppajjanti, khattiyecāpi brahmaṇe*
Mahādhane mahābhoge, mahācakulamuttame

"They are born in two casts, of warriors or even brahmins, of great wealth (and) great enjoyment, even in the best of great families."

211 Of the four Castes (*Brahmana, Kattiya, Vessa, Sudda*) at the time of the Buddha; *Kattiya* means the royal caste, the noble landlord, or the warriors' deals with ruling people; *Brahmana* means the priestly, caste deals with ceremony and rituals. See http://www.wisdomlib.org/

25. *Ñātiyo sukhino honti, arogāca matāpitā*
Antokucchi vasantānaṃ, koci rogo nuppajjati
"(Their) relatives are happy, and mother (and) father are without sickness, being inside the womb, whatever sickness (it may be,) it does not arise."

26. *Asuci makkhitā na honti, asuci rudhirānica*
Visuddhavimalā honti, kālinga[212]*vatthamaṇiyathā*
"Dirty, smeared and of blood dirt they are not, purified (and) unstained are they, like if (they had) jeweled clothes of Kalinga."

27. *Adhosirā uddhampādā, aññe janā nikkhamanti*
Tathā te na nikkhamanti, karitvā bimbamuttamaṃ
"Other people are born, head-down (or) legs-upward, (but) these are not born so, (who) made the excellent image."

28. *Samaṃ katvā ubhopāde, kucchimhā nikkhamantica*
Suvaṇṇena kataṃ bimbaṃ, devakāyāva dissare
"Both legs being (made) same, and they leave the womb (that way), (having) body (like if) made by gold, it looks like a divine body."

29. *Sabbe piyā manāpāca, candimāca yathā narā*
Sukkhaṃ vaḍḍhati niccato, koci rogo nuppajjati
"Pleasant (and) beloved to all, like the moon (are) these men, continuously (their) happiness increases, though no sickness doesn't arise."

30. *Pūjakā sangaṇā nandā, vasundarāca pūjakā*
Pathaviṃ anusāsanti, caritvā dhammamuttamaṃ

212 A country: the Kalingarattha. It is one of the seven political divisions mentioned in the time of the mythical king Renu and is given first in the list, its capital being Dantapura and its king Sattabhu. See http://www.wisdomlib.org/definition/kalinga/index.html

"Making merits *[pūja+akā]* in group (they) rejoice, making merits (they) are beautiful, (they) advice those of earth, practicing the best teachings."

31. *Navakappasahassesu,*[213] *koṭijātiṃ anussare*
Anubhavanti sabbabhavaṃ, paṇḍitāca visāradā

"In nine thousand eons, remembering ten million births, (they) enjoy every life, also (as) knowledgeable experts."

32. *Sattiṃsakappe devindā, sattiṃsaca cakkavattī*
Padesarajjaṃvipulaṃ, gaṇanato asankhiyaṃ

"Sixty eons (as) kings of gods, and (another) sixty (as) universal monarchs, of a large region of kingdom, of an uncountable crowd."

33. *Mahiddhikā mahāpaññā, vaṇṇavantoyassasino*
Sirīca rūpasampannā, satthubimbassidaṃ phalaṃ

"Of great (magical) powers, of great wisdom, of good complexion (and) glorious, endowed with (good) body (and) luck, this is a fruit of (making) the Buddha's image."

34. *Aḍḍhe ete mahābhoge, mahāseṭṭhikulesuca*
Khattiyecāpi brahmaṇe,[214] *satthubimbassidaṃ phalaṃ*

"Opulent (is) their great wealth, (they are) also among the families of great bankers, among *Khattiyas* (caste of warriors) and even *Brahmins,* this is a fruit of (making) the Buddha's image."

---

213 Periodic manifestations and dissolutions of universes that go on eternally. Great kalpas consist of four asamkhiya kalpas corresponding to childhood, maturity, old age, and the death of the universe. See http://www.wisdomlib.org/definition/kalpa/index.html

214 See above.

35. *Buddhe*[215] *paccekabuddhe,*[216] *arahante*[217] *mahiddhike*
Yaṃ yaṃ patthitaṃ sabbaṃ, taṃ taṃ labhanti pāṇino

"Buddhas, silent-Buddhas, Arahants of great (magical) powers, all whatever they wish, they receive, (these) living beings."

36. *Lohakāḷāyasadanta, dārūhi candanehivā*
Visāṇehi aṭṭhīhivā, mattikāhiṭṭhakāhivā

"By copper, (black) iron, ivory, wood, or sandal, by horns or bones, by clay, or (whatever they) wish,"

37. *Nānāvaṇṇehi vatthehi, selehivajirehivā*
Khuddakaṃvā mahantaṃvā, saddhā cittena sāsane

"In various colors, clothes, stones, or diamonds, whether small or big, with faithful mind toward the Teachings."

38. *Likkhitvā satthussa bimbaṃ, limpetvā rajatehica*
Saddhācittena modanti, passamānā bahuguṇe

"Having drawn the Buddha's image, having smeared it also by silver, they, by faithful mind rejoice, seeing so many qualities."

---

215 *Lit.* the Awakened One; One who through eons of spiritual development has attained Sammasambodhi. A being who has completely abandoned all delusions and their imprints. In general, "Buddha" means "Awakened One," someone who has awakened from the sleep of ignorance and sees things as they really are. A Buddha is a person who is completely free from all faults and mental obstructions. Every living being has the potential to become a Buddha. See http://www.wisdomlib.org/definition/buddha/index.html

216 *Lit.* Private Buddha; One who, like a Buddha, has gained Awakening without the benefit of a teacher, but who lacks the requisite store of paramis to teach others the practice that leads to Awakening. On attaining the goal, a paccekabuddha lives a solitary life. See http://www.wisdomlib.org/definition/pratyeka-buddha/index.html

217 *Lit.* Worthy One; A being who has eliminated the entirety of mental impurities (kilesas) and who, in consequence, is free from all attachment and from all forms of suffering. See http://www.wisdomlib.org/definition/arahanta/index.html

39. *Tasmāhi paṇḍito poso, sampassaṃ attamattano*
Kareyya satthussa bimbaṃ, suvaṇṇarajatehivā
"Therefore, the wise man, reflecting himself about himself, should make the image of the Buddha, by gold or by silver."
SatthubimbaSuttaṃ niṭṭhitaṃ
"The discourse on the Buddha's image is finished."

4.7. Developments of Indian Buddhism

Different schools of thought had already arisen among the followers of the Buddha within a hundred years of his *mahāparinibbāna*, and these were being gradually systematized into various well-defined orders of the Buddhists. When Emperor Asoka accepted the creed as his own personal religion after the *Kaliṅga* war, several such orders were in existence, and the king espoused the cause of that school regarded at the time as the most orthodox among them.

The most generally accepted division in most division in most modern studies on Buddhism is the one between *Hīnayāna* and *Mahāyāna.* The first is a derogatory term understood to be used by Mahāyānists to designate schools other than the *Mahāyāna* one. However, the word "*Hīnayāna*" is not used consistently in all *Mahāyāna* scriptures.[218] Terms used to refer to schools other than *Mahāyāna* are "*Srāvakayāna*" and "*Pratyekabuddhayāna.*" In place of *Mahāyāna*, a commonly used term is "*Buddhayāna.*"[219]

Traditional accounts list eighteen schools of Buddhism that existed before the rise of the *Mahāyāna* school, which are divided into two main groups: the *sthavira* and the *Mahāsaṃgika.* These two, in

218 This term appears in the *Suvarṇaprabhāsottamasūtra* and the *Mahāvyutpatti*, the latter of which is a glossary of Buddhist terms.

219 This term appears in the *Saddharmapuṇdarīka.*

turn, are divided into subgroups of different schools, one of which is the *Theravāda* school. Usually, *Theravāda* is synonymous with the Buddhism of Sri Lanka. But there is confusion here as well. Some scholars are reluctant to use the word "Hīnayāna" because it signifies the "Lesser" Vehicle. They instead use the word "*Theravāda*" to signify Buddhist schools which do not belong to the *Mahāyāna*. In this case, *Theravāda* has the same meaning as its Sanskrit counterpart, *Sthaviravāda*. However, because the term *Theravāda* does not include the *Mahāsaṃghika*, it is an inadequate term, if the purpose is to contrast it with other schools from *Mahāyāna*. The word "*Hīnayāna*," derogatory or not, can serve a useful purpose here, by separating all other schools of Buddhism from *Mahāyāna*.

Furthermore, if, as a principle of clarification, we look at the languages used in the scriptures, there are three to take into account: Sanskrit, Buddhist Sanskrit, and *Pāḷi*. *Pāḷi* is used extensively by the *Theravāda*, and Sanskrit and Buddhist Sanskrit are used by different schools within *Hināyāna* and *Mahāyāna*. One might assume that in that case, it could be said that *Theravāda* is *Pāḷi* Buddhism. The situation is, however, not simple, because some inscriptions have been found using *Pāḷi* that may or may not belong to the *Theravādins*.[220] Moreover, if the term "*Theravāda*" is used to denote Sri Lankan Buddhism, which had three main schools, the *Mahāvihāra*, *Abhayagiri*, and *Jetavana*, then one must consider that the *Abhayagiri* School is reported sometimes to have used Sanskrit as a sacred language. Therefore, to equate *Theravāda* with *Pāḷi* Buddhism does not resolve the confusion.

4.8. Asoka Mission

It is generally accepted that Buddhism is a missionary religion, and that is the reason why is spread so effectively both within India

220 Vogel, J. Ph. "Prakrit Inscriptions from a Buddhist Site at Nāgarjunakonda" *EI* 20, no. I (1929): pp. 1–37.

and beyond. In fact, Buddhism was the only Indian religion that was able to flourish outside the confines of the subcontinent. Even though Hinduism reached Southeast Asia at about the same time as Buddhism, it never became the principle creed of the common people. This does not mean that Hinduism did not play a role in Southeast Asia religion, but by its very nature Hinduism was unable to attain a status equal to Buddhism. The success of the Buddhist mission also reveals the "portable" sanctity of Buddhism. Its sacredness was not bound by territory as was Hinduism, which forbade its chief representatives, the Brahmans, form travelling abroad.

The second introduction of Buddhism is said to have received by the peoples of Rakhaing during the reign of King Suriyacakka, the sixth successive king of King Candasuriya, in the third Dhaññavatī period.[221] In view of that nine Buddhist missionaries were sent to evangelize nine different lands away from *Maghada* Empire after the third Buddhist council headed by *Mahāthera Moggaliputtatissa* supported by the Emperor Asoka of India. A group of five monks out of nine led by the *Thera Mahādeva* went to *Mahisamaṇḍala* (*Mahinsakamandala*). The connection between Rakhaing land and Indian Buddhism or, to be more precise, the introduction of Buddhism into the land is found not in Indian literature, but in the *Pāḷi* literature of Sri Lanka: the *Dipavaṁsa*, and the *Mahāvaṁsa*, and the *Samantapāsādikā*.

The tradition rests primarily on the authority of the two Sinhalese narrative chronicles, the *Dipavaṁsa* and the *Mahāvaṁsa*.[222] This is also recorded in the *Pārājikakaṇḍaṭṭhakathā* as the following: *Mahādevatheropi mahinsakamaṇḍalaṁ gantvā devadhūtaSuttaṁ kathesi Suttapariyosāne cattālisapāṇasatassāni dhammacakkhuṁ paṭilabhiṁsu*

221 *Op. cit.*, "*New Razawon*" Vol. 1, p. 163f
f

222 Geiger, *Dipavaṁsa*, 8:1–13; *Mahāvaṁsa* 12:1–54.

cattālisayevapaṇasahassāni pabbajiṁsu (Venerable *Mahādeva* also, having gone to *Mahinsakamaṇḍala,* preached the *Devadhuta Sutta,* after the end of the discourse, forty thousand people had got the eye of the Dhamma, another forty thousand had been ordained as monks.)[223] In the section of *Navaṭṭhānāgata* of the *Sāsanavamsa,* it states that the name *Mahinsakamandala* is *Andaka* country which is called the city country of ogres *(mahinsakamandalaṁnāma andhakaraṭṭhaṁ yaṁ yakkhapura raṭṭhanti vuccati).*

According to the local accounts,[224] *Mahinsakamandala* is assigned to be Rakhaing region at that time, but others say it is modern Mysore, southern India. Ven. *Candamālālaṅkāra*'s "*Jambudipa India Map Treatise*" states that southern *Rājagaha* regions (*janapadas*) such as *ahinsaka, andhakavida,* Orissa, Bengal, Chittagong, *Phalungchit, Panva,* etc., all the region of the northern Madras including Rakhaing is called *Mahinsakamandala.*[225]

Therefore, even though the *Maṇḍala* is not at all northern region of Rakhaing completely, some parts of northern Rakhaing is supposed to be connected with. According to the *Nāgājunakoṇḍa* inscription supposed to be written in the third century AD, a Buddhist missionary was sent to the southern regions of ancient India, *Andhara* country of Deccan: Kāsmira, Gandhāra, Cīna, Cilāta, Tosali, etc. Dr. Ray says that the place Cilāta (Kirāta) of the third century AD mentioned in the inscription might have been the region now known as Arakan and lower Burma. It says, "for the benefit of the fraternities (of monks) of Tambapamna who had converted Kasmira, Gandhara, Cina, Cilāta, Tosali, Avaramta,

223 Translations are mine.

224 Mahadhamma Thurn-gran, *Sāsanālaṅkāra Sadan,* Rangoon, Hansāvatī Press, 1928 p. 21; Aung Tha Oo, *The Buddhasāsana and the Land Rakhing,* 1974 Nov. p. 9.

225 Pru (Sandoway), Maung. "*Early History of Buddhist Rakhing*" Sittwe College Magazine (1982–83) p. 59.

Vamya, Vannavasi, Yuvanna (?), Damila (?), Palura (?), and the isle of Tambamni."[226] As the record was inscribed in the fourth reignal year of king Madhariputa, the scholars think this king seems to be identical with King Madhariputa Sri Virapurisadata of the Issavaku dynasty (third century AD).[227] Dr. Ray had attempted to identify the Cilāta (Kirāta) country with the regions of Arakan and lower Burma.[228] Besides, there is a strong tradition that Kirāta was a province of Burma as indicated by a bell inscription, though modern (*viz.* AD 1811) at the Mahāmuni pagoda, Mandalay.[229] Therefore it has a define reference to the prevalence of Buddhism not only in Arakan, but in Burma as well sometimes before the third century.[230]

As the *Nāgārjunakoṇḍa* inscription was issued in the third century AD[231] the sending of the Buddhist mission must have been sometime before the third century. If so, it would not be wrong to conclude that Buddhism had already arrived at Rakhaing in the third century AD. At this point, the popular tradition, which says Buddhism came to Rakhaing at the reign of king *Candasuriya*, should be considered in the context of Phayre and Gutman's opinion of putting king *Candasuriya*, contemporary with the Buddha in India, to the second century AD.

---

226 Vogel, J. Ph. "Prakrit Inscriptions from a Buddhist Site at Nāgarjunakonda" *EI 20*, no. I (1929): pp. 1–37. pp. 22–23.

227 Ray, Nihar Ranjan. "*An Introduction to the Study of Theravāda Buddhism in Burma*" Calcutta: University of Calcutta (1946) p. 14 ff.

228 *Op. cit.*, Ray (1946).

229 Inscription collected in Upper Burma, Vol. II, 1903, p.2.

230 *Op. cit.*, Ray (1946).

231 *Op. cit.*, Ray (1946).

The above assumption is supported by the fact that the ancient Buddhist buildings of *Nāgājunakoṇḍa* city flourished during the third and fourth centuries AD and influenced both ancient cities of Vishnu and Srikettra.[232] Moreover, Prof. Luce says that Pyu used Rakhaing as a transit land when they made contacts with southern India such as Andhara and Orissa.[233]

Dr. Gutman approximates in her thesis that the Buddhist missionary would have reached to the land of Arakan during the third century AD if not earlier, comparing some sculptures of Vesālī of Arakan bear a resemblance to that of *Nāgājunakoṇḍa.*[234]

Dr. Ray also suggests that even apart from the tradition of Asoka mission, it is not impossible to assert the prevalence of Buddhism in Burma sometime before the third century AD.[235] However, only a few indigenous pieces of evidence as indicated above relating to this period is found in Rakhaing.

Additionally, Coedes remarks is worthy of note, "Because of their geographical position it would seem that they ought to have been penetrated by Indian culture earlier and more profoundly than Funan, Campa, and other kingdoms of farther India. They offer, however, only rare and quite late archaeological and epigraphical remains for the period before the middle of the sixth century. It would be imprudent to conclude from this negative argument that they were Indianized later, for various circumstances may have caused the disappearance or delayed the discovery of older remains. The almost total silence of Chinese sources for the

232 Sein Maung Oo, "Old Srikettara City," *University Padesa Journal*, Vol. 3, Part 1, (1960). p. 177.

233 Gutman (1976) p.110.

234 *Ibid.*, p.222.

235 *op. cit.*, Ray (1946)

period in question is due to the fact that the envoy from China to the kingdoms of the south at that time used the sea route and countries situated farthest from China for the seamen were the last to establish relations with her."[236]

Summary

To what extent the accustomed ways of life of the king and people were changed by the acceptance of Buddhism as the official creed in the reigns of King Candasuriya and his sixth successive king Suriyacakka in the third Dhaññavatī period, it is difficult to gauge today. In the conversion—if we may use that term—of a person to Buddhism, there are several degrees of earnestness. One may formally take refuge in the Three Jewels (i.e., the Buddha, the *Dhamma,* and the *Saṁgha*). This generally implies that such a person accepts that the Buddha and his teachings would lead him to ultimate salvation, and abjures faith in gods, other prophets, or teachers as efficient for that purpose. Such a person may, however, invoke the aid of a divine or human agency for worldly ends. To the three Refuges, a more earnest convert may add the Five Precepts, the vows to abstain from taking life, stealing, wrongful conduct in matters sexual, untruthfulness, and addiction to intoxicants. Still more earnest devotees may observe the eight precepts on fast days, or take the ten vows to be observed every day. All this may be done while one remains in the world. But the really earnest believer in the Buddha (i.e., he who wishes to realize for himself the Truth realized by the Buddha) has to give up all social obligations and family ties, and take to the life of the almsman by being formally admitted to the *Saṁgha.*

The presence of Indian elements, in whatever role, be they princes, *Brahmanas,* hermit then-kings, traders, or artisans, must have resulted from the customary, age-old law of succession which prevented

236 Coedes (1968), p. 62.

those who followed the first son in the Hindu family, however personally accomplished they may be, from enjoying the fruits of parental or hereditary wealth and status. At any rate, the percentage of Indian migrants physically present at any given time in the Southeast Asian kingdoms appears to have been small if not negligible, and it was only local royal patronage that enabled Indian religious, cultural, linguistic, and, more importantly, scriptal elements to seep generously into the Rakhaing social fabric. This largely perhaps largely due to the successive migration, under hope of royal patronage, of educated Brahmanas and Buddhist clergy as well as educated as well organized members of trade guilds who must have carried with them to the Rakhaing shores the latest of what was Indian in their days, including to the scriptal changes. Thus far, we have seen how Indian Buddhism played a major role in the development of social and religious affairs in Dhaññavatī Kingdom of Rakhaing in ancient time.

As mentioned above, the local chronicles traditionally assert that during the reign of king Candasuriya in the Dhaññavatī City Gotama the Buddha, while visiting, converted the court and cast the image, *Mahāmuni*, and preached *Sutthubimba Sutta*. According to this tradition, Buddhism is supposed to be introduced to Rakhaing since Buddha's lifetime in the sixth century BC. It was also in the Dhaññavatī dynasty that *Thera Mahāreva* was said to have come to *Mahinsakamaṇḍala* for conversation, after the third Buddhist synod was held at *Pātaliputta*. Some consider that *Mahinsaka* as the present Rakhaing land or the land was once part of *Mahinsaka*. However some scholars insist that *Mahinsaka* was at one time the same of Mysore at the southern part of India. Aforementioned traditions hint that Buddhism came to Rakhaing in the sixth and third centuries BC respectively by means of missionary activities. Unfortunately, however, no contemporary record is found relating to these traditions. It has been for the tradition that many local archeological and literary evidence in later dates so far been found firmly claim that present available Buddhism relates to those traditions. Their religious devotion in Buddha image, *stūpas*, relic, etc. would have made them to advance their culture in the successive early periods in Rakhaing, which we will see in later chapters. The Buddhist portability might have enhanced to replace the then existing Brahmanical cults, their former religion, and suddenly might have spread all over ancient Rakhaing.

CHAPTER 5

THE DEVELOPMENT OF BUDDHISM IN RAKHAING

In this chapter, first, we attempt to see the developments of Buddhism in *Vesālī* period in fairly details based on the available epigraphic and archeological sources we have. After that, a short description of Buddhist developments in the Lay-mro and Mrauk Oo periods will also be included. It is undeniable that by far the most interesting and astonishing by its Buddhist art and culture is the *Vesālī* period in Rakhaing history, as far as Buddhism and its culture in Rakhaing land are concerned.

5.1. *Vesālī* Period

A study of development of Buddhism during *Vesālī* period is a highly significant phenomenon in Rakhaing history. We will see in the following that a number of epigraphic and archeological remains unearth tells us religious aspects of this period. Most of the donors who recorded their deeds were Buddhists.

Vesālī is the most famous period in the history of Buddhism in Rakhaing, but in one spot of that *Vesālī* it is now a poor village, about fifty miles away from present capital Rakhaing State, Sittway (Akyab), in the northeastern about six miles away from the last capital of Rakhaing land, Mrauk Oo (old city, Mrohaung).

The *Vesālī* is known in the chronicles as Kyauk Hlay Gar City because the founder King Dvencandra or Mahātaicandra, son of King Suriyaketu the last king of the third Dhaññavatī, built a stone pier about one mile in length on the bank of the river Randanadī near the city. It became a noted trade port to which as many as a thousand ships from abroad came annually.[237] *Vesālī* phase that started from the early fourth century AD, about 327 witnessed all round development including political stability under a long line of kings, known by the surname "Candra." Though, according to the old glory till about AD 818, we notice a shift of political activities from *Vesālī* of Kaladan River to Pañcā of Lay-mro River. At least nine kings are believed to have ruled during this dynasty, but it is more than nine. According to the *Ānandacandra* Inscriptions and numismatic evidence, there have been fifteen Candra kings altogether. We came across four more kings of the same dynasty who denied "Candra" as their surnames; in other words, the four others came from the families other than Candra.

Certain scholars[238] are of the opinion that the following dynasty of this Candra in Rakhaing may have been connected to the Candra dynasty Harikela in southeast Bengal or to a Candra ascendancy of Gupta Empire of Magadha who might come to rule in Rakhaing land without evidence. It was, however, only Indian

237 Aung Tha Oo, *Arakanese Culture: Vesālī period*, p. 10.

238 Gutman (1976) p. 2; Leider (2002) p.144

influences not only in Rakhaing but in Southeast Asia as reflected in the personal names. As the contacts between India and Southeast Asia have a long and checkered history and had many dimensions—commercial, religious, and cultural—the names mostly derived from Sanskrit, Prakrit, or Pāḷi obviously as a result of the spread of Buddhism and Hinduism (i.e., Brahmanical faith).[239]

One of the verses on the *Ānandacandra* pillar describes the King Dvencandra, founding father of the city that could well laugh at the beauty of the home of celestial beings. The other twenty kings who ruled between the fourth and eighth centuries are also recorded. *Vesālī* thrived with trade and commerce, and gold and silver coins of five denominations were used. Earlier coins had only the king's seal, but later, the author kings' names were also stamped. Coins bearing the names of fifteen kings have so far been found.

It is, however, certain coins of King Rājacandra and King Devacandra having stamped with conch in obverse side. *Vesālī* coins are stamped with a sitting bull on obverse side and the crown flanked by two *thazurn* (a traditional and national orchid of the state) stalks on the reverse. The latest collection of Rājacandra coins from Kharine Island in Taung-goke Township were found in two types: the first with a conch in an obverse side and the crown flanked by two *thazurn.* The other type is with a bull on obverse and the crown on the reverse. The collections of Dvencandra coins from Kha-rine Island possess three types: first, with conch (*srivatsa*); second, with bull left turn (*srivatsa*); and third, bull right turn (*srivatsa*).

Inhabitants of *Vesālī* city with great effort built a civilization that bears the name *Vesālī* up to this day. The abundant findings of inscribed *ye dhammā* verse, which is considered as the essence of

239 Aung Tha Oo, *Buddhasāsana and Rakhaing Land,* typeset (in Burmese) (1974, Nov.), p. 14.; Raman, K. V. "Indian Influences in Southeast Asia as reflected in the Personal Names" Ancient and Medieval Commercial Activities in the Indian Ocean: Testimony of Inscriptions and Ceramic-sherds, *Report of the Taisho University Research Project 1997–2000,* Ed. by Noboru Karashima, pp.184–206.

Theravādin spirit in nooks and corners of Rakhaing land bears testimony to the fact that Buddhism flourished to an utmost degree. *Vesālī* folks built pagodas, *stūpas* and temples, etc. They cast Buddha images. They established illustrious Buddhist monasteries. They donated lands, copied old treatises. Pāḷi and Sanskrit were officially used and widely learned. The *Ānandacandra* Inscriptions, copper plate land grants and bell inscriptions, bear testimony to the heritage. Besides the prevailing faith of Buddhism, Brahmanism practices also coexisted.

The old palace city wall encompassing an area of 2.7 square miles forming an oval shape can still be traced easily. Pibaungrong village lying west of it serves in the outer city. Palace site situated in the center of the palace city, serves today on the settlement ground of *Vesālī* village. Brick rubbles going hints to what it once was adjacent to the eastern of the palace city is Lat Khatt Gung or Loon batten hill lock where some *Vesālī* artifacts from nearby are displayed. This is believed to be the original site of the Ānandacandra pillar now preserved at Shitthung Pagoda in Mrauk Oo.

In this period, territory of *Vesālī* extended to the southeastern part of Bengal known as twelve towns of Bengal *(Banga Sae Na Mro)* in Rakhaing, or twelve provinces of Banga, viz. (1) Mushidabad, (2) Dakha, (3) Cambila, (4) Shilat, (5) Pattikara, (6) Gangacara, (7) Chittagong, (8) GandawPāḷin, (9) Kansa, (10) Talinga, (11) Barisal, and (12) Rangpur. In other words, the Rakhaing territory in Bengal was from the east bank of Ganges River to the mouth of Naff River.[240]

According to the Sanskrit Stone and copper plate inscriptions, the possibility of close contact between the Candra of *Vesālī* and Candra of Harrikela Samatata has been hinted. Both the groups of rulers were Buddhists. Traditional history of Bengal refers that

240 Zan, U Shwe. "*Wethali: The Land of Historic Finds*" p. 2.

Candra dynasty ruled the Bengal region from AD 825 to 1035. Based on the *Ānandacandra* stone inscription, we have known that *Vesālī* of Rakhaing flourished in trade and commerce from the fourth to the eighth century AD.

In Rakhaing Chronicles, the name of a queen of the founder king Mahātaicandra was Supabhā Devī, who was happened to be a most pious queen. When the couple ascended to the *Vesālī* throne, they requested to dispatch a rear Buddha image by her father king from India. On the way from to Rakhaing, that very Buddha image was lost in the sea near present Mrauk Oo. It was happened due to the heavy stormy weather. The queen became so much grieved for the unfortunate event. To ease her grief and its substitute the image the king planned to erect a new great image made of bronze as a founding image to commemorate of their completion of the *Vesālī* city. And she worshiped and prayed the new image that she be the first person to be worshiped to the lost image when it reappears again one day.

For the reconstruction of Buddhist history of this period there are a variety of sources: epigraphic, archeological, and literary. But we will base our study on the former two; the latter, literary, is less important.

5.1.1. Epigraphic Sources of Buddhist *Vesālī*

Most of the inscriptions found in Rakhaing land are religious in nature, to the regret of some historians who long for more data describing secular events. However, due to some specific dates, proper names, or names of particular schools of Buddhism, the inscriptions yield little information that can be used for the study of the history of Buddhism. The majority of the quotations from canonical texts in the inscriptions are ones common to all sects, although the language used can, in some instances, help to identify the sects or schools to which they belong. However, the situation is not so straightforward as to automatically ascribe all Pāḷi inscriptions to the *Theravāda* tradition, or all Sanskrit inscriptions to the *Sarvāstivāda* or the *Mahāyāna* traditions.

Inscriptions other than the so called "quotation inscriptions" can mostly be categorized as "eulogy inscriptions," which often serve as prefaces to "donation" or "royal inscriptions." These two types of inscriptions are recorded of kings' meritorious deeds. Eulogy inscriptions and royal inscriptions can be composed in either Pāḷi or Sanskrit. Donation inscriptions that belong to people other than royalty or nobility are few in number.

Grouped according to language, there are three linguistic categories of inscriptions: Pāḷi, Sanskrit, and the vernacular. Four categories by subject matter can be discussed: quotation, eulogy, royal, and donation. These categories are provisional ones used only for the sake of research, for there is no absolute distinction among them. For example, quotations taken from texts might be used as eulogizing stanzas prefacing a royal inscription, in which case, three categories would appear in the same inscription.

Inscriptions are dated in paleographic terms from the fourth to the beginning of the tenth century CE. The scripts used closely resemble the so-called "Gupta," "Devanāgari" scripts, but sometimes resemble the Nālanda style. Over time, from around the fifth and sixth centuries, the Rakhaing "Gupta" script evolved into distinctive local or regional scripts. Devanagari scripts were used in the famous *Ānandacandra* pillar inscription in the Sanskrit language.

All the available inscriptions will be briefly examined as a group, and even though the scripts may change, the texts used remain constant in the same tradition. For centuries, the quotation inscriptions primarily cited the same passage, but this does not mean that no development in the selection or presentation of quotation occurred. It just means that there is no real distinction between the two sets of data.

Problem concerning language, paleography, and the relationship between epigraphic and archaeological data will be set aside temporarily. Even if the data ultimately cannot be distinguished by means of categorization of subject matter, for the sake of convenience, it will be presented in that manner.

5.1.1.1. Quotation Inscriptions

The inscriptions in this category come from quotations found in texts, both canonical and extracanonical. They can be written either in Pāḷi or Sanskrit, but with different provenances. Where Sanskrit inscriptions are found Pāḷi inscriptions are also found.

In paleographic terms, both the Pāḷi and Sanskrit inscriptions of the *Vesālī* tradition date from the late fifth century on. The texts found are inscribed on stone, on copper, on *stūpas*, on the base of Buddha images, and bells.

Quotations inscriptions contain material drawn from canonical texts and, to a lesser extent, noncanonical ones as well. They usually consist of a short stanza that summarizes the doctrine.

Ye Dhammā or *Ye Dharmā* Inscriptions

This is by far the most common quotation inscription. Textual sources for this stanza include the Mahāvagga of the Vinayapitaka from the Pāḷi canon and the Buddhist Sanskrit text the Mahāvastu of the Lokottaravādin Mahāsaṃghikas. The Pāḷi version form the Mahāvagga of the Vinaya Pitaka is as follows:

ye dhammā hetuppabhavā
yesaṃ hetuṃ tathāgato āha
tesañ ca yo nirodho
evaṃvādī mahāsamaṇo ti.

In most cases, the Pāḷi inscriptions agree with the Mahāvagga, except when tesaṃ is sometimes inscribed as yesaṃ. The Sanskrit version differs slightly from the Mahāvastu and could have come from another text, which is now lost.[241] A Sanskrit version found in Rakhaing reads as follows:

ye dharmmāḥ hetuprabhavāḥ
hetun teṣan tathāgato hy avadat
teṣañca yo nirodho hy- [var. yo nirodha evaṃvādī/yo nirodho evaṃvādī]
evaṃvādī mahā'sramaṇaḥ.

A third type is written mainly in Pāḷi but with the addition of one or two words in Sanskrit. These inscriptions cannot be described as being Buddhist Sanskrit ones, because they could not be the result of scribal errors or slips due to a familiarity with Sanskrit. A number of such inscriptions found in *Vesālī*, and in paleographic terms dated to the seventh century, use the Sanskrit word *hetuprabhavā* in place of the Pāḷi word *hetuppabhavā*, but otherwise, the declension and euphonic rules follow Pāḷi grammar. In an inscription from Sārnāth in India dated to the second century, the Sanskrit forms, *hetuprabhavā* and *Mahā'smaṇa*, replace the Pāḷi forms of *hetuppabhavā* and *Mahāsamaṇo*, although the declension remains Pāḷi throughout.[242]

---

241 For this type of inscription found in Yunnan, see two articles by Libenthal, "*Sanskrit Inscriptions from Yunnan I*;" and "*Sanskrit Inscriptions from Yunnan II.*" The stanza is also often placed at the end of chapters or at the end of Mahāyāna sūtras or Tantric texts such as the Ratnaguṇasamccayagātha and the Pañcakrama. See Yuyama, ed., Prajñā-pāramitā-ratna-guna-samcaya-gāthā. For the stanzas found in India, see Shizutani, Indo bukkyo himei mokuroku; and Yuyama, "Jūni innenju' oboegaki."

242 See Oertel, "*Excavations at Sārnāth,*" 74. Interestingly, this inscription is found with other inscriptions that mention the name "*Sarvastivādin.*"

Inscriptions of this third type are found in abundance in Rakhaing land. Of them, Vesāli period inscriptions, the *ye dhammā* is accompanied by other stanzas reproduced here from Prof. San Tha Aung's writing:

Nīticandra[243] and Vīracandra[244] Inscriptions of *Vesālī*

The first inscription, which is the inscription of the time of Nīticandra, is engraved on a slab recovered from the ruins of an old *stūpa* on the Unhissaka hill situated to the east of *Vesālī* in 1956.

The second inscription, which is the inscription of Vīracandra, is engraved on a slab belonged to what is called the *Ānandacandra stūpa* standing on Thinkyat-taw hill which is closely situated to the Unhisaka hill. It was found about the same time.

The name of Nīticandra and Vīracandra are mentioned in Ānanadacandra inscription inscribed on the west face of the pillar now at Shitthaung Pagoda at Mrauk Oo, Rakhaing. The first part of this inscription contains three sections quoting the names of the kings together with the durations of their reigns.

In the second section of the first part, we found the names of Nīticandra and Vīracandra. The verses 28 and 29 described them very briefly. Verse 28: "Then the renowned Nīticandra, who removed strife by policy, reigned like Mahendra for fifty-five years." Verse 29: "After him, King Vīracandra reigned three years; then King Pritticandra (ruled) for twelve years." Dr. Sircar's chronology gives Nīticandra's ruling period as AD 520–575 and Vīracandra's as AD 575–578.

The alphabets of both the records have a close resemblance with the alphabets used in certain Eastern Indian inscriptions of the fifth

243 Regarding Nīticandra inscription, Gutman (1976) p. 83 mentioned to Sircar, D. C. "*Inscriptions of the Candras of Arakan*" EI XXXII, 2 (1957) pp. 103–109; ASB 1958–59 pl. 37, San Tha Aung. (1974) pl. 15. Now at Mrohuaung (*Mrauk Oo*) Museum.

244 Regarding Vīracandra inscription, Gutman (1976) p. 86 mentioned to Sircar, *loc. cit.*; ASB 1958–1959, 38, San Tha Aung. *Loc. cit.* pl. 16. Mrauk Oo Museum.

and sixth centuries AD. However, a certain amount of local development is noticed in the paleography of these inscriptions. Careful study of the consonants, initial vowels, and medial vowels revealed this. The inscriptions can also be dated paleographically as those belong to the last quarter of the sixth century. Comparative studies of the alphabets, initial vowels, and medial vowels of Rakhaing script (Rakkhavaṇṇa) with those of Eastern India will reveal very interesting information about the Rakhaing scripts.

Nīticandra Inscription Text

1. *ye dhammā hetu-prabhavā hetuṃ tesha tathāgata*
2. *āha tesham ca yo nirodho evaṃ vādī mahāsramana*
3. *sri niticandra sya candravat-parchi na sya devī savitaṃ*
4. *candrasriya nama pa re mo pa si ka sya*
5. *deyya dharmmo yam sarvvo satvanamm auka (tta) ma*

Translation: Out of all the laws, the law of cause is the origin. Tathāgato (i.e., Buddha) has spoken of the conditions arising from a cause. He has also spoken of their cessation. This is the doctrine of the great Sramaṇa (i.e., Buddha).

This is the pious gift of the queen of Sri Nīticandra, who is likened to the moon. The queen by the name of Savitam Candrasriya is a devout lay worshiper of the Buddha. Let all creatures acquire the best knowledge (acquiring *Nirvāna*) as a result of having given this meritorious gift.

Vīracandra Inscription Text

1. *satya-dharmmanu ragena kritamsvarthena bhubhuja*
2. *parartha ghatanodyoga damyanni hita ceti sa*
3. *sri-viracandradevena mahi mandala mandanam*
4. *dharmama dhigata rajyena buddha stupa satam (ceti)*

Translation: Sri Vīracandradeva, the king who obtained sovereignty through righteousness (*dharmma*), whose heart is fully set on exertions for effecting good to others, constructed a hundred Buddha *stūpas*, which are the ornaments of the earth, with his own wealth, owing his love for the true law.

These two dedicatory inscriptions are very important for us as they are the only epigraphic so far found of kings Nīticandra and Vīracandra of the Buddhist royal family of the Candras of Rakhaing. Of course, the names of these rulers are known from the coins issued by them as well as from the *Ānandacandra* inscription of Shitthaung Pagoda in Mrauk Oo as mentioned above.

Prof. San Tha Aung remarks that the inscriptions give us the information: first, flourishing of Buddhism in *Vesālī* during the sixth century AD, second, the existence of many Buddha-stupas built by the kings of that period, partial confirmation of the genealogy of the Candras of Rakhaing given in the *Ānandacandra* inscription, the name of the queen of Nīticandra was Sāvitam Candrasiya, type of scripts used during this period, the use of Sanskrit literature by royal families.

Additionally, these inscriptions can be classified as "*pattidāna*" inscriptions because the donors share their deeds to others, let others known, so that they will delight upon (*pattānumodana*), as far as Buddhist literature is concerned.[245] It is clear that such inscriptions were considered sacred, since they contained the doctrine in summary form. We cannot assume that all of the patrons who sponsored these inscriptions were able to read Pāḷi, but at least we can say that they must have known the essential import of the stanza of Pāḷi canon. So far as the context shows, the tradition appears to be closely connected

245 According to Mahā Thera Nyanatiloka, "pattidāna" literary means "giving of the acquired," (i.e., "transference of merit"). Though in the older texts very seldom mentioned (e.g., A VII, 50), it is, however, a widespread custom in all Buddhist countries. It is presumed that moral merit, especially that acquired through giving food, can be transferred to others, apparently for the reason that one's own good actions may become to others, especially to departed relatives and friends reborn in the ghost realm, an inducement to a happy and morally advantageous state of mind. Transference of merit is advocated though without mentioning the term patti-dāna in the Tirokudda Sutta Khp. and Petavatthu and its Comp. Khp. Tr. It is one of the ten "bases of meritorious action" puññakiriyavatthu, called there pattānuppadāna. See, Nyanatiloka, Mahā Thera. "*Manual of Buddhist Terms and Doctrines,*" BPS, 1st Ed. 1952.

to worshipping Buddha and *stūpa* construction and the cult of relics. And their literarily skills are superb like, "likened to the moon," in the Nīticandra inscription, and "whose heart is fully set on exertions for effecting good to others," "which are the ornaments of the earth" in the Vīracandra inscription. As mentioned above, persons who commissioned in the inscriptions had a good knowledge of Sanskrit.

According to the facts in the second inscription, King Vīracandra in his reign built a hundred *stūpa*s with his own wealth (possession). It seems everyone would appreciate upon his noble action done to his religion. It can also assume that kings of *Vesālī* were Buddhist missionary kings like emperor Asoka of India (274–237 BC). Here, by means of "his own wealth," seems to denote "finance possessed by royal family or king maintained alone by the royal lineage." There are three kinds of finance of kings of Rakhaing: (i) royal owned finance (*rājabaṇṭa*), (ii) state owned finance (*janabaṇṭa*), and (iii) finance for religious purposes (*sāsanabaṇṭa*). It is said that it has to be used separately, cannot be transferred from one to another.[246]

Moreover, as to the inscriptions found in this period, it can be seen a tradition that soon after consecration ceremony (*abiseka*) to ascend throne, kings of *Vesālī* used to make coins, built religious building such as *stūpa*s, etc., and record donations made. It at least shows the flourishing Buddhism in *Vesālī*.

Historians mostly agree that the Buddhist culture and writing system (i.e., script) entered into different parts of Southeast Asia in the course of Indianization. Observing the epigraphic evidence found in Rakhaing, the earliest inscriptions are Buddhistic. Inscribed scripts are Brāhmī or its ascendancy of later times like Gupta. The language is northern Indian Sanskrit, while literature is southern Pāḷi in Rakhaing inscription mostly. Pāḷi had been primarily used by Theravādīns. Both

---

246 Oo, Aung Thar. "*Rakhaing Culture: Vesālī Period*," Vol. 1, No. 1, Aung Ratana Press, Rangoon. (1966 Sep.) p.6.; Khine, Tun Shwe. "*Buddhist Art of Vesālī Period, Arakan*," Site-thay-daw Sarpay, Rangoon. (1990 Jan.), p. 33.

Sanskrit language and Pāḷi literature had influenced Rakhaing to a great extent.

What is *ye dhammā* verse? Since when, thus far it frequently been used throughout Rakhaing?

The verses from the Vinaya[247] beginning "*ye dhammā hetuppabhavā*" are the words spoken by the Arahant Assaji (Sanskrit: Aśvajit) to Upatissa, later to become known as Sāriputta (Sanskrit: Śāriputra). Sāriputta along with his boyhood companion Kolita, later called Moggallāna (Sanskrit: Maudgalyayana), was one of the two chief disciples of the Buddha. Upon meeting Assaji, Sāriputta was impressed and asked after his teacher and the dhamma that he taught. Assaji demurred, being "only a beginner," but eventually responded with the now famous verse, and before he had finished Sāriputta had a decisive break through. Nyanaponika says: "Upon hearing the first two lines, there arose in the wanderer Upatissa the dust-free, stainless vision of the Dhamma—the first glimpse of the Deathless, the path of Stream-entry—and to the ending of the last two lines he already listened as a stream-enterer."[248]

Prof. San Tha Aung writes referring to Georges Coedes, a celebrated Southeast Asian historian, "The *ye dhammā* verse, therefore, gives the cream of Buddhism. According to the comments made by Coedes, 'The extraordinary conciseness of this stanza, that gives in four verses the quintessence of the teaching of the Master, might alone be considered sufficient justification for its choice and explanation of its popularity. But there is more in it than that. According to the tradition preserved in the most ancient writings, it was by means of this stanza that the Buddha secured the adherence of the two disciplines Sāriputta and Moggalāna, afterward revered in the circles of the Brotherhood

247 Sāriputtamoggalānapabhajjakathā, Mahāvagga Pāḷi, Vinaya Piṭaka, CSCD

248 Thera, Nyanaponika., and Hecker, Hellmuth., "*Great Disciples of the Buddha: Their Lives, Their Works, Their Legacy*" ed. Bhikkhu Bodhi, BPS, Kandy, (2003). p.7.

as second only to the Master himself. A formula which had so speedily convinced the two most notable followers of the Master, must rapidly have acquired in the eyes of the ancient Buddhists a sort of magic virtue, and may well have seemed to them a quite irresistible charm for the conversion to the Faith of any how had not yet heard it."

Including the above mentioned two inscriptions, Pamela Gutman[249] presented a number of inscriptions engraved with *ye dhammā* verse in her thesis, *viz.* (i) votive inscriptions found in the vicinity of Dhaññavatī, (ii) inscribed votive *stūpa* from Selagiri, (iii) inscription from Minthachaung, (iv) two inscribed votive *stūpa*s from Meewa village near Kyauktaw, (v) inscription of the time of Nīticandra, (vi) inscription of Vīracandra, (vii) inscription from Payagyi, (viii) inscribed *stūpa* from Tezarama monastery, (ix) inscription from Thinkyitaw, (x) fragmentary inscription from Thinkyitaw, (xi) inscription from Letkhat-taung, (xii) inscription from Kyaukphyu, (xiii) inscription from Ngalunmaw.

Ye dhammā verse is found throughout Rakhaing from the fifth to the eighth century AD. It is used to ascribe whether as verse alone or as introductory one above other lines. It is "namo tassa bhagavato..." verse in the present day we have found in almost every Buddhist books in Burma. Concerning why this has been frequently been used is, Tun Shwe Khine reasons, "because (i) it can grasp what the Buddha taught with a few lines, (ii) by it, as mentioned in the story above, Sāriputta and Moggalāna have enlightened, and (iii) believing that thus inscribing *ye dhammā* verse, their religious works had accomplished."[250]

Briefly, most of the inscriptions belonging to the fifth and ninth centuries AD were engraved with *ye dhammā* verses, the cream of Buddhism. It indicates that Buddhism, most probably *Theravāda* Buddhism, was flourished in *Vesālī* period.

---

249 Gutman (1976) pp. 79–95.

250 *Op. cit.*, Tun Shwe Khine (1990 Jan)

5.1.1.2. Eulogy Inscription (*Ānandacandra* Inscription)

This type of inscription occurs both as an independent eulogy and as a benediction preceding the body of an inscription. A eulogy inscription consists of verses praising precursor kings, of what they did, of how they were, etc. and religion. By far the most important eulogy inscription of Rakhaing is the famous *Ānandacandra* Inscription.

Concerning Rakhaing Razawons (chronicles) there have been forty-eight chronicles. There is a saying in Rakhaing that one has to read or study all those forty-eight chronicles in order to comprehend fully about Rakhaing history. Only a few of them has been come across for this study. In them, chronologies of kings differ to each other mostly. It is, therefore, not easy to choose by far the most correct one to pick up from. Being written in modern alphabets of Rakhaing, those chronicles cannot be ascertained about history happened before AD 1000. *Ānandacandra* Inscription is like a chronicle which tells the Rakhaing history before AD 700; it is, therefore, a more authentic and reliable source as well. It is also not easy to identify the names of the kings mentioned in the inscription with any literary evidence. We have, however, coins and other epigraphic evidence for that concern. In a single stone slab, a few inscription lines help to know the chronology of kings ruled in Rakhaing before AD 700. It is invaluable for the Rakhaing history.

The *Ānandacandra* Inscriptions Pillar now on the hill of Chitthoung Pagoda in Mrauk Oo is the most important backbone to reconstruct the actual religious history especially the Buddhist history of Ancient Rakhaing. It is also one of the most important archaeological representations of the past of what Rakhaing is now. This inscription was written by King *Ānandacandra*, one of *Vesālī* kings flourished between the fourth century and the tenth century AD. It is said that it was written after nine years of ascending the throne by King *Ānandacandra* (i.e., about AD 729 or for some around AD 650). Prof. Johnston and Dr. Sircar have studied the inscriptions and dated it paleographically to be the beginning of the eighth century AD.

Sometimes in the inscription, Brahmanical gods are placed the Buddhism, but there is no indication that Buddhism was regarded as inferior to the Brahmanical gods. This type of inscription has not been found in either the Pyu or the Dvāravatī traditions. In fact, Sanskrit *Ānandacandra* inscription, Brahmanical or Buddhist faith combined, is rare occurrence in Southeast Asia. Certain stanzas mentioned in the inscription honor a king or a noble, using Buddhist terminology to praise the royal's qualities and deeds. These are evident to insight into how Buddhism was regarded at that time. Sometimes, Buddhism is mentioned along with Brahmanism, especially Saivism. Sometimes Buddhism appears to be less prominent than Brahmanism. However, most of the verses have a royal provenance, and with Brahmanism playing a more important role as a political instrument, it is not uncommon to find inscription eulogizing Brahmanical gods, Buddhas, as well as bodhisattvas. Supposing that inscriptions that are purely Buddhist definitely belong to the Mahāyānistic or Tantric tradition would be mistaken because the *Ānandacandra* inscription has its distinctive character of Buddhism, but not either Mahāyānistic or Tantric. This will be explained in later section briefly.

In the inscriptions, king *Ānandacandra*, Asoka of ancient Rakhaing, supporter of Buddhism, calls himself as an *Upasaka*, but following the Buddhist tradition of religious tolerance he did not neglect the Brahmanas in this display of liberty. Many monasteries named *Ānandodaya* have been built. There have been made gold and silver *catiyas* containing the relics of Buddha. There have been images of Lord of Sages (Buddha) composed of brass bell metal and copper. There have been made many pleasing and well-executed images of the Buddha (*Sugata*) made of ivory, wood, terracotta, and stone. Innumerable clay *cetiya* models and also books of the Holy Law (*Dhamma*) have been caused to be written by the good king in large numbers. He has out of reverence given many robes and copper bowls to monks coming from diverse places. The king has also dug two delightful wells named after the monastic communities called Pundinga and Soma.[251]

Therefore, we have found in the famous *Ānandacandra* Inscriptions that king *Ānandacandra*, being a Buddhist *Upasakā* king, let to be reconstructed then collapsed many famous religious monuments of gods built by his ancestral kings.[252]

In verse 46, "many monasteries named *Ānandodaya* have been built," in verse 47, "there have been made gold and silver *cetiya*s containing relics of the Buddha, Bodhisattvas, Cunda, and others according to power" are mentioned clearly.[253]

251 See Verse Nos. 47, 48, 49, 50, 51, 54 of the Inscriptions.

252 See Verse No. 54 of *Ānandacandra* Inscription. See Aung, San Tha. *Ānandacandra: Eighth Century Rakhaing Vesālī King.* Rangoon: Nov. 1975, p. 142.

253 Verse Nos. 46 and 47 of *Ānandacandra* Inscription. See Aung, San Tha. (1975 Nov). *Op. cit.*, p. 134–135.

While narrating the eventful reign of king *Ānandacandra*, it gives us about his relationship with the rulers of a number of countries living far beyond the realm of his kingdom. It is evident that *Ānandacandra* formulated diverse policies relating to the establishment of friendly relations with these far away kingdoms. Of these motives, two can easily be identified: signing a treaty of amity with King Silamegha of Sri Lanka by showing generosity to the Buddhist clergy in his kingdom and contracting matrimonial alliances with royal family of Tamraptna, which can be identified with Tamralipta in Madnapure district of West Bengal or Tamrapartna (i.e., Sri Lanka).[254] This may be by far the firmest earliest epigraphic reference to communication between Rakhaing and Sri Lanka.

In the inscription, verse 53 tells, "donations of copper bowls and good silk robes to the monks come from eight different directions (by the king *Ānandacandra*)."

Moreover, verse 61 of the inscription states the king sent a number of necessities, such as a seat for Dhamma preacher (dharmāsana), a good female elephant, and brilliant cotton robes to the congregation of monks residing in the land of king Silamegha. According to Pamela Gutman, the king mentioned in the inscription has been identified as Aggabodhi IV of Sri Lanka (AD 727–766) by referring, "Whose throne name was Silamegha (Silameghavaṇṇa of Sri Lanka) mentioned in Cūlavaṁsa I, chapter 46 (41–67)

254 We can also identify Tamraptana with Sri Lanka on the basis of evidence furnished in literary as well as epigraphic sources. The Puranic literature mentions Tamraptna as one of the nine fold divisions of India. This Tamraptna, according to H. C. Raycauduri, is usually identified with Sri Lanka. The ancient Greeks called it Taprobane and Asoka referred to it as Tambapanni in his inscriptions. See Raychaudhuri, H. C., "Political History of Ancient India" 7th Ed., Calcutta (1972), p.294 and note 2; see also by the same author, "Studies in Indian Antiquities," Calcutta (1958), p.84.

by Geiger."[255] But according to the list of kings in the works of the late Ven. Dr. Wapola Rāhula, the king can be identified as Aggaboddhi VI (AD 727–766). He also based his list on Geiger's list: Cūlavaṁsa translation, part II, p. ix ff.[256] It should be noted that Dr. Pamela Gutman has mistaken regarding the identification of the king Silamegha of Sri Lanka. It appears that after fulfilling his kingly obligations toward the different religious communities at home, he embarked on similar activities places far away from home. In one of these ventures he was pleased to have sent presents to the Buddhists living in Sri Lanka.

An interesting incident of king *Ānandacandra*'s life is narrated in the inscription. In verse 62 of the epigraph, it is mentioned that he married to Dhenda, the daughter of King Tamrapatna. Okkantha suggests that his Tamraptna is Tamluck in present West Bengal.[257] But he did not cite any evidence in support of this suggestion. It could be Dhenda from Sri Lanka, because as mentioned above Tamrapatna has been identified with Sri Lanka in ancient days.

It can be suggested that without a number of affiliations with Sri Lanka in earlier century, there would not be possible for king *Ānandacandra*'s sending a number of gifts to the congregation of noble monks in Sri Lanka.

Johnston suggested the reignal duration of King *Candrodaya* of *Ānandacandra* inscription as AD 201–229 and was inclined to equate with *Candasuriya* of the chronicles.[258]

255 Gutman (1976), p. 37.

256 Rahula (1993) *History of Buddhism*, p. 310.

257 *Op. cit.*, Okkantha (1999), p. 56.

258 Johnston (1944) p. 368.

In this *Ānandacandra* inscription the modifications for the kings previous to *Candrodaya* are read as "zealous in doing kindness to the world," "the able," "eminent for soothedness," "fair of form and heroic in policy." *Candrodaya* and successors were, however, modified as "approved by the good," "giving of countless gifts," "want to heaven," and "eminent in religious practices." In contrast with the former one the later ones sound a bit religious. This fact also seems to provide us the liability to assume that at the reign of Candrodaya, in the third century AD, a particular kind of religious had been introduced in Rakhaing land. This fact is firmly confirmed by a number of *ye dhammā* quotation inscriptions.

The following text and translation of, the inscription on Western Face of Pillar at the Shitthaung Pagoda, Mrauk Oo, Rakhaing, is reproduced from Dr. Pamela Gutman's PhD thesis, "Ancient Arakan with special reference to its cultural history between the fifth and eleventh centuries" in the Australian National University. August 1976, (Unpublished) pp. 51–67, with a number of certain consultations with Dr. Johnston's posthumous article, "Some Sanskrit Inscriptions of Arakan" in *BSOAS* XI (1944) pp. 373–382. For further details explanations and comments are be available in the aforementioned authors' works. All the notes have been retained where applicable from aforementioned works, and are indicated by the initials preceding them as EHJ for Dr. E. H. Johnston, LDB for L. D. Barnett, and PG for Dr. Pamela Gutman.

Note: Doubtful letters are enclosed in square brackets, and letters which cannot be read are placed by a dot. Omitted characters, when restored, are shown in angular brackets: thus, < >. For convenience of reference, while the text is arranged and numbered marginally according to the verses, the line of the inscription is also noted in brackets in the body of the text. [To mark the elision of initial *a-* after a final *-o* a raised comma has been used (e.g., *tinītimān* [v. 23d]).][259]

Immediately below the inscription are two lines in a later hand, more or less contemporary with that on the north face of the pillar. It is uncertain whether they were intended to have any connection with *Ānandacandra*'s *praśasti.* For convenience of reference, while the text is arranged and numbered marginally according to the verses, the line of the inscription is also noted in brackets.[260]

Text

[Verses 1–3 are not transcribed.]

v.4 (4) tato ri[ṣya ?]d...[sa ?] –ja[ha] jagata d[e]va |
[Mahātma...?][261] bhupālo varṣa[ṁ] viṁśādhikaṁ śataṁ ||

v. 5 [Pu]rva[rtho]pi[262] mahīpālo (5) lokānugrahatatparaḥ |
Rajyaṁ[263] tena kṛtaṁ tas[m]ād varṣaviṁśottaraṁ śataṁ ||

v. 6 Śaṭyāyana nāmā tato rājā lok...janita-ṣa- (6) kāt[264] |
Cakārārīṁtapo[265] rājaṁ varṣaṁ viṁśādhīkaṁ śtam ||

---

259 In EHJ

260 of PG

261 PG; Footnote: [The name looks like *Narappagamāśva.*] (in EHJ, of LDB)

262 [.arvaryavi ?] Footnote: [Possibly the true reading may be *Purvartho' pi.*] (in EHJ, of LDB)

263 Read *Rājyaṁ* (of PG)

264 [For *vat* Professor Johnston gives an alternative *kam.*] (in EHJ, of LDB)

265 EHJ read *cakāra...;* LDB suggested *cakārārīṁtapo,* although there is no clear trace of a long vowel after the first *r,* and *rī* would be a mistake for *ri.* (of PG)

v. 7 Tasmād Bahubalī bhūbhṛt [pu]nar dhairyyaviśāradaḥ |
Kṛtaṁ ca kṛti- (7) nā tena rājyaṁ viṁśa[bd]ikam[266] śatam ||
v. 8 Tato Raghupatīr[267] bhūpaḥ surūpo nītivikra[maḥ] |
[Cakāra]...ta[ṁ] rājyaṁ var[ṣa] (8) viṁśottaraṁ śatam ||
v. 9 Ta[sya] Viśratadevya[268][vaṁka][269]...mahābālaḥ |
Viṁśabdā[ny]...............................rājyaṁ kṛtaṁ ||
v. 10 (9) Tataś Candrodayo nāma bhūpālaḥ sādhusammataḥ |
Saptaviṁśati varṣāṇi rājyam yenātmasatkṛtaṁ[270] ||
v. 11 Aṇṇaveta- (10) mahīpālā dānaṁ datvā tv anekadhā |
Bhuvi lokasukhaṁ jñātvā [paṁcābdāna][271] divaṁ gatāḥ||
v. 12 Tatpaścān nṛpavara...(11) caryāsu viśāradaḥ |
Cakāra matimāṁ rājyam abdāni saptasaptatiḥ ||
v. 13 Riṁbhyappo bhūpatis tasmāc caran dāna...(12) tiḥ |
Tryadhikaṁ viṁśad abdāni rājyaṁ puṇyena nītavān ||
v. 14 Kūverāpi[272] tato devī dānaśīla.........|
(13) Saptābdāni tato rājyaṁ cakārārivivarjitāṁ ||

---

266 [Alternatively the reading in *d* is *viṁśadhikaṁ*, in which case there is no word for "year."] (in EHJ)

267 [Presumably read *Raghupatir*.] (in EHJ, of LDB)

268 EHJ read *Ta[sya]vi...*; LDB suggested *tasyavi...Devaḥ* (of PG)

269 [The first syllable of this *pāda* is possibly *vaṁ*, the second perhaps *ka*.] (in EHJ, of LDB)

270 [As the rubbing shows, the true reading is definitely *tenātmasātkṛtaṁ*.] (in EHJ, of LDB)

271 For *paṁcabdani* (of PG), [There seems to be no trace of a vowel *ī* on the rubbing.] (in EHJ, of LDB)

272 [Possibly *Kūverāpī*.] (in EHJ, of LDB), EHJ read *kūverāmi* (of PG)

v. 15 [Omvirya] patis[273] tasyās tato bhūpo 'tinīti<mān|>
<Rā-> (14) jyaṁ viṁśati varṣāṇi cakāra mahimākṛtī[274] ||
v. 16 Jugnāhvayas[275] tato bhubhṛt sarvasattvahitārthakṛt |
Sa[pta] <saṁva> (15) tsarāṇy evaṁ tadā rājye pratiṣṭhitaḥ ||
v. 17 Lāṅkīnāmā[276] tato rājā kṛtvā varṣadvayaṁ kṛtī |
Rājyaṁ papā[da][277] (16) vīraḥ krameṇa trīdivaṅgitaḥ[278] ||
v. 18 Kathyate varsasaṁkhyātra devānāṁ kulakartṛṇāṁ[279] |
Eteṣāṁ bhūbhṛtāṁ n[ū]n[aṁ] (17) sahasraṁ ṣaḍdaśādhīkam[280] ||

---

273 EHJ *Umāvīrya*; LDB *Oṁppavīrya* (of PG); [The first two letters *pāda* look more like *Oṁppa-*. Possibly, too, the stone-cutter has omitted a *visarga* before *patīs*.] (in EHJ, of LDB)

274 *Mahimākṛtī* is an old compound. [Comparison with verse 42d (see note on latter) suggests that the poet wrongly took *mahimā* as a fem. vowel-stem.] (in EHJ, of LDB)

275 If the pillar has been correctly read in *a*, it should read *Jugnāhvayas*. [It has *Jugnahvayas tato bhūbhṛt*.] (in EHJ, of LDB)

276 EHJ read *Laṅkī* but LDB suggested that the first vowel is a short curve above the *l* to the right, somewhat like the *ī* in *sphīta°* in the inscription of Yaśovarman, line 12 (E.I. XX, p. 43). A similar ī is also found in the Tipperah grant of Lokanātha at E.I., XV 301–15; N. Chakravarti *loc. cit.* p. 369. (of PG)

277 A syllable is missing here. EHJ read *v*[ipu], while LDB suggested a reading of *prapa-*; *papā*[*da*] the Vedic perfect of √*pad*, is unusual in Classical Sanskrit. *Navīna*, "new," "young" is also possible. (of PG)

278 for *°gataḥ* (of PG)

279 EHJ: the *ṝ* in *°kartṛṇaṁ* has been shortened for metrical reasons.

280 EHJ: *Saḍdaśādhikaṁ* presumably means "+ 60," not "+ 16." In either case it is not clear how the total is made up from what can be read of the inscription. (cf. p. 41 and n. 16 above) (of PG)

v. 19 Tatpaścād apare kāle puṇyatakṣmīyuto balī |

Dvaṅ[281] Candranāmako dhīmaṁ (18) yo 'bhuvi bhūbhṛtām patiḥ[282] ||

v. 20 Nṛpaikottaraśataṁ jitvā punyato bāhuś[ā]linā |

Prakārakhātasaṁyuktaṁ (19) nagarā[bhūṣa]ṇam kṛtam[283] ||

v. 21 Tena niṣpādya nagaraṁ[284] svarggasaundaryahāsinam |

Paṁcapaṁcāśad abdā-(20)ni kṛtaṁ rājyaṁ yaśasvinā[285] ||

v. 22 Rāhacandras tataḥ śrīmāṁ viṁśavarṣāṇi rajyakṛt |

Evam svargasukhaṁ (21) jñātvā divaṁ yāto mahīpatiḥ ||

v. 23 Tasmān navābdiko rājā [B]ālacandro[286] Mahārdhikaḥ |

Kṛtvā kīrttimayī<ṁ> (22) mā[l]ām svargaṁ yato 'tinītimān ||

v. 24 Devendreva Sa[kr]o[287] 'bhūd Devacandra mahīpatiḥ |

Tato dvāviṁśavarṣāṇi (23) rājyaṁ kṛtvā tu svargabhāk ||

---

281 EHJ read *Dveṁ*. The medial *'e'* is doubtful. (of PG)

282 EHJ: The reading in *b* looks like *yo bhūt bhū*°, and it is not certain what the correct reading is. LDB: [The stone certainly has *yo bhūt bhū*°, but a syllable is lacking to make up the meter.] *Bhuvi* appears to be an anomalous aorist "was" (of PG).

283 EHJ: The first *pāda* of v. 20 is hypormetric. *Ābhūṣaṇa* is a possible synonym of *bhūṣaṇa*, the prefix having the slight force of "additional" (of PG); Pāda a is hypermetric. In *d* the consonant fourth letter is either *bh* or *s*, and the next syllable should contain either *r* or *ṣ* because of the following *ṇa*, but looks more like sva than anything else. The reading adopted seems the only possible one, though *ābhūṣaṇa* in this sense is unrecorded. [The rubbing is in favor of reading *nagarāsūtraṇaṁ*, which may be an error for *nagarasūtraṇaṁ*.] (in EHJ, of LDB)

284 *Nāgara* is treated as masculine. (of PG)

285 EHJ: read *jaśasvinā*. (of PG)

286 EHJ suggested Kālacandro or possibly Rālacandro; however, the reading Bāla° is confirmed by a comparison of the rubbings. (of PG)

287 Read *Devandra iva Śakro*. (in EHJ)

v. 25 Saptavārṣikas tasmād[288] Yajñacandraḥ prakīrttitaḥ |
Candrabandhus tato loke ṣaṭsa-(24)mvatsararājyabhāk ||
v. 26 Pṛthivyām uditaś candro Bhūmicandrās[289] tato 'paraḥ |
Sapta saṃvatsarāṇy eva rājyaṁ puṇyena (25)ta nītavān[290] ||
v. 27 Caturviṁśati varṣāṇi rājyaṁ sambhujya nītimān |
Bhūticandras tato yāto divyaṁ sukham avāptaye ||
v. 28 (26) Nīticandras tataḥ khyāto nītyutsāritavigrahaḥ |
Paṁcapaṁcāśad abdāni so 'bhūd rājā Mahendravat ||
v. 29 Abdatra-(27)yikas tasmād[291] Vīryacandro nareśvaraḥ |
[Ta]to dvādaśa varṣāṇi Priticandro mahīpatiḥ ||
v. 30 Sapta<sa>ṁvatsarāṇy a-(28)smāt Pṛthvīcandreṇa bhūbhujā |
Rajyopabhogaṁ[292] saṁbhuktaṁ nityaṁ dharmānuvarttinā ||
v. 31 Jagaddhṛtiṁ karoty asmād Dhṛ-(29)ticandro narādhipaḥ |
Prajām apālayat tasmāt tṛbhir[293] varṣair divaṁ gataḥ ||
v. 32 Īśānvaya[-][294] prabhavaṁ ṣoḍaṣaṁ (30) bhūpatīnāṁ
Candrābhiramayaśasām iha Candranāmnām |

---

288 A syllable is lacking in this *pāda*. (in EHJ, of LDB)

289 EHJ: read *Bhūmicandras* (of PG)

290 EHJ line begins *tanītavān*, but *ta* is marked above for erasure; LDB line begins *nanītavām*. (of PG)

291 [This *pāda* is a syllable short.] (in EHJ, of LDB)

292 EHJ °*upabhoga* is treated as neuter. (of PG)

293 EHJ read *tribhir.*

294 A character has been erased after *īśānvaya*. In *a* read *Īśānvaya prabhavatrayodaśabhūpatīnām*, and note a short before *tr*. In *b* read °*yaśasām*. (of EHJ) [We should read °*ṣoḍaśa*. The emendation *trayodaśa* would gratuitously introduce a short syllable before *tr-* and make the *pāda* a syllable too long. The better course is to read *ṣoḍaśa* and risk the possibility that the author's reckoning was wrong; moreover, he may have intentionally omitted the names of some kings who were too insignificant for mention.] (of LDB in EHJ)

Triṁśā[dh]ikaṁ pragaṇitāni [ś]atadvayaṁ syād
Varṣāṇi rājyaśubha-(31)bhogakṛtāni nūnam ||
v. 33 Tataṁ[295] paścān Mahāvīraḥ Purempure[296] nareśvaraḥ |
Tena dvādaśavarṣaṇi dharmarājyaṁ(32)kṛtam tadā ||
v. 34 Vrayajapnāmāpi yo rājā[297] dvādaśābdāni bhovibhuḥ |
Bhuktvā rājyasukhaṁ vīras tata svargopa-(33)bhogabhāk ||
v. 35 Seviṅreṅ bhūpatis tasmāt smṛto[298] dvādaśakarṣikaḥ[299] |
Rājyasampatsukhaṁ tena bhuktaṁ Māvukaghātinā[300] ||
v. 36 (34) Kṣitiṁ rarakṣa dharmeṇa Dharmaśūras tato nṛpaḥ |
Trayodaśābdasaṁpūrṇṇe svargaṁ yāto Mahārddhikaḥ ||
v. 37 Bhaktimān iva bhaktyā(35) vai yo vajrīva mahībhṛtām |
Vajraśaktis tata[301] khyāto rājā devānvayodbhavaḥ ||
v. 38 Pratipālya jagat sarvaṁ rājyaṁ ṣo(36)ḍaṣavatsarām[302] |
Dānaśiladisaṁyukto devalokaṁ sa yātavan ||
v. 39 Śrūdharmajayasaṁyukto lokābygrahatatparaḥ |
(37) Tatpaścād abhavad dhīraḥ Śrīdharmavijayo nṛpaḥ ||
v. 40 Ṣaṭtriṁṣad[303] abdāny upabhujya rājyaṁ
Dharmeṇa nītyā ca jayena caiva |

295 *anusvāra* for *viṣarga* (of PG)

296 EHJ read both *Pureppura-* and *Purempura-*. The rubbings seem to give *Purempura*; however of *mpa* in l. 33 l. 47 l. 66 (of PG)

297 LDB: The *pāda* is hypometric. (of PG)

298 [In *a* the name may be read as *Doviṅreṅ*. In b the letters on the stone may be read as either *smṛto* or *smṛtā*; they should be *smṛto*] (of LDB in EHJ)

299 EHJ read °*vāṣikah* (of PG)

300 *Māvuka* may be a proper name or a word indicating kinship. (of EHJ)

301 Read *tataḥ*. (of EHJ)

302 Read *ṣoḍaśa*. (of EHJ) (cf. 32b) (of PG)

303 for *ṣaṭtriṁśad* (of PG)

Ratna-(38)trayanusmaraṇābhiyogāt
Sa devalolaṁ Tuṣitaṁ prayātaḥ[304] ||
v. 41 Narendravijayenāpi tatputreṇa mahīmat[305] |
(39) Navamāsādhikaṁ rājyaṁ bhuktaṁ varṣadvayaṁ satā ||
v. 42 Īśanvayaḥ samabhavad vijitārivargaḥ
Śaktitrayapra<ṇa>[306]-(40)yalabdhamahāpratāpaḥ |
Yo Vajraśaktisutavīranarendracandraḥ[307]
Śrīdharmacandramahimāprathitaprabhāvaḥ[308] ||
v. 43 Śrimā-(41)n ṣoḍaṣa[309] varṣāṇi bhuktvā rājyaśriyaṁ nṛpaḥ |
Datvā sutavare rājyaṁ paścāt svargaṁ prayātavān ||
v. 44 Yas tatsu-(42)taṁ[310] praṇatabhūpatimaulimālā-
Ratnadyutiprasararaṁjitapādapadmaḥ |
Ānandacandra[311] bhuvanaikayaśo-(43)'tituṅga
Ānandayaṁ jayati vairitamovibhūma[312] ||

---

304 [The stone has *prayāt*, with a final *t*.] (of LDB in EHJ)

305 LDB suggests *mahīpateḥ*, but there is no sign of a medial *e*. We suggest *mahīmatā*, a word coined from *mahī*, "earth." There is a faint trace of a vertical to the right of the *ta*, which may be the remains of an *ā* vowel mark. (of PG)

306 [At the end of line 39 there seems to be a faint trace of *ṇa*.] (of LDB in EHJ); Another syllable is missing at the beginning of line 40 (of PG).

307 EHJ cf. verses 44 and 62. One should probably understand *Vajraśaktisutovīra°* for *°sutavīra°*. (of PG)

308 cf. v. 15d above, where the poet seems to have taken *mahimā* as a feminine vowel stem. Here, apparently, *śrīdharmacandra* is treated as a nominative, cf. v. 62c and v. 64c. (of PG)

309 Read *ṣoḍaśa*. (of EHJ); cf. 32b and 38b. (of PG)

310 It should presumably be *tatsutaḥ*. (of EHJ); Again, *anusvāra* for *viṣarga*. (of PG)

311 *°candra* for *°candro*: the nominative ending *–o* shortened to *–a* to suit that metre. (of PG)

312 Apparently to be corrected to *vibhūma*. (of EHJ)

v. 45 Dāne ca Karṇṇasamo rājā satyenāpi Yudhiṣṭhiraḥ |
(44) Pradyumnaiva[313] rūpeṇa tejasā bhānuvad bhuvi ||
Tena mahārājādhirājena parahitotsukadhiyā svarā-(45)
jyaprathamasaṁvatsarataḥ prabhṛti yāvad ā navamābdāt
svakṛtakāritānumoditāni sucaitāni sa-(46)tvānāṁ
darśanaprabodhānumodanapuṇya- vistaram icchatā
pravakṣyaṁte ||
v. 46 Ānandodayanāmāno vihārā-(47)neka[314] kāritāḥ |
Dāsadāsībhiḥ sampannāḥ kṣetragomahiṣaiḥ saha ||
v. 47 Sugatabodhisattvānāṁ(48) Cundādīnaṁ ca śaktitaḥ |
Pratimādhātumaccaityāḥ kāritā raukmarājatāḥ ||
v. 48 Rītīmayāni bi-(49)mbāni kāṅsatāmramayāni[315] ca |
Kāritāni munīndrasya bharasaṁkhyāpramāṇataḥ ||
v. 49 Paśudāru[316] (50) mayānekāṁ[317] Pustaśailas[318] tathaiva ca |
Sugatapratimāḥ saumyāḥ kāritās sādhucitritāḥ[319] ||

---

313 Read *Pradyumna iva.* (of EHJ)

314 EHJ [The poet has used] double samdhi shortening *vihārā anekāh* to *vihāranekah* to suit the metre, cf. v. 49. (of PG)

315 Read *Kāṁsya°.* (of EHJ)

316 EHJ read *paśadāru,* and suggested that it "may be the name of a particular kind of wood, or it may be a compound implying images made of leather (?) and wood," which is unlikely. The medial u is quite clear and Monier Willaims, *s.v. paśu* gives the lexical meaning as *Ficus glomerata,* the Clustered Fig known in Pagáninscriptions as the Bodhi tree of Koṇāgamana—see *OBEP* III, p. 321. However, cf. the compound in b, perhaps we should translate as ivory, an animal product suitable for image making. (of PG)

317 EHJ: for *mayā anekāḥ*; the long syllable has been shortened to suit the metre. LDB noted that the poet may possibly have meant to write *°mayā naikaḥ.* Note the *anusvāra* again used for *visarga.* (of PG)

318 *Pusta* is presumable "plaster" here, and *śaila* "stone" (of EHJ); "terracotta" is more appropriate for the former. (of PG)

319 [The stone has *kāritāsādhu°.* Read *kāritāḥ.*] (of LDB in EHJ); There is an indication of a second *s* however. (of PG)

v. 50 Mṛtsaṁhā?<ra>(51) kṛtasaṁkhyāni bimbāni caityakarmaṇaḥ |
Saddharamapustakāś[320] cāpi lekhitā bhuśaḥ satā ||
v. 51 Sau-(52)varṇṇarājatānekān padmān sadratnakarṇṇikān |
Nityaṁ[321] śrīdhātupūjārtham adād bhūpo 'tiśraddhayā ||
v. 52 (53) Dadau prahṛṣṭaḥ suviśuddhacetasā
Saddharmapūjāṁ prati taṇḍakān[322] bahūn |
Dine dine sarvajanā-(54)numoditān
Narādhipo dharmakathānurāgataḥ ||
v. 53 Lauhapātrāṇy anekāni sannetracīvarāṇi[323] ca |
Nā-(55)nādeśāgatānāṁ ca bhikṣūṇāṁ gauravād dadau ||
v. 54 Dānapāramitā hīnā mā me bhavantu jantuṣu |
Tasmād upāsa-(56)kenāpi sarvasatvahiteṣiṇā[324] ||
v. 55 Paṁcāśadbrāmaṇāvāsaṁ kṣetrabhṛtyasamanvitaṁ |
Vādyavādakasaṁyuktaṁ kā-(57)ritaṁ maṭhacatuṣṭayam ||

---

320 Probably *Saddharmapuṇdarika* is suggested here, cf. 52b. (of PG); We suggest only this *Saddharamapustakāś*, if not, otherwise, impossible.

321 EHJ: a short vowel remains before *śr.*

322 None of the recorded meaning of *taṇḍaka* fits here; possibly for *tāṇḍavan.* (of EHJ); [The actual reading of the rubbing seems rather to be *vanṭakan*, though the letter below *ṇ* is not clear. *Vanṭaka*, "share" (found in Sanskrit and Kanarese lexx; from √vaṇṭ, whence Hindi *bāṇt*) occurs in the sense of a holding or portion of land, forming part an estate in the Yādava Rāmacandra's Thana grant of Śaka 1194 (*E.I.* xiii, p. 199).] (of LDB in EHJ)

323 The first certain instance of *netra* in the same of silk; cf. *Raghauvaṁśa*, vii, 36. (of EHJ); There is no reason why this should not be good cloth. (of PG)

324 Read *°hitaisiṇā.* (of EHJ)

v. 56 Somatī[rthe][325]dvijāvāse maṭhaś cānandamādhavaḥ |
Ānandeśvaranāmīpi[326] (58) Naulakke ca maṭha smṛtaḥ[327] ||
v. 57 Pīlakkavanakuhve 'pi Daumaghe[328] pūrvanāmakau[329] |
Vīthikā[330] vividhārāmā[331] (59) kāritā setuaṁkramā<ḥ> ||
v. 58 Pratyahaṁ bhaktaśālāyāṁ sadā satraṁ pravarttitaṁ |
Ativadhyāś ca kārun<ā>[332]-(60)t prāṇino mocitāsadāḥ[333] ||
v. 59 Daṅkaṅgamargaṅgaḍuvārasaṁjñite
Bhūrokanaulakkalavārakāhvaya |
Puṇḍi(61)ṅgasomāhvayasaṁghasaṁjñikau
Manāpavāpyau[334] nijakhāna bhūpathiḥ[335] ||

---

325 There is no evidence of a superscript r; however *Somatīrtha* seems meant. (of PG)

326 [The p has been almost entirely cut out.] (of LDB)

327 [Read *maṭhaḥ*.] (of LDB); Apparently these two *maṭhas* are in addition to the four of the previous verse. (of EHJ)

328 *Domaghe* in EHJ.

329 In a presumably read °*vanakākve*, and in b read °*nāmake*. (of EHJ); [The reading of the rubbing is possibly °*vaḍakuhve* and *Daumaghe*.] (of LDB)

330 See D. C. Sircar *Indian Epigraphical Glossary, s.v. vīthi, vithī*, "a territorial unit, the subdivision of a district" (of PG).

331 The stone is broken here. (of PG)

332 -*Ā*- is missing through breakage of stone. (of EHJ)

333 Read *sadā*, as *mocitāsadāḥ* as a compound is hardly possible.(of EHJ) [Also read *mocitāḥ*] (of LDB)

334 [The rubbing gives –*vāpyo*.] (of LDB); PG gave the wrong footnote here.

335 Read *nicakhāna*. (of EHJ)

v. 60 Pūrvarājakṛtā ye'pi devaprā-(62)sādatīrthikā<ḥ>[336] |
Naṣṭā niṣpāditās tena sarvathā dhīmatā punaḥ ||
v. 61 Dharmāsanaṁ hastiniko-(63)ttamaikā[337]
Bhupena netrojvalacīvarāṇi|
Bhikṣvāryasaṁghasya hi nāyitāni[338]
Deśe Śila-(64)meghanarādhipasya ||
v. 62 Vikhyātaśauryagaṇadharmayaśonurāgād
Devāṇḍajā-(65)nvayasamudbhavapārthivasya |
Śrītājmrapattananarādhipa bhaktinamro[339]
Dhendā[ṁ]dadau sva-(66)tanayām paramādareṇa ||
Aparaṁ ca |
v. 63 *Ānandacandra*kṣitipārthivasya
Śridharma-(67)rajāṇḍajavaṁśajasya |
Śrutvā vaco dharmahitārthayuktaṁ
Śauryānvayatyāgaguṇā[dh]i-(68)kaṁ ca ||
v. 64 Bhaktipraṇāmena prakurvatājñāṁ
Śaivāndhravaṁśodbhavapārthivena |
Śrimanma-(69)nodhīraMahārddhikena
Kalyāṇamitratvam upāgatena ||
v. 65 Vāpīviharau tvaritena (70) kṛtvā
Śrīpattanātmīyamahīpradeśe |

---

336 *Visarga* omitted. (of PG) Read °*tīrthikāḥ* in *b*. (of EHJ) [*Tirthikāḥ* can only mean "heretics'. Probably the poet meant to write *tīrthakāḥ*, in the sense of *tīrthāḥ*.] (of LDB)

337 I do not know if *hastinikā* is to be taken seriously. (of EHJ)

338 In *b* read *netrojjvala*°. *Nāyitāni* in *c* is odd, and *dāpitāni* would be better. (of EHJ); Although *yi* could be read as *pi*, the *na* is quite clear. (of PG)

339 One must understand that °*narādhipo bhaktinamro*, which is impossible metrically, is indicated. (of EHJ)

Strīratnadhendā svasutātibhaktyā
Saṁpreṣite-(71)hāsamabhūtiyuktā ||[340]
(line 72) Śri[kī]rttisaṁpū[rṇa] vijaya
(line 73) ekādaśame[341] 'bde

Translation

(verse 4) Then the king (Mahātma...?) ruled for one hundred twenty years. (v. 5) There was a king, Purvartha (?) zealous in doing kindness to the world; he reigned afterward for one hundred twenty years. (v. 6) Then a king, Saṭyāyana by name...ruled for one hundred twenty years. (v. 7) After him, the able Bahubalī, eminent for stout-heartedness, ruled for one hundred twenty years. (v. 8) Then king Raghupati, fair of form, heroic in policy, reigned one hundred twenty years. (v. 9)...his puissant...ruled...one hundred twenty years. (v. 10) Then (was the king Candrodaya by name, approved by the good; he made the kingship his own for twenty-seven years. (v. 11) The Aṇṇaveta kings, givers of countless gifts, having experienced earthly pleasure on earth for five years, went to heaven. (v. 12) After that an excellent king...eminent in religious practices, possessing wisdom, reigned for seventy-seven years. (v. 13) After him, king Rimbhyappa, bestowing bounty...reigned in righteousness for twenty-three years. (v. 14) Then Queen Kūverā, bountiful...for seven years after him, made the

340 The inscription ends with three double *doṇḍas*, between the first pair of which is a sign, identified by Barnett as a "Garuda symbol" "appropriate in the edict of a king claiming to belong to the 'bird-ribe.'" The symbol also appears at the end of the fragmentary *caitya* inscription (see below, p. 99 of PG) and the sixth century Vesālī bell (below, p. 95 of PG) which definitely belongs to the first Candra dynasty, and appears to be merely a decorative element marking the end of the inscription. (of PG)

341 EHJ: The form *ekādaśama* is odd, but similar forms are found in the other late inscriptions (i.e., north face of the pillar) and it possibly shows Prakrit influence, cf. Pischel, §449, who says these forms are only authenticated so far in Jaina Prakrit works. For other instances note the *apparatus criticus* of the colophons to *Saundar* Ānanda XI and XVIII (ed. A. N. Upadhye, Bombay, 1938), colophons to XI, XII and XIII. (by PG)

kingdom free from foes. (v. 15) After, Omavīrya her son, a most politic king, ruled for twenty years, the performer of (deeds of) glory. (v. 16) Then a king named Jugna, who benefitted all beings, was likewise established on the throne for seven years. (v. 17) Then the able king name Liṅkī, a young man, having held the kingdom for two years, in due course went to heaven. (v. 18) Here is now proclaimed the number of years of the ancestral monarchs; verily 1060 (1016?). (v. 19) After that, at a later time, there was one possessed of righteousness and fortune, puissant, sage, Dvaṅ Candra by name, who was a lord of kings. (v. 20) He, strong of arm because of righteousness, conquered 101 kings, built a city (which was) adorned by surrounding walls and a moat. (v. 21) Having constructed the city, which laughed at the beauty of Paradise, reigned for fifty-five years. (v. 22) Then the fortunate Rājacandra reigned twenty years; having thus known the pleasure of Paradise, the king went to heaven. (v. 23) After him, Rālacandra, a very prosperous and exceedingly politic king, who reigned nine years, went to heaven after making a garland of glory. (v. 24) Then king Devacandra, like Śākra king of the gods, after ruling twenty-two years, enjoyed heaven. (v. 25) After him, the renowned Yajñacandra reigned seven years. Then Candradandhu enjoyed a reigned of six years in the world. (v. 26) Then arose Bhūmicandra, a second moon on earth; he reigned with righteousness for seven years. (v. 27) Then politic Bhūticandra, having enjoyed kingship for twenty-four years, then went to gain heavenly happiness. (v. 28) Then the renowned Nīticandra, who removed strife by policy, reigned like Mahendra for fifty-five years. (v. 29) After him, King Vīryacandra reigned three years; then King Priticandra (ruled) for twelve years. (v. 30) After that, King Pṛthvicandra, constantly following the royal law enjoyed the pleasures of kingship for seven years. (v. 31)After him, King Dhṛticandra supported the world; he protected his people, then after three years went to heaven. (v. 32) The years spent in happy enjoyment of kingship by the sixteen monarchs sprung from the lineage of Īśa (=Śiva), who bore the name

Candra and whose glory was as delightful as the moon, when counted up will be verily 230. (v. 33) Afterward, Mahāvīra, king of Purempura then had a righteous reign of twelve years. (v. 34) Also, the king named Vrajajap, a valiant lord of the earth, having enjoyed the happiness of kingship for twelve years, thereupon enjoyed the pleasures of Paradise. (v. 35) After him, King Seviṅreṅ, recalled as having ruled twelve years; slaying Māvuka, he enjoyed the happiness of prosperity in kingship. (v. 36) Then King Dharmaśura protected the earth in accordance with the law; greatly prosperous, on the completion of thirteen years he went to heaven. (v. 37) Then was the devout famous king, sprung from the gods' (=Deva) lineage, Vajraśakti, who because of his devotion was like a Vajrin (Indra) among monarchs. (v. 38) Possessing beauty, virtue and other qualities, he went to the world of gods having protected the entire universe for a reign of sixteen years. (v. 39) After him, there was a brave king, the fortunate Dharmavijaya, attended by fortune, religion and victory, intent on doing kindness to the world. (v. 40) After enjoying kingship for thirty-six years, by reason of religion (dharma) policy and victory, and through practicing remembrance of the Three Jewels, he passed away to the Tuṣita heaven. (v. 41) That king's good son, the lord of the earth, Narendravijaya, also enjoyed the kingship for two years and nine months. (v. 42) There arose one belonging to the lineage of Īśa (Śiva), a conqueror of troops of enemies, gaining great majesty by manifestation of the three powers[342], a moon of valiant kings, son of Vajraśakti, the fortunate Dharmacandra, having majestically celebrated puissance. (v. 43) That fortunate king, having enjoyed a prosperous reign for sixteen years, handed over the kingdom to [his] excellent son, and afterward passed away to Paradise. (v. 44) His son *Ānandacandra* is victorious, having lotuses of his feet reddened by the brilliant gleams of gems in the garlands of the diadems of reverently bowing monarchs, exceedingly lofty in fame

342 *viz.* lordship, counsel, and enterprise. (of EHJ)

unequalled on earth, causing gladness, rising (like the sun) above the darkness of his foes, elevated above the legions of his enemies. (v. 45) [He is] like Kaṛna in bounty and also Yudhiṣṭhira in truthfulness, Pradyumana in beauty and like the sun on earth in splendor. The good deeds in beauty by that emperor, whose thought yearned for the welfare of others, from the first year of his reign until the ninth year, whether done by himself or caused to be done, and approved [by him] because he desired for living beings an abundance of merit, through enlightenment of vision and acceptance will be declared. (v. 46) Many monasteries named Ānandodaya have been built, provided with men and women slaves, together with fields, kine, and buffaloes. (v. 47) There have been made gold and silver caityas containing relics of the Buddha, Bodhisattavas, Cundā, and others according to power. (v. 48) There have been images of the lord of sages (= Buddha) composed of brass bell metal and copper, according to the weight, number, and size. (v. 49) There have been made many pleasing [and] well-executed images of the Buddha (Sugata) made of ivory, wood, terracotta, and stone. (v. 50) Innumerable clay caitya models [have been made] and also books of the Holy Law have been caused to be written by the good [king] in large numbers. (v. 51) The king, with exceeding faith, has constantly given for the purpose of worship of the blessed relics, numerous lotuses made of gold and silver, and having pericarps of goodly gems. (v. 52) The king, rejoicing with very pure spirit, because of his delight in religious discourses, bestowed day after day many shares, approved by all the people for the purpose of worship of the Holy Law. (v. 53) He has out of reverence given many robes and copper bowls to monks coming from diverse places. (v. 54–5) "Let not the protection of bounty toward creatures fail me": [with this intent] therefore, he, seeking the welfare of all beings, although he was only a lay-worshipper, caused to be built four monasteries, lodging fifty Bramans, provided with fields and servants, furnished with musical instruments and musicians. (v. 56) The Ānandamādhava monastery at the residence of the Somatīrtha Brahmans and also the monastery called Ānandeśvara at Naulakka are recorded. (v. 57) In the quarter called Pīlakka, formerly named Daumagha, he made an area with various pleasure gardens and a walk on the causeway. (v. 58) Every day a session has been held in the dining hall; and because of his mercifulness, capital offenders have always been released. (v. 59) At the place styled Ḍaṅkaṅgamargaṅgaḍuvāra [and] at that named Bhūrokanaulakkavāraka, the king has dug two delightful wells named after (for?) the monastic communities (belonging to the places) called Puṇḍiṅga and Soma. (v. 60) The temples of gods[343] and holy places built by former kings that had perished have also been restored by him, who is wise. (v. 61) A seat of the law (? pulpit),[344] an excellent cow elephant[345] [and] robes, brilliant to the eye[346] have been dispatched by the king to the noble congregation of monks in the land of king Śilāmegha. (v. 62) Out of regard for the renowned quality of valor, religion, and fame of the monarch sprung from the Deva and egg-born linage, the king of the fortunate Tāmrapattana, making devout obeisance, gave [to him] with the highest respect his daughter Dhendā. Moreover: (v. 63–64) Having heard the speech of *Ānandacandra,* monarch of the earth, scion of the egg-lineage of fortunate righteousness kings, [speech] fraught with meaning and helpful to the religion and with all the qualities of valor, [high] descent, and bounty—the king sprung from the Śaivandra lineage, the fortunate and highly prosperous Manodhīra, fulfilling his command and devout obeisance,

343 i.e., non-Buddhist. (of PG)

344 Probably one of the beautifully carved stone *dhramasana* still to be seen at Kyauktaw and Mrohaung, see below pp. 236–237, no. 105. (of PG)

345 *Hastinikā* may here denote a particular kind of elephant, as a "small cow elephant" would certainly not be a tusker appropriate for the fostering of the export trade. (of PG)

346 Johnson prefers "brilliant robes of silk" (of PG)

entered into happy friendship [with him]. (v. 65) Having promptly made a well and a monastery in the district belonging to his fortunate city, he sent here with extreme devotion his daughter Dhendā, a gem among women, endowed with incomparable fortune.

(ll. 72–73) In the eleventh year, the fortunate victory (is) declared accomplished.

5.1.1.3. Donation and Royal Inscriptions

Inscriptions of this type are incorporated in the above mentioned quotation and eulogy inscriptions, but need a certain clarification. They are found in Pāḷi, Sanskrit, and local languages, which often the second part of the inscription. In both Nīticandra and Vīracandra, inscriptions are this type too. There are examples of donation inscriptions of common people from even southern Rakhaing land, unique to this tradition. In other areas, most of the inscriptions, which are usually of a later date, relate to kings, the royal family, or high officials. The historical content of the inscriptions mainly concerns royal deeds and biographies or lineages of kings. Buddhist concepts are used in the eulogizing stanzas.

The donation inscriptions of this period provide a great deal of information regarding how Buddhist merit was made in those days and with what intentions and goals. The inscriptions, dated from the fifth to the eighth century, are written in Gupta or Rakkhavanna (Rakhaing script).

The meritorious acts recorded in these inscriptions are typically Buddhist and ones that are common to India, Sri Lanka, and even present-day Buddhist countries. They include casting of Buddha images, repairing damaged images, building *stūpa*s and *vihāras*, donating gifts to monasteries, and even freeing prisoners.

The donors came from all walks of life: from royals to normal citizens. The inscriptions show that during this period there were close ties between a ruler and his subjects, and close ties between Sri Lanka. The donors express the wish to transfer merit to the living and to the dead as well as to themselves. They also aspire to see the Buddha Maitreya or to become a Buddha. Some donors wish for the well-being of all living beings.

While the language used is late Brahmi, Gupta, or Rakkhavanna, there are also Pāli and Sanskrit loaner words such as puñña and puṇya. They often appear in both Pāḷi and Sanskrit forms, sometimes within the same inscription. Some terms cannot be said to be either Pāḷi or Sanskrit, but rather, seen to be a hybrid.

Among many donations and royal inscriptions, a few of them are rediscussed from U Sandamuni's work mentioned in U Shwe Zan's book.

Inscription of Candrasiri from Sandway[347]

An inscription inscribed in late Brahmi script and in corrupt Sanskrit was found on November 20, 1994, at Sandway, a place of hoary antiquity, rich in archaeological materials which are of immense help for the reconstruction of the early history of Rakhaing. Tradition and archaeological documents point out the existence of Sandway as a significant and important site that served as a link between early Rakhaing and old Pyu capital named Sriksetra before the emergence of the Pagan phase.

The inscription, on a square stone slab was for many years hidden within the premise of Andow *Stūpa* in Sandway. The writing field is sixteen inches long and ten inches wide. There are eight lines of writing in

347 *Op. cit.*, Zan, U Shwe. (2010) "The Land of Historic Finds" pp. 88–89.

late Brahmi of about the sixth century AD the content of this inscription is almost the same as found in the inscription of the Nīticandra with the difference that the expression "sri niticandrasya candravat pachinasya" has been omitted. The script of the inscription is late Brahmi of about the first quarter of the sixth century AD, and the language is corrupt Sanskrit. Presently preserved at the New Andow Monastery, Sandway, the contents of the inscriptions are being discussed here for the first time.

The discovery location of the inscription in a remote place of southern most Rakhaing indicates that the domain of the Candra rulers extend up to the region (Sandway) at least from the sixth century AD. It shows that the queen of Nīticandra of the royal family was devoted to Buddhism, and the queen built numerous Buddhist *stūpa*s throughout the kingdom. Many of these religious places contained inscribed *ye dhammā* verses on various objects, which are now being found everywhere in Rakhaing.

According to *Ānandacandra* Pillar inscription, which still stands on Phokaungtaung at Mrauk Oo, the reign of king Nīticandra lasted for fifty-five years, from about AD 520 to 575 the characters of the inscription are similar to those of the inscription of the Nīticandra (mentioned above), but the shapes of the letters from Sandway are, unlike the characters of the inscription from *Vesālī*, uneven. It is likely that the engraver concerned was not an accomplished artist.

The text

1. *ye dhammā hetu prabhavā*
2. *hetumtesaṃ tathāgato hyavo*
3. *dattesanca yonirodho*
4. *evaṃvādī mahāsamaṇa*
5. *devisāvitaṃ candrasiriya nama*
6. *parame pasikasya deyya dharmma*
7. *yam ma sarvva satvanaṃ manu*
8. *kattama*

Stone Slab Inscription from Ohtein, Taunggouk[348]

Ye dhammā verses in inscriptions are found not only in the vicinity of old *Vesālī* which is full of ancient ruins, but also in the southernmost areas of Sandway and Taunggouk. An inscription engraved on a stone slab was discovered from a ruined *stūpa* named Ohtein *Zeti*. It has four lines of writing on a space of about twelve inches long and ten inches wide. It appears to have contained three or four more lines below. The letters engraved are small and smooth as found in the inscriptions from Kyauktaw and Lanmwon-taung and are similar in forms to those recorded in the east face of *Ānandacandra* Pillar inscription is in late Brahmi, and the language is in corrupt Sanskrit. A number of scholars have commented upon this inscription (e.g., San Tha Aung,[349] Tun Shwe Khine,[350] U Kosalla,[351] and Gutman).[352]

Being of a uniform type of writing, the inscription prominently extends an unusual passage at the end of third line of the verse, which can apparently be read as "*Gottamah.*" The name of *Gottamah* is not mentioned in any known inscription from Rakhaing. The verse in the first three lines has Pāḷi word *pabhava* for Sanskrit *prabhava*, and *sriva* in fourth line is reminiscent of *savitam candrasriy* Nīticandra inscription form Sandawy, and may be compared with certain use of this type of word in India.

In this inscription *hetutesanca* likely indicates the more usual *hetutesam.* The expression *hyavaocare* seems to have been used for *hyavadattesanca*, and the plural *upasakadi* in forth line is notable.

---

348 *Op. cit.*, Zan, U Shwe. (2010) pp.94–95.

349 *Op. cit.*, p. 113.

350 Khine, Tun Shwe. (1990) p. 35.

351 Kosalla, U. *Journey of Arakanese Literature.* Yangon: Burmese, pl. 87.

352 *Op. cit.*, Gutman (1976) p. 93.

The Text

1. *ye dhammā*
2. *tathāgato hyavocare yo nirodha evaṃ*
3. *VadiMahāsramana gottamah*
4. *Upsakadi sriyya ctupam krito*

Stone Slab Inscription from Grat-ga-rwa-ma, Kyauk Phru[353]

An inscription from Grant-ga-rwa-ma village in the district of Kyauk Phru, is found engraved on a stone slab which is a bit damaged at the right upper corner. The script of the inscription is late Brahmi, and the language is corrupt Sanskrit. The inscription has been commented upon by Prof. San Tha Aung,[354] Tun Shwe Khine,[355] and Gutman,[356] and is also referred to in the State Gazetteer (Culture).[357]

The inscription seems to have contained eight lines of writing, but only five lines remain legible due to the ravages of nature. The letters in this inscription are large, uneven, and carelessly engraved. The first three lines of the verse are usually sanctified in *ye dhammā* verse. The characters are very much akin to those of Selāgiri inscription, and the script indicates a date of about the sixth century AD. Presently, the inscription is preserved at Archaeological Office, Mandalay.

The Text

1. *dhrmma heturabhava hetum*
2. *(te) samtathagato...yoniro (o)*

353 *Op. cit.*, U Shwe Zan (2010), pp. 95–96.

354 *Op. cit.*, San Tha Aung, "Buddhist Art" (1979) pl. 18.

355 *Op. cit.*, Tun Shwe Khine, (1990) p. 35.

356 *Op. cit.*, Gutman (1976) p. 92.

357 *State Gazetteer (Culture)*. pl. 25.

3. *evaṃ (va) di mahāsarmana*
4. *yapabhuta...nama...*
5. *...Sri...prati...tu*

Stone Slab Inscription from Nga-lone-maw[358]

In the vicinities of the cities of Sandoway and Taunggauk, in the southernmost site of Rakhaing, a number of epigraphs belonging to ancient period, were often found form the ruins of *stūpa*s or of religious structures. In 1872, during English rule in Rakhaing, an inscription bearing seven lines of writing was accidently discovered by Phayre from a cavity in a hill which is close to Nga-lone-maw village in the district of Sandoway. Before the Second World War, the inscription was sent to Oxford, but it is claimed that at the present it is in the possession of the Asiatic Society, Calcutta.[359]

The record is inscribed on a stone slab measuring seven inches in length, five in width, and an inch in thickness. The first three lines of the inscription contain mixed Pāḷi and Sanskrit. The letters are uniform in size, but omit some words in some cases, and even a superscribed sign for vam under third line is noticeable. Such a superscribed letter is never found in any known inscription of *Vesālī*, scholars who commented upon this epigraph are, among others, San Tha Aung,[360] Tun Shwe Khine,[361] U Kosalla,[362] and Gutman,[363] and Johnston.[364]

358 *Op. cit.*, U Shwe Zan (2010), pp. 97–99.

359 *Op. cit.*, San Tha Aung (1979), "Buddhist Art" p. 114.
360 San Tha Aung, (1979) *ibid.* p. 20.

361 *Op. cit.*, Tun Shwe Khine, (1990) p.35–37.

362 *Loc. cit.*, U Kosalla, pl. 65.

363 *Op. cit.*, Gutman (1976) pl. XXVIb

364 *Loc. cit.*, Johnston (1944) IV, fig. 2.

The Text

1. *ye dhammal hetuprabhavā hetu*
2. *tesaṃtathāgata hyavoda tesancayo*
3. *nirodho evaṃ diMahāsrana*
4. *upasaka maiga upasa*
5. *kasakoma vanmma makara*
6. *yimatapita ku*
7. *sala*

The paleography of the present inscription is remarkably similar to that of the copper plate inscription (will be discussed later). In this inscription the personal name is tentatively read as Kimmayana, which is connected with the name of one of the Candra queens given in the copper plate inscription dated about AD 507.

The object of the record is to notify the gift of the bell to the *Zeti*, probably of Apaung-daw. A pious wish expressed in the inscription is that the dedication of the bell was meant for the welfare of the father and mother of the donor. The suffix *Āyana* in the name of *Kimmāyana* can be referred to one *Āyana* in the inscription of bronze lamp at *Vesālī*. We know again the copper plate grant issued by a *Vesālī* king saying that a village by the name of Dengutta was granted by Kimmajudevi in favor of a *vihāra* built by her. Therefore, the prefix names of the bell donor and the village donor, if not point to one and the same woman, at least point to the popularity of the name. We have *om nama* at the beginning of the verse, which is rarely found only in this inscription during the *Vesālī* period. The *garuda* symbol noted at the end of the verse is also found in certain inscriptions of the eighth century AD and particularly in the *praśasti* of King Ānanadacandra of Rakhaing.

The Text

1. *om nama matapitroh (hiritathetra) kimmayanadhanayah*
2. *nirayanta yaddatte yam samarirasvarah*

Bhanta Inscription of Dharmavijaya, *Vesālī*[365]

In Rakhaing, the old *Vesālī* region has been yielding many inscriptional materials. They are engraved on either stones or bricks. Recently, an inscription on a stone slab was discovered at the place of Bhanta in the vicinity of old *Vesālī*. Now it is preserved in the Mrauk Oo Museum. It contains twenty-two lines of writing. The upper portion of the inscription is, however, badly damaged. The inscription remained unnoticed. The stone, measuring 1′10″ in length and 1′ in breadth in the writing field, is engraved with small, neat letters measuring between 15 and 18 mm, excluding some ornate medial vowels. The language of the inscription is Sanskrit, and the script is latter Brahmi of the northern class. As the inscription does not bear any date, we have to take into account paleographical features of the inscription itself. The characters with thick nail-heads are very much similar to those found in the east face of the Shitthaung pillar.[366]

Fortunately, in line 16 we have the name of King Sri Dhammavijaya during whose reign in the inscription was engraved. He assumed the title of Mahārajadhiraja, indicating independent and imperial status. In the *Vesālī* period there were a number of rulers who use this epithet

365 *Op. cit.*, U Shwe Zan, (2010) pp. 102–103.

366 Shitthaung *prasasti*, a monolith inscribed with Sanskrit stanzas and housed in a grille structure on the left side of the main stairway of the Shitthaung temple, may be considered as the earliest history book in Arakan. Three of its four faces are inscribed. Originally the pillar was believed to have been erected in Vesālī from where it was removed by King Murn Ba Gree (also called Mong Bong), the thirteenth king of the Mrauk Oo age, in 1536. This square pillar rises 3.3 m (9ft 7 in) from ground level, and each side is 0.7 m (2ft 4 in) broad. The material used is the fine-grained sandstone common at Dhaññavatī and in the early sculpture of Vesālī. Zan, U Shwe. *op. cit.*, pp. 47–56, 206. Aung, San Tha. *op. cit.*, p. 159.

like their counterparts in India in the Gupta period.[367] The name of kings who are known to have ruled during the third period, a category divided on the basis of the names of kings found mentioned in the Shitthaung *praśasti* of King Ānanadacandra at Mrauk Oo. This is the first ever known inscription of the reign of Dhammavijaya. D. C. Sircar tentatively placed the reign of the king between AD 665 and 701, but Dr. Johnston dated his reign period between AD 645 and 681. We have also a coin bearing the name of Dhammavijaya from Rakhaing.

Besides, Mahārājadhirāja, we have Paramabhattaraka as an epithet used by King Dhammavijaya in the manner used by king of India from at least the Gupta period. In line 17 we may read *Rajyodayadvitiyadamvatsara* indicating the second reignal year of the king. According to the Shitthaung pillar inscription of Ānanadacandra he reigned for thirty-six years. The king seemed to have granted a piece of land to the monks residing in the monastery called *Mahāramavihāra*, mentioned in line 18, for the enjoyment of four artifacts, namely: robe, food, bedding, and medicine (*Mahāramaviharaяyya bhiksusainghaparibhogaya*).

In line 19, we can read (*hareinge saku*) *la catu saityassimaparyandatta* (*paryantan data*). The land donated probably extended up to the embankment on the river called *Haremga*. It may be pointed out that in the vicinity of the side, yielding the inscription under inscription, there is a river called Tin Nyo, which was possibly known as *Haremga* (or *Radananadi*) in early days.

In line 19 again, we have *catu caityassimaparyyantan*, which may explain the intended tentative boundary of the *cetiya*. At the beginning of the last verse, we may read *Matapitu purvamga samkritva sakalasya ca (sattvarase)*, a well-known expression used in Indian inscriptions referring to gift in favor of Buddhist establishments. The phrase reminisces to that found in the votive *stūpa* inscription from *Vesālī*. The last two

367 It is interesting to note that a number of Gupta rulers, whose inscriptions have been discovered in north Bengal, used at least three epithets before their names, (e.g., Paramadaivata, Paramabhattaraka, Mahārajadhiraja). See: Majumdar, R. C. (Ed.). "*The Classical Age*" Bombay, (1998). pp. 348–349.

lines are imprecatory verse and basically identical with those found in India inscriptions from about the fifth century AD.

The Text starting from line 14 is as follows:

14.... *matapitro Mahāraja*

15. *padanudhaytataparah tena u (danva?) yavijamulodita parma*

16. *paramabhattaraka mahrajadhiraja sri dharmmavijaya*

17. *devena prajya rajyodaydvitiya samvatsraca (vaha)*

18. *samva (stha ca) Mahāramaviharyya bhiksu samgha paribhogaya*

19. *haramgesa (ku) la (se tu) ncatu ssimaparyyan tandatta matapi*

20. *tupurvvage samkritva sakulasyaca (sattavaraseh?) rajchanada (pruye?)*

21. *sadattam paradattam va yo hareta (vasundharam) sa visthyam krmi*

22. *rbhutvapitrbhissaha (pacyatati)*

A Ceti Dedicatory Inscription from Eight Century *Vesālī*[368]

A notable stone inscription is found in *Vesālī* village, which is situated five miles north of Mrauk Oo. It was actually found somewhere on the brick mound which is situated at the edge of the so-called canal. This place is situated at the southwest corner of *Vesālī* village and the northwest corner of Tharlarwaddy village.

The upper portion of the stone slab has broken off and been lost. The missing part probably contained the beginning of the inscriptions, which normally would have mentioned the name of the donor and of his ancestors. We are left with only ten lines of inscription. The language of the inscription is Sanskrit. The inscription commemorates the construction of a *cetiya*.

The Text

Verse 1. (lost)

Verse 2. *punyam mayaptamatulam yamihadya caityam nispadya tena bhavasagrato hi param, trsan tranga*

368 Aung, San Tha. (1979) p.45–47.

bhrsa cancala raudra nadat satvah prayantu sukhina trimala prahinah.

Verse 3. *yati prajvalitam ghoram bhedako rauravam param divyakalpa sahasrani svarge tisthati palaka iti*

Translation

Verse 1. Lost. Might have contained the names of the donor and his ancestors.

Verse 2. As I have completed the building of the *cetiya* in this place today, I have gained the incomparable merit. For the meritorious deed I have done let all beings be able to discard the three impurities (*lobha, dosa, moha*) and cross the ocean of becoming, which is roaring fiercely due to the waves of craving and striking violently, and reach the other shore (nibbāna) happily.

Verse 3. The one who destroys the *cetiya* goes to the terrible and flaming "*roruwa*" hell after death, and the one who looks after (it) stays in heaven for thousands of heavenly eons. This is the end.

We should note that the attain *nibbāna*, one has to discard the three impurities (*lobha, dosa, moha*). This is stated in the inscription. Discarding the three impurities is nothing but purifying one's own mind. This is the teaching of the Buddha, and Buddhism at that time was based on the teachings of the Buddha.[369]

The *cetiya* mentioned in the inscription is no longer in existence. But we still have the dedicatory inscription with us. What was the shape of the *cetiya*? How large and how beautiful was it? We can only speculate and dream about what the answers to these questions may be.

The inscriptions mentioned above reveal that a mixed religious situation existed between the sixth and eighth centuries AD in ancient Rakhaing between Buddhism, most likely not advanced *Mahāyāna*, and Brahmanism (i.e., Hinduism).

369 Verse no. 183, Dhammapada, Khuddapatha, CSCD ROM

Thus far, Buddhist inscriptions in Rakhaing can be divided into two main parts. Pāḷi inscriptions are found in the old *Vesālī* in the middle of the fifth century or even in the sixth century AD. The majority of them are quotations from canonical texts with the exception of a few royal inscriptions in Pāḷi and mostly Sanskrit. Most of those with Mahāyānistic elements belong to the later seventh century AD and are also found because of Sanskrit influence. Donation inscriptions that record the aspirations of the donor and the transfer of merit are written solely in Sanskrit and vernacular language and are found.

The *ye dhammā* stanza is the most frequently used one. They popularity of the stanza is not limited to India, Sri Lanka, or Southeast Aisa, it is largely found in Rakhaing land. The stanza occurs in inscriptions with Sanskrit *Mahāyāna* elements and in the case is associated with those traditions within majority *Theravāda* Buddhist or community, side by side as well. Otherwise, when the stanza is found alone, either in Pāḷi or Sanskrit, it cannot simply be identified as either *Theravāda* or *Mahāyāna*. A language similar to Pāḷi was evidently used in the inscriptions of sects other than the *Theravāda* in South India[370] or in Sri Lanka, and the

370 For examples, see *Epigraphia Indica*, Vol. 20 (1929–1930): 16–17, 19ff., 21ff., *Epigraphia India*, vol. 35 (1963–1964): 6ff. One difference is that in the inscriptions, consonant clusters are usually written as a single consonant clusters are usually written as a single consonant. For example, *raño* is written as *rañño* and *budhasa* as *buddhassa*. Declensions like *nānadesasamanagatānaṃ* and verb forms like parigahitam or hotu are essentially the same as in Pāḷi. it is worth noting that the inscriptions that use a language with close affinities to Pāḷi are from sites in the Andhara area, such as Nāgājunakoṇḍa and Amarāvatī, while to Sanskrit are the sites in the Nālanda and central India. The schools mentioned mostly might be associated with the "*Theriyānaṃ Tambapaṇṇakānaṃ*'. Inscriptions from northern (i.e., Nālanda) or western India usually use a language closer to Sanskrit. The language associated with a particular school probably arose out of the local dialect rather than *vice versa*. It is logical to assume that a regional *Sangha* would use the forms and sounds to which it was accustomed. The Saṅgīti of the Buddhists written in a northern location, for example, would probably sound closer to Sanskrit, and over time, the text becomes Sanskritized. The same would be true for the south with a language that sounds like Pāḷi, and after time and use, the text becomes standardized in that language. The true significance of the word *saṅgīti*, which we suggest may be a form of "aural editing" or "proofing by the sounds," differs from the present visual system of reading a text.

Mahāyāna school was not the only one to use Sanskrit as a sacred language.[371] To further complicate the issue, Sanskrit was sometimes used as a scared language by the *Abhayagirivihāra* in Sri Lanka.[372]

The inscriptions are closely related to religious buildings or religious objects. By examining the archaeological data, we shall be able to discover the nature of the context in which the inscriptions appear.

5.1.2. Archaeological Sources of Buddhist *Vesālī*

Our knowledge in this field is rather inadequate. There is less archeological data from south than there is from northern Rakhaing land. Due to lack of sustained and systematic excavations, the archeological evidence available to us is like a jigsaw puzzle with missing pieces. This evidence, for the most part, has been interpreted by art historians, who even among themselves, cannot agree on dates or artistic styles.[373] Any statements made by art historians on the subject should be regarded as provisional.

There are four principal schools or periods of Indian art that influenced the art of Southeast Asia: the *Amarāvatī* (second to third centuries AD); the *Gupta* (fourth to sixth centuries AD); the *Pallava* (AD 550 to 750); and the *Pāla* (AD

371 For example, the *Sarvastivādins*, the *Mahāsaṅghikas*, and the *Dharmaguptakas* also used their own versions of Sanskrit.

372 See R. A. H. L. Gunawardana, Buddhist Nikāyas in Medieval Sri Lanka. *Sri Lanka Journal of Historical and Social Sciences IX*, (1966), p. 57.

373 San Tha Aung, (1979) "*Buddhist Art*"; Gutman (1976); Khine, Tun Shwe. (1990) "*Buddhist Art of Vesālī period*"

750 to 900).[374] Another important influence from Sri Lanka, especially during the Anurādhapura period (third century AD to the eight century AD) that affected the development of Southeast Asian art no less than did India.[375]

These influences do not mean that no process of localization took place. Quite the contrary, the various Southeast Asian cultures in different regions modified these outside influences and made them their own, from as early as the fourth or fifth centuries.[376] There had been certain characteristic of Rakhaing art itself different from those of India and Sri Lanka. In addition to localization, there was also sublocalization among different traditions, especially at times when a shift in political or cultural part of Rakhaing and in the region. Mixed styles developed in areas where the boundaries of different cultures overlapped. Styles developed unevenly, inconsistently, and influences from India and Sri Lanka were not the same in all areas. Furthermore, in some areas a certain style persevered, while in others new styles replaced previous ones. Even though we have not found explicit Buddha images during the third and fourth centuries AD, we have discovered a number of sculptures related to Theravāda Buddhism. It is due mainly to

---

374 Paul Wheatley, "Golden Khersonese: Studies in the Historical Geography of the Malay Peninsula before AD 1500. Kaula Lumpure: University of Malaya Press, (1961), p. 193. The list comes from Wales, H. G. Quaritch, "Making of Greater India" London: B. Quaritch, 1951.

375 See Sirisena, Sri Lanka and South-East Asia. See also Auboyer et al., Oriental Art, 97ff, where Sri Lanka is included in the section on Southeast Asia. The authors note that: "It is mainly on the accounts of Sri Lanka's (Sri Lanka's) influence that the chapter devoted to that country has been placed as an introduction to the section of this book dealing with South-east Asia...It seems likely that Sri Lanka served as a link between India and South-east Asia during the very earliest centuries of Indian influence in that part of the world, and the development of the island's influence there has continued almost unbroken to this day."

376 Gutman (2001)

the fact that Rakhaing people may have avoided to make one else existing Mahāmuni Images, either a number of fires burn out the Mahamuni Temple in chronicles, or weather condition and foreign attacks. Regarding the Rakhaing sculptures during the third and fourth centuries AD such as devapala, yaskhas, etc. found in Sririgutta Hill, Prof. San Tha Aung is of the opinion that those are the contemporary of Gupta sculpture of Mathura of India.[377] According to Pamela Gutman, sculptures of pre-*Vesālī* period are close resemblance with that of Nagājunakoṇḍa, Andhāra of southern India.[378]

Since it is not possible to present here the full extent of archaeological data pertinent to our discussion, we shall try to summarize it under topics related to the type of archeological find.

5.1.2.1. *Stūpas*

Only a few ruins of the ancient buildings have survived intact, and not one is free from reconstruction, repairs, or additions. This is partly explained by the fact that Buddhism continues to be a living faith in Rakhaing. In addition, not only did various schools of Buddhism flourish in different phase of *Vesālī*, but also Hinduism was always present on the scene. Sometimes the different religions were on equal footing, but other times one or the other predominated. This can be seen in buildings that were originally Buddhist, but later were "converted" for Hindu cultic use, and *vice versa.*

Most of the Buddhist buildings in the Rakhaing were *stūpa*s. The *stūpa*s show influence from the *Andhara* area,

---

377 *Op. cit.*, Aung, San Tha. "Buddhist Art" (1979) p. 115.

378 Gutman (1976) p. 222

especially *Amarāvatī*. Originally the *stūpa*s were hemispherical mounds, but later a square or rectangular base, sometimes very elaborate, was added.

A hundred stone *stūpa*s were donated by a *Vesālī* king (i.e., Vīracandra). As the epigraphist Dr. Sircar mentioned, "A hundred Buddha-*stūpa*s (i.e., structures enshrining relics of the Buddha) which are the ornament of the earth: are made owing to his love for the true faith (and) with his own money the illustrious King Vīracandradiva who has his heart fully set on expectations for effecting good to other (and) who obtained Kingdom or sovereignty through righteousness."[379]

Due to a number of researchers studied *stūpa*s of different parts of Rakhaing since nearly thirty years ago, a specific number of *stūpa*s have been discovered to supplement as a chapter in the history of Rakhaing significantly. A number of art historians of Rakhaing have studied the *stūpa*s of Rakhaing land. Firstly, distinguished Prof. San Tha Aung presented about three *stūpa*s from Kyauktaw Township together with their photos in chapter 5 of his famous book, "Buddhist Art of Ancient Arakan." A retired township education officer, Maung Ba Thein discovered thirty-one *stūpa*s from the island of Sandowshurn near Sittway (formerly Akyab). Additionally, *stūpa*s from Krein Khwe Maw village of Taung Run Island, Pauk Taw Township, and Doiṇe Thein, Buthitaung Township have also been discovered. Notably, Pamela Gutman also discussed some *stūpa*s from Mrauk Oo Township in her PhD thesis.[380] Besides,

379 Sircar (1957) pp. 103–109.

380 Gutman (1976) pp. 229–234.

the State Gazetteer (Culture Section) presents some of it.[381] Researcher Aung Hla Thein together with U Aung Murn from Murn Bra discovered some *stūpa*s from Sa Aun village, Murn Bra Township and presented about it in a state magazine with English language. U Tun Shwe Khine also mentioned about *stūpa*s in his book, "Buddhist Art in *Vesālī* period."[382] Additionally, a special booklet called "Rakhaing Miniature *Stūpa*s" by Murn Bra Murn Thein Zan has been published.[383] It presents most of all Rakhaing *stūpa*s as far as available in previous studies, but it is not yet a complete one because there have many other *stūpa*s in Rakhaing unknown. It is a matter of later scholarship. In addition to these, a number of articles on Rakhaing *stūpa*s has hitherto presented in different Rakhaing magazines and local journals.

*Stūpa*s are found in abundance in Rakhaing. Of them, three miniature *stūpa*s of *Vesālī* period engraved with *ye dhammā* verse reproduced here from Prof. San Tha Aung's work:[384]

> To Buddhist the world over, the stupa is an emblem of Buddha's prinibbāna, for the *stūpa* is a monument erected over relics of the Buddha. And because Buddhists revere the relics of the Blessed One, it naturally follows that the stupa should play a leading role in Buddhist architecture.

---

381 *State Gazetteer (Culture)* pp. 38–39.

382 Khine, Tun Shwe. (1990) "*Buddhist Art in Vesālī period*" pp. 43–48.

383 Zan, Murn Bra Murn Thein. "*Arakan Miniature Stūpas*" PEAL, Rangoon. (2003 Nov.)

384 Aung, San Tha. (1979) "Buddhist Art" pp. 16–17.

The oldest *stūpa*s extant are full hemispherical domes constructed of brick or stone, usually reised on a terrace. The *stūpa*s of Sanchi, Andhāra and Mankiala near Rawalpindi, in India and Pakistan, all belong to such a type. At a later period, a solid cylinder or drum was added beneath the hemisphere, thereby gradually raising it above the ground-level. Later still a square piece acted as the support for the *hti* or finial. Still later on the architect added a niche to one side of the drum, each niche facing one of the cardinal points. Today these niches each contain an image of the Buddha. Generally, four Buddhas are figured around votive *stūpa*s.

Today almost every hillock in Arakan is crowned with a pagoda, but old *stūpa*s dating before 1000 AD are now extremely rare. They have either collapsed due to weathering, (annual rainfall in the Arakan State is over 200 inches), or have been destroyed by vandalism, or been encased in pagodas built by later kings. There is no doubt, however, that they were once plentiful. The inscription of Vīracandra, a king of the Candra dynasty states that a hundred *stūpas* were constructed and dedicated by King Viracandra because of his love for the True Law. (*mentioned above about it*) To date, over thirty stone inscriptions bearing, in Gupta characters, the *ye dhammā* verse in full, have been found all over Arakan. These stone inscriptions are the remains of the old *stūpa*s before the sixth century AD.

After describing about three *stūpa*s, Prof. San Tha Aung comments further on the *stūpa*s, "These three surviving miniature *stūpa*s carved out of stone in a bygone age, and by chance spared by the climate, together with other stone inscriptions fallen from old pagodas, each bearing the *ye dhammā* verse in Gupta characters, are sufficient to establish positively, the fact that Buddhism flourished in Arakan not later than the fourth or fifth century AD."[385]

Concerning meaning of the word "*stūpa*" in Rakhaing, we need to discuss two inscriptions of the *Vesālī* period. First, according to O Htein inscription engraved on *stūpa* from Taungguake Township, *stūpa* means 'small *cetiya*.' Second, according to a *stūpa* at Mrauk Oo Museum, marked no. ca/23, it means the same as the first.

Building of *stūpas* in *Vesālī* period was not only by kings, but by normal people alike. In the Vīracandra inscription, King Vīracandra engraved, "constructed a hundred buddha *stūpas*, which are the ornaments of the earth, with his own wealth, owing to his love for the true law." It is also evident that O Htein inscription reads, "This *stūpa* is built for the prosperity of the people living in the place who faith in the Three Jewels (*tiratana*)"

Additionally, it is interesting to note that inscription engraved on the *stūpa* at Mrauk Oo Museum, marked no. ca/23 from old *Vesālī* reads, "This *stūpa* is built dedicating the Lord Buddha by an *upasaka* who observes five precepts. By this deed, may my parents and all beings by observing eight and nine precepts see the doctrine of *anattā* and finally realize the four noble truths."[386]

Observing words *anattā, cattāri ariyasaccānī* engraved in the seventh line of the inscription on the *stūpa*, we can surmise that people in *Vesālī* period were purely just Buddhist,

385 *Op. cit.*, Aung, San Tha. (1979) "Buddhist Art" p. 18.

386 *Op. cit.*, Zan, Murn Bra Murn Thein. (2003) p. 41–42.

but not *Mahāyāna* type. In fact, many *stūpa*s were built by Buddhist kings, normal people as well in *Vesālī* period with good will.

The objective of building *stūpa* is different from each other. According to the Vīracandra inscription, it is because, "*stūpa*s are the ornaments of the earth." As for O Htein inscription from Taungguke Township, it is, however, "for the prosperity of the people living therein." "Dedicating the Lord Buddha" is mentioned in the inscriptions of the *stūpa* marked ca/23 at the Mrauk Oo Museum.

The *stūpa* has symbolic significance on several levels.[387] It is not simply a symbol of the Buddha's attainment of *nibbāna* but also a symbol of the Buddha himself, especially when it houses his physical relics (*sarīradhātu*).

5.1.2.2. Images

The earliest style of Buddha image found in Rakhaing is that labeled as "*Amarāvatī*." Buddha images are in the standing or upright posture, with hands in the *vitarka* or *abhaya mudrā*, a style that prevailed in Andhara Pradesh and in Aurādhapūra at approximately the same time. Later, the favorite *mudrā* for the standing Buddha in the Gupta style was the *varada* or *abhaya mudrā*, and for the seated Buddha, the *dhammacakka mudrā*.[388]

---

387 For studies on the concept of "*stūpa*," see Snodgrass, Adrian. "*Symbolism of the Stupa*." Studies on Southeast Asia. NY: Southeast Asia Programme, Cornell University. (1985)

388 See Auboyer, et al., "*Oriental Art: A Handbook of Styles and Forms*." Translated by Elizabeth and Richard Bartlett. New York: Rizzoli International Publications, Inc. (1980) pp. 364ff; and for explanations of these *mudrā*s, see Saunders, E. Dale. "*Mudrā: A Study of Symbolic Gestures in Japanese Buddhist Sculpture*." Bollingen Series, No. 58. Princeton, NJ. Princeton University Press. (1960).

According to Prof. San Tha Aung, *mudrās* found in Rakhaing can be classified into six: 1. The *Bhumiphassa mudrā*, 2. The *Dhana mudrā*, 3. The *Dhammacakka mudrā*, 4. The *Abhaya mudrā*, 5. The *Abhaya* and *Varada* Combined *mudrā*, 6. The Internal *Varada mudrā*.[389]

Not only stone images, but also images made of bronze, gold, silver, and copper are found. One of the stone images out of many, *Vesālī* Phara Gree (Great Buddha Image from *Vesālī*) made of a single marvelous stone still can be seen. Moreover, certain sculptures of angels, spirits, and demons such as *devapala*, *yakkhapala*, etc. would have been made to guard the premises of the pagodas. Different kinds of *mudrās* (styles) made of gold, silver, copper, or other metal are found in Rakhaing. *Mudrās* found in Rakhaing can be into two kinds: crowned and uncrowned. Again, uncrowned images can be classified into two according to the representations of the head: (i) The head with long flowing locks gathered together on top of the head to form a topknot, (ii) The head with a cranial protuberance (*Usnisa*). The whole head together with the protuberance are being covered by small curls.[390] Many crowned images have been found throughout different ages in Rakhaing. Concerning the Rakhaing version of crowned Buddha images, Prof. San Tha Aung explained by referring an ancient palm-leaf manuscript, "According to unbroken tradition, the kings of Arakan, during their Coronation Ceremonies, take their oath of Office by holding aloft a specially cast image of the Buddha, beautifully ornamented and depicted in full royal regalia. For this reason, such images of the Buddha have

389 See details about Arakanese *mudrās*: Aung, San Tha. (1979) "*Buddhist Art*" p. 71.

390 *Ibdi.* Aung, San Tha. (1979) "Buddhist Art" p. 58.

come to be known either as Mahākyain Phara (Royal Oath Buddha) or Nantet Phara (Coronation Buddha). Later, due to the passage of time, the word Mahākyain became corrupted, and the image also came to be called Mahākyain Phara."[391]

Additionally, he insisted that, "Arakan has ever been a land where Buddhism has flowered and its kings have been devout Buddhists. At the ascension of each king the first requisite is the casting of a Mahāyain Phara (also called a Nantet Phara). This image then plays an important part in the Coronation Ceremony. Although, it is not certain at what period and in which reign this practice began, a study of the style and workmanship of the old Mahākyain Phara images extant, reveals that they were probably cast during the fourth century AD during the reigns of the *Vesālī* kings."[392]

Again, Prof. San Tha Aung clarified, "For his Coronation Ceremony, an Arakanese king first selects the most renowned pagoda within his kingdom as the site, and then proceeds toward it in Royal Procession, passing out of the Palace grounds through the Mangala Gate. Arriving at the platform of the selected pagoda, each personage takes up his assigned position. The king then raises the Mahāyain Phara to the top of his head, and holding it there, he makes three circuits of the pagoda. He completes the third circuit at the temporary Hall, where the coronation is to take place. The Coronation Ceremony itself follows traditional rites. At the conclusion, the Thathabaing Sayadaw (the patriarch or principal monk of the kingdom) and a number of monks who can recite from memory the

391 Aung, San Tha. *op. cit.*, p. 67.

392 *Op. cit.*, p. 67.

whole of the Tipitakas (the three main canonical divisions of the Buddha's teachings are divided into Vinaya, Code of Discipline; Sutta, Discourses; and Abhidhamma, Higher Doctrine), then hold the Mahākyain Phara over the king's head and exhort him to uphold justice in the tradition of his forefathers, to venerate the Triple Gem (Buddha, Dhamma, and Saṁgha), to encourage the Buddhist religion within his kingdom, and to suppress the enemies of Buddhism. The king has to take an oath and declare that he will faithfully discharge his duties as enumerated above. This oath-taking is the high point of the ceremony."[393]

And he further explained a Rakhaing tradition as model of king's royal oath-taking, "The Arakanese peasantry in olden days very often used a Buddha image to take an oath in trying to settle conflicting claims or even criminal cases. This practices was no doubt, in some measure, due to their belief and faith in Buddhism but could just as easily have derived from the king's Royal Oath-taking."[394]

There are many types of Buddha images in *Vesālī*. A few of them are presented here. First, *Vesālī* Great Image (*Vesālī* Phara Gree) is located in Buddhist synod hill. This image is donated by Queen Supabhādevī of King Mahātaicandra (Mahā Dvencandra in the inscription). It has own a beautiful story. The story reads, "In Rakhaing Chronicles, the name of a queen of the founder king Mahātaicandra was Supabhādevī, who was happened to be a most pious queen. When the couple ascended to the *Vesālī* throne, they requested to dispatch a rear Buddha image by her father king from India. On the way from to Rakhaing, that very

393 *Op. cit.*, p. 70.

394 *Op. cit.*, p. 71.

Buddha image was lost in the sea near present Mrauk Oo. It was happened due to the heavy stormy weather. The queen became so much grieved for the unfortunate event. To ease her grief and its substitute the image the king planned to erect a new great image made of bronze as a founding image to commemorate of their completion of the *Vesālī* city. And she worshiped and prayed the new image that she be the first person to be worshiped to the lost image when it reappears again one day."

The seventeen-foot-high Great Image of *Vesālī* carved of a single block of sand stone rests on a hill half a mile north of the palace city, *Vesālī*. It was built in AD 327, the same year that *Vesālī* was established. Lying east to the Great Buddha Image is the seventy-foot-high Saṅgāyana or Buddhist synod hill. The crowned queen mansion is said to lie to the north of the people. Close to the western palace city wall on the Ran-chaung tributary stood the stone piers that helped earn the name of the Stone Pier City (Kyauk Haly Gar Mro). See Plate.

In 1956, a stone slab inscription was recovered from the ruined *stūpa* behind the image on the same hill. The script of the inscription is in late Brahmi, and the language is Pāḷi. Among many, the scholars who have taken note of this inscription are: Prof. San Tha Aung,[395] Tun Shwe Khine,[396] Ven. Kosalla,[397] and Dr. Pamela Gutman.[398]

---

395 San Tha Aung, *Scripts of Arakan: Sixth Century and Before*, Rangoon: (1974). pp. 115–116. pl. 22.

396 Tun Shwe Khine, *Buddhist Art in Vesālī Period*, pl. 8.

397 U Kosalla, *Journey of Arakanese Literature*, Yangon: Burmese, pp. 26–27.

398 P. Gutman, *op. cit.*, pp. 87–88.

In addition to this, only three types of *mudrās* of *Vesālī* period are presented here. The first one is standing figure bronze Buddha images with his right hand raised and the palm turned to the front with figures directed upward. The second and the third are *bhumiphassa mudrā* and *dhanyamudrā* respectively, both are legs crossed and crowned bronze images.[399]

5.1.2.3. Miniature Bronze *Zetis*

Regarding about *zetis*, Prof. San Tha Aung explains, "A solid religious edifice of the Buddhists is called a *zeti*. This is an abbreviation of the Pāḷi word '*cetiya*', which generally be translated as something built or piled up. The word is used for funeral mounds; built in honor of heroes, teachers, or prophets. The *zeti* is an object of veneration and serves as a place of worship. The *zetis* are memorials in monumental form, constructed mainly to preserve the memory of the Buddha. Most of these contain relics of the Buddha, his images or scripture, recording his teachings. They are placed in sealed chambers known as relic chambers often located in the basement, and sometimes up in the datu-gabbha, which lies between the bell and the finial. In the building of *zetis*, Buddhists are motivated by certain sentiments. The building of a ceti is considered an act of great religious merit for the person or persons concerned. The merit, thus gained, spells elevation to a better life in the hereafter or elevation to some heavenly abode or even to nibbāna in some future existence. People, by the generations, can also use these *zetis* for religious worship and for the practices of Buddhism. The *zetis* themselves help

399 See details about Arakan *mudrās* in Chapters XV and XVI of San Tha Aung's work "*Buddhist Art*" pp. 60–82.

ensure the preservation and perpetuation of the religion for a long time."[400]

Additionally, Prof. San Tha Aung presented three miniature bronze *zetis* to be noticed. According to him, the first was found in Tharlawaddy village, which is located within the southern city walls of old *Vesālī* city. The second one was found in Dharmarit village, which lies very close to the old *Vesālī* site. The exact location where that third one was found is unknown. He explained in details about those three.[401]

By observing these three Buddhist architectural designs of bronze *zetis* of *Vesālī* period, we can surely say that there was prevailing advanced Buddhist art and Buddhism thus far flourishing in ancient *Vesālī* of Rakhaing.

5.1.2.4. Copper-Plate Land Grant

Giving (*Dāna*) is a customary way of practice by the Buddhists. We have found earlier that construction of *cetiyas*, of monastery, of wells; giving food, robes to monks; casting of Buddha images, etc. by not only ancient kings and royal peoples, but by common citizens in Vesāli, Rakhaing, are evident of Buddhism flourished in ancient in *Vesālī* period. What we are going to present here now is a copper-plate land grant sealed by a king of *Vesālī*. According to Prof. San Tha Aung, "This copper plate was a royal document issued by a *Vesālī* king of a sixth century AD. The grant of land for religious purposes was engraved

400 *op. cit.*, Aung, San Tha. (1979) "Buddhist Art" p. 48.

401 *Op. cit.*, pp. 50–51.

on it. It contained well known imprecatory and benedictory stanzas written on the reverse side."[402]

We have known that lines 1 and 2 are lost. Lines 3–8 mention six kings and describes them as padanudyata (meditating on or favored by the feet of his predecessor), as Paramamahesvara (a devout worshiper of the god Mahesvara or Śiva) and as born of a particular Mahādevi (chief queen). The kings enjoyed the title of Mahārajadhirāja, indicating independent and imperial status in the Gupta age. The names of the queens can be read in lines 4–8, the queen's name in line 3 being damaged. It is privileged to know the donor's mother, grandmother, great-grandmother, great-great-grandmother, and great-great-great-grandmother, viz. Kalyanadevi, Kyawdevi, Sukanyadevi, Kimdaldevi and Kimtondevi respectively. In lines 9–10 the issuing king addresses the character to the rulers of his own family and of other dynasties in respect of the grant. Lines 10–13 state that a village called Dengutta was granted by Kimmajuvdevi in favor of a *vihāra* (Buddhist monastery) built by herself.[403]

Prof. San Tha Aung remarked, "Kimmajuvdevi was doubtless a Buddhist, although her husband and his ancestors were mentioned as Paramamahesvara. So far as I have noticed, there is practically no evidence of Śaivism in the archeological assemblage of Arakan. *It may be conjectured that Śaivite ritual may have been confirmed*

402 Aung, San Tha. (1979) *Buddhist Art* p. 33.

403 *Op. cit.*, p. 35.

to certain court ceremonies necessary to legitimize kingship, but incompatible with Buddhism, performed by a small group of court Brahmins."[404]

It is again mentioned in the lines that the income derived from the gift village was meant to be utilized on behalf of the *ratntrayopayogaya* (*rattanattya*) (i.e., the Buddha, the Dhamma and the Saṁgha, in respect of the *catushpratyana* (*catupaccaya*) [i.e., the four requisites *viz. cīvara* (clothing), *piṇḍapāta* (food), *senāsana* (bedding), and *bhesajja* (medicine), and the repairs of breaks, cracks, etc. in the monastery]).

According to a damaged passage in lines 12–13, we have known that the gift village was replaced in charge of the fraternity of the holy monks of the all lands including the elders of *Jetavana*, who were already in the monastery and who might in future come to reside there in. Here, the elders of *Jetavana* may represent to those who might have contacts with monks of *Jetavanavāsins* from ancient Sri Lanka. As Rakhaing might have had contacts with Sri Lanka times immemorial, Rakhaing monks in *Vesālī* may have used the famous names, not only monks of *Mahāvihāravāsins*, but also of *Jetavanavāsins* and *Abhayagiriyavāsins* from Sri Lanka.

5.1.2.5. Bronze Bells[405]

Two inscribed ancient bells preserved in Akyab Buddha Museum(present Sittway) at present, made of bronze (i.e., an alloy of copper and tin), from the vicinity of *Vesālī* in Rakhaing, one of the bells seems to be a *cetiya* bell and

404 *Op. cit.*, p. 36.

405 *Op. cit.*, p. 38–40.

the other a monastery bell have been presented by Prof. San Tha Aung. Paleographically, date of their casting is dated in sixth century AD by him. The first bell's two lines of writing, according to him, have been inscribed around the center. The first line contains eighteen words endowed with vowel marks or conjunct and the second line fourteen words. The language is a mixture of ancient Rakhaing and Sanskrit. Texts are below.

1. mataitroh hiritathettr kimmayana dhanayah...Nama

2. naraghantayad datteyam samarira svarah

Prof. San Tha Aung's rough translation reads, "Obeisance...for the welfare and Punna of (my) mother and father, kimmayana...this nara bell with a sweet sound is given."

According to Prof. San Tha Aung's remarks, the writing can be paleographically assigned to the pre or early Niticandra period around AD 520. The writings reveal the dedication by a monk for the benefit of his spiritual preceptors, etc. and his mother and father. The second bell's two lines of inscription are presented below.

1. Deyyadharma' yam sakyabhikso...yac atra punyam tad bhavatu matapitropurvangamam krtva

2. caryyopadhyayanam sarvvasatvanan ca anuttarajnanavaptaye iti.

A rough translation is presented by Prof. San Tha Aung: This is a pious offering of the Buddhist monk...May my merit that is therein be for the gaining of supreme knowledge (acquiring *nirvāna*) by teachers, tutors and all beings in company with his mother and father. He remarked finally that these bronze bells show us that the people of Rakhaing of that age already possessed an advanced metallurgical technology.

Addition to Prof. San Tha Aung, these two bronze bells have been studied and commented upon by Dr. Gutman,[406] Tun Shwe Khine.[407]

5.1.2.6. Bronze Lamps

A number of lamps made of bronze have been found in Rakhaing. They were usually found in the vicinity of old Dhaññavatī, and old *Vesālī.* They have also been found in other places of Rakhaing. They are varied in design, but all the forms of the lamp are meant for worshipping. An old lamp found by the late U San Shwe Bu at Paring-daung village, about six miles to the north of *Vesālī* bearing an inscription represents a woman holding out in front of her, a rather elongated spear-shaped receptacle, intended to hold the oil, which is meant to be lighted before the image of Buddha by means of wicks. Six indentations at the edges of the receptacle may be noticed for placing such wicks. The woman stands on a high pedestal in which a line of inscription in Rakhaing characters appears.

The writing in the lamp pedestal may be read as "*Āyanā kaungmutaw*" (i.e., "gift of Āyana"). Including this lamp, another four more lamps, one similar to the foresaid style, the remaining three in different were also presented in Prof. San Tha Aung's book. Regarding Rakhaing bronze lamps, he commented, "A lamp is a vessal for burning oil with a wick, and so giving light. The oil used may be animal, fish, or vegetable oil. Of all the forms of gifts to the gods (*devadanam*), there is perhaps none which can equal in merit-winning capacity, that which is offered in the form

406 Gutman (1976) p. 96.

407 Kine, Tun Shwe. (1990) "*Buddhist Art of Vesali Period*" pl.13

of lamps or *dipan*, (from the Sanskrit *dipa* "to light"). All over the world, the lighting of lamps forms an essential part of temple and shrine worship."[408]

5.1.3. Fourth Buddhist Council in *Vesālī* of Rakhaing

Geographically, Magadha and northern Rakhaing are so close to contact by land to each other. Cultural connections might be surely possible, no doubt. Which is why we have to consider the fact that geographical feature is a great factor to the development of Buddhism in Rakhaing along the centuries past, even though there is no epigraphical evidence to be proven. Due to various other reasons, most importantly geographical fact, it is undeniable logical fact that missionary Buddhist monks from Magadha would have reached into Rakhaing land and Buddhist pilgrims and traders would also travelled to Magadha, and *vice versa.*

After the third Buddhist council held in India by the support of Emperor Asoka and by the patronage of Ven. Moggaliputtatissa, Buddhism travelled not only to the western parts of India, but also, spread to all over Southeast Asia region, it now includes Rakhaing coastal strip as its westernmost part.

By the time of the Fourth Buddhist council, Buddhism had long since splintered into different schools. The *Theravāda* had a Fourth Buddhist Council in the last century BC in Tambapanni (i.e., Sri Lanka), at Aloka Lena now Alu Vihara during the time of King Vattagamani-Abaya. However it should be clarified that an anonymous local chieftain had given patronage and not the king, since he was a firm follower of the Abayagiri School (a *Mahāyāna* Sect.). In fact one of the

408 *Op. cit.*, p. 41.

main reasons for the Council was the cruel policy the king held against the Mahāvihāra priests who were Theravadins who were once attacked at the Mahāvihāra Premises killing many and driving away the others. The temple was destroyed, and in its place, a *Mahāyāna* Temple was built. The other main reasons for the Council were the unstable political situation within the country due to constant invasions which lead the king himself to flee several times and also severe famine. It is said to have been devoted to committing the entire Pāḷi Canon to writing, which had previously been preserved by memory. No mention had been made as to who led this Council, for which the approximate cause would have been the deteriorating status of Buddhism then, and the collective effort by the priesthood to preserve the religion in its purest form therefore not needing a leader (only the fact that the Mahāvihāra priesthood [i.e., *Theravāda* school] took part in this recital and compilation had been mentioned).

Another Fourth Buddhist Council was held in the *Sarvāstivāda* tradition, said to have been convened by the Kushan emperor Kanishka, in AD 78 at Jalandhar or in Kashmir. It is said that Kanishka gathered five hundred Bhikkhus in Kashmir, headed by Vasumitra, to systematize the Sarvāstivssdin Abhidharma texts, which were translated from earlier Prakrit vernacular languages (such as Gandhari in Kharosthi script) into the classical language of Sanskrit. It is said that during the council, three hundred thousand verses and over nine million statements were compiled, a process which took twelve years to complete. Although the *Sarvāstivāda* are no longer extant as an independent school, its traditions were inherited by the *Mahāyāna* tradition. The late Monseigneur Professor Etienne Lamotte, an eminent

Buddhologist, held that Kanishka's Council was fictitious.[409] However, David Snellgrove, another eminent Buddhologist, considers the *Theravāda* account of the Third Council and the *Sarvāstivāda* account of the Fourth Council "equally tendentious," illustrating the uncertain veracity of much of these histories.[410]

After nearly four centuries, a Buddhist council was held under the leadership of Ven. Cūlareva in *Vesālī* of Rakhaing during the reign of King Sridhammavijaya (Sricandra in the chronicle) in AD 638 for the purpose of inscribing the Tripiṭaka. This convention was the crowing event in the history of Buddhism in Rakhaing. A total of two thousand monks, one thousand from Sri Lanka and one thousand from Rakhaing, participated in the council. According to the contemporary epigraphical accounts, the language in which the words of the council were written at the council would either be Sanskrit or Pāḷi. Pāḷi is more plausible for the canonical literature, while Sanskrit for the commentarial literature, or Pāḷi would be for the both literatures because being *Theravādins* all the venerable monks participated the councils would be favor Pāḷi as their sacred language of their Master more than Sanskrit.[411]

409 The teaching of Vimalakīrti (Vimalakīrtinirdeśa): from the French translation with introduction and notes (L'enseignement de Vimalarkirti), translated by Sara Boin, pub. by The Pāḷi Text Society, London, (1976). p. XCIII.

410 *Snellgrove, David. "Indo-Tibetan Buddhism"* Boston, *Shambhala* (1987), vol. 2, p. 46

411 Medhapaññā Mawgwan Laṅkā (Record of Medhapaññā) is a lyrical poem, which briefly records about cancellation of era, holding Buddhist councils, coming of missionary monks from India, written by Minister Medhapaññā, one of leading ministers during king Sridhammacandra (Sricandra) (in Vesālī period). See about Minister Medhapañña and the poem in the State Gazetteer (Culture) (1984), pp. 185–188; Aung Thar Oo, U. "Buddhasasana and Rakhaing Land" (1974 Nov). pp. 19–20.; Rakhing Cultures and Traditional Customs (1976 Jan) p.144; State Gazetteer (Culture) (1984) p. 3.

According to the Medhapaññā account, by the following method, both canon and atthākathās were written down on the copper plates in the council. It can be seen as follows:

Canonical Literature	number of books	number of copper plates
Vinaya	5	250 golden copper plates
Suttanta	3	910 *ibid*
Abhidhamma	7	840 *ibid*
Commentarial literature	number of books	number of copper plates
Vinaya	5	750 reddish copper plates
Suttanta	3	1500 *ibid*
Abhidhamma	7	690 *ibid*
Visuddhimagga	1	60 *idid*
	Total plates	5000

Thus far, after the council was held during of reign of King Sridharmavijaya, in the reign of King Ānanadacandra, grandson of King Sridharmavijaya, dispatched, according to the verse 61 of the *Ānandacandra* inscription, a number of gifts to Sri Lanka. Additionally, it is also to verse 50 of the inscription, books of the Holy Law (Buddhist scriptures) have been caused to be written by the King *Ānandacandra* in large numbers. It is evident that Rakhaing relationships with Sri Lanka had been since King Sridhammavijaya, grandfather of King *Ānandacandra.*

Many artifacts were discovered from the Saṅgāyanā hill. Now the hill is covered by trees and many other plants. A *devapāla* sculpture mentioned in Pamela Gutman's PhD thesis plate number LXXIIa was found in this hill.[412] The art

412 *Op. cit.*, Gutman (1976), Part II, pl. LXXIIa

style of artifacts found in this hill areas bear a resemblance to that of *Nāgajunakoṇḍa*, Andhra, Southern India.[413] It may be connected with *Nāgajunakoṇḍa* inscription written before the third century AD mentioning monks from Sri Lanka went to the Bengal region for a Buddhist mission. The Sri Lanka Buddhist missionary monks could reach the Rakhaing region since the beginning of Christian era.[414] Concerning the fourth Buddhist council held in *Vesālī* of Rakhaing, Dr. Pamela Gutman remarks in her PhD thesis, "It is probable that the tradition of a fourth synod is associated in Arakanese Buddhist hagiography with the joint decision of the Phyu and Arakanese kings to begin era in 638."[415]

Additionally, the council is proven by two other facts as well. First, it would not be impossible that at the council the words of the Buddha were committed into writing on five thousand copper plates at that time because there have been a land grant copper plate written by King Būticandra (AD 496–520) a hundred year earlier before the council was held in AD 638.

Another fact, in verse 50 of the *Ānandacandra* inscription engraved a hundred year after the council, the grandson of the fourth council supporter King Dhammavijaya, King *Ānandacandra* recorded "books of the Holy Law have been caused to be written by the good king in large numbers."[416] of what his predecessor did in the year AD 638. But here the Holy Law could either be the Buddhist canonical and commentarial

413 See Gangoly, O. C. "*Andhara Sculptures*" Hyderabad. (1973). pls. XVIII, XXXIX, XL.

414 Khine, Tun Shwe. (1990) "*Buddhist Art in Vesālī period*" pp. 15–16.

415 *Op. cit.*, Gutman (1976) p. 222, footnote no. 73.

416 See details in the translation of Ānandacandra Inscription provided above.

literature from Sri Lanka or be Hāyāma scripture from Nālanda University.

As mentioned above, before sectarian Buddhism, Buddhist in Rakhaing had flourished. After the sectarian Buddhism break out India, Hinayāna Buddhism entered into the land by land and sea. This fact has already been proven by means of *Nagājunakoṇḍa* inscription. According to the inscription, monks from Sri Lanka went for a Buddhist missionary work to Bengal region. Here Bengal is not western bank area of Ganges, but eastern part of it. That means including to northern Rakhaing Land. According to Luce, quoting Ptolemy [who in turn was citing Pomponius Mela (circa 43) on the location of ancient Rakhaing, said:

> "Descending the coast south-eastward from the mouth of the Ganges, he names first the Airrhadoi (with the port Barakoura) [this was presumably in the Chittagong region]; then the country of Argyre["Silver Land" i.e., Arakan] with [the towns of] Sambra, Sada, Berabonna and Temala [which Gereni believed was cape Negrais]; then a Cape; then the cannibals of Besynga [thought to be in the region of the mouth of the Irrawaddy River, in the Sarabak Gulf [most likely to Gulf of Martaban].[417]

It is, therefore, Rakhaing is in the location of eastern part of Ganges, *Nagājunakoṇḍa* names it "Cilāta or Kilāta country" as the same as the name given by Pomponius Mela (circa 43), which is "Argyre," meaning the same "Silver Land."

We do not know yet about when and how northern Mahāyanist Buddhism entered into the land. Chinese pilgrim

417 Luce, G. H. "The Tan (AD 97–132) and the Ngai-Lao." *JBRS, XIV*, (1924). p. 232.

Fa-hien reported that he did not find any written Pitaka in the Ganges plain during the end of the fourth century AD, only in the beginning of the fifth century AD he had found Vinaya texts written in Sanskrit with other Buddhist texts in Pataliputta, city of Magadha; then he learned Sanskrit and copied them.[418] If it is so, only we can say that *Mahāyāna* Buddhism entered from Magadha to the land, not earlier than the fifth century AD.

Rakhaing was a country in which 'freedom of worship' was given to all creeds. Therefore, after sectarian Buddhism, there was no distinction or discrimination whether *Mahāyāna* or Hinayāna in the country. According to the verse 47 in the *Ānandacandra* inscription, it is firmly stated that, "There have been made gold and silver *ceityas* containing relics of the Buddha, Bodhisattvas, Cunda, and others according to power." In this "Boddhisattvas and Cunda" are *Mahāyāna* type of worship. But some scholars assert by quoting verse 55 of the inscription that Buddhism was mixed with other cults, (i.e., Brahmanism). In fact, as "right to religion" was given in the city of ancient *Vesālī*, everyone had right to choose any kind of worship, but Buddhism was not mixed with any cults. As mentioned earlier, it is evident in the epigraphic records of the time that most of the Buddhists were the same as the very basic of present *Theravāda* Buddhism (i.e., *ye dhammā* verse), and types of donation they did. By observing this, Buddhist peoples in ancient *Vesālī* of Rakhaing practiced Buddhism to a great extent, and they experienced "freedom of religion" since this time onward, if not earlier.

Even traditionally Buddhism had been flourished since Dhaññavatī period, owing to sectarian Buddhism and

418 *Hien, Fa; Tr. from the Chinese by Herbert A Giles.* Record of the Buddhistic Kingdoms by Fa Hien (414 AD). Trubner & Co., London. (1877). *Chapter XXXVI*

Brahmanism entered in the fifth century AD *Vesālī* by force in to the land, holding a Buddhist council by then existing orthodox Buddhists was seen in the year AD 638. By observing especially *Ānandacandra* inscription and other epigraphic evidence mentioned above, without doubts, people of *Vesālī* well experienced Buddhism a great deal. In the first half of the seventh century, a Buddhist council of one thousand monks from the land joined by one thousand Sri Lankan monks was held in *Vesālī*. Rakhaing's intercourses with Sri Lanka in history are primarily religious purposes. Thus far, we have known that Buddhism flourished throughout *Vesālī* period.

5.1.4. Patterns of Buddhist Developments in *Vesālī* Period

Never has there been impediment in the practice of *Theravāda* Buddhist faith since it has introduced in Rakhaing. The copious findings of inscription *ye dhammā* verse were practical evidence that *Theravāda* was dominant faith if epigraphic and archaeological sources were to be believed.

It is common practice for scholars to label the Buddhism in *Vesālī* period as *Theravāda* or *Mahāyāna* on the basis of the language of inscriptions or of archeological remains identified by art historians as either *Theravāda* or *Mahāyāna*. This, however, is an oversimplification.

In the case of language, any document using Pāḷi is usually labeled as belonging to the *Theravādins*, or occasionally narrowed further to the belonging to the *Theravādins* of Sri Lanka. Sanskrit inscriptions that do not show any overt influence of the *Mahāyānists* have been assigned to the *Sarvāstivādins*.[419]

---

419 For this type of reasoning, see de Casparis, *Prasasti Indonesia II*, p. 69; N. R. Ray, *Sanskrit Buddhism*; and Piriya Krairiksh, *Buddhist Folk Tales*.

Because Pāḷi is used only in the *Theravāda* tradition, the first conclusion seems more secure.[420] However, the language used in inscriptions of other sects found in the Andhara Pradesh area of India and dated to around the third and fourth century is very similar to Pāḷi. The differences may stem from the orthographic or epigraphic conventions of the time, as, for instance, the absence of double consonants or long vowels. But these conventions do not appear in the Pāḷi inscriptions of *Vesālī* period, which were written in what is known as "standard" Pāḷi. This would seem to indicate that the Pāḷi used in the region does indeed belong to the *Theravāda* and most probably the *Theravādins* of Sri Lanka as well. However, it is worth noting that there is evidence that Pāḷi was still in use in *Vesālī* during the sixth century AD. A number of inscriptions engraved by using Pāḷi dated to *Vesālī* period (from the fourth century to the tenth century AD) have been found side by side with inscriptions inscribed by using Sanskrit (e.g., Phara Gree Inscriptions from *Vesālī* and Thinkyittaw Hill Pillar Inscriptions, *Vesālī* inscribed with the *ye dhammā* verse in Pāḷi).

Sanskrit, which became the *lingua franca* of India, was more widely used then Pāḷi for that reason, and its use was by no means limited to the *Sarvāstivādins.* Sanskrit made its impact felt in Buddhism rather early, as seen in the progressive trend toward a Sanskritized Prakrit language. The languages used in Buddhist texts become more and more Sanskritic over time, and even Pāḷi did not escape this trend.[421] The Mahāvastu of the *Mahāsanghika-Lokottaravādins* is written in Buddhist Sanskrit, and *Mahāyāna* texts are written either in Buddhist

---

420 For the origin and development of Pāḷi, see Bechert, "*Some Sidelights on the Early History of Pāḷi Lexicography*;" Norman, *Pāḷi Literature,* pp. 1–14; and Norman, "*Pāḷi Language,*" pp. 29–54.

421 See Norman, "*Pāḷi Literature,*" and Norman, "*Pāḷi Language.*"

Sanskrit or in more or less standard Sanskrit. The *ye dhammā* in Sanskrit was widely used and adopted by the *Mahāyāna* tradition, but the evidence is inconclusive to pinpoint the sect to which the *ye dhammā* inscriptions belong. The issue is further complicated by the *Theravādins* of the *Abhayagirivihāra* in Anuradhapura, who are said to have used Sanskrit alongside Pāḷi and whose monastery served as a center for the *Mahāyānists* as well as the *Theravādins.*[422] It is reasonable to conclude that the Sanskrit texts found in *Vesālī* could have come from Sri Lanka or directly from Magadha in later time. In this case, the term "*Theravāda*" only adds to the confusion, since the *Abhyarigivihāvasins*, even if they were open-minded toward the *Mahāyāna* doctrines, were still regarded as belonging to the *Theravādins* of Sri Lanka. Thus, an inscription that cited a stanza from a Buddhist text in Sanskrit could belong to any one of at least three schools: *Sarvāstivādins*, *Mahāyānists*, or the *Abhayagirivihāravasins* of the *Theravādin* of Sri Lanka.

In summary, what can we say about the religious situations of Rakhaing? Canonical texts were quoted in inscriptions, which leads us to the assumption that the Pāḷi canon existed in some form in the Rakhaing *Vesālī* coastal region by the fifth century AD at least. The inscriptions were compiled consciously from several texts in such a way as to show a mastery of diverse sources. There is also some evidence for the presence of other Hinayāna sects, but due to the paucity of data, they cannot be identified with any certainty.

Beginning with the eighth century AD, traces of *Mahāyāna* Buddhism were found mainly in the reign of King Ānanadacandra. Even though *Mahāyāna* Buddhism influenced *Theravāda* Buddhist culture, the older, local traditions continued to flourish.

422 Paranavitana, "*Mahāyānism in Ceylon.*"

5.2. A Brief Account of Buddhism in Lay-mro Period (AD 818–1430)

After *Vesālī*, Pañsā was found by Lay-mro dynasty in AD 818. Changing the capital at least five times over its five centuries a series of small Rakhaing cities: Pañcā, Parien, Narañjarā Taungoo, Launggret along the bank of Lay-mro River (formerly Añjananadī) succeeded each other. The transfer was done most probably owing to the shiftless course of the Lay-mro currents. Little apart from the remains of city walls survives from the Lay-mro period. As in former *Vesālī* period Buddhism continued to flourish in Lay-mro valley. All the cities had been located near the river, as times went by, most of all old remains were disappeared by the river erosion apart from some, which are in the high mounts. As this period was contemporary of Bagan and Innwa of Burma, Anawrahta and his grandson Alaungsithu of Bagan Empire made two unsuccessful attempts to carry off the Mahāmuni Image during this time. Inscriptions with Rakkhavanna (Rakhaing alphabets) evolved from Brahmi script are evident in this period. Some of the inscriptions linked with Buddhism are presented here.[423]

Launggret Taung Maw Inscription: It was written in the beginning of the twelfth century AD by King Koliya (AD 1118–1123). It is so called because of written on the rock of Launggret Taung Maw (Launggret Mount). The old palace wall (half a mile long, one thousand feet wide, and twenty feet high) was washed away by the mighty Lay-mro currents by the turn of century. Today scarcely anything except the Launggret Taungmaw hill stone inscription (thirty feet long and twenty feet high), which throws light on the deeds of merit of the Lay-mro kings, is left of the period.

Mahāhtee Kyauk Mi Jaung Inscription: Popularly known as crocodile inscription the name of the inscription took its name

423 *State Gazetteer (Culture)* pp. 29–32.

from the crocodile shape of the stone. The inscription is carved on a slope of a small hillock south of Mahāhtee Buddha Image. This land grant was given in 1356. Three miles west of Launggret, King Koliya built Mahāhtee or Great Monk (Mahāthero or the Buddha himself) Pagoda was built to mark the victory over the lesser kings and lords and in decentralizing power in order to establish a greater Rakhaing. The present image was newly built after the original red sandstone image had been destroyed by the downpour English shells upon the Burmese troops haltered in the temple, in the first Anglo-Burmese War (1824–1826).

Nan Kya Gree Inscription: This inscription was written on the back of a Varada*mudrā* (standing Buddha Image) in Nan Kya village. The image was discovered from a place near See Thay village south of Nan Kya village. It was donated by King Latyar Murn Nan in AD 1125. The date of the inscription was written a litter later than Mya*zeti* Inscription of Pagan, the earliest inscriptions of Burma.

Nan Kyar Gree Buddha Image Inscription: It was engraved in AD 1238. Only the written year can be read, else characters are disappeared.

Mahābodhi Inscription: This was written in Mahābodhi Temple in India mentioning about the reconstruction and renovation of the temple by King Murn Htee in AD 1295, and after the renovation of the temple, a great donation ceremony was held three years later in AD 1298. It comprises nineteen lines of inscription by Rakkhavanna.

King Aloma Phru Inscription: It mentions about the visit of King Aloma Phru, founder of Launggret city, to Sri Lanka in AD 1256. In the inscription it has engraved "Thein Kho Ruck Murn" (king who reached Thein Kho, Sri Lanka) referring to King Aloma Phru.

Manaung Budaung Kwae Inscription: It was written in AD 1063 mentioning about ordering law with Rakkhavanna mixed Sanskrit language.

Prun-laung-rwa-thone-tan-su Inscription: In the inscription, it was written in AD 1238 mentioning about King Murn Htee's visit to Sri Lanka.

This period culture was not much influenced by India. Chewing betel during King Murn Htee was significant. The Rakhaing traditional way of striking drum started King Nan Kyar Gree's reign. Pāḷi was largely used here and there. Rakhaing literature of its own character was born, rich with poetry, and many other styles of literature flourished in this period. Rakhaing Revered Aggasara wrote the famous "Lokasara Pyot Poem" during King Murn Htee's reign (AD 1333–1343). Shuk Htoone literature along the period was famous. Of them Minister Kavi Kyaw, The Wise Purohita Guru, Minister Vijala, and Chittagong Governor Vimala were noteworthy.[424] The following narratives are taken from Ven. Candamalalankara's "New Rakhaing Chronicle" and translated very briefly related to Buddhism.

5.2.1. Pañcā city

In Pañcā city, fifteen kings reigned for 285 years (AD 818–1103). In this dynasty Arahat Saccapaṇṇava Thera was noteworthy during King Khetta Thein. Panca is located to the east of Mrauk Oo. Almost nothing remains of this old city except some one hundred odd ponds in the northern part. Across the Lay-mro opposite Panca, Naranjara Taungoo is said to have flourished between AD 1160 and 1250. The city flourished before Launggret appeared on the scene.

It is found in Razapon manuscript that great King Murn Run Phru turned his attention toward the development of Buddhism, and in AD 847 he convened the second Buddhist council in Rakhaing attended by eight hundred Arahants.

424 *State Gazetteer (History)*, p. 78

Rakhaing Chronicles report that therein the Tipiṭaka and Aṭṭhakathā were inscribed on the golden plates by Rakhaing script using the Pāḷi language and enshrined later in U Reit Taung pagoda by King Murn Phalaung in Mrauk Oo period. Twenty-eight crossed-leg Buddha images were commissioned to cast by pañcalohā (*viz.* of gold, silver, copper, iron, and tin). In his reign it had relationship with Sri Lanka as earlier in *Vesālī* period.[425]

5.2.2. First Purein City

Because of Minister Asankhaya's aggression, King Murn Ray Baya, son of King Bilu, the twelfth king of Pañcā city, fled together with his son and daughter to Pagan king Anawratha. Latyat Murn Nan and Shwe Gu Thar Devi, son and daughter of King Murn Ray Baya, returned back to Rakhaing to regain the throne with the help of Pagan king. And he established the first Purein city in the nineteenth year of King Kyan Sit Thar of Pagan.

North of Launggret lies the old city of Parein. Twelve kings came to its throne between AD 1103 and 1160. Only vanishing trails of King Koliya's palace site and Pah-ree and Nah-ree Pagodas remain as silent testimonies to the existence of the splendorous city.

5.2.3. Second Purein city

In AD 1123 the city was built by King Dasarāzā, son of King Koliya. According to chronicle, he donated many things to his people and ruled his subjects righteously. He rediscovered hidden Mahāmuni Image, and housed for the Image.

---

425 Oo, Aung Tha. *Rakhaing Razawon Cultural History and View of Scholars.* p. 25–31; *State Gazetteer (History)* p. 77.

5.2.4. Naranjara Taungoo city

The city was established by King Manju Thein in AD 1171. He was a great supporter of Buddhism building of many Buddha images, *cetiya*s by recording 'Donation of Rakhaing king' to commemorate his donation in later time.

During the reign of King Thetkya Won Nge, a great donation ceremony was held at Mahāmuni Temple in AD 1222. He also distributed many copies of Tipitakas all over Rakhaing land, and supported bhikkhus in this country and abroad.

During King Tha Nat Pum Phru, son of King Thetkya Won Nge, followed suit with the way his father did, nourishing the Buddhasāsana. His son, King Nga Na Lone was also like his father.

5.2.5. Launggret city

By the Lay-mro River, five miles east of Maruk Oo, city of Launggret flourished from AD 1250 to 1430 under seventeen kings. King Murn Htee happened to be the longest-living and the most prominent ruler of this city. Merely seven when he ascended the throne in AD 1283, his legendary uprightness in making and following the law is still remembered. Internal strife and the power play of invading Inwa and Hanthawaddy troops drew the last days of Launggret into chaos. King Alo Ma Phru, the founder of Launggret city is reported to have been visited to Sri Lanka, the heartland of Buddhism after its demise in India. He was called "Thein Kho Ruck Murn (king who has been in Sri Lanka). The Rakhaing relations with Sri Lanka were mostly religious purpose in this period too, for example seeking to bring copies of Pāḷi tipiṭaka and their Aṭṭhakathā to Rakhaing land. The Royal patronage has always been significant factor contribution to stability and progress of the religion in Rakhaing.

North of Launggret Taungmaw, Pharabaung, and Tissa Phara Temple lies Nangya village. The 2′ 9" Tissa Phara stone image of King Murn Htee was built in the line of the Lay-mro period iconographic style. One-line inscription on the image cushion (asana, or seat) accounts the land grant of the meritorious king, supposed written in AD 1330. A little further west stands Mayrung Phara of King Dasarāzā.

Purification of Sāsana was done in AD 1394 during the reign of King Rāzathu, son of King Murn Htee.

5.3. A Brief Account of Buddhism in the Mrauk Oo Period

5.3.1. Political History

The period AD 1430–1530 is known as the first golden Mrauk Oo period. King Murn Saw Munn's brother, Naranu, came to power in 1433 and shortly thereafter concluded a bilateral agreement with the king of Burma, Min Khaung, which recognized the sovereignty and territorial integrity of both nations as independent states. The treaty established a border that lasted even through the British colonial era, separating the countries along the crest line of the Rakhaing Roma mountain range, down to the Ngawan River, to the Bassein River, and to the Martaban Sea. Haigree Island, Pagoda Point, and Cape Nagris were also recognized as Rakhaing territory.

The second golden Mrauk Oo period lasted from AD 1530 to 1620. In the early sixteenth century, around the time of King Henry VIII's coronation in England, King Murn Bun of Rakhaing ruled a thriving empire. Rakhaing was renowned for its modern army and advanced trade network, which covered the known world and extended as far as Portugal and the Netherlands. Mrauk Oo during this period enjoyed similarly far-reaching diplomatic relations, notably with India,

Sri Lanka, the Burmese, the Mon, Siam (Thailand), Indonesia, Java, Japan, and several western countries. Much closer links with the Muslim states and peoples to the west appear to have been made during this period, although it is unclear exactly why this occurred. Some historians have suggested that a debt was owed to the Sultan of Bengal for supporting King Murn Saw Munns's return to power. At this time, many Rakahing kings adopted Islamic names, coins were inscribed with Persian as well as Rakhaing, and hundreds of Muslims from Bengal migrated to the area in and around Mrauk Oo.

During this era, many areas of modern Bangladesh and West Bengal were fought over by the kings of Rakhaing, Mughal emperors, Afghan kings, and various Bengali Sultans. A city of particular importance was the booming commercial center of Chittagong. Few details of these conflicts have survived, but it is known that during the reign of King Murn Bunn (1531–1553) Rakhaing forged close ties with the Portuguese, whose presence (and influence) in the region was quickly expanding. These ties helped the Rakhaing to develop a superior military and navy, which helped them defeat several rival kingdoms in the region, and capture Chittagong. According to various Rakhaing scholars, by 1532 the Rakhaing frontier extended up to Calcutta in West Bengal, India, encompassing the whole of modern day Bangladesh. By the end of the sixteenth century, noblemen in Mrauk Oo received tribute from cities as far away as Mushidabad in the west, to the Mon capital of Pegu in the east, and much of lower Burma. Their power was maintained in these areas by thousands of Mughal, Burmese, Japanese, Mon, Siamese, and Portuguese mercenaries.

The dominant theme of seventeenth-century Rakhaing history was the kingdom's struggle to preserve its vast empire. During the early part of the century, border tensions between the

Rakhaing and Mughal empires escalated and developed into full-blown conflicts. Most of East Bengal came firmly under the authority of the Mughal king; around the same time the Kingdom of Ava rose to power and Rakhaing lost its grip on Pegu and much of lower Burma.

Its huge, modern navy helped Rakhaing hold power in Eastern Bengal throughout the first half of the seventeenth century. During this period, thousands of Bengali slaves were taken by the Rakhaing, and many were sold to the Dutch to work on nearby plantations.

In the 1730s a number of internal disputes in the Mrauk Oo administration led to a breakdown of national unity and significant political instability. In 1638, King Sirisudhamma died, followed by his only heir. A powerful lord named Launggret then took the throne by force and executed most of the royal court. His reign was the first of several that brought about the gradual demise of Rakhaing's prosperity.

In the late seventeenth century, the Mughal Empire forged closer relations with the Dutch and was able to significantly modernize its military. In 1660, the Mughals took Dhaka, previously under the rule of the Bengali sultan Shah Shuja, precipitating a notable influx of Muslims to Mrauk Oo. In 1666 they annexed Chittagong after almost a century-long struggle, depriving the Rakhaing Kingdom of a key source of income. The Mughal Emperor subsequently allowed the expanding British East India Company to establish a *diwan,* or de facto governmental body, in the area; in 1772, the Company established a capital at Calcutta and took control of the majority of what had been Western Rakhaing.

In mid-November 1784 a Burmese army led by King U Wine (Bodaw Phaya) invaded Mrauk Oo without declaring war. U Wine likely received some help from the inside, by exploiting some of the many feuds among the Rakhaing nobility. By the end of that year, the Burmese had occupied the whole country, and "The Dark Age of Rakhaing" had dawned.

5.3.2. Buddhist Culture

There is a saying verse in Rakhaing regarding how many Phara are in Mrauk Oo:

"*Thazurn*[426] pan khaing ta mraing mraing
Rakhaing phara paung"[427]
The *Thazurn*'s sprigs in cheer clusters
Sum the total of Rakhaing phara grandeur.[428]

Not only Rakhaing is rich in natural resources, but it is also rich in the establishment of the Buddhist monasteries, pagodas which play a very creative role to development of Rakhaing culture and civilization. Rakhaing offers some of the richest archaeological sites in the Southeast Asia. A number of Buddhist landmarks erected by the Rakhaing are still be found intact or the archaeological ruins under the earth. In the city of golden Mrauk Oo, there are innumerable temples and pagodas that

426 "Thazon" is a kind of orchid.

427 The verse enunciates multitude of phras by placing letters for numbers using a formula in which the alphabets are assigned in the order thus arranged to represent the days of the week.
Formula: Tha-zon pan khaing ta mraing mrain
6 3 5 2 7 5 5

According to Days of the week	Letters assigned
2. Monday	ka, kha, ga, gha, nga;
3. Tuesday	sa, has, za, zha, nya;
7. Saturday	ta, hta, da, dha, na;
5. Thursday	pa, hpa, ba, bha, ma;
4. Wednesday	la, wa;
* Rahu (midday to midnight Wednesday)	ya, ra;
6. Friday	tha, ha;
1. Sunday	ah.

428 Hla, U Tha. *The Rakhaing Magazine*. Vol.1. No.7 (2000)

are preserved as places, thereby exerting a great influence on spiritual life of the people.

Rakhaing chronicle records that more than six million shrines and pagodas flourished in Mrauk Oo. In fact, they formed the pride of golden Mrauk Oo. Dr. Forchhammer described in his "Arakan," "In durability, architectural skill, and ornamentation the Mrohaung (*Mrauk Oo*) temples far surpass those on the banks of Irrawaddy."[429] Buddhist arts both in the field of architecture and Buddha-image constructions are on the same line of flourishing. An illustrative example of this fact can be seen in the temple of Chitthaung pagoda and colossal Dukekanthein temple. Hence Rakhaing with its rich legacy has been able to achieve a great success in enriching and disseminating their culture and civilization. Even at the present, these cultural heritage lives sources are precious legacies of sacred symbols of Buddhism since the Rakhaings are conscious of the contributions of their country toward the growth and development of their culture, literature, and spiritual heritage, they are anxious to see their ancestral land once more restored to its pristine glory.

The old capital of Mrauk Oo was founded in 1430.[430] It was built upon a far older city with first-millennium walls and earthen works probably used for the management of water. It is mostly known now, however, for it scores of spectacular stone monuments spread over many kilometers built in the Mrauk Oo period (1430–1784). The city flourished between the fifteenth and seventeenth centuries when it was a regional

429 Forchhammer, Dr. E. *Arakan.* p. 31.

430 Tun Aung Chain (2004) p. 129

commercial and cultural center.[431] Its lavish court life was described by a seventeenth-century Portuguese Augustinian monk, Father Sebastian Manrique, whose account was immortalized by Maurice Collis in his 'The Land of the Great Image.' In the same century another description with engravings made from drawings was made by Wouter Schouten, an employee of the United East India Company, or the Verenigde Ostindische Compagnie (VOC).[432]

In Mrauk Oo itself the most important shrine today is the Shitthaung Pagoda, nestled against a ridge just north of the old palace site. Shithaung literally means "eighty thousand," rounded off from eighty-four thousand, the number immortalized by Asoka who enshrined that many relics in stupas throughout India. The unspecified relics are believed to be inside the central stupa placed over the sanctum. The Shithaung was founded in 1536 by King Murn Bunn, according to the chronicles. The temple is thought to commemorate his victories in Bengal over twelve provinces, or the "twelve towns of Bhanga."[433] For this reason, the temple is also called "Temple of Victory," or Ran Aung Zeya. This association with military might and the eighty-four thousand relics are the only two features underlying the sanctity of the monument today. The central stone Buddha statue, now gilded, is seated upon its original sixteenth-century ornamented stone base. The image dominates its small camber, access to which is via a narrow corridor. The sanctum is surrounded by two concentric corridors. On either side of the inner corridor are twenty-eight Buddhas,

431 Leider (2002)

432 Raymond (2002)

433 Leider (2002) p. 145

representing the twenty-eight Buddhas in *Theravāda* belief. Figural carving is lavished on the inner side wall of the outermost corridor where its surface is divided into six horizontal registers with hundreds of figures. Collectively, the imagery may represent the 'world of desire' in a structured Buddhist universe.[434] Some of the sculptures still retain bits of original colored glazing. The most complex figures are on the corners, with at least one representing Indra upon his elephant and flanked by his four loyal but troublesome wives. The nicest are whimsical depictions of wrestlers and everyday scenes. Earth goddesses are shown wringing out their hair at the time of Mara's defeat.[435] A small number of *Jatakas* are also said to be depicted, but this is difficult to prove.

The court and Saṁgha also had strong ties to Sri Lanka, with missions from the island bringing the Tipiṭaka from time to time. For example, the Andaw stupa in Mrauk Oo is thought to contain a tooth-relic from Sri Lanka. There was even a time in the seventeenth century when a reform movement was began in Sri Lanka, with Rakhaing monks at the center, with Dutch ships facilitating the exchanges. There were also bronze Buddha figures probably sent from Sri Lanka to Rakhaing.[436] Casting ateliers were also influenced from China, notably during the Yongle period (1403–1424) when Sino-Tibetan styles converged.[437]

434 Gutman (2001) p. 96

435 Raymond (1998)

436 Raymond (1999)

437 Gutman (2001) p. 149

Remarks

As we have presented above, Sanskrit influence in *Vesālī* does not mean that Buddhism flourished in ancient *Vesālī* period was Mahāyānist; it was mainly because of geography—Rakhaing Land had been directly by land connected with northern India (i.e., Nālanda). And during that period, Sanskrit had been a *lingua franca* and the official language of the Rakhaing court. But almost all the evidence shows that it was *Theravāda* type of Buddhism that flourished throughout the *Vesālī*, Lay-mro, and Mrauk Oo periods. Notably, during the *Vesālī* period, the practice of *Theravāda* Buddhism with Brahminal background are found, but not in the successive Lay-mro and Mrauk Oo periods.

CHAPTER 6

ARAKAN BUDDHIST RELATIONS WITH SRI LANKA

Introduction

The present day Arakan was known as *Rakkhaṅgadesa* to most of the Islanders in ancient days, while the present day Sri Lanka was known as *Thein Kho Kywan* (*lit.* Lion Island) or *Thein Kho Pray* (*lit.* Lion Country) to Arakanese peoples in the times past.

Only after western people arrived to the east especially the English people, recent political boundary speaks in the studies difficult.

They have divided South Asia, Southeast Asia, East Asia, etc.[438] Geographically Arakan has been by far the nearest frontier to India in relation between so-called South Asia and Southeast Asia. It is however more appropriate to take into account Arakan as an easternmost part of India for its distinct culture.

As Sri Lanka contributed by far the most in the history of Buddhism especially for the advancement of Buddhist learning not only in the land but abroad as well, the Buddhist land like *Rakkhaṅgadesa* (Arakan) had to pay back their outmost gratitude to Sri Lanka, then-source of Buddhist knowledge, when Sri Lanka had to go through difficult times of its deterioration of *Buddhasāsana* sometimes in the history due to its political instability.

The propagation and successive growth of Buddhism in Arakan (*Rakkhaṅgadesa* or *Rakkhaṅgapura*) reveal the treasured relations that exist between the Island of Sri Lanka and Arakan land, not for a

438 The term "Southeast Asia" is of recent vintage. German writers of the late nineteenth century occasionally used the term. It gained some currency when the British during the Second World War created Lord Louis Mountbatten's Southeast Asia Military Command which included Ceylon, now Sri Lanka. It became more or less a household term when the Cold War was already raging in earnest in the mid-1950s and the West was impelled by regional events to create a military alliance called the Southeast Asia Treaty Organization (SEATO). Source: http://www.aseansec.org/11834.htm

Before the Second World War, the term "Southeast Asia" was scarcely a geographic expression and was rarely used. The region of the peninsula between India and China was included in the term "Far East." Some authors called the region "Further India." During the Second World War, the Japanese army used the term "Greater East Asia" to include countries of Southeast Asia. The term "Southeast Asia" is credited to the Indian historian K. M. Pannikar, who used it in the title of his book, *Future of Southeast Asia*, published in 1943. Due to military and strategic considerations during the Second World War, the region came to be regarded as a separate geographic entity, and the Allied Supreme Command adopted the term "Southeast Asia." By the end of the war, the term was well established and was used as a collective for the peninsula between India and China. The countries include Brunei, Burma, Thailand, Laos, Cambodia, Vietnam, Malaysia, Singapore, and Indonesia. Some organizations include the Philippines in Southeast Asia. Countries in and adjacent to the Indian subcontinent, namely, India, Pakistan, Bangladesh, Nepal, Bhutan, Sri Lanka, and Maldives are considered as belonging to "South Asia."

Source: http://www.searo.who.int/en/Section898/Section1443.htm

period of barely a few centuries earlier, but for a long epoch, well over two millennia since the visit of the Buddha to both countries in their stories handed down from generation to generation. Similarly, the *Dhammadūta* missions of Emperor Asoka, with the proper guidance of *Mahāthera Moggaliputtatissa* who presided over the third Buddhist council held in *Pātaliputta* (modern Patna) on the conclusion of which *Thera Mahinda* and his retinue came to Sri Lanka and *Thera Mahādeva* accompanied by five monks are said to have visited Arakan[439] in order to establish the *Buddhasāsana*, the noblest services to humanity ever known to the history and religions of the world, contemporaneously sprinkled the spirit of a new enlightened life to both countries, as recorded in the annals of history, a blessing that benefitted the peoples who lived and are living in both countries, basically following the *Theravāda Pāḷi* Buddhism.

The Rakhaing Chronicles unanimously state that the Buddhist relationships between the two countries had existed since two centuries after the Christian era, long before the great commentator Buddhaghosa who translated the *Sinhalaṭṭhakathās* into Pāḷi at Anuradhapūra in the fifth century AD.[440]

No one who writes any Buddhist history in Southeast Asia or even a history of Buddhism in general can leave out the important role of Ceylon. Eventually, after the third century BC, the Buddhist scholarship from India moved to the island, where present available source what it is called Pāḷi Buddhism has survived in the hands of Sinhalese

439 See 4.8. of Chapter IV, Asoka Mission

440 Candamalālaṅkāra, Ven. "*Rakhaing Razawon Theik Kyan*" (New Arakan Chronicle Vols. I and II in Burmese), 1st pub. Hanthavadi Press, Rangoon, 1931, reprinted by Publishers of Eminent Arakan Literature (PEAL), Rangoon, November 1997.; Ñāṇa, Ven. "*Dhaññavatī Razawon Theik*" (New Dhaññavatī Chronicle), Vols. 1 and 2, 1st pub. Hanthavadi Press, Rangoon. (1954), reprinted by PEAL, Rangoon, July 1996.; Oo, Aung Tha. "*Rakkha Maṇḍala Arakan Razawon*" (Rakkhamaṇḍala Arakan Chronicle), Mraratana Press, Rangoon, 1955.

monks at the Mahāvihāra (Great Monastery) in the city of Anurādha.[441] Therein the Buddhist scriptures have developed and spread to other shores through the Bay of Bengal throughout centuries. Whereby, the Buddhist scriptures have reached into *Rakkhaṅgadesa* that we have known with the help of the Rakhaing Chronicles.

Dr. Wagenaar observes that the "Golden Age" of Arakanese Theravāda Buddhism was unthinkable without the import of many copies of the *Tipiṭka* or scripture form Sri Lanka; and close to the *Mahāmuni* the famous image of Buddha, libraries had been built to keep those holy texts, to be venerated by the *Saṅgha*. Long before the gift to Siam of a replica of the tooth of the Buddha, Arakan had got one from Sri Lanka in the reign of Min Bin (1531–1571), placed in a relic shrine in the Andaw Stupa. This demonstrates how much the two countries esteemed each other.[442]

Studies into the history, religions, language, literature, arts, sciences and social conditions of the present and former peoples of the Island of Sri Lanka connected with Arakan, if any, has been neglected or not paid attention to it deserves, especially when they have studied Sri Lankan Buddhist interactions with Burma. This has encouraged me to take into the study of Sri Lankan–Arakan Buddhist relationships.

The main objective of this chapter, therefore, is to reelucidate relationships between the two Buddhist countries as revealed by the local accounts together with the existing secondary literature, and to attempt to give a fairly over all feature of Buddhist intercourses between them. It is especially to correct some mistaken names of Arakan (Rakhaing) and to supplement some missing points in the writings of earlier scholars in this field.

441 Rahula, Wapola. "*History of Buddhism in Ceylon*" Colombo: BCC, 3rd Ed., 1993; Adikarama, W. "*Early History of Buddhism in Ceylon*" Colombo: BCC, 1994; Panabokke, Gunaratne. "*History of the Buddhist Sangha in India and Sri Lanka*" PGIPBS, 1993.

442 See de Silva (2006), pp. 175–176.

6.1. Sources

Arakan is unknown to most of Sri Lankan academics[443] in different fields especially in the cultural history mainly due to the land has no longer been an independent sovereign in present days. Dr. Pamela Gutman,[444] an expert in the cultural history of Arakan, notes, "In 1784 it was conquered by the Burmese ruler Bodawpaya (February 11, 1782–June 5, 1819) and the revered Mahāmuni Image was taken to Mandalay. With its loss, the Arakanese people seemed to lose heart, and its shrines and images were largely neglected for the next 200 years. It is only recently, with the emergence of Mrauk Oo as a tourist destination, that the Burmese government has begun to restore some of the monuments."

The primary sources in which this chapter is based are sources mostly stone inscriptions and Arakanese and Sinhalese literary sources.

Concerning Arakanese Buddhist relations with Ceylon and *vice versa,* recent Sri Lanka scholars have come to the conclusion that the relation of both Ceylon and Arakan was around the fourteenth century AD. Here, as stated above, it is however to be noted that the Buddhist links between the two countries had been since the second century AD according to the Rakhaing sources. For the later

443 Wickremasinghe, Sirima. "Ceylon's Relations with Southeast Asia with special reference to Burma" *The Ceylon Journal of Historical and Social Studies*, Vol. 3 (1960), pp. 38–58.; Pe, U San. "*Cultural Links between Ceylon and Burma.*" The New Lanka A Quarterly Review, Vol. 1, No. 4. (July 1950), pp. 45–52.; Dias, Malini. "Historical Relations of Ancient Sri Lanka and Myanmar." *Ancient and Medieval Commercial Activities in the Indian Ocean: Testimony of Inscriptions and Ceramic-sherds, Report of the Taisho University Research Project 1997–2000*, Ed. by Noboru Karashima, pp.170–183.

444 http://www.rakhapura.com/scholars-column/22-between-india-and-southeast-asia-arakan-burmas-forgotten-kingdom.html accessed on March 9, 2012.

centuries, Sinhalese sources: the Colombo Museum *Cūrṇṇikā-pota,*[445] *Kaḍadora Grant,*[446] the British Museum *Rakkhaṅga-sannas-cūṇikāva,*[447] *Cūlavaṁsa,*[448] *Sāsanavaṁsa,*[449] *Sūlurājāvaliya*[450] reveal information about Buddhist missions sent by Arakan to Sri Lanka owing to the diplomatic requests made by the kings of Lanka in regard to the Buddhist revivals in the Island.

Referring to Dr. Fernando, a scholar who read this manuscript earlier, Nanadasena Mudiyanse says that the *Rakkhaṅgasannascūṇikāva* is a short document of eight palm leaves, now available at the British Museum Library, London, gives the contents of the text and says that it is a very brief account of the first mission sent by Vimaladharmasūriya II to Arakan, of the eight leaves of that manuscript, only three leaves and the first page of the last leaf are said to contain this brief account.[451]

Again, it is mentioned by Mirando that another work that belongs also to the reign of Vimaladharmasūrya II is the *Rakkhangasāsanacūṇikāva* which contains besides a collection of formal address adopted in writings to the king, also an account of the enquires Vimaladharmasurya II made in regard to the ordination

---

445 "*Curnika Pota*" Catalog no. J -3. (Deposited at the National Museum of Colombo, Sri Lanka)

446 Godakumbara (*Edit. and trans.*), C. E. "Kaḍadora Grant, an ola leaf manuscript from the Kadadora vihara in the Central Province" *JCBARS*, New Series, Vol. II, 1952.

447 See Fernando (1959)'s work.

448 "*Culavaṁsa*" Pt. II. Ch. 94, pp. 228–229; Ch. 97, pp. 239–240.

449 "Sāsanavaṁsa" p.27.

450 "*Sulurājāvaliya*" Published by C. D. S. K. Jayawadena, 1914, p. 22

451 See Mudiyanse (1971): pp. 26.

from the Rakkhangadesa," referring the British Museum manuscript number Or. 6611 (258).[452]

About the *Cūrṇṇikā-pota* at the National Museum Library, Colombo, Nandasena Mudiyanse remarks, "It may be that these notes were read aloud before the king-in-council. The manuscript, which is marked *J.3* is made up of 60 ola leaves written on both sides. In W. A. de Silva's *Catalogue of Palm Leaf Manuscripts,* it is referred to as a collection of letters dispatched by the kings of Kandy. The subject matter of the *Cūrṇṇkā-pota* is varied. The first five leaves deal with such matters as administration of justice (*rāja-nīti*) and the arrival in the Kandyan Court of an ambassador from the Dutch Governor in Colombo. Leaves numbered six to fifteen contain detailed accounts of the two embassies to Arakan, dealt with by Sir D. B. Jayatilaka. Each page consists of about 8 or 9 lines of writing which admits of no difficulties in reading. As usual in ola manuscripts of the Kandy period, there has been no consistency in the use of *n ṇ l ḷ*. There are also some other irregularities in spelling, typical of this period..."[453]

Additionally, the studies by Sir D. B. Jayatilaka[454] (using the Sinhalese text Curnika: British Library and Colombo Museum), Dr. Fernando[455] (using the same sources), Nandasena

452 Mirando, A. H. "Buddhism in Sri Lanka in the Seventeenth and Eighteenth Centuries with Special Reference to Sinhalese Literary Sources." *The Ceylon Historical Journal Monograph Series,* Vol. X, Pub. Tisara Prakasakayo Ltd., (1985), pp. 84.

453 See Mudiyanse (1971) pp. 26–27.

454 Sir D. B. Jayatilaka, "Sinhalese Embassies to Arakan." *JRASCB* Vol. XXXV (1940): 1–6.

455 P. E. E. Fernando, "The Rakhanga—Sannas-Curnikava and the Date of the Arrival of Arakanese Monks in Ceylon." *UCR* Vol. XVII, Nos. 1&2 (1959), pp. 41–46.

Mudiyanse,[456] Dr. Raymond,[457] Dr. Lodewijk Wagenaar,[458] Bandu de Silva,[459] Hema Goonatilake,[460] etc. are useful for this study.

Notably, only Buddhist mission that Arakan sent to Sri Lanka in order to reestablish the Buddhist order during the reign of King Vimaladhammasuriya II in 1697 has been inserted in the volume two of the History of Sri Lanka edited by Prof. K. M. de Silva published by the University of Peradaniya.[461] Using above mentioned sources especially the *Cūlavaṁsa* and articles integrated in the Journals of the Royal Asiatic Society of Sri Lanka, Kanai Lal Harza discuses two Buddhist missions from Arakan to Sri Lanka in the reigns of Vimaladhammasuriya I and II.[462] In fact, they have done some good work on its subject of links between the two countries. It is, however, worthy to note that according to available local

456 Nandasena Mudiyanse, "Cultural Missions to Arakan (Rakkhanga-Desa)," *JCBRAS* (new series) Vol. XV (1971): pp. 26–35.

457 C. Raymond, "Archaeological Evidence of Buddhist Links between Sri Lanka and Arakan." *Ancient Ceylon: Journal of the Archaeological Survey Department of Sri Lanka, No. 12, Vol. 6.* Colombo: Commissioner of Archaeology, Department of Archaeology, 1990, pp. 9–26

458 Lodewijk Wagenaar, "Looking for monks from Arakan, a chapter of the Kadyan-Dutch relations in the Eighteenth century" *JRASSL* (new series) Vol. XLVIII, 2003, pp. 91–110.

459 D. G. Bandu de Silva, "A Study on Trincomalee in the Sixteenth and Seventeenth centuries with Special reference to relations with Arakan as revealed by Portuguese Sources" *JRASSL* (new series) Vol. LII, 2006, pp. 175–208.

460 Hema Goonatilake, "Sri Lanka-Myanmar Historical Relations in Religion, Culture and Polity." *JRASSL* (new series) Vol. LV, 2009, pp. 77–114.

461 K. M. de Silva (ed.), 1995. *History of Sri Lanka*, Vol. 2, Colombo: University of Ceylon Press Board. p. 202.

462 Kanai Lal Harza, *History of Theravāda Buddhism in Southeast Asia with special reference to India and Ceylon.* New Delhi: Munshiram Manoharlal Publishers, Second edition (2002). pp. 121–125.

literary accounts,[463] Sri Lanka and Arakan had religious contacts since the second century AD onward.

Moreover, Arakanese sources on Sri Lanka and Arakan relationships being scattered in recent writings of the eminent local scholars such as U Aung Tha Oo, U San Tha Aung, U Tun Shwe Khine, Ven. Cakkinda, and Goyamray Saw Won, and in different magazines, periodicals, and journals published in Arakan and Burma proper based primary on the chronicles and a number of Arakanese ancient lyrical poems, have been also read for this study as the secondary sources.

6.2. Pāḷi: The Identity of Thera Tradition and Tool of Communication

Without having a number of connections with Sri Lanka since the beginning of Christian era, Arakanese Buddhist society would never have been a Theravāda proper among religious milieus in ancient Arakan. Despite the fact that the ascendency of *thera* tradition of the third century BC Buddhist missionary monks has been found in the local chronicles, our present knowledge never reaches concrete into that area owing mainly to lack of supporting evidence.

It was possible to establish a cordial relationship between Sri Lanka and Arakan as both had widespread association on Theravāda Buddhism, and both depended on each other for the higher ordination of *bhikkhūs* when this facility was not available in one country. Such historical information makes local chronicles of both countries unique, sometimes supplemented by epigraphic evidence, which not only gives the sketches of the Buddhist relationships between these countries but also provides the building blocks for the development of the religious history

463 *New Razawon*; *State Gazetteer (Culture)*

of the two countries. With the spread of Buddhism, the two countries gained mutual cooperation under the common banner of Buddhism.

Buddhist studies in Arakan and Sri Lanka have been mainly in the Pāḷi language, even though they pronounce it phonetically different owing to the geographical and ethnographical backgrounds. The Pāḷi has been employed and exercised as what the Buddha taught. In Theravāda tradition it is firmly believed that Māgadhī has been used by the Buddha to teach his *Dhammavinaya,* that language was yet to be called Pāḷi. It is undeniable fact that among *Theravadins* monks might have used Pāḷi to communicate each other even though the difference in race or land may be, in other words, the language of Pāḷi might have been *lingua francs* among the Theravāda milieu.

The cordial relationship between Sri Lanka and Arakan could be attributed to Pāḷi, in which language the doctrines of the Buddha were known to both countries. There were opportunities to the scholars of the two countries to be acquainted with the books available to both countries. In addition to this, it is evident in the famous *Ānandacandra* Inscriptions that there had been a practice for both countries to exchange costly gifts and maintain cordial friendship. A number of Arakanese inscriptions bear testimony to the historical relations that had existed between Arakan and Sri Lanka.[464]

Mirando mentions, "We have already observed that the study of *Pāḷi* existed to some extent from the time of Alagiyavanna. It is also known that Vaṭaṁbuḷuve Mahāthera was proficient in *Pāḷi* as to have been able to converse in that language at the higher ordination ceremony conducted by the monks from

464 Ānandacandra Inscriptions (c. AD 729), King Alomāphru Inscription (AD 1256); Prun-laung-rwa-thone-tan-su Inscription (AD 1238)

Rakkhaṅgadesa in the reign of Vimaladhrmasūriya II." referring Samgharājasādhusariyāva p.2.[465]

Going through the Sinhalese literary sources available as far as the Buddhist relationship between the two countries, it is evident that Pāḷi as a communication might have been used by the ambassadors sent from Sri Lanka to Arakan.

6.3. Unknown in the Sri Lankan Sources

In order to reveal Arakanese sources unknown in Sri Lanka, here it will be appropriate to describe a short introduction of the background situations in Buddhist Sri Lanka.

In the middle of the third century BC[466] during the reign of Devānaṁpiyatissa, the great Buddhist missionary Thera Mahinda arrived in Laṅkadīpa: in short, Buddhism gained the status of the state religion of the island by the firm support of the king. The Mahāvihāra was well-established at Anurādhapura by the close of the third century BC.[467] A century later, Vattagāmaṇiabaya (29–17 BC)[468] built the Abhayagirivihāra, a second major school of monastic learning in the city of Anurādha.

By the close of the first century BC, there was a surfeit of important events in Anuradhapura: the city was ruled by five Hindu Tamil kings from 43 to 29 BC, and the Buddhist King Vattagāmani went into hiding. In 13 BC, Mahācūlika Mahātissa was succeeded by Vattagāmani Abhaya's son, Coranaga. He was hostile to Buddhism and destroyed eighteen vihāras, where he had been

465 *Ibid.* Mirando (1985) p.97.

466 *Dipavaṁsa* Vol. 7, p. 18 and pp. 39–54; *Mahāvaṁsa* Vol. 5, p. 195.

467 Rahula "*History of Buddhism in Ceylon.*" BCC, Colombo, 3rd Ed., 1993. p. 52.

468 *Mahāvamsa*, XXXIII, p. 18.

denied shelter earlier when he was staging a rebellion against his cousin, Mahācūlika Mahātissa (17–3 BC).[469]

During this era of disturbances the country was ravaged by a famine, popularly known as the Bramaṇatissa famine: according to myths, starving people were compelled to commit such atrocities as killing—and then eating—those same Buddhist monks whom they had previously venerated. With or without cannibalism, thousands of Buddhist monks and lay-people doubtless perished. Vihāras were deserted, even the Mahāvihāra was abandoned to the jungle, and the Mahāthūpa lay in complete neglect. Many monks left the island for India. The country was physically and spiritually devastated.[470]

Elder Sinhalese monks perceived that the future of Buddhism was endangered, since the continuation of the oral tradition of conveying the *Tipiṭaka* from teacher to pupil appeared no longer possible in such as tragic and murderous period. Attempting to safely preserve the Teachings of the Buddha (*Dhamma*) in a time of chaos, the far-sighted *mahatheras*—under the patronage of the local chief—assembled at Aluvihāra at Mātale (in the south of the island), and for the first time in Sri Lankan history, committed to writing the whole of the *Tipiṭaka*, along with the full commentaries (*aṭṭhakathās*), *in order that the True Doctrine might endure.*[471]

In the first century AD, dissension began to show up in the *Saṅgha,* which had till then had been united the influence of the *Mahāvihāra.* Later, the *Dhammarūci* sect (the *Abhayagirivihāra* group) separated from *Mahāvihāra* and founded *Jetavanavihāra,* which eventually became *Mahāyānā*-oriented.

---

469 *Ibid.* Rahula (1993) p. 85.

470 *Vibaṅga Aṭṭhakathā*, *Aṅguttaranikāya Aṭṭhakathā*, CSCD.

471 *Mahāvaṁsa*, XXXIII, pp. 100–101; *Dipavaṁsa*, XX, p. 45.

According to available Arakanese literary sources, Arakan had a contact with Ceylon in Dhaññavatī period, as the earliest relationship, in the reign of King Suriyasīri (AD 201–221), the twenty-second successor of historic King Candasuriya.[472] The account says "From Dhaññavatī city of Arakan, twenty *bhikkhus* led by Ñāṇasīrīdhipadi Mahāthera were sent to Lankadipa for a Buddhist missionary works in the reign of king Suriyasīri, after a period of Hindu ascendance in the Island."[473] The information has, however, not been supported by any Sinhalese sources, if any, as far as Arakanese contacts with Sri Lanka are concerned.

It has been recorded in the Rāzawon that in Vesālī period, King Siri Chandra (Siri Dhammavijaya) in AD 384, seeing the danger of advancing Mahayanist Bodhisava idea from India, that idealism would reached to Arakan and would be embraced by Brahamanas, approached to Cūlarevata Mahāthera, discussed about to hold a Buddhist council. Thus, a council, the fourth council as in the Arakanese chronicle, was held under the leadership of Cūlarevata Mahāthera at mount of Shwe Taung Gree in Arakan with the royal support. It took three years to write five thousand records of scriptures on the copper plates. In this council, one thousand monks from Sri Lanka and one thousand monks from Arakan gathered together. This information has been mentioned in verse 50 of the famous *Ānandacandra* Inscriptions, "many noble scriptures had been copied."

It is reported to Arakanese by a group of unknown epigraphists while they visit to Mrauk Oo that some of the recorded scriptures on the copper plates were deposited somewhere in Sri Lanka.

The earliest inscription in which Arakan interaction with Ceylon has been traced is in the *Nāgājunakoṇḍa* Inscription which

472 Rakhaing Magazine, Vol. IV, 1977, p.132.

473 Utinnalanka Nigone *(ola leaf Manuscript)* by U Pandi (formerly monk) of Rambree Bamboo Monastery (1873).

mentioned about a country called Kirāta or Cilāta resemblance with Arakan and lower Burma (i.e., *Suvaṇṇabhūmi* of the *Pāḷi* texts and medieval tradition) by Dr. Ray referring *Epigraphia Indica*, XX, pp. 22–23, Second Apsidal Temple, Insc. F. He remarks, "as the inscription is dated in the reignal year of the Ikṣvāku kings of the eastern Deccan who flourished in the third century AD, the conversion of the Kirāta country by the fraternity of monks of *Taṁbapaṁna* must have taken place sometime before that date."[474]

Dr. Sircar mentioned that Vanga (Bengal) province was a flourishing Buddhist center. The Buddhist missionary monks from Ceylon went to the region, according to the *Nāgājunakoṇḍa* Inscription inscribed in the third century AD.[475]

Referring to large footnoted references, Dr. Gutman remarks in her thesis, "Contact with the west via the Bay of Bengal was no doubt well-established by the beginning of the Christian era. The early references to "The Islands of Gold and Silver," which must have included Arakan, are vague."[476]

Moreover, with the help of the Ānandacandra Inscription in verse 62, the relationship between the two countries has been firmly identified. It is mentioned that the Arakanese king Ānandacandra sent a seat for Dhamma preacher (dharmāsana), a good female elephant, and brilliant cotton robes to the congregation of noble monks in the land of king Silāmegha. This might have happened earlier than AD 729 because scholars assigned the writing date of the inscription in AD 729 as King Ānandacandra mentioned the inscription was engraved after ninth year of his righteous ruling.

474 Ray (1946) p. 18.

475 D. C. Sircar, "Nagarjunikonda Inscription of Virapurushadatta." *Select Inscriptions bearing on Indian History and Civilization, Vol. I. from Sixth Century BC to Sixth Century AD.* Calcutta, 1965, p. 219.

476 Gutman (1976) p.7.

This king can be identified as Aggabodhi VI of Ceylon.[477] This fact is supported by many scholars, but Pamela Gutman misguided identification as Aggabodhi IV of Ceylon with King Silamegha.[478]

In Lay-mro period of Pañcā dynasty, in the reign of king Murn Run Phru (AD 843), a Buddhist council was held according to the Pāḷi Canon manuscripts of the fourth synod held at Aluvihāra in central Ceylon in the reign of Vaṭṭagāmaṇi Abaya. This was, as the eleventh council (ekādassama) held in Arakan, the council headed by Theras named Uttamasiri, Nandiya, Baddiya, Revata, Paduma, participated by eight hundred monks from Sri Lanka and eight hundred from Arakan.

Additionally, in the same period of Parein dynasty, in the reign of King Dasarāza (1123–1139), degeneration of Sāsana in Sri Lanka due to *adhammavādins* (unrighteous people), the king re-nourished Sri Lanka Buddhism by sending a group monks headed by Mahāthera Atulavijayagaṇapāmokkha accompanied by twenty-six monks.[479] Conducting religious exchanges with Sri Lanka by Arakan during this period has been mentioned thus in the local accounts, despite Sri Lankan sources are silent on this matter.

The Polonnaruva stone inscription of the Velaikkaras (AD 1137–1157) notes a purification revival conducted within three sects in Sri Lanka during the reign of Vijayabhahu I, with the assistance of Sangha delegates from *Arumana.* Referring to the

477 "*Culavamsa*" Pt. I, 48, 42; "*History of Ceylon*" University of Peradeniya Sri Lanka, Vol. I, Part I, p. 319.

478 Aung Tha Oo, "*Rakhaing Culture: Vesāli Period*" (1966), pp. 27 and 29; San Tha Aung, "*Ānanda Chandra Eighth Century Rakhaing Vesali King,*" (1975), pp. 149 and 180; *Rakhing Cultural and Traditional Customs* (1976 Jan), p.156; Gutman (1976), pp.37 and 49.

479 *Rakhaing Magazine*, Vol. IV, 1977, p.132.

Rakhaing chronicles, Raymond assumes that *Arumana* mentioned in the inscription can be one of the names for Arakan.[480]

Moreover, in the same period of Narañjarā Taung Ngu dynasty, in the reign of Nga Ra Man Murn Gree (AD 1166–1168), a delegation of Buddhist missionary headed by Mahāthera Uttaradhammasanghādhipadi accompanied by his thirty-six pupil monks were sent to Sri Lankan King Parakramabahu I (AD 1153–1186).[481] It is, however, the period between Vijayabahu I and Parakrambahu I can be considered as a dark chapter in Sri Lanka history. During this period neither Burmese sources such as the Sāsanavamsa and the "Glass Palace Chronicle," nor Sinhalese sources like the Cūlavamsa mention any religious or political contact between Sri Lanka and Burma.[482]

Additionally, according to the king Alomāphru Inscription in Lay-mro period, King Alomāphru visited the Lanka Island in AD 1256. In the inscription the king is inscribed as *Thein Kho Ruck Murn* (king who reached Ceylon -*Thein Kho*).[483]

In the inscription of Prun-laung-rwa-thone-tan-su, written in 600 RE (+638=AD 1238), mentions about King Murn Htee's visit to Sri Lanka.[484] According to Mahābodhi Inscription written in Rakkhavaṇṇa alphabet altogether nineteen lines, King Murn Htee

---

480 C. Raymond, "*Archaeological Evidence of Buddhist Links between Sri Lanka and Arakan.*" Ancient Ceylon, Journal of the Archaeological Survey Department of Sri Lanka, Papers submitted to the International seminar—Toward the Second Century of Archeology in Sri Lanka on July 7–13, 1990, Colombo, Vol. 6, Pub. the Commissioner of Archaeology, Dep. Of Archaeology, Colombo – 07, Sri Lanka, 1990. p. 14.

481 Candamalalankara, Ven. "*Rakhaing Rāzawon Theik Kyan*" Vol. I, 1931, p. 347.

482 *Ibid.* Raymond (1990)

483 *State Gazetteer (Culture)* p.31

484 *Ibid.*, p.32,

also paid a pilgrimage to Bodh Gaya in AD 1295 and repaired Mahābodhi Cetiya. When the renovation was finished in AD 1298 he had done a great donation therein.[485]

Unfortunately the detail descriptions of what the two aforementioned kings did in Sri Lanka are unknown to us. What we know is only their visit to Sri Lanka in their reigns.

The Golden Age of Mrauk Oo, extending from the fifteenth to the beginning of the seventeenth century, was also a high point of cooperation between Arakan and Sri Lanka. Considerable evidence indicates the close political, cultural, and religious ties then existing between these two countries: King Ba Saw Phru (AD 1459–1482) received the Tipitakas from Sri Lanka in AD 1476 and in return, sent a religious delegation to Lanka led by the famous Ven. Mahāthera Siddhatthāna along with fifty accompanied monks.[486]

During Murn Ba (Ba Saw Thiri) (AD 1525), while he was a king-to-be ruling in Sandoway at that time, Venerable Tejobhasa from Sandoway and Venerable Dhammavilāsa from Mrauk Oo were sent as Buddhist missionary to Sri Lanka. When they returned, they brought a tooth replica of the Buddha, and handed over to the king.

In the reign of King Murn Phalaung (AD 1571–1593), a missionary head by Venerable Nandicakka accompanied by forty monks was sent to Sri Lanka.

To sum up, thus far presenting only what in the light of available sources so far been found there might have remained many other instances of relationship between the two countries as both long histories of the countries had prevailed throughout centuries.

485 *Ibid.*, p. 31.

486 Candamalalankara, Ven. "*Rakhaing Rāzawon Theik Kyan*" Vol. II, 1931, p. 31.

6.4. Sri Lankan Buddhist Revivals in the Sixteenth and Seventeenth Centuries by Arakanese Saṅgha

An ola leaf manuscript, the Kaḍadora Grant found in Sri Lanka, refers to religious intercourse between Laṅkādīpa and Rakkhaṅgapura (Arakan) during the sixteenth century AD. The Arakanese missions to Sri Lanka during Vimaladhramasuriya I and II have been found, most of the contacts mentioned are the same with only slight difference, in the Sinhalese sources such as *Cūlavamsa, Nikāyasangaraha, Sulurājavaliya,* and the *Narendracaritavalokapradipikava,* the Colombo Museum *Cūrṇṇikāpota,* the British Museum *Rakkhaṅga-sannas-cūṇikāva.*

The following will discuss how Buddhism in Sri Lanka deteriorated under the Portuguese occupation, which led to Arakanese Buddhist monks being sent to Sri Lanka.

In a Christian monastery, life with rigorous schedules was centered around prayer and communal living. Prayer was to the Christian "God" and constituted a monk's main work which took up most of a monk's existence. While not praying, monks were given time to work on their activities of writing, copying, or decorating books. In this latter sense, Christian monasteries were centers of education and intellectual life.

Yet, the predominant ideology in these monasteries was that of the Dark Ages whose beginnings coincided with the burning of the excellent Library of Alexandria and other acts against free thought. And in the nearly one-thousand-year reign of the Inquisition, churches became the major center for torture and murder of persons who challenged the Pope's version of truth. This ideology of intolerance was transferred to Sri Lanka in the sixteenth century where the Portuguese burnt all the Buddhist centers.

The political intrigues of the country reached such a high climax, that the ruler of Kotte, Dharma Parakramabahu IX (AD

1506) invited the Portuguese to assist him in ousting his rivals. This gave the later an incentive to involve themselves in the political affairs of the country. The Portuguese by now had established a strong Empire in the West and were a powerful seafaring nation, bent on commercial enterprise and territorial expansion. Their policy of expansion was marked with a strong proselytizing movement. The request of the king of Kotte gave them a stepping stone toward the establishment of their claims in the island, and eventually the monarch granted them free trade rights for the assistance he received. Within a short time, numerous trade settlements were opened up in the Maritime Provinces of the island. Very soon, with characteristic duplicity, the Portuguese effected internecine warfare in the country, and demanded that the king place more faith in them and act according to their demands. The unscrupulous diplomacy of these aliens even estranged the chiefs from their king, and every inducement was made to the minor chiefs to break away from the allegiance they owed to the rightful sovereign. It was also part of Portuguese policy to inflame their apprehensions, one against the order and excite their jealousy. By AD 1540, Portuguese treachery have even succeeded in estranging the Sinhalese monarch from the sympathies of his own countrymen, so that he now found himself entirely at the mercy of his foreign allies, and he appealed to them to ensure the succession of his family to the throne.

To give solemnity to their acquiescence an image of Dharmapala, the grandson of the ruler, was depatched to Lisbon, where a coronation of the effigy was held by the Portuguese Emperor. In return for this recognition, Dharpala eventually abjured the national faith and professed himself a baptized convert to Christianity. He also conceded to the request of the Portuguese monarch who was a pronounced fanatic and was controlled by peculiarly aggressive ecclesiastical advisers, to accept a party of the island. As a result of this the first Christian communities were organized in various places in the Maritime Districts.[487] Thus began the gradual destruction of Buddhism the only organization which existed for the spiritual and intellectual education of the people. By the seventeenth century the Portuguese directly governed the whole of the Maritime areas, including Jaffna, and their influence extended inland up to the frontiers of the kingdom of Kandy.[488]

Contemporary historians have left an account of the ferocious atrocities committed by the Portuguese in the early part of their rule. Malalasekera described them in the following manner:

> "Even stage of their progress was marked by a rapacity, bigotry, cruelty, and an inhumanity, unparalleled in the annals of any European Colonial powers. Their ferocity and their utter indifference to all suffering increased with the success of their army; their inhuman barbarities were accompanied by a callousness which knew no distinction between man, women, and child, no feeling of compassion was strong enough to stay their savage hands in their fell work. To terrify their subjects and to bring home to them the might of Portuguese power, they committed atrocities, which, had they not been found recorded in the annals of their own friendly historians, seem too revolting to be true."[489]

The official who acted as administrators had almost absolute power, and the people were ground down by heavy taxation and

487 Tennent "*Christianity in Ceylon*" Ch. 1.

488 *Ibid*, Ch. 11, 26.

489 Malalasekera (1994) "*Pāḷi Literature of Ceylon*" p. 262

laws of terrible severity. Those who followed their policies were favored with ranks and high posts. The tenants of village land were so oppressed that they were even compelled to sell their children to procure the barest necessities of life. The whole country under their control suffered from cruel oppression, and whatever produce their soil was made to yield was misappropriated. The kingdom was thus depopulated and the land mostly left uncultivated. The Sinhalese were left entirely disorganized and decadent, without a proper king and devoid of leaders of ability.[490] The Franciscan friars did further damage by launching an active scheme of proselytization, whereby the high spiritual values and traditional beliefs and customs of the people were entirely undermined. Many people from the Maritime Provinces gave up their faith and embraced Christianity with a view to enhancing their own material gains. Lucrative posts, honors, and distinctions were assigned by the Portuguese to those who embraced their faith. This ultimately led the people to disregard the values and cherished ideas that had been dominant in the life of the Sinhalese nation and that had been manifested in Buddhism. Those who stopped being loyal to their own faith were severely affected by these measures and led a very hard and miserable existence. The missionaries and the Portuguese leaders in their fanatical frenzy pulled down monasteries, burnt the temple libraries, and even slaughtered the monks.[491] This was further aggravated when Dharmapāla granted the revenues of the rich temples to the furtherance of Christian missionary activities. This spelled further doom for the monastic organizations in the island. The *Cūlavaṁsa* says that the enemy (Portuguese) "broke into relic shrines and monasteries, destroyed

490 *Ibid.*

491 Knox, Robert. *A Historical Relations of Sri Lanka.* London, 1958. p. 333.

image houses, Bodhi trees, Buddha statues, and so on, and did grant harm to the laity and the Order."[492]

The ravages and the destructions of the Portuguese went unabated till Mayadunne, a brother of Bhuvanaikebahu VII (AD 1521–1550) was able to marshal troops at Sitavaka and set himself the task of freeing the island of foreign domination. In his attempt he received the assistance of his son Tikiri Bandara. Fired with a sense of nationalism, these two heroes gathered round them whatever forces they could form among the gallant young Sinhalese men and launched severe attacks on the Portuguese and paralyzed their power. Their attempts were exceedingly successful, and they were able to stem the rising tide of Portuguese domination within the country. Though the Portuguese were not finally driven out of the country, from now onward their powers were weakened, a fact which enabled later rulers to oust them easily.

After the victory of these two princes, the *Cūlavaṁsa* account states that the hasty prince Tikiri Bandara slew his father Mayadunne and established himself as king of Sitavaka. There is no other evidence to show that Mayadunne was killed by his son. Geiger in fact doubts the statement of the chronicles.[493] The description of Rajasinghe as detailed in the *Cūlavaṁsa* states that he became a convert to *Saivism* and ruthlessly persecuted the Saṅgha. Here the account in the chronicles seems to be prejudiced. The real facts that motivated the king to antagonize the Saṅgha were that they joined in a conspiracy against him, which was planned by the Portuguese. To justify their treacherous conduct these clerics had made Rajasinghe I a parricide.[494] However, under Rajasinghe's

---

492 "*Culavaṁsa*" Pt. II, Ch. 95, p. 231.

493 *Ibid.*, p. 225.

494 Peries, "*Sri Lanka and the Portuguese*" pp. 11–94.

rule the Sangha benefitted the least and the wrathful king according to the description of the Chronicles, annihilated the Order, slew the monks, and destroyed the monastic establishments.[495] He gave over to Hindu ascetics the charge of the shrine of the Sacred Footprint (Samantakuta) which was the most esteemed possession of the Buddhists, apart from the Tooth Relic. Thus whatever was left the Sangha and Buddhism which survived the onslaughts of the Portuguese was totally annihilated by the vengeance of Rajasinghe I.

Rajasinghe died in AD 1562 and was succeeded by Vimaladharmasuriya I, a prince of the Gampola dynasty. Originally a Christian, married to Dona Catherina, this prince renounced the faith at the opportune time, which won him the sympathy of the masses and the Sangha.[496] Early in this rule the Portuguese made an attempt to seize the Kandyan kingdom but this king was able to repulse their attacks. In his defense he was assisted by the Thera Ratnalankara of Devanagala Vihara who was instrumental in marshalling all forces and assisting the king in checking the inroads of the foreigners.[497] All damage done to the religion and the Sangha by Rajasinghe was made good by this ruler. Most temples and shrines that had been destroyed were repaired, and the Tooth Relic was housed in a magnificent temple at Senkadagala (modern Kandy), the capital of the ruler. The custody of Samantakuta was restored to the Buddhists, and in the period of peace which prevailed in his rule, the monarch devoted his attention to the development of Buddhism and the monastic Order.[498] Whether it

495 Culavamsa. Ch. 93, 10–11.

496 "*Rajavaliya*" p. 87.

497 *EZ.* III, p. 320.

498 Culavamsa Pt. 2, chap. 94.

be as a consequence of the alleged hostile attitude of Rajasinghe of Sativaka, or due to the generally disturbed state of the country and the antagonism of the Portuguese, the Buddhist Order at that time of Vimaladharmasuriya I was in a state of decay, and, to quote the words of Cūlavamsa, "there were no bhikkhus of the Island of Lanka on whom the ceremony of admission to the Order had been performed."[499]

As he was aware that there was a scarcity of fully ordained monks in the island which prevented monks from performing higher Ordination and other ecclesiastical rites, he dispatched a mission to Arakan (Rakkhaṅgadesa) and brought back ordained monks to reestablish the monastic Order, and perpetuate he necessary monastic duties. As a result of this mission in AD 1597 a group of monks led by the Elders Nandicakka, Candavilāsa and other monks (*atireka dasavaggiya bhikkhu*)[500] arrived from Arakan. A ceremony was performed for the admission of novices to the higher ordination in Udakukkhepa Sīmā, demarcated in the river Mahāveli at the landing place called Gettumba or Gatambe near Kandy. Perhaps because of the depleted numbers of the Buddhist Order the opportunity thus presented was availed of to make "many sons of good birth submit themselves to the ceremony of renunciation of the world."[501]

Vimaladharmasūriya I and his Queen Donha Catherina had earlier lived for a considerable time in an environment dominated by the Christian and European way of life, and they were therefore expected to have strong European sympathies. Mālalasekera, referring to the times of Vimaladhramasūriya I, says that "Portuguese

499 *Ibid.* Pt. 2, chap. 94, p. 228.

500 "*Sulurājavaliya*" Published by C. D. D. K. Jayawardena, 1914. p. 22

501 "*Culavamsa*" Pt. II, Ch. 94, p. 229.

ideas moulded the fashions at the Kandyan Court and their influence—not always for the best—has come down as a legacy even to the present day."[502] The apparent European sympathies of Vimaladhramasūriya I and his past career, led another historian to comment that he protected Buddhism and restored its neglected rites not for the love of Buddhism, but with the intention of consolidating his position by enlisting the support of the people through appealing to their religious sentiments.[503]

Additionally, Mirando points out, "This course of action was perhaps deemed necessary for more than one reason; firstly he had to allay the suspicious of his subjects and win their confidence, for it was not long before that Vimaladhrmasūriya I had renounced his traditional religion and aligned himself with the Portuguese; secondly he had to depend on the support of his subjects and keep his kingdom contented if the Portuguese were to be effectively encountered. Whatever the motives may have been for his religious undertakings, Vimaladhramasūriya I certainly paved the way to a Buddhist revival."[504]

Vimaladharmasūriya I was succeeded by his brother Senerat, who renounced the monastic life to take over the reins of government.[505] A fierce battle was fought against the Portuguese at Gannoruva, where the forces of the Portuguese were completely routed and their general massacred. Following this victory Rajasinghe II the successor of Senerat was able to deliver the death blow to the Portuguese, and this king, with the assistance of the

---

502 Malalasekera (1994) "*The Pāḷi Literature of Ceylon*" p. 269.

503 Pridham "Ceylon and Its Dependencies" *Vol. I, Ch. V.* London: T. and W. Boone, 1849. p. 98

504 Mirando (1985) *ibid.* pp. 36–38.

505 "*Nikayasangaraha*" ed. V. Amaramoli (1955), Colombo.

Dutch, was able to drive the Portuguese completely away in AD 1658. Thus the first lap of foreign domination which lasted nearly half a century was eliminated. The Dutch, unlike the Portuguese, were more tolerant, and their policy was of a military tenure and not of civil colonization. They were also more diplomatic in their relationships and assisted the ruler on a number of occasions to bring monks from Arakan and Siam. The period of peace which followed the expulsion of the Portuguese enabled the Sinhalese ruler Rajasinghe II and Vimaladharmasūriya II to devote more time to the development of Buddhism and the enhancement of the Sangha. Not only for the purpose of contending against a foreign power like Portuguese and internal political insurgencies, but also for the purpose of the advancement of Buddhism and the cultivation of the finer arts, the need for establishing political stability throughout the country was essential, and these two kings seems to be achieved by their efforts in Buddhism. The great days of Buddhism in Sri Lanka as well as Arakan as history reveals, have always synchronized with periods during which prevailed political stability, peace, and contentment. The political climate that obtained under Vimaladharmasūriya seems to be propitious for the furtherance of Buddhism and literary activities that had earlier suffered considerably owing to the unsettled state of the country, even though now engaged with the Dutch. All monastic land that had been forcibly taken away by the Portuguese and former royal land grants to the Sangha which had lapsed from its ownership, was regranted to the monasteries.[506]

There had been frequent religious intercourse between the Buddhists of Sri Lanka and Southeast Asia. These contacts had been disturbed throughout the seventeenth century due to the presence of the Portuguese and the constant wars that prevailed.

506 *Cūlavaṁsa.* Pt. II, Ch. 96, p.41.

It was seen that the Sangha or order of monks which was once revived by Vimaladharmasūriya II at the end of sixteen century had become extinct.

The *Cūlavaṁsa* and *Sāsanavaṁsa* each contain important evidential records of religious intercourse between Arakan and Sri Lanka during King Vimaladhammasurya II's reign. Both chronicles refer to the arrival of the Sinhalese envoy in Rakkhaṅgapura and the restoration of the Sri Lankan Buddhist Saṅgha by Arakanese monks. In the reign of King Murn Rāzā Gree (AD 1593–1612), a request made by Vimaladhamma- suriya I to send a group of monks from Arakan in order to reestablish monk lineage in Sri Lanka, presiding Ven. Candavilāsa and accompanied by twenty monks set forth for a mission to Sri Lanka.[507]

Again, King Vimaladhammasuriya II (AD 1687–1707) requested to send a Buddhist mission for the continuation of *thera* linage in the Island to the King of Arakan, Māruppiya (AD 1696–1697). Thus a Buddhist reestablishment had been performed. The heads of the mission were Thera Indamañjū, Abbot of Sattathāna Monastery of Mrauk Oo and Abbot of Laung Grat, accompanied by forty monks. Interestingly, when Arakanese monks went to worship the tooth relic of the Buddha, the doorkeepers did not open the gate of the relic. Then, when Sattathāna Mahāthera recited "*Rajanatala ākāsaṁ nakkhattāra parikkhettaṁ*" etc. fourteen verses by firm decision, the lockers were automatically opened. After then, they worshiped the tooth relic. Seeing such, the doorkeepers said pardon to the monks. Here, the chronicles mentions about forty monks, but in Sinhalese sources, it was only thirty-three monks.

It is interestingly to note that at the opening ceremony of the International Theravāda Buddhist Missionary University (ITBMU) in Rangoon, Myanmar (Burma) in December 9, 1998,

507 Oo, Aung Tha. "*Rakkha Mandala Rakhaing Razawon*" Mra Ratana Press, Rangoon. (1955).

on behalf of the Sri Lanka government, Nimal Samarasundera, secretary of Ministry of Buddha Sāsana, delivered a speech. The detail speech has been mentioned correctly in the newspaper, New Light of Myanmar (English) dated on December 10, 1998, published by the Ministry of Information, Myanmar. It has to be cited an abstract from it here, "Subsequently during the reign of King Wimalasooriya I, higher ordination of Sangha was taken to Sri Lanka from Myanmar as which was then known as Arakan or Rakkhaṅgadesa (Rakhaing)." However, the mentioned abstract has been changed or replaced or mistaken, "...higher ordination of Sangha was taken to Sri Lanka from Myanmar Shin Arahan..." in the Myanmar version of the paper. Arakan or Rakkhaṅgadesa (Rakhaing) has been replaced by Myanmar Shin Arahan.[508]

Rājasinghe II was succeeded by his son Vimaladhrmasūriya II, who as enjoined by his father, followed a policy of peace. His reign of twenty-two years (AD 1684–1706) was marked by friendly relationships with Dutch and by the absence of destructive warfare. This period of respite from war allowed him to direct his energies toward religious and cultural matters. Urgent reforms of the Buddhist Order received his attention. The Buddhist Order at the time had degenerated, in that "not more than five Upasampadā monks were to be found in the whole Island," and it was therefore essential and indeed imperative that for the reorganization of the Order there should be the reestablishment of the Upasampadā or the Higher Ordination.

Vimaladharmasūriya II despatched two embassies to Rakkhanga (Arakan), the first of which under the three Chiefs Bāmṇivatte Disānayaka Mudiyanse, Doḍanvala Herat Mudiyanse and Sivāgama Paṇḍita Mudiyanse was of an exploratory nature, undertaken with a view to find out whether Buddhism existed in

508 *New Light of Myanmar* published by the Ministry of Information of the Union of Myanmar dated on December 10, 1998 (both English and Myanmar versions)

its purity in Rakkhangadesa.[509] The result of this enquiry proving fruitful, the second embassy under the three chiefs who had already been to Rakkhanga and two others, Gampaha Vijetunga Mudiyanse and Galagama Mohoṭṭāla, were dispatched to obtain monks for the performance of the Upasampadā ceremony,[510] the Dutch providing ships to convey the monks from Arakan to Sri Lanka. This mission arrived with thirty three monks led by the Abbot of Sattaṭhāna Monastery, Ven. Indamañjū, and the Abbot of Laung Grat Monastery from Mrauk Oo City, Arakan. In 1697, at the landing place called Gatambe in the river Mahāvali, the monks from Arakan performed the ceremony for the admission to the Higher Ordination at which "thirty three sons of good family received the Upasampadā."[511]

It is indeed striking that the number of monks who received the Upasampadā should correspond to the number of Arakanese monks who arrived who arrived in the Island. Perhaps it was customary with the Arakanese monks that each Upājjhayā or Preceptor should have no more than one newly initiated Upasampadā Bhikkhu under his turtorship, or it may be that the number initiated was so restricted for effective supervision. Besides the sāmaṇeras or novices who were admitted to the Higher Order, Vimaladhramasuriya II also caused, "120 sons of good family to be admitted to the Order of the Novitiate."[512] By these measures, he brought about the reorganization of the Buddhist Order, and restored it to something approaching its pristine purity.

509 Jayatilaka (1940) "*Mission to Arakan*"

510 "*Culavaṁsa*" Pt. II, Ch. 97, p. 239.

511 *Op. cit.*, Pt. II, Ch. 97, p.240; *JRASCB* Vol. XI No.41–14

512 *Ibid.*

By this act the king assisted the cause of Buddhism and the Sangha. Yet the smaller numbers to receive admission and higher ordination at this time, as compared to the larger numbers in earlier ages, show that less people were really anxious to pursue a religious life, notwithstanding the customary way mentioned. The king and his people wished to continue this kind of cultural relations with other Buddhist centers in Southeast Asia and for this purpose the ports had to be left open. By this time all Kandyan foreign contacts and trade were effectively channeled through the company. Within the kingdom, the position of the king *vis-à-vis* his chiefs deteriorated considerably. It is only in the realm of religion that Vimaladharmasūriya II asserted his personality, and henceforth Buddhism began to play a more important part in politics than it did in the seventeenth century. A significant achievement of the king was that he revived the Sangha and reestablished international contacts. As a result he won the loyalty of Sinhalese Buddhists all over the island.

Thus in the sixteenth and seventeenth centuries, the relationship between Sri Lanka and Arakan had been critical to the reestablishment and restoration of Buddhism in Sri Lanka, especially in the performance of religious ceremonies and higher ordinations (*upasampāda*).

6.5. Religious and Cultural Syncretism

Why Buddhist Arakanese interactions with Ceylon for a number of times in the history can be assumed: first, Arakanese wanted to have Buddhist scriptures; second, to be validated with Sinhalese Theravāda Pāḷi Buddhism; third, and to check and adjust the variations between Sri Lankan Pāḷi scriptures and theirs, if found any.

The crowing event in the history of Rakhaing was the Convention of the Buddhist Council at the top of golden hill of Vesālī under the royal patronage of King Dhammavijaya in AD

638 through joint effort of two countries, Rakhaing and Ceylon. This momentous triumph of the great council was participated by one thousand monks from Ceylon and one thousand monks from Rakhaing kingdom. As a fitting celebration of the occasion, the lavish construction of pagodas, statues, and monasteries were undertaken for the purpose of inscribing the Tipiṭaka.[513]

It is well known fact that the words of the Buddha were committed to writing in palm-leaf manuscript for the first time in the history of Buddhist literature by Arahats of Sri Lanka at the Aluvihāra near present Kandy in Sri Lanka during the very beginning of years of the Christian era. The previous three councils held in India did not record the teachings by any means of writing. We have also read that around the time the council held in Sri Lanka, there was also a council held in Gandhara, north India, in the city of Pashava, sponsored by king Kanishka.[514] The teachings of the Buddha were written down in copper plates. It is not accepted by most owing to the real words of the Buddha were not in the records and those were mixed with Brahmanism. Since that time on, Buddhism divided into two in the history of Buddhism as northern Buddhism and Southern Buddhism. The first one is so called because it was born in northern India, and the later in Sri Lanka, southern India. It is developed to be called in later years as *Mahāyāna* and *Hīnayāna* (*Cūlayāna*) respectively.

Due to those two schools reached to Ganges plains in successive centuries, we cannot say that both northern and southern schools may not reach to Arakan. Students of different backgrounds either *Mahāyāna* or *Hīnayāna* came to study at the Nālandamahāvihāra, a Buddhist center of learning from the fifth or sixth century AD to

---

513 See details on the Arakanese Buddhist Council in chapter 5.

514 *Snellgrove, David. "Indo-Tibetan Buddhism"* Boston: *Shambhala*, 1987, vol. 2, p. 46

1197 CE.[515] It has been called "one of the first great universities in recorded history."[516] The Gupta Empire also patronized some monasteries. Nālanda flourished between the reign of the Śakrāditya (whose identity is uncertain and who might have been either Kumara Gupta I or Kumara Gupta II) and 1197 CE, supported by patronage from the Hindu Gupta rulers as well as Buddhist emperors like Harsha and later emperors from the Pala Empire.[517] They could choose to study any subject among varieties of subjects under different faculties. We cannot say no that there would not be any from Arakan to study with different aliens. Thus far, both *Mahāyāna* and *Hīnayāna* would have reached Arakan since the beginning of Christian era. But later, *Theravāda* Buddhism prevailed over Arakan.

It is growing of writing and speaking about the fourth Saṅgāyanā at Shwe Taung Gree hill, in Vesālī in AD 630, although is not counted or accepted by Theravādins now. According to Arakanese records relating Buddhism in Arakan, there are two kinds of Saṅgāyanā: Saṅgāyanā Gree (*lit.* big council) and Saṅgāyanā Nge (*lit.* small council). In Arakan, we have found both kinds of council. What is meant by Saṅgāyanā Gree held in Arakan is that it has been regarded and successively numbered as one of the councils held in India being internationally participated eminent scholar Arahat bhikkhus who were skillful in the words of their Master. Meanwhile, Saṅgāyanā Nge is regarded as a small domestic council. During the reign of king Murn Ran Phru of Lay-mro period in Arakan, the fifth Saṅgāyanā Gree and the

515 Jeffrey E. Garten, "Really Old School," *The New York Times*, December 9, 2006; Sukumar Dutt, *Buddhist Monks and Monasteries of India: Their History and Contribution to Indian Culture*, George Allen and Unwin Ltd, London. (1962).pp. 329.

516 *Ibid.* Sukumar Dutt, (1962). pp. 329.

517 *Op. cit.*

eleventh Saṅgāyanā Nge were held, according to Medhapañña literary record.[518]

In Arakan the ascendancies of Buddhism, of ethnicity, of ruling administration are different to each other. According to a number of epigraphic and archaeological accounts, Vesālī from the fourth century to the ninth century AD was the era in which Buddhism flourished. Due to Vesālī kings were Buddhists, they had relations with Sri Lanka socially and religiously from the beginning of Christian era. Thus, in AD 630, King Dhammavijaya invited one thousand eminent scholar *bhikkhus* from Sri Lanka, including five hundred *ganthadhūra* and five hundred *vipassanādhūra,* to the fourth Buddhist council in Vesālī. Likewise, one thousand monks from Arakan, altogether two thousand monks participated in that council. The council was held at the Shwe Taung Gree hill near Vesālī. The presiding Mahāthera was Arahat Cūlareva. It took three years to complete writing the words of the Buddha on copper plates. Before the council, the king had to build five big monasteries for the invited *bhikkhus* to reside therein. We can even find the ruins of those monasteries at the present time. This council is regarded as the fourth Saṅgāyanā Gree in Arakan. Peoples of Arakan regard a Saṅgāyanā Gree, which is properly accomplished only participated by leading Arahats who are mastered in the words of the Buddha. The fourth Vesālī Buddhist council is proven by later literary and archaeological evidence, but there is no contemporary and parallel evidence.

After Vesālī, Pañsā was found by Laymro dynasty in AD 818; the great king of dynasty (AD 818–1430) was king Murn-Yin-Phru, who turned his attention toward the development of Buddhism, and in AD 847 he convened the second Buddhist council in Rakhaing attended by eight hundred Arahants. Rakhiaing chronicles report

518 See detail *State Gazetteer (Culture)* (1984), pp. 185–188

that therein the Tipiṭaka and Aṭṭhakathā were inscribed on the golden plate and enshrined. Never has there been impediment in the practice of Theravāda Buddhist faith since it has introduced in Rakhaing. The copious findings of inscription *ye dhammā* verse were practical evidence that Theravāda was dominant faith if epigraphic and archaeological sources were to be believed. The royal patronage has always been a significant factor contributing to stability and progress of the religion in Rakhaing.

Resume

We have presented a detailed account of sources that reveal that the Arakanese Buddhist intercourses with Sri Lanka produced a number of Buddhist revivals in Sri Lanka, and Arakanese monks may have brought Sri Lankan *Thera* traditions and customs to their land for the advancement of Buddhism therein. Although Arakan had received Buddhism directly from its origin land, India, as early as the emergence of Buddhism according to local accounts, without Sri Lankan Theravāda Buddhist literature, a successor of the Third Buddhist Council, Arakanese Buddhism might have not developed that much in the concept called *Thera* tradition in Araka.

CHAPTER 7

CONCLUDING REFLECTIONS

Before we give a general impression of our subject (of Historical and Cultural Study of the Influence of Buddhism on Inhabitants of Rakhaing Land) we would like to raise a few points about Buddhism and Indian culture. Buddhism was born in India. From the moment we start to have a discussion about Buddhism and the Buddhist developments in Rakhaing coastal region we must immediately look to India. Whenever we consider any cultural aspect of Rakhaing life—particularly religious, social, educational, literary, or artistic—our attention goes to that great country of India.

Nobody would deny that India is one of the cradles of world civilization because of her outstanding contributions in diverse fields. In the history of human thought and culture, India has played an important part, and her contributions are second to none. It is the birthplace of several important world religions such as Brahmanism, Buddhism, and Jainism, which influenced the culture and civilization of the many parts of the world that accepted India as their "motherland." They are indebted to India in many respects.

Indians who came to settle in different countries of Southeast Asia and the Far-east had their first contacts with the primitive tribes of those regions. By virtue of their superior military campaigns, cultural heritage, and advanced civilization, the local inhabitants were largely Indianzed culturally. They gradually occupied some certain regions and converted them into their colonies. The Indians spread their own culture and traditions all of these territories, and this marked the great beginning of the progressive stage of their cultural expansion.

Once Buddhism had a strong footing in Rakhaing Land, Buddhist art was strongly influenced and greatly stimulated by the creative genius of many people with whom it came in contact, and this led to great complexity and diversity. It never possessed an underlying unity. This unity is illustrated by the fact that the problems it was to solve, and the forms it developed have a certain constancy and continuity.

In the field of Buddhism in Rakhaing, especially Buddhist art, we have religious buildings, edifices for ritualistic purposes and for monastic life and the creation of impressive images to convey the idea of the Buddha. Boddhisattas, monks, and other sacred personages and the treasury of stories and legends together with their abundance of narrative motifs, set up a vocabulary of symbols to convey the main religious idea. The art of Buddhism devised convincing visual images of the world's metaphysical structure, especially the structure of the spheres lying beyond the limits of the empirical, terrestrial world.

In the third chapter of this study, we have embraced the natural boundaries of mountains Rakhaing Roma and sea Bay of Bengal protecting a compact area suited to dry and wet rice cultivation factors which led to the evolution of the urban settlement of ancient people in Rakhaing Kaladan-Laymro Valley and centralized organization, while both sea and land routes made direct contact with India possible.

CONCLUDING REFLECTIONS

From the viewpoint of historical development of Rakhaing, it is interesting to note that it has been an independent kingdom throughout its history. Besides, the Rakhaing people were able to control large tracts of area along the sea-coasts to the east, west, and south, far beyond borders of the Fatherland. The Rakhaing Empire extended westward to Dacca and Tripūra for a long time and also conquered Bago. For a short time, Rakhaing held the lower part of Burma and even extended its influence to Martaban. On one hand, the physical boundaries of Rakhaing determine the extent of control by a central authority. On the other hand, as shown in the chapters, it was helpful in giving rise to a good opportunity for the growth of the Buddhist religion and Indian-influenced culture, which should be seen not only as an introduction of Indian Buddhism itself, but as help of three ways of trade, missions, and pilgrimage.

Ancient Rakhaing's geographical background, its peoples, and its cities with their unique position on the eastern bank of the Bay of Bengal where South and Southeast Asia meet, with both land and sea routes to the east and west, resulted in the development of political and cultural traits, especially that of Buddhism and later in emergence of it as a "maritime kingdom" or a "cultural frontier" in the region.

To what extent the accustomed ways of life of the king and people were changed by the acceptance of Buddhism as the official creed in the reigns of King Candasuriya and his sixth successive king Suriyacakka in the third Dhaññavatī period, it is difficult to gauge today. In the conversion—if we may use that term—of a person to Buddhism, there are several degrees of earnestness. One may formally take refuge in the Three Jewels (i.e., the Buddha, the *Dhamma*, and the *Saṅgha*). This generally implies that such a person accepts that the Buddha and his teachings would lead him to ultimate salvation, and abjures faith in gods, other prophets, or teachers as efficient for that purpose. Such a person may, however, invoke the aid of a divine or human agency for worldly ends. To the three Refuges, a more earnest convert may add the Five Precepts, the vows to abstain from taking life, stealing, wrongful conduct in matters sexual, untruthfulness, and addiction to intoxicants. Still more earnest devotees may observe the eight precepts on fast days, or take the ten vows to be observed every day. All this may be done while one remains in the world. But the really earnest believer in the Buddha (i.e., he who wishes to realize for himself the Truth realized by the Buddha, has to give up all social obligations and family ties, and take to the life of the almsman by being formally admitted to the *Saṁgha*).

The presence of Indian elements, in whatever role, be they princes, *Brahmanas*, hermit then-kings, traders, or artisans, must have resulted from the customary, age-old law of succession which prevented those who followed the first son in the Hindu family, however personally accomplished they may be, from enjoying the fruits of parental or hereditary wealth and status. At any rate, the percentage of Indian migrants physically present at any given time in the Southeast Asian kingdoms appears to have been small if not negligible, and it was only local royal patronage that enabled Indian religious, cultural, linguistic and, more importantly, scriptal elements to seep generously into the Rakhaing social fabric. This largely perhaps largely due to the successive migration, under hope of royal patronage, of educated Brahmanas and Buddhist clergy as well as educated as well organized members of trade guilds who must have carried with them to the Rakhaing shores the latest of what was Indian in their days, including to the scriptal changes. Thus far, we have seen how Indian Buddhism played a major role in the development of social and religious affairs in Dhaññavatī kingdom of Rakhaing in ancient time.

As mentioned above, the local chronicles traditionally assert that during the reign of King Candasuriya in the Dhaññavatī City Gotama the Buddha, while visiting, converted the court and cast the image, Mahāmuni, and preached *Sutthubimba Sutta*. According to this tradition Buddhism is supposed to be introduced to Rakhaing since Buddha's lifetime in the sixth century BC. It was also in the Dhaññavatī dynasty that *Thera Mahāreva* was said to have come to *Mahinsakamaṇḍala* for conversation, after the third Buddhist Synod was held at *Pātaliputta*. Some consider that *Mahinsaka* as the present Rakhaing Land or the land was once part of *Mahinsaka*. However some scholars insist that *Mahinsaka* was at one time the same of Mysore at the southern part of India. Aforementioned traditions hint that Buddhism came to Rakhaing in the sixth and third centuries BC respectively by means of missionary activities. Unfortunately, however, no contemporary record is found relating to these traditions. It has been for the tradition that many local archeological and literary evidence in later dates so far been found firmly claim that present available Buddhism relates to those traditions. Their religious devotion in Buddha images, stūpas, relics, and so on would have made them to advance their culture in the successive early periods in Rakhaing, which we have seen in the chapters. The Buddhist portability might have helped replace the then existing Brahmanical cults, their former religion, and suddenly might have spread all over ancient Rakhaing.

As has been presented above, Sanskrit influence in Vesālī does not mean that Buddhism flourished in ancient Vesālī period was Mahāyānistic; it was mainly because of geography— Rakhaing Land had been directly by land connected with northern India (i.e., Nālanda). And during that period, Sanskrit had been a *lingua franca* and the official language of the Rakhaing court. But, almost all the evidence shows that it was Theravāda type of Buddhism that flourished throughout the Vesālī, Lay-mro, and Mrauk Oo periods successively. Notably, during Vesālī period the practice of Theravāda Buddhism with Brahminical background are found, but not in the successive Lay-mro and Mrauk Oo periods.

Many sources reveal that Rakhaing Buddhist intercourses with Sri Lanka produced a number of Buddhist revivals in Sri Lanka, and Arakanese monks may have brought Sri Lankan *Thera* traditions and customs to their land for the advancement of Buddhism therein. Although Rakhaing had received Buddhism directly from its origin land, India, as early as the emergence of Buddhism according to local accounts, without the connection with Sri Lankan Theravāda Buddhist literature, a successor of the Third Buddhist Council, Arakanese Buddhism might have not developed that much in the concept called *Thera* tradition in Rakhaing.

Last, but by no means least, as has already been pointed out, this study is just an introduction to the historical and cultural study of the influence of Buddhism on the peoples of Rakhaing Land. It therefore remains one of many works on Rakhaing, a transit land where South Asia and Southeast Asia meet in which rich Buddhist traditions prevailed. No doubt new evidence on Rakhaing studies also awaits discovery.

APPENDIXES

Appendix 1: Maps

Map 1

Map 1. Dhaññavatī with respect to Ancient India and Ceylon

Map 2

Map 2. Arakan (Rakhaing) with respect to South Asia and Southeast Asia

Map 3

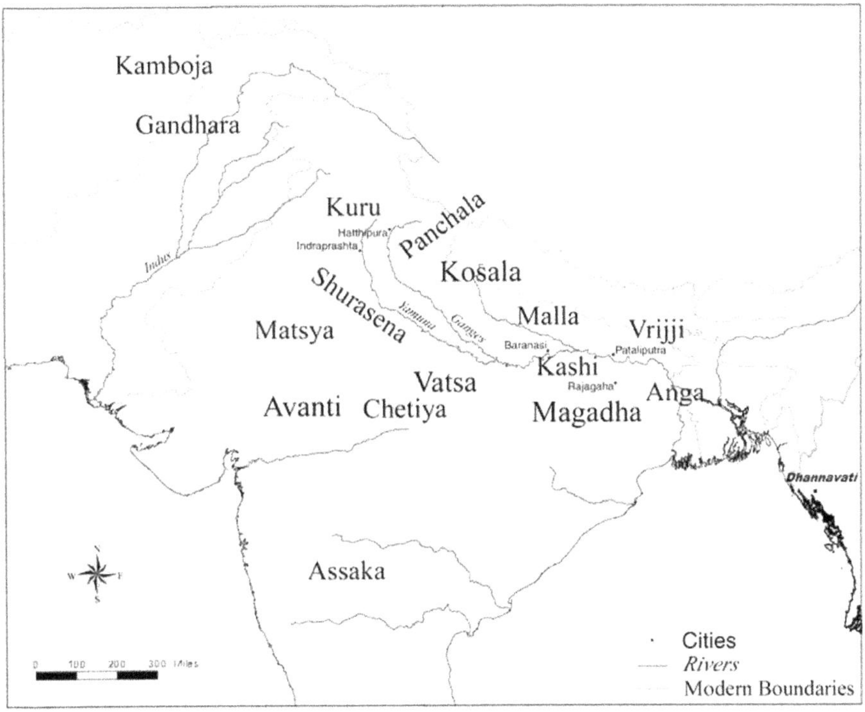

Map 3. Dhaññavatī with respect to Ancient India

Map 4

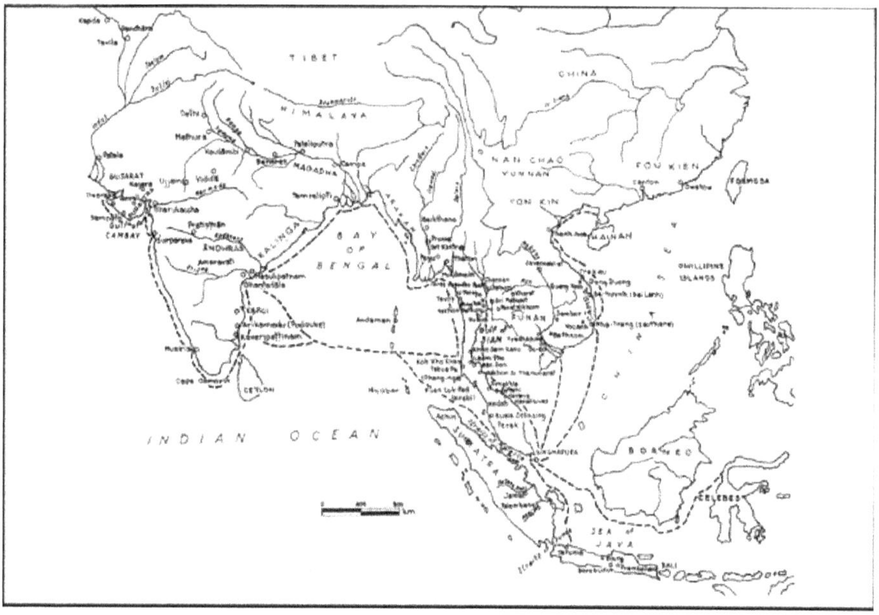

Map 4. Sea routes and ancient ports in India and Southeast Asia

Map 5

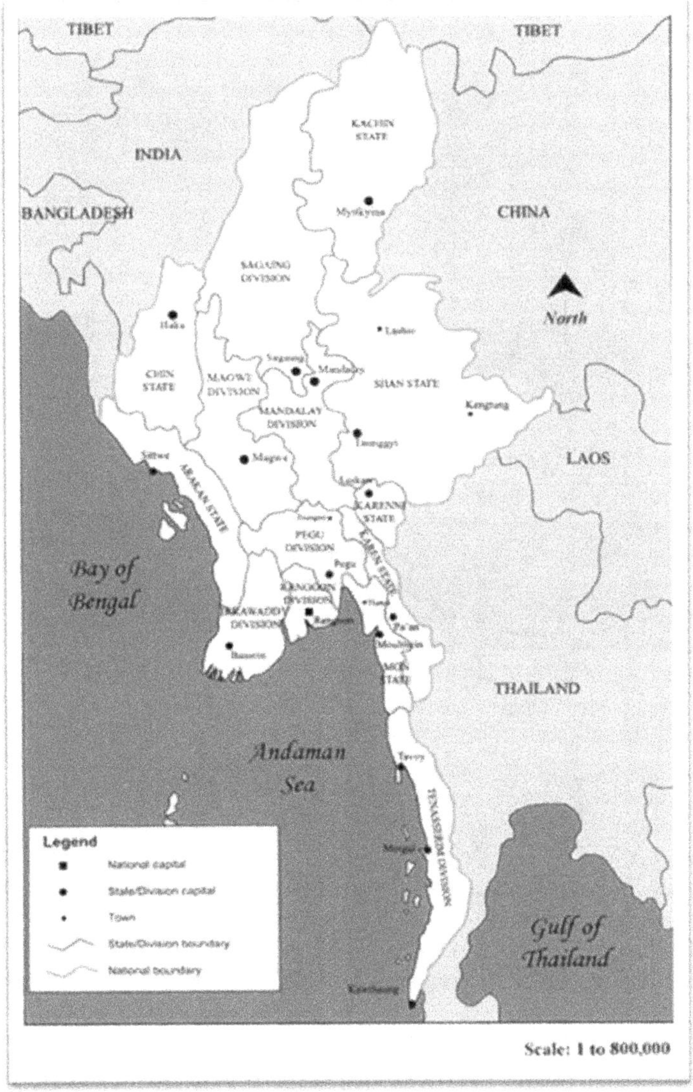

Map 5. Present Arakan State in Burma

Map 6

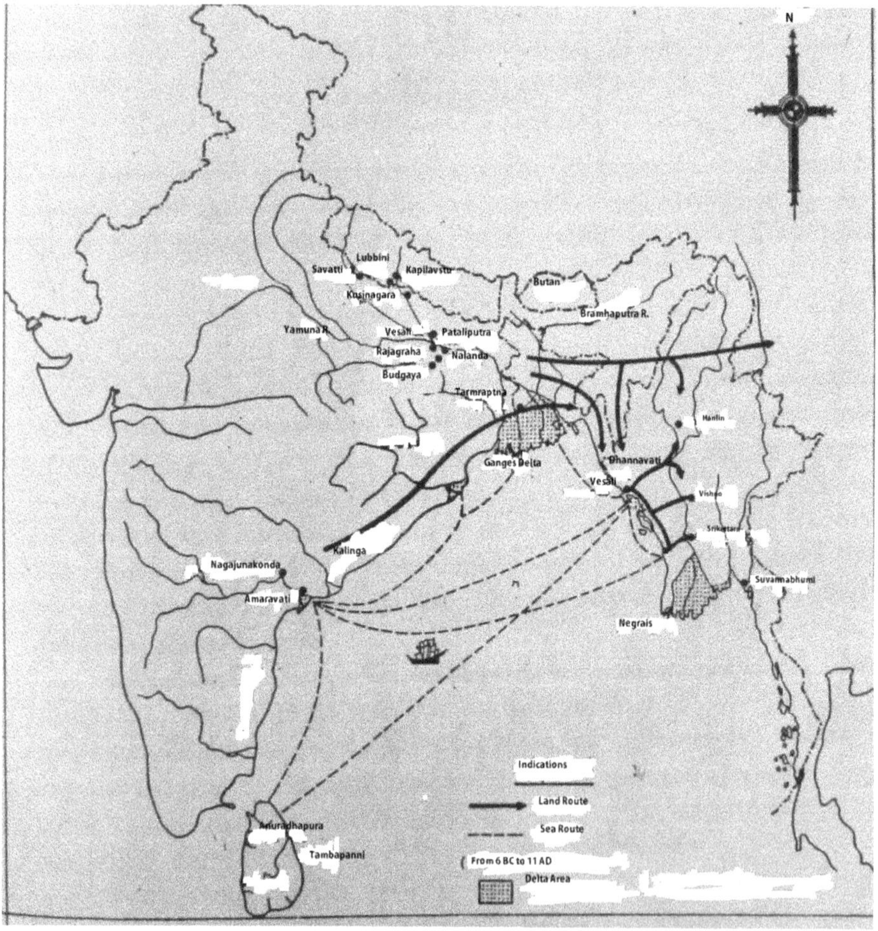

Map 6. Rakhaing Links with India and Ceylon (c. sixth century BC and eleventh century AD) adapted from Tun Shwe Khine (1990)

Map 7

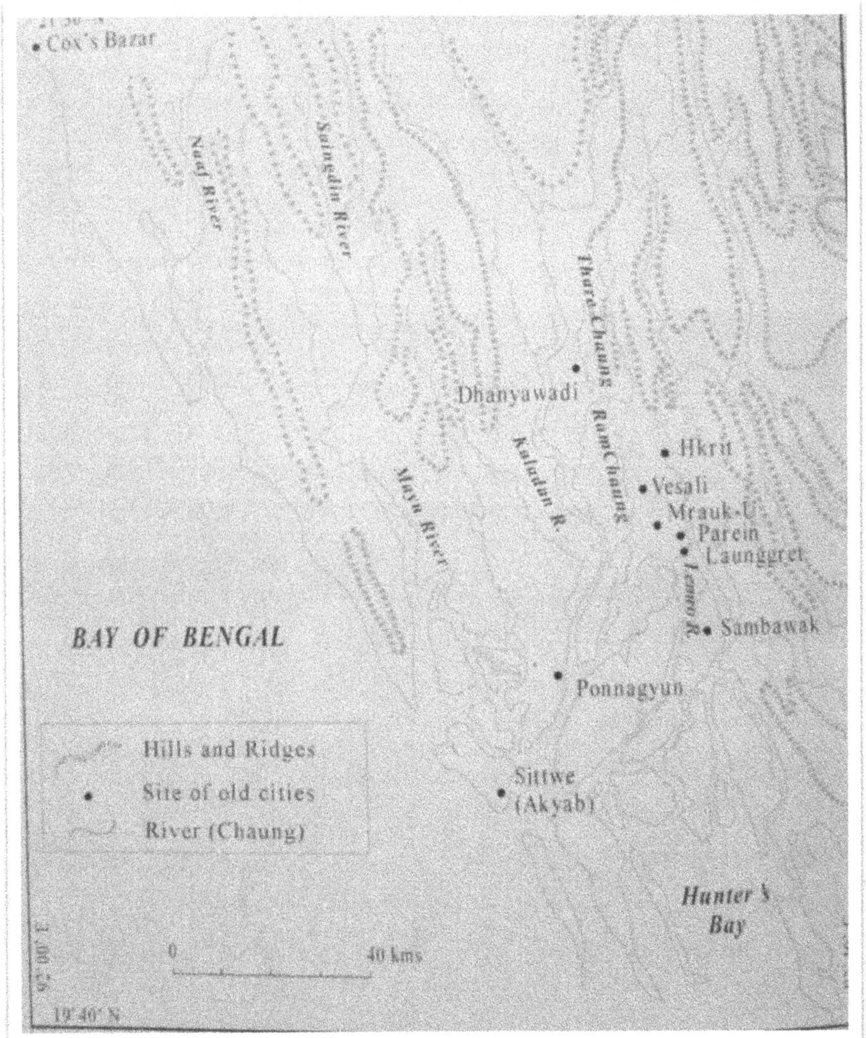

Map 7. Sites of Old Capitals of Rakhaing from Gutman (2001)

Map 8

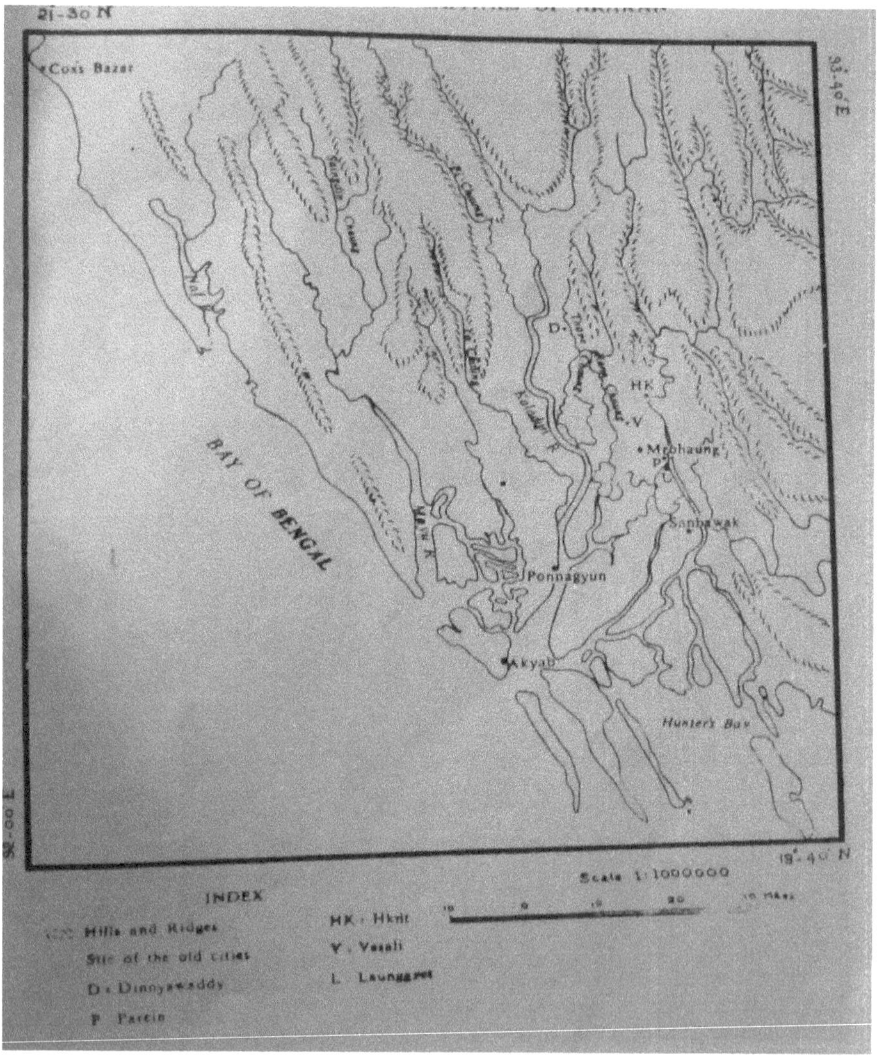

Map 8. Sites of Old Capitals of Arakan from Thin Kyi (1970)

Map 9

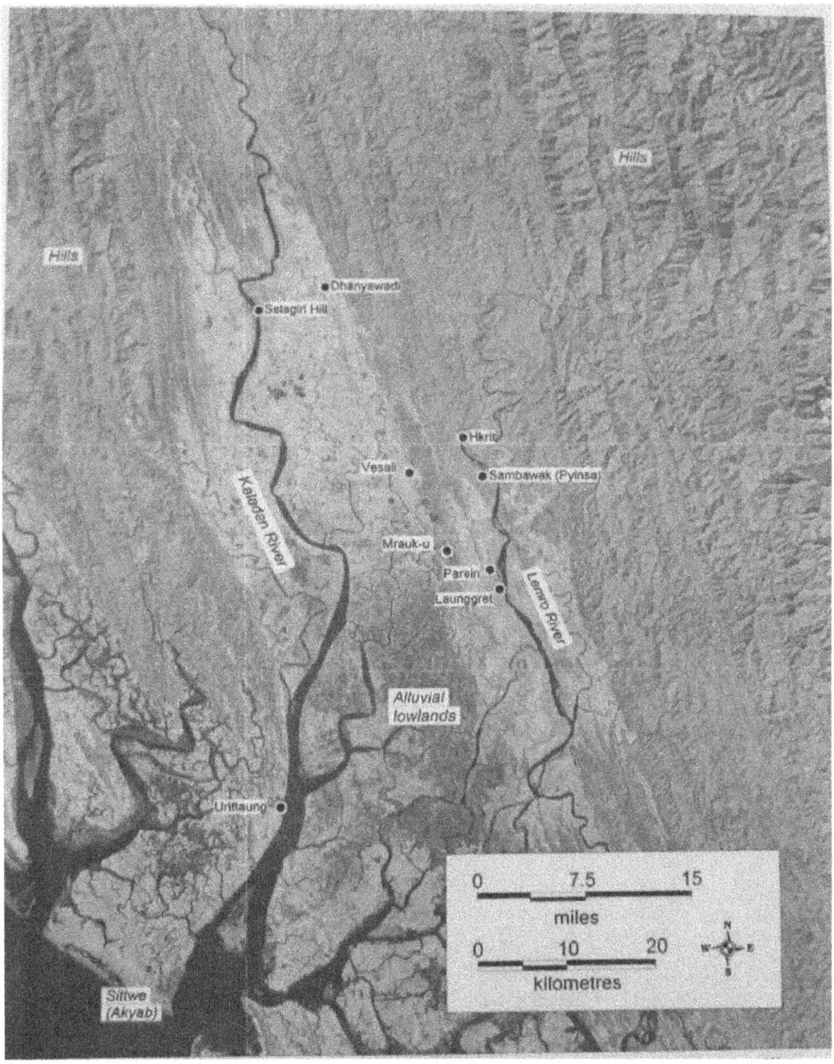

Map 9. Location of the old cities and some major landmarks in Rakhaing (LandSat 2000 satellite image) from Hudson (2005)

Map 10

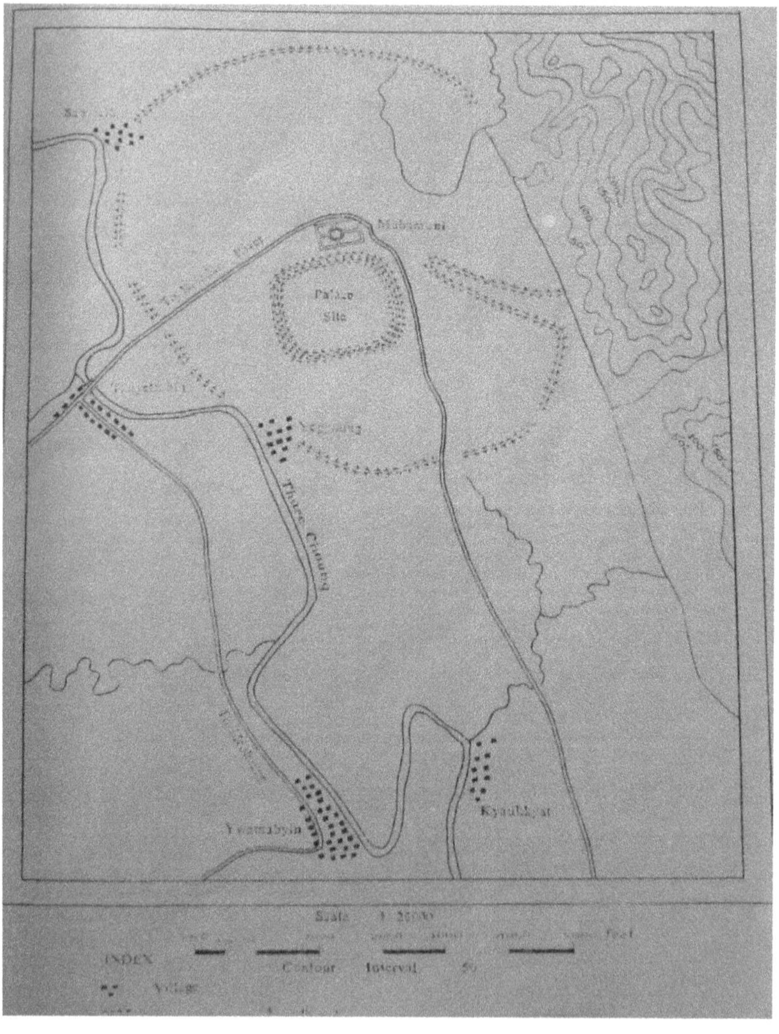

Map 10. Old Dhaññavatī Ground Plan without Eastern Wall from Thin Kyi (1970)

Map 11

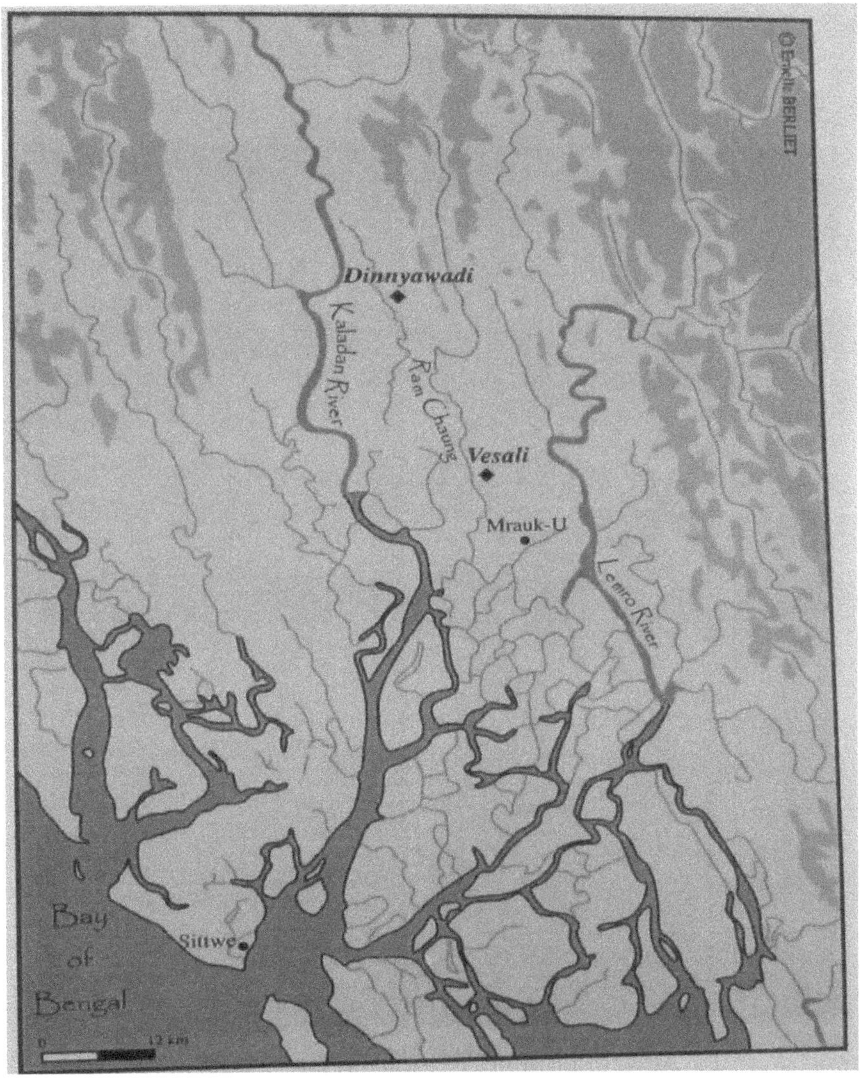

Map 11. The old sites of Dhaññavatī and Vesālī from Berliet (2004)

Map 12

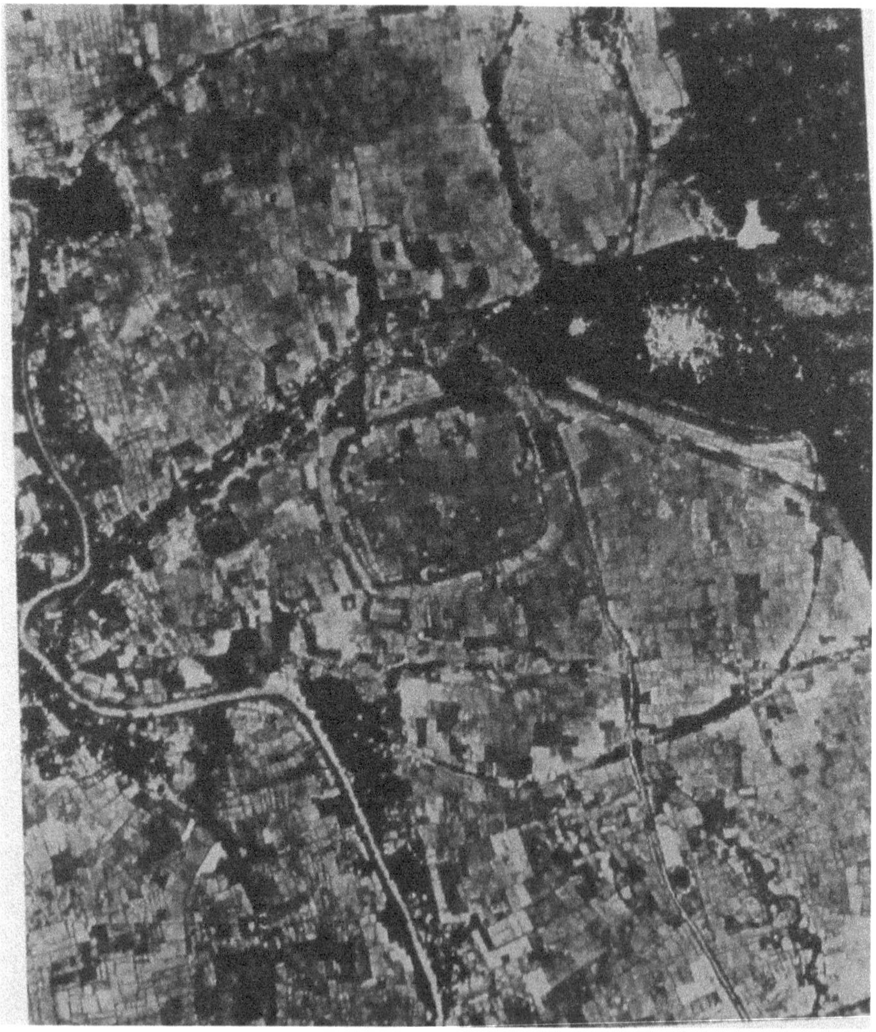

Map 12. Aerial Photo of Dhaññavatī from Gutman (1976)

Map 13

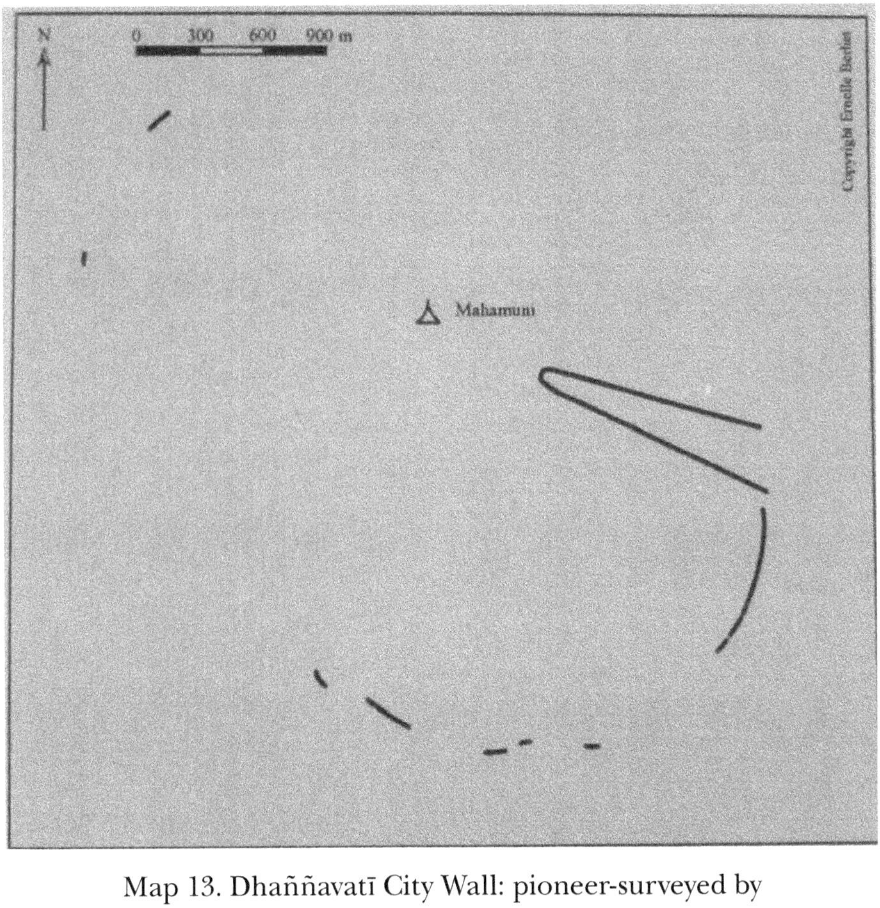

Map 13. Dhaññavatī City Wall: pioneer-surveyed by GPS in 2002 from Berliet (2004)

Map 14

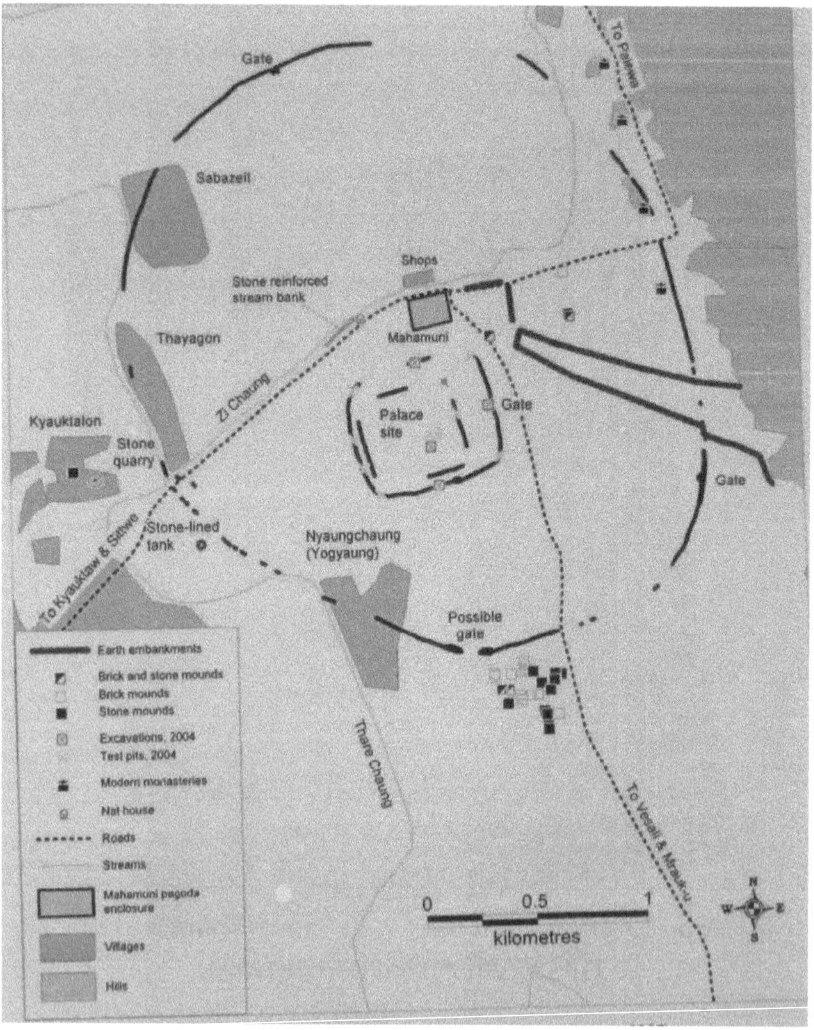

Map 14. New Dhaññavatī Ground Plan confirmed by GPS from Hudson (2005)

Map 15

Map 15. Satellite Photo of Dhaññavatī from Google Earth

Map 16

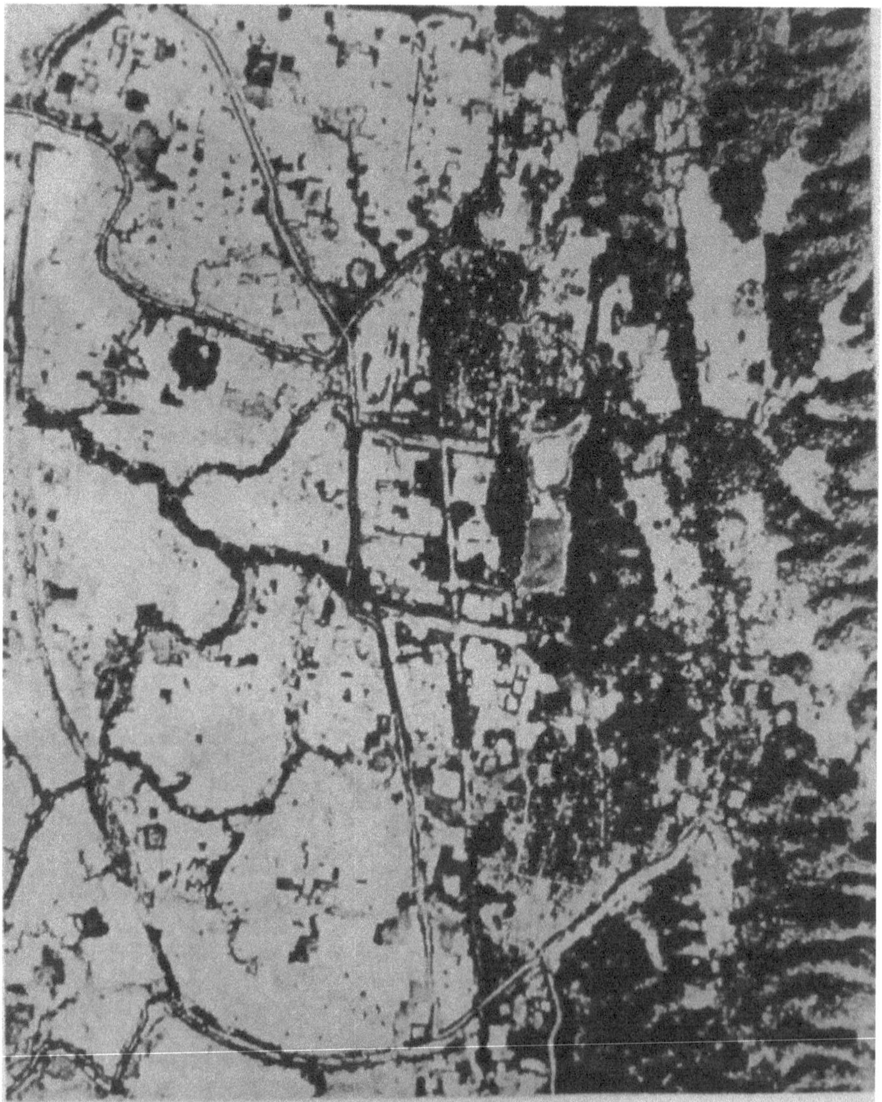

Map 16. Aerial Photo of Vesālī from San Tha Aung (1979)

Map 17

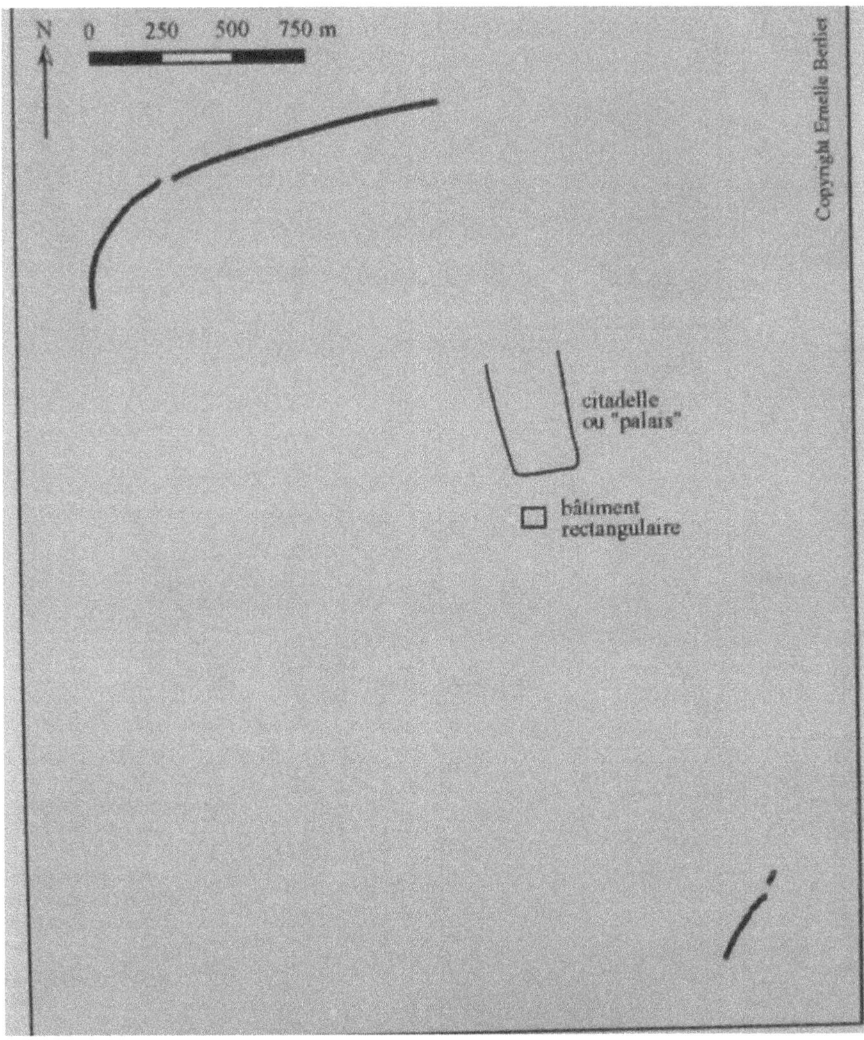

Map 17. Vesālī City Walls: pioneer-surveyed by GPS in 2002 from Berliet (2004)

Map 18

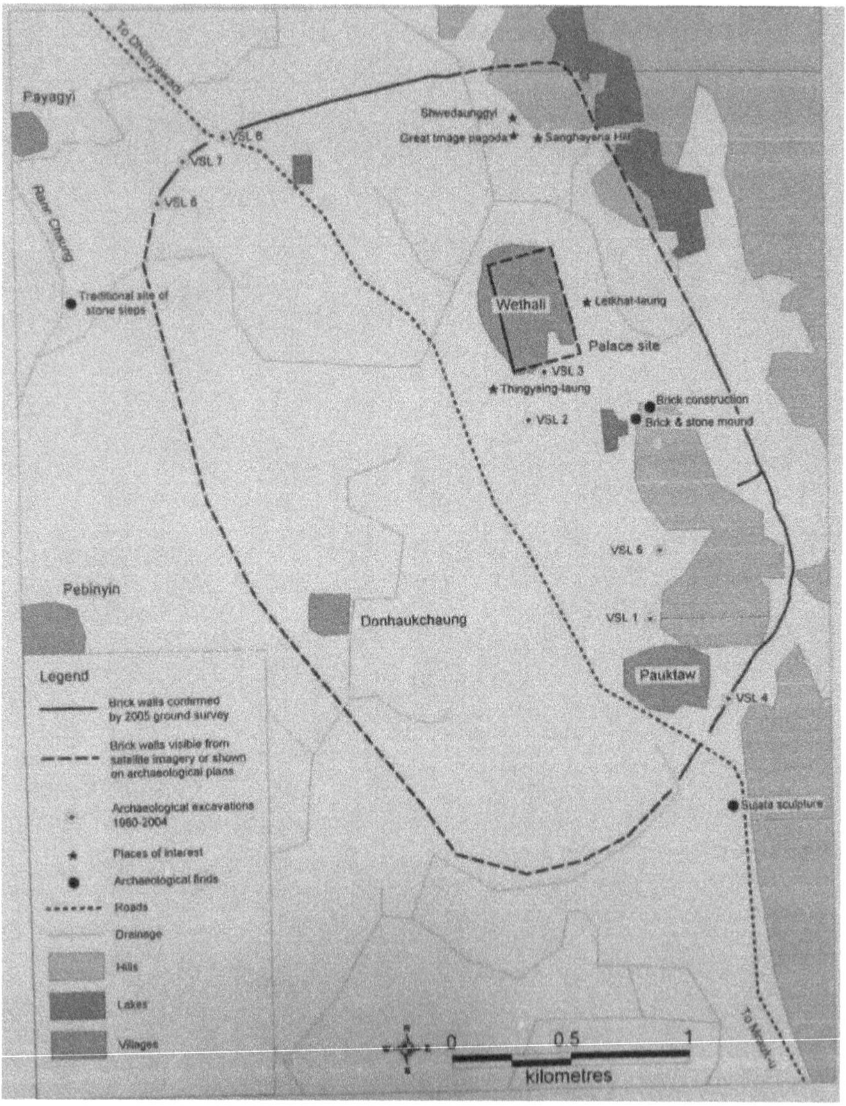

Map 18. New Map of Vesālī surveyed by GPS from Hudson (2005)

Map 19

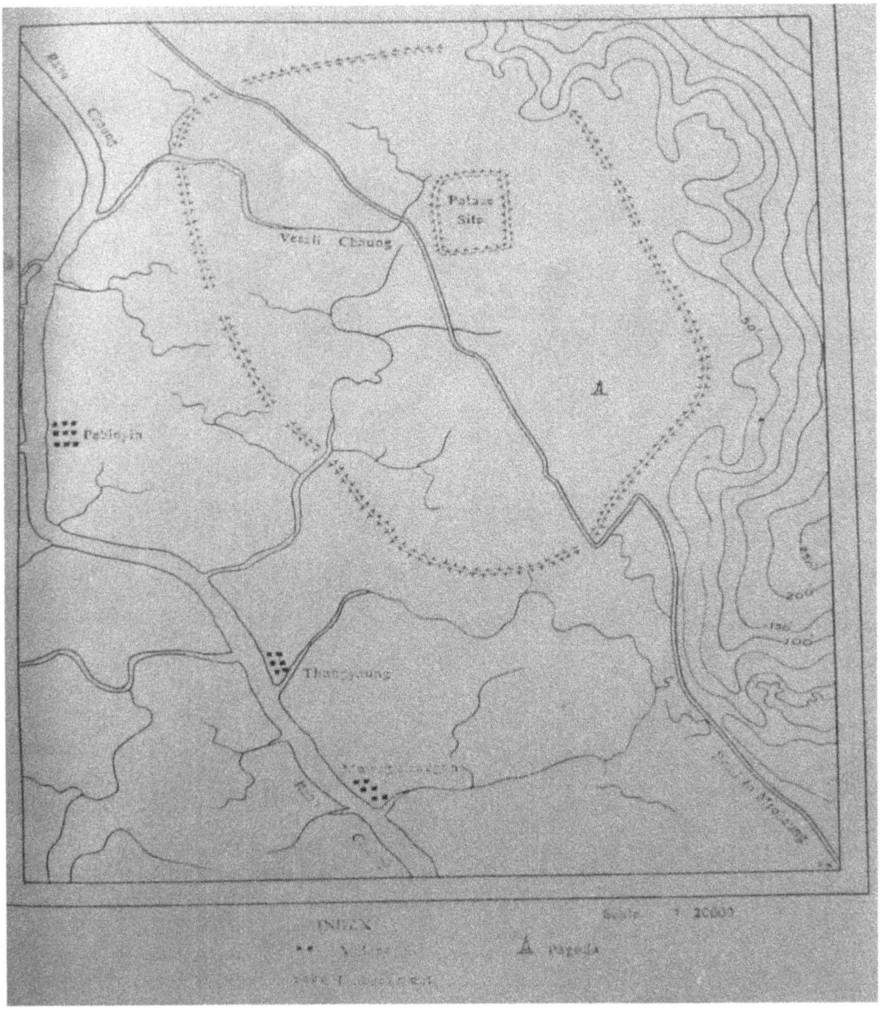

Map 19. Old Map of Vesālī from Thin Kyi (1970)

Map 20

Map 20. Satellite Photo of Vesālī from Google Earth

Appendix II: Tables

Table 1

Table showing Arakan dynasties by foreign scholars

Notion of different Scholars	Notion of different Scholars	Regime [Starting and ending dates]
1. Hall, European group	BC 2666	Starting date of Mārayu
2. -do-	BC 825	-do- Kan Rāzā Gree
3. -do-+Dr. Gutman	AD 1	-do- Añjana and Rālamārayu
4. -do-+-do-	AD 146	-do- Candasūriya
5. Dr. Johnstan	AD 350	-do- Dvencandra
6. Dr. Sircar & Dr. Gutman	AD 370	-do- Dvencandra
7. Dr. A.M.B. Irwin	AD 638	Sūriyarenu & Popa Saw Rahan
8. Dr. Sircar & Dr. Gutman	AD 729+ 10	Ānandacandra-ending date
9. Dr. Gutman	AD +49	Unsettled period
10. Dr. Forchhammer	AD 788-9	Starting date of Mahā Taingcandra
11. -do-	AD 810	-do- Sūriya Taingcandra
12. -do-	AD 935	-do- Taingcandra
13. -do-	AD 951	-do- Sūla Taingcandra
14. -do-	AD 964	-do- Pe Pru
15. -do-	AD 994	-do- Ngaton Murn

16. -do-	AD 24	Ending date of Ngaton Murn
17. -do-	AD 1018	Ending date of Vesālī
18. -do-	AD 1086	Athinkhayar (Usurper)
19. -do-	AD 1096	Starting date of Parein Period by Letyar Murn Nan reigned Arakan throne by the help of Alaungsithu of Bagan.
20. -do-	AD 1153	Starting date of Datha Rāzā (2nd Parein)
21. -do-	AD 1239	Starting date of Alomā Phru
22. Dr. Gutman	AD 1279	Ending date of Vesālī
23. Dr. Forchhammer	AD 1430	Starting date of Mrauk Oo (Murn SawMon) End of
24.	AD 1785	Mrauk Oo
		AD 4451+621 = 5072 2666+621 = 3287

Source: U Shwe Zan's *Wethali* (November 2010)

Table 2

Comparative Statements between Rakhaing Scholars and Arthur P. Phayre Showing Ancient Dynasties and Different Periodizations

Rakhaing Scholars

Sir Arthur P. Phayre

(A) (B)

SN	Dynasties	Christian Eras	Rakhaing Eras	Span	Rulers	Christian Eras	Rakhaing Eras	Span	Rulers
1	Dhaññavatī -								
	(Mārayu	Started				2666–825		1841	54
	Kanrājā Gree	3287 BC				BC		840	23
	Rālamārayu					825 BC–		131	5
	Candasuriya)			3651	110	AD 15		642	25
2	Vesālī	Ended AD		492	25	AD	150–		
		364	155–156	1	-	15–146			
	Sambawak	AD	156–180	24	1	AD	-380	230	12
3	Pañcā	364–793	180–465	285		146–788	380–465	85	15
4	Parein	AD	465–504	39		AD 788	465–529	64	8
5	Khraik	793–794	504–513	9			529–542	13	4

6	Second	AD	513–523	10		AD	AD 1018		
	Sambawak	794–818				1018–1103	542–599	57	16
7	Nerañjarā	AD	523–612	89	61	AD	599–766	167	17
8	Taungoo	818–1103				1103–1167	766–792	26	1
9	Second	AD	612–792	180	48	AD	792–1146	354	48
	Pañcā	1103–1142			245	1167–1180		4450	288
10	Launggret	AD	792–1146	354					
		1142–1151		5071					
	Mrauk Oo	AD				AD			
		1151–1161				1180–1237			
		AD				AD			
		1161–1250				1237–1404			
						AD			
		AD				1404–1430			
		1250–1430				AD			
						1430–1784			
		AD							
		1430–1784							

Source: U Shwe Zan's *Wethali* (November 2010)

Table 3

Table Showing Various Periodizations

Events 1	Añjana Era 2	Ajatasattu Era 3	Kawzā Era 4	Kaliyug Era 5	Asokan Era 6	Hall and Europeans 7	Rakhaing 8	Dr. Sircar Era 9	Dr. Gutman 10
First cancellation	*1 8645	To 2		690 BC	638 BC	AD 1	626 BC		
Buddha's date of birth	68			624 BC	572 BC		609 BC		
Ascension date if Candasuriya	97			594 BC	542 BC	AD 146	680 BC		AD 146
Buddha's enlightenment	103			589 BC	537 BC		545 BC		
Buddha's visit to Dhaññavatī	123			569 BC	517 BC		525 BC		
Buddha's Parinibbāna	148			544 BC	492 BC		500 BC		

Second cancellation	148	1	1	544 BC	429 BC		500 BC		
Candasuriya's death	149	2	2	503 BC	491 BC		499 BC		
Third cancellation Vesālī Kyauk Hlay Gar founded		 856	609 249		AD 117 AD 364	 AD 789	AD 79 AD 326	 AD 370	 Fourth century AD
Fourth cancellation		1184 1169	1332 to 2 560 to 2	AD 638	AD 677		AD 638	AD 677	
Vesālī ended and Lay-mro started		1310	180	AD 818	AD 818	Twelfth century	AD 818	AD 818	Twelfth century
Lay-mro ended and Mrauk Oo began		1974	792	AD 1430			AD 1430		

Mrauk Oo captured and Rakhaing lost his sovereignty		2329	1146	AD 1785			AD 1785		

Source: U Shwe Zan's *Wethali* (November 2010)

Table 4

Comparative Dates between Chronicles and Inscription Sides of Vesali Period
Source: U Shwe Zan's *Wethali* (November 2010)

		S.N.	King	Reign	Kawza Era	Sasana Era	Christ Era 1	Christ Era 2	Dr. Sircar Date	Sasana Era	Kawza Era	Reign	King	S.N.
27	758	1	Taicandra	57	249	856	327	364	370	858	249	55	Dvencandra	1
20	810	2	Rajacandra	49	306	911	382	419	425	913	304	20	Rajacandra	2
			Suriyacandra			931	402	439	445	933	324	9	Kalacandra	3
						940	411	448	454	942	333	22	Devacandra	4
					355	962	433	470	476	964	355			
			2	106	106	106	106	106	106	106	106	106	4	
	830	3	Molacandra	49	355	962	433	470	476	964	355	7	Yajnacandra	5
	849	4	Polacandra	46	404	969	440	477	483	971	362	6	Candrabandu	6
	875	5	Kalacandra	48	450	975	446	483	489	977	368	7	Bhumicandra	7
	884	6	Htulacandra	19	498	982	453	490	496	984	375	24	Bhuticandra	8
						1006	477	514	520	1008	399	55	Niticandra	9
						1061	532	569	575	1053	454	3	Viracandra	10
						1064	535	572	578	1066	457	12	Priticandra	11
						1076	547	584	590	1078	469	7	Pathvicandra	12

						1083	554	591	597	1086	476	3	Dhrticandra	13
						1086	557	594	600	1088	479	12	Mahavira	14
						1098	569	606	612	1100	491	12	Varajayap	15
						1110	581	618	624	1112	503	12	Sevinren	16
					517	1122	593	630	636	1124	515			
					162	160	160	160	160	160	160	160	12	
32	903	4	Siricandra		517	1122	593	630	636	1124	515	13	Dharmasuriya	17
					587/29	1135	606	643	649	1137	528	13	Vjaskti	18
						1151	622	659	665	1153	544	36	Dharmavijaya	19
						1187	658	695	701	1189	680	3	Narendravijaya	20
					29	1190	661	698	704	1192	23		14	
				72	72	68	68	68	68	68	68	68		
16	935	8	Singhacandra	66	29	1190	661	698	704	1192	23	16	Dhrmacandra	21
					95	1206	677	724	740	1208	39	9	Anandacandra	22
					1	1225	696	733	759	1227	58	10	2	
				66	66	35	35	35	35	35	35	35		
6	951	9	Sulacandra	36	95	1225	696	733	720	1227	58	36	Sulacandra	23
7	957	10	Ahmrathu	7	131	1261	732	769	756	1263	94	7	Ahmrathu	24
30	964	11	Pephru	17	138	1268	739	776	763	1270	101	17	Pephru	25
		12	-		155	1285	756	793	780	1287	118	+	-	26
24	994	13	Nga Ton	0	156	1286	757	794	781	1288	119	24	Nga Ton	27

					180	1310	781	818	805	1312	143			
			4		85	85	85	85	85	85	85		4	
				491	491	454 37	454 37	454 37	454 37	454 37	454 37	454 37		
				491	491	491	491	491	491	491	491	491		

Chronicle Side Inscription Side

S.N.	Number of Years	Number of Kings	Number of Years	Number of Kings	Remarks	
1	106	2	106	4	2–4 (1:2)	
2	162	4	160	12	4–12 (1:3)	+2
3	72	1	68	4	1–4	+4
4	66	1	35	2	1–2	+31
5	85	5	85	5	5–5 (1:1)	
	491	13	+454	27	37	

37 13–27

Table V

CHRONOLOGICAL TABLE OF THE KINGS OF ARAKAN.
Source: Phare, Sir Arthur P. *History of Burma* (1967 ed.) (1883)

Dhy-nyga-wa-ti Dynasty.

No.	Name of Sovereign	Date of Accession, B.C.	Date of Accession, At Era.	Reign, Yrs	Reign, Ms.	Relationship of each Succeeding Sovereign.
1	Ma-ra-yo	2666	...	62	0	
2	Ma-ra-dzi	...	...	32	0	Son.
3	Ma-ra-on-leng	...	...	53	0	"
4	Ma-ra-rway-leng	...	...	48	0	"
5	Ma-ra-bengh	...	...	55	0	"
6	Ma-ra-dzi	...	...	33	0	"
7	Ma-ra-keng	...	..	32	0	"
8	Nga-tshup-o	...	..	21	0	An usurper.
9	Dwa-ra-tsan-dra	...	..	40	0	Son of Má-ra-keng.
10	Tho-la-tsan-dra	...	..	33	0	Son.
11	Tsan-da-thu-ri-ya-tsan-dra	...	..	37	0	"
12	Ka-la-tsan-dra	...	...	40	0	"
13	Ti-tsan-dra	...	..	31	0	Son.
14	Ma-dhu-tha-tsan-dra	...	..	20	0	"
15	Dze-ya-tsan-dra	...	..	40	0	"
16	Mok-kha-tsan-dra	...	..	26	0	"
17	Gun-na-tsan dra	...	..	12	0	"
	Three nobles reigned for seven days, three months, and eight months successively	...	...	0	11	Usurpers.
18	Kan-Ra-dza-gyi	...	...	41	0	Grandson of Gun-na-tsan-drá.
19	Kan-Ra-dza-ngai	...	...	36	0	Brother.
20	In-da-thu-ri-ya	...	...	35	0	Son.
21	A-thu-rin-da-thu-ri-ya	...	...	30	0	"
22	Tha-ra-me-ta	...	...	28	0	"
23	Thu-ri-ya	...	...	31	0	"
24	Meng-thi	...	...	22	0	"
25	Meng-ba	...	...	22	0	"
26	Tsi-oung	...	...	28	0	"
27	Ta-taing-theng	...	...	31	0	Brother.
28	Kyau-khoung-weng	...	...	31	0	Son.
29	Thu-ri-ya-nan-da-mit	...	...	21	0	"
30	A-thu-rin-da-bha-ya	...	...	31	0	"
31	Let-ya-tsi-thu-kyi	...	...	32	0	"
32	Thi-ha-ka	...	...	43	0	"
33	Meng-bhun-than	...	..	31	0	"
34	Tha-ret-hmwe	...	..	49	0	"
35	Dze-ya-nan-da-thu	...	..	51	0	"
36	Tek-ka-thu	...	..	46	0	"
37	Lek-kha-na	...	...	37	0	"
38	Gun-na-rit	...	...	48	0	"
39	Thi-wa-rit	...	...	41	0	"
40	Meng-hla-hmwe	...	...	31	0	"
41	Ma-rin-da	...	...	62	0	"
42	Thi-dhat-kum-ma-ra	...	...	22	0	"
43	Meng-hla-kyi	...	...	47	0	"
44	Meng-hla-ngay	...	...	24	0	Brother.
45	Nga-tsa-rit	...	...	38	0	Son.
46	Myet-hna-wun	...	...	31	0	"
47	Let-thut-kyi	...	...	27	0	"
48	Thi-ri-kam-ma-thun-da	...	...	31	0	"
49	Nan-da-ko-ta-bha-ya	...	...	27	0	"
50	Meng-nan-hpyu	...	...	20	0	"
51	Meng-ma-nu	...	...	28	0	"
52	Meng-khoung-ngay	...	..	19	0	"
53	Louk-khoung-ra-dza	...	..	40	0	"
54	Meng-ngay-pyau-hla-tsi	...	..	6	0	"
	Three nobles usurp the throne	...	..	6	8	

Dhi-ngya-wa-ti Second Dynasty.

No.	Name of Sovereign.	Date of Accession. B.C.	Date of Accession. Ar. Era.	Reign. Yrs.	Reign. Ms.	Relationship of each Succeeding Sovereign.
1	Kan-Ra-dza-gyi	825	...	37	0	
2	Thi-la-Ra-dza	...	...	48	0	Son.
3	Wa-tsa-thu-ra	...	...	31	0	”
4	Nan-da-wi-thu-ra	...	...	40	0	”
5	Pu-na-thu-ri-ya	...	...	32	0	”
6	Thu-ran-da	...	...	23	0	”
7	Tsan-di-ma	...	...	37	0	”
8	Thi-ri-tsan-da	...	...	40	0	”
9	Thi-ha-ran	...	...	46	0	Brother.
10	Thi-ha-nu	...	...	20	0	Son.
11	Pa-ya-ka	...	...	31	0	”
12	Ne-la-gun	...	...	41	0	”
13	Roha-ha-gua	...	...	31	0	”
14	Thi-ri-gun	...	...	24	0	”
15	Tha-ma-dza	...	...	35	0	Nephew.
16	Kum-ma-ra	...	...	20	0	Son.
17	Thek-hteng-hypu	...	...	40	0	”
18	Tha-bheng-u	...	...	42	0	”
19	Te-dza-wun	...	...	36	0	”
20	Mun-dza-ya-ba	...	...	34	0	”
21	Kum-ma-ra-wi-thud-dhi	...	...	87	0	”
22	Wa-thu-mun-da-la	...	...	34	0	”
23	Thu-rin-da	...	...	31	0	”
		A.D.				
24	Ra-la-ma-yu	15	...	22	0	Brother.
25	Na-la-ma-yu	37	...	31	0	Son.
26	Wa-dha-gun	68	...	22	0	”
27	Wi-thu-ra-dza	90	...	21	0	”
28	Thi-ri-ra-dza	111	...	35	0	”

Dhi-ngya-wa-ti Dynasty of the Religion of Goad-a-ma.

No.	Name of Sovereign.	Date of Accession. A.D.	Date of Accession. Ar. Era.	Reign. Yrs.	Reign. Ms.	Relationship of each Succeeding Sovereign.
29	Tsan-da-thu-ri-ya	146	...	52	0	Son.
30	Thu-ri-ya-di-ti	198	...	47	0	”
31	Thu-ri-ya-pa-ti-pat	245	...	53	0	”
32	Thu-ri-ya-ru-pa	298	...	15	0	”
33	Thu-ri-ya-man da-la	313	...	62	0	”
34	Thu-ri-ya-wan-na	375	...	44	0	”
35	Thu-ri-ya-na-tha	418	...	40	0	”
36	Thu-ri-ya-weng-tha	459	...	9	0	”
37	Thu-ri-ya-ban-da	468	...	6	0	”
38	Thu-ri-ya-ka-lya-na	474	...	18	0	”
39	Thu-ri-ya-muk-kha	492	...	21	0	”
40	Thu-ri-ya-te-dza	513	...	31	0	”
41	Thu-ri-ya-pu-nya	544	...	8	0	”
42	Thu-ri-ya-ku-la	552	...	23	0	Son.
43	Thu-ri-ya-pa-bas	575	...	25	0	”
44	Thu-ri-ya-tsi-tra	600	...	18	0	”
45	Thu-ri-ya-the-tha	618	...	22	0	”
46	Thu-ri-ya-wi-ma-la	640	...	8	0	”
47	Thu-ri-ya-re-nu	648	...	22	0	Brother.
48	Thu-ri-ya-geng-tha	670	...	16	0	Son.
49	Thu-ri-ya-thek-ya	686	...	8	0	Paternal uncle.
50	Thu-ri-ya-thi-ri	794	...	20	0	Son.
51	Thu-ri-ya-ke-thi	714	...	9	0	”
52	Thu-ri-ya-kut-ta	723	...	23	0	”
53	Thu-ri-ya-ke-tu	746	...	42	0	”

Dynasty of the City We-tha-li.

No.	Name of Sovereign.	Date of Accession. A.D.	Date of Accession. Ar. Era.	Reign. Yrs.	Reign. Ms.	Relationship of each Succeeding Sovereign.
1	Ma-ba-taing-tsan-dra	788	150	22	0	Son.
2	Thu-ri-ya-taing-tsan-dra	810	172	20	0	”
3	Mau-la-taing-tsan-dra	830	192	19	0	”
4	Pau-la-taing-tsan-dra	849	211	26	0	”
5	Ka-la-taing-tsan-dra	875	237	9	0	”
6	Du-la-taing-tsan-dra	884	246	19	0	”
7	Thi-ri-taing-tsan-dra	903	265	32	0	”

8	Thing-gha-tha-taing-tsan-dra	935	297	16	0	"
9	Tsu-la-taing-tsan-dra	951	313	6	0	"
10	A-mya-thu	957	319	7	0	A chief of the Myu tribe.
11	Pai-phyu	964	326	30	0	Nephew.
12	Nga-meng-nga-tum	994	356	24	0	Son of Tsu-la-taing-tsan-dra.
	Dynasty of Ping-tsa City.					
1	Khet-ta-theng	1018	380	10	0	Grand-nephew to Tsu-la-taing-tsan-dra.
2	Tsan-da-theng	1028	390	11	0	Brother.
3	Meng-reng-phyu	1039	401	10	0	Son.
4	Na-ga-thu-ri-ya	1049	411	3	0	"
5	Thu-ri-ya-Ra-dza	1052	414	2	0	"
6	Pun-na-ka	1054	416	4	0	"
7	Meng-phyu-gyi	1058	420	2	0	"
8	Tsi-tha-beng	1060	422	1	0	Usurper.
9	Meng-nan-thu	1061	423	5	0	Son of Meng-phyu-gyi.
10	Meng-la-de	1066	428	6	0	Son.
11	Meng-ku-la	1072	434	3	0	"
12	Meng-Bhi-lu	1075	437	3	0	"
13	Theng-kha-ya	1078	440	14	0	Usurper.
14	Meng-than	1092	454	8	0	Son.
15	Meng-pa-di	1100	462	3	0	"
	Dynasty of the City Pa-rin.					
1	Let-ya-Meng-nan	1103	465	6	0	Grandson of Meng-Bhi-lu.
2	Thi-ha-ba	1109	471	1	0	Son.
3	Ra-dza-gyi	1110	472	2	0	Son.
4	Tha-ki-weng-gyi	1112	474	3	0	"
5	Tha-ki-weng-ngay	1115	477	18	0	"
6	Gau-li-ya	1133	495	20	0	"
7	Da-tha-Ra-dza	1153	515	12	0	"
8	A-nan-thi-ri	1165	527	2	0	"
	Dynasty of the City Khyit.					
1	Meng-Phun-tsa	1167	529	7	0	Brother.
2	Pin-tsa-ka-wa	1174	536	2	0	Son.
3	Gan-na-yu-ban	1176	538	3	0	"
4	Tsa-leng-ka-bo	1179	541	1	0	Usurper.
	Second Dynasty of the City Ping-Tsa.					
1	Mi-dzu-theng	1180	542	11	0	Son of Pin-tsa-ka-wa.
2	Nga-ran-man	1191	553	2	0	Son.
3	Nga-pug-gan	1193	555	2	0	"
4	Nga-ra-khoing	1195	557	3	0	"
5	Nga-kyun	1198	560	3	0	"
6	Nga-tshu'	1201	563	4	0	"
7	Nga-tswai-theng	1205	567	1	0	"
8	Meng-koung-gyi	1206	568	1	0	"
9	Meng-khoung-ngay	1207	569	1	0	"
10	Kam-bha-loung-gyi	1208	570	1	0	"
11	Kam-bha-loung-ngay	1209	571	1	0	"
12	Let-ya-gyi	1210	572	8	0	"
13	Let-ya-ngay	1218	580	11	0	"
14	Tha-na-beng	1229	591	3	0	"
15	Nga-na-thin	1232	594	2	0	"
16	Nga-na-lum	1234	596	3	0	"
	Dynasty of the City Loung-Kyet.					
1	H-lan-ma-phyu	1237	599	6	0	Son.
2	Ra-dza-thu-gyi	1243	605	3	0	"
3	Tsau-lu	1246	608	5	0	"
4	Uts-tsa-na-gyi	1251	613	9	0	"
5	Tsau-mwun-gyi	1260	622	8	0	"
6	Nan-kya-gyi	1268	630	4	0	"
7	Meng-Bhi-lu	1272	634	4	0	"
8	Tsi-tha-beng	1276	638	3	0	Usurper.
9	Meng di	1279	641	106	0	Son of Meng-bhi-lu.
10	Uts-tsa-na-ngay	1385	747	2	0	Son.
11	Thi-wa-rit	1387	749	3	0	Younger brother.
12	Thin-tse	1390	752	4	0	" "
13	Ra-dza-thu	1394	756	1	0	Son.

14	Tsi-tha-beng	1395	757	2	0	Usurper.
15	Myin-tsoing-kyi	1397	759	0	5	"
16	Ra-dza-thu (restored)	1397	759	4	0	
17	Thing-ga-thu	1401	763	3	0	Brother.
	Dynasty of the City Myouk-u.					
1	Meng-tsau-mwun	1404	766	2	0	Son of Ra-dza-thu
	Interregnum	...	...	24	0	
	Meng-tsau-mwun (restored)	...	792	4	0	
2	Men-kha-ri	1434	796	25	0	Brother.
3	Ba-tsau-phyu	1459	821	23	0	Son.
4	Dau-lya	1482	844	10	0	"
5	Ba-tsau-nygo	1492	854	2	0	Uncle, a son of Meng-kha-ri.
6	Ran-oung	1494	856	0	6	Son of Dau-lya.
7	Tsa-leng-ga-thu	1494	856	7	0	Uncle by the mother's side.
8	Men-ra-dza	1501	863	22	0	Son.
9	Ga-dza-ba-di	1523	885	2	0	"
10	Meng-tsau-o	1525	887	0	6	Brother to Tsa-leng-ga-thu.
11	Tha-tsa-ta	1525	887	6	0	Son of Dau-lya.
12	Meng-beng	1531	893	22	0	Son of Men-Ra-dsa.
13	Dik-kha	1553	915	2	6	Son.
14	Tsau-lha	1555	917	9	0	"
15	Meng-Tsek-ya	1564	926	7	0	Brother.
16	Meng-Pha-loung	1571	933	22	0	Son of Meng-beng.
17	Meng-Ra-dza-gyi	1593	955	19	0	Son.
18	Meng-Kha-moung	1612	974	10	0	"
19	Thi-ri-thu-dham-ma	1622	984	16	0	"
20	Meng-Tsa-ni	1638	1000	...		Son reigned only 28 days.
21	Na-ra-ba-di-gyi	1645	1000	7	0	Great-grandson of No. 11, Tha-tsa-ta.
22	Tha-do	1638	1007	7	0	Brother's son.
23	Tsanda Thudhamma	1652	1014	32	0	Son.
24	Thiri Thuriya	1684	1046	1	0	"
25	Wara Dhamma Rádzá	1685	1047	7	0	Brother.
26	Munithu Dhamma Rádzá	1692	1054	2	0	"
27	Tsanda Thuriya Dhamma Rádzá	1694	1056	2	0	"
28	Naurahtá Dzáu	1696	1058	...		Son, reigned 15 days.
29	Mayuppiya	1696	1058	1	0	Usurper.
30	Kalamandat	1697	1059	1	0	"
31	Naradhibadi	1698	1060	2	0	Son of No. 27, Tsanda Thuriya.
32	Tsanda Wimala	1700	1062	6	0	Grandson of No. 22, Thado.
33	Tsanda Thuriya	1706	1068	4	0	Grandson of No. 23, Tsanda Thudhamma.
34	Tsanda Widzaya	1710	1072	21	0	Usurper.
35	Tsanda Thuriya	1731	1093	3	0	Son-in-law.
36	Naradhibadi	1734	1096	1	0	Son.
37	Nara Pawara Rádzá	1735	1097	2	0	Usurper.
38	Tsanda Widzala	1737	1099	0	8	Cousin.
39	Katya	...	...	...		A foreigner; held the palace for three days.
40	Ma-da-rit	1737	1099	5	0	Brother to No. 38.
41	Na-ra-a-pa-ya	1742	1104	19	0	Uncle.
42	Thi-ri-thu	1761	1123	0	3	Son.
43	Pa-ra-ma-Ra-dza	1761	1123	3	0	Brother.
44	Ma-ha-Ra-dza	1764	1126	9	4	Brother-in-law.
45	Thu-ma-na	1773	1135	4	0	" "
46	Tsan-da-wi-ma-la	1777	1139	...		Usurper, reigned forty days.
47	Tha-di-tha-dhamma-yit	1777	1139	5	0	A chief from Ram-byi.
48	Tha-ma-da	1782	1144	2	0	A chief in whose reign the Burmese conquered the country.

APPENDIXES

Appendix III: Plates

Plate 01

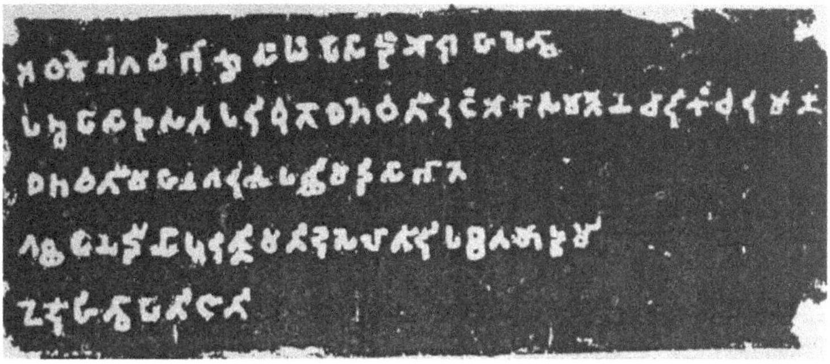

01. Taungbauk Gree Inscription [from Goyamray Saw Won (1994 Dec)]

02. Fat Monk Image Inscription from Pan-Zee-Mraung-Phar, Mrauk-U, (c.2nd century B.C to 2nd Century A.D) [from San Tha Aung (1979)]

Plate 02

The Buddha in preaching style to the King Candasuriya in attentive listening to the Buddha's sermon, Kyauk-taw, Arakan [from San Tha Aung (1979)]

[from U Shwe Zan (1997)]

Slab 01 Slab 02

Slab 03 Slab 04 Slab 05

[from Gutman (2001) except Slab 02]

Plate 03

Yaksa General Panada

Legible Inscription of the Yaksa General Panada

01

Naga King of
Mahamuni Shrine

02

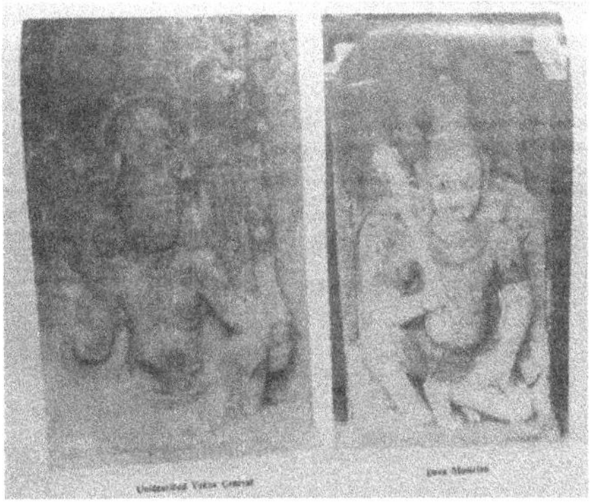

03

Unidentified Yaksa General
& Deva Musician

Source: San Tha Aung (1979)

Plate 04

04

Kinnara

05

Kinnara

06

Bodhisattva

Source: San Tha Aung (1979)

Plate 05

07

Lokapala

08

Lokapala Diad

Source: San Tha Aung (1979)

Plate 06

09

Diad

Triad

10

Dorapala & Squating Figure

Source: San Tha Aung (1979)

Plate 07

01

Miniasture Stone Stupa with niches   Miniasture stone stupa from Kyauktaw Hill

02

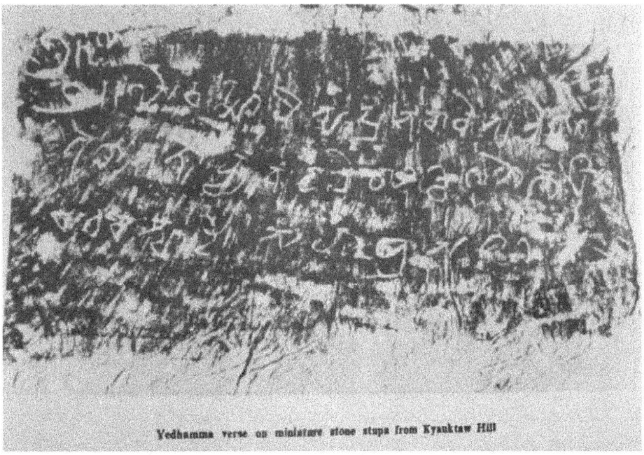

Ye dhamma Verse on Miniature stone Stupa from Kyauktaw Hill

Source: San Tha Aung (1979)

Plate 08

03

Miniature stone stupa 1 from Meechaungwa

Ye dhamma verse on miniature stone stupa 1 from Meechaungwa

04

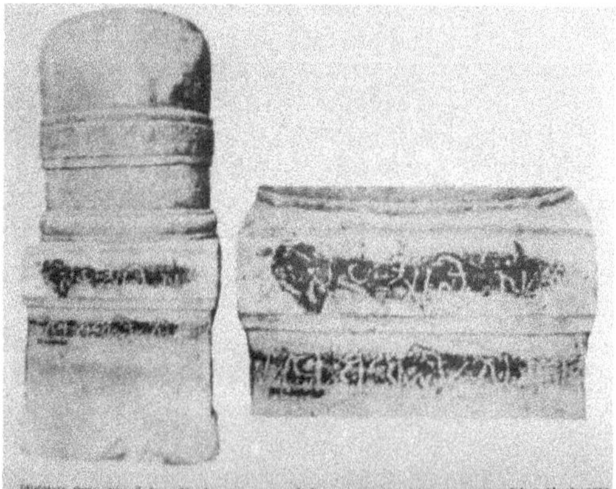

Miniature stone stupa 2 from Meechaungwa

Ye dhamma verse on Miniature stone stupa 2 from Meechaungwa

Source: San Tha Aung (1979)

Plate 09

01

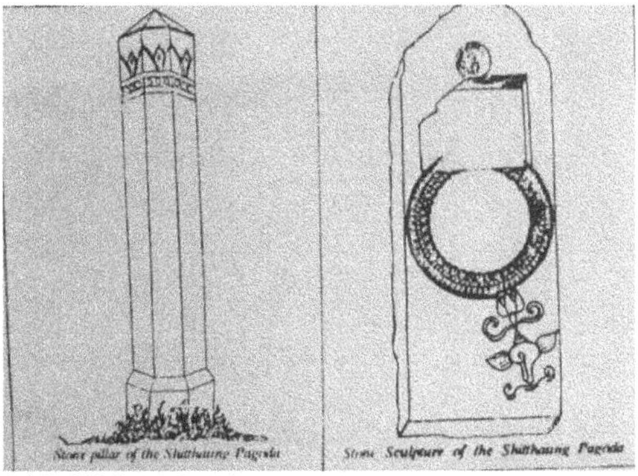

Stone pillar of the Shitthaung Pagoda

Stone Sculpture of the Shitthaung Pagoda

Source: U Shwe Zan (1997)

02

Photo of Stone Sculpture of the Shitthaung Pagoda

Plate 10

Plinth Inscription of Buddha Image From Vesali (c.5th - 6th century A.D.)

Source: U Shwe Zan (2010)

Plate 11

01 Photo of Mahamuni Shrine, Kyauktaw Source: U Shwe Zan (1997)

02

Mahamuni Buddha Image, Kyauktaw

Plate 12

03

Old Photo of Mahamuni Buddha Image, Mandalay

Source: U Shwe Zan (1997)

04

Present photo of Mahamuni Buddha Image, Mandalay

Plate 13

05

Old Photo of Ran Aung Mrun, Zalun

06

Present Photo of
Ran Aung Mrun, Zalun

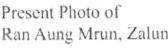

Plate 14

07

Photo of Candamuni,
Buddha Image, Mrauk Oo

08

Photo of Cakkramuni
Buddha Image, Sittway

Plate 15

Photo of the Great Buddha Image of Vesali

Plate 16

01

Niticandra Inscriptions of Vesali

02

Viracandra Inscriptions of Vesali

Source: San Tha Aung (1979)

Plate 17

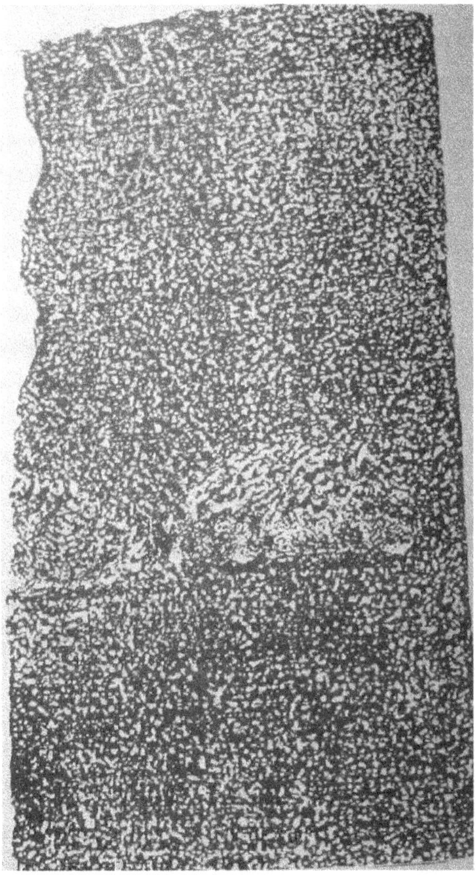

01 Anandacandra Pillar Inscription (East Face Upper Part I (c. 5th-6th Century AD)

Source: U Shwe Zan (2010)

Plate 18

02 Anandacandra Pillar Inscription (East Face Upper Part II (c. 5th-6th Century AD)

Source: U Shwe Zan (2010)

Plate 19

03 Shitthaung Pillar Inscription of Anandacandra, Mrauk Oo
(West face Part I) (c. 8th Century AD)

Source: U Shwe Zan (2010)

Plate 20

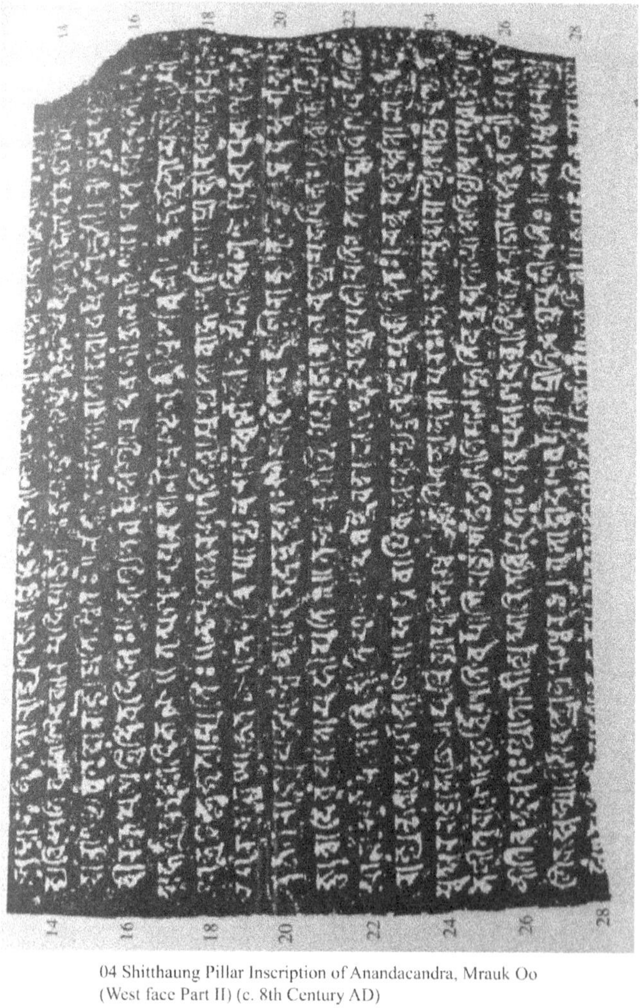

04 Shitthaung Pillar Inscription of Anandacandra, Mrauk Oo (West face Part II) (c. 8th Century AD)

Source: U Shwe Zan (2010)

Plate 21

05 Shitthaung Pillar Inscription of Anandacandra, Mrauk Oo
(West face Part III) (c. 8th Century AD)

Source: U Shwe Zan (2010)

Plate 22

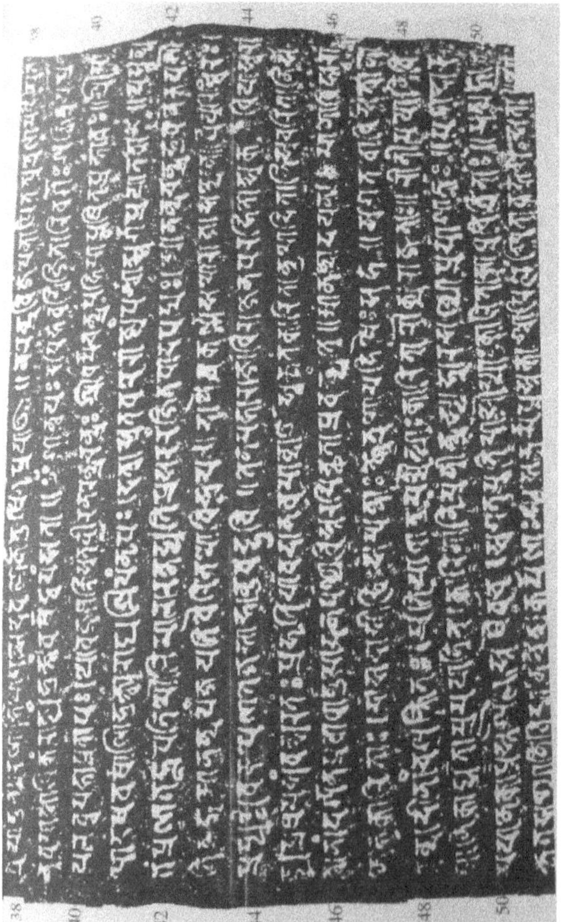

06 Shitthaung Pillar Inscription of Anandacandra, Mrauk Oo
(West face Part IV) (c. 8th Century AD)

Source: U Shwe Zan (2010)

Plate 23

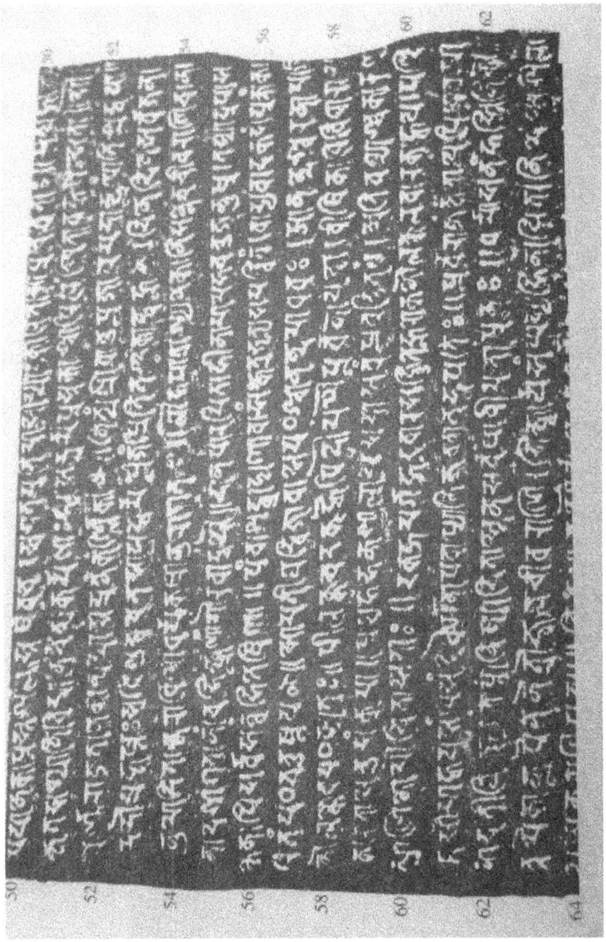

07 Shitthaung Pillar Inscription of Anandacandra, Mrauk Oo (West face Part V) (c. 8th Century AD)

Source: U Shwe Zan (2010)

Plate 24

08 Shitthaung Pillar Inscription of Anandacandra, Mrauk Oo (West face Part VI) (c. 8th Century AD)

Source: U Shwe Zan (2010)

Plate 25

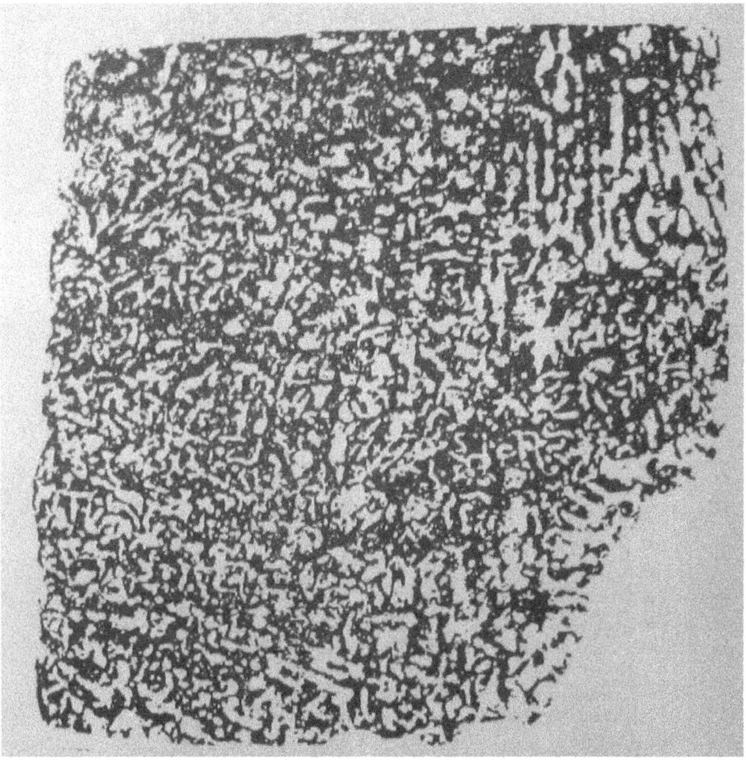

09 Shitthaung Pillar Inscription of Anandacandra, Mrauk Oo
(North face Top Part II) (c. 9th-10th Century AD)

Source: U Shwe Zan (2010)

Plate 26

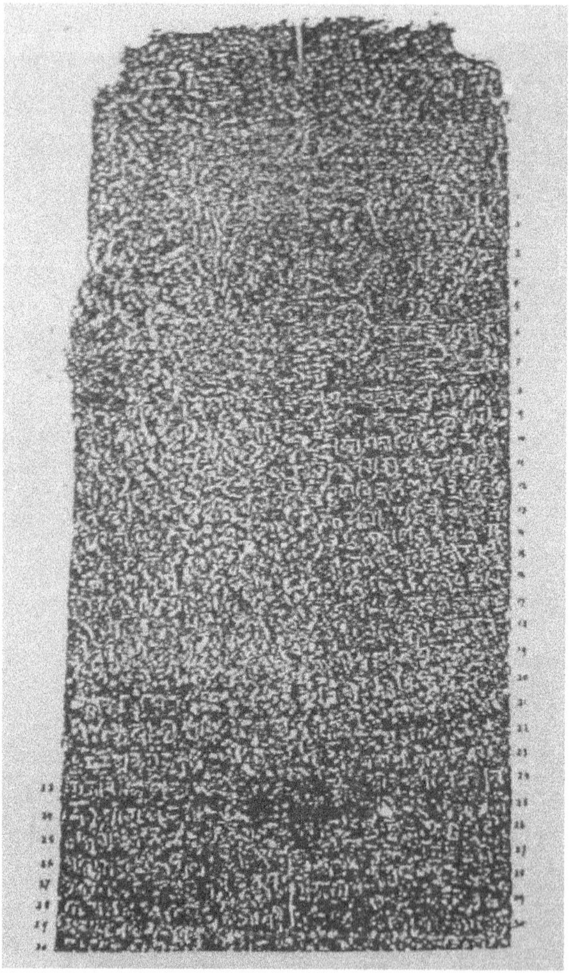

10 Shitthaung Pillar Inscription of Anandacandra, Mrauk Oo
(North face Upper Part I) (c. 9th-10th Century AD)

Source: U Shwe Zan (2010)

Plate 27

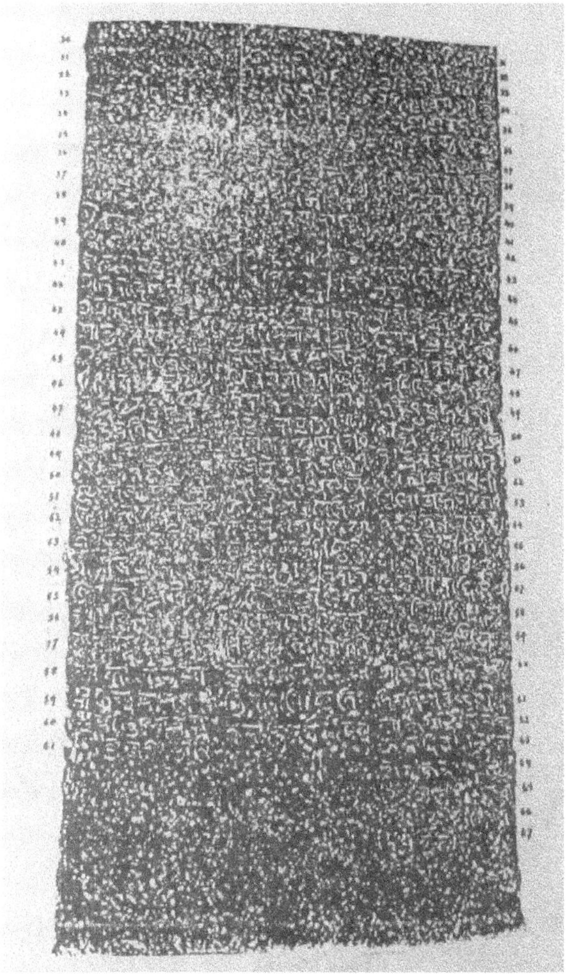

11 Shitthaung Pillar Inscription of Anandacandra, Mrauk Oo
(North face Lower Part II) (c. 9th-10th Century AD)

Source: U Shwe Zan (2010)

Plate 28

Inscription of Candrasiri from Sandway

Source: U Shwe Zan (2010)

Plate 28

Inscription of Candrasiri from Sandway

Source: U Shwe Zan (2010)

Plate 29

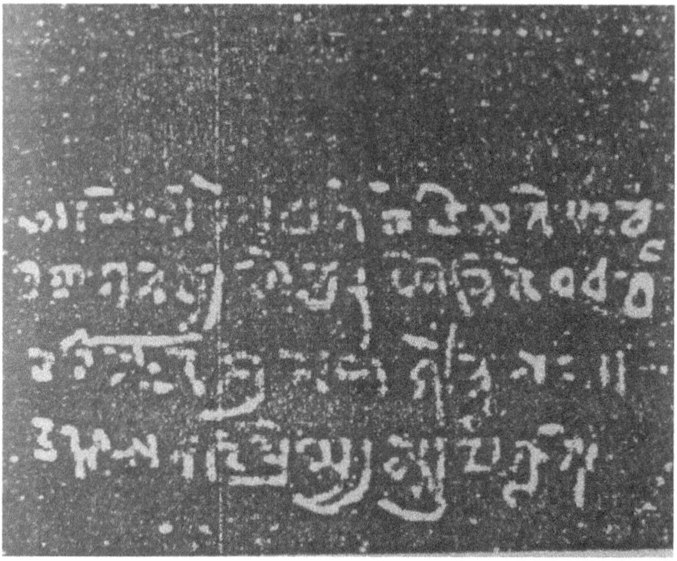

Stone Slab Inscription from Ohtein, Taunggouk

Source: U Shwe Zan (2010)

Plate 30

Stone Slab Inscription from Grat-ga-rwa-ma, Kyauk Phru

Source: U Shwe Zan (2010)

Plate 31

Stone Slab Inscription from Nga-lone-maw

Source: U Shwe Zan (2010)

Plate 32

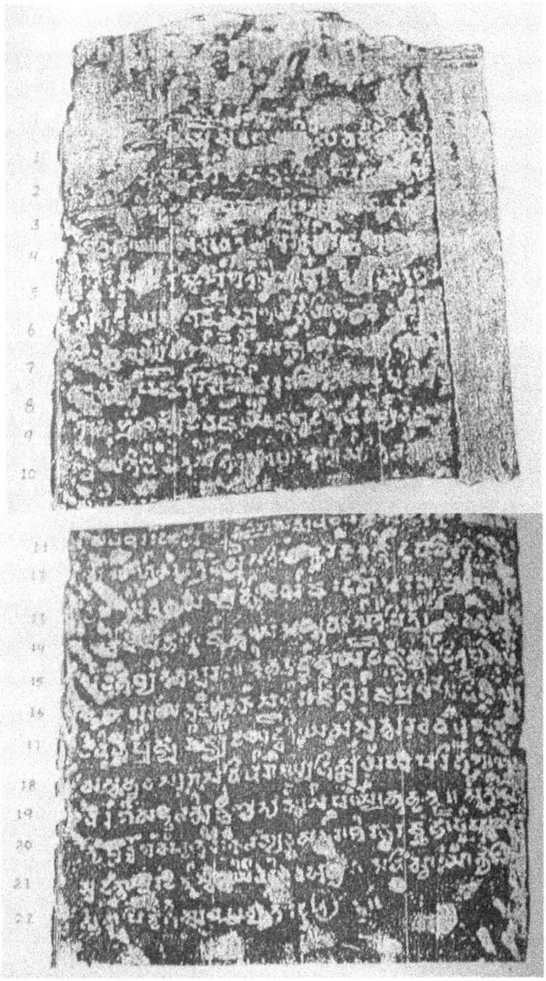

Bhanta Stone Slab Inscription of Dharmavijaya, Vesali
(c. 6th-7th Century AD)

Source: U Shwe Zan (2010)

Plate 33
Buddha Images from Rakhaing

Source: San Tha Aung (1979)

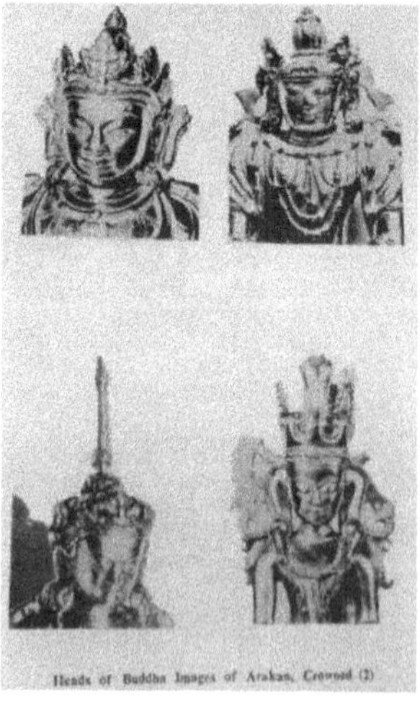

Plate 34

Buddha Images from Rakhaing

Source: San Tha Aung (1979)

Plate 35

Buddha Images from Rakhaing

Crowned Buddha of Arakan. Bronze. Dhyana Mudra. Right leg on left leg.

Crowned Buddha of Arakan. Bronze. Dhyana Mudra. Right leg on left leg. Two broken caityas, Vasumdhari and a guardian Lion.

Crowned Buddha of Arakan. Bronze. Dhyana Mudra. Legs crossed.

Source: San Tha Aung (1979)

Plate 36

Buddha Images from Rakhaing

Source: San Tha Aung (1979)

Plate 37

Buddha Images from Rakhaing

Crowned Buddha of Arakan. Bronze. Dhyana Mudra. Legs crossed

Crowned Buddha of Arakan. Bronze. Dhyana Mudra. Legs crossed

Crowned Buddha of Arakan. Stone. Bhumisparsa Mudra. Right leg on left leg

Source: San Tha Aung (1979)

Plate 38

Buddha Images from Rakhaing

Crowned Buddha of Arakan. Bronze. Bhumisparsa Mudra. Right leg on left leg.

Crowned Buddha of Arakan. Bronze. Bhumisparsa Mudra. Legs crossed

Crowned Buddha of Arakan. Bronze. Bhumisparsa Mudra. Right leg on left leg.

Crowned Buddha of Arakan. Bronze. Bhumisparsa Mudra. Legs crossed.

Source: San Tha Aung (1979)

Plate 39

Buddha Images from Rakhaing

Source: San Tha Aung (1979)

Plate 40

Buddha Images from Rakhaing

Source: San Tha Aung (1979)

Plate 41

Buddha Images from Rakhaing

Source: San Tha Aung (1979)

Plate 42

Buddha Images from Rakhaing

Right leg on left leg. Two attendent figures in Bhumisparsa Mudra.

Bronze Buddha of Arakan. Bhumisparsa Mudra. Right leg on left leg. Two attendent figures in Bhumisparsa Mudra and Yasamdhari.

Source: San Tha Aung (1979)

Plate 43

Buddha Images from Rakhaing

Bronze Buddha of Arakan. Bhumisparsa Mudra. Right leg on left leg. Two attendant figures in Bhumisparsa Mudra and Vasundhari.

Bronze Buddha of Arakan. Bhumisparsa Mudra. Right leg on left leg. Two attendant figures in Bhumisparsa Mudra and Vasundhari.

Bronze Buddha of Arakan. Bhumisparsa Mudra. Right leg on left leg.

Bronze Buddha of Arakan. Bhumisparsa Mudra. Right leg on left leg.

Source: San Tha Aung (1979)

Plate 44

Buddha Images from Rakhaing

Source: San Tha Aung (1979)

Plate 45

Buddha Images from Rakhaing

Source: San Tha Aung (1979)

Plate 46

Buddha Images from Rakhaing

Source: San Tha Aung (1979)

Plate 47

Buddha Images from Rakhaing

Standing Buddha. Bronze. Abhaya Mudra.

Standing Buddha. Bronze. Abhaya and Varada Mudra.

Standing Buddha. Bronze. Abhaya and Varada Mudra.

Crowned Buddha of Arakan. Bronze. Internal Varada Mudra. Right leg on left leg.

Crowned Buddha of Arakan. Bronze. Internal Varada Mudra. Right leg on left leg. Two praying attendants.

Source: San Tha Aung (1979)

Plate 48

Buddha Images from Rakhaing

Crowned Buddha of Arakan. [illegible] Varada Mudra. Right leg on left leg. Two attendants in Bhumisparsa Mudra. Two praying attendants. Two Caityas. Guardian animals and Vasundhari

Ten Scenes Plate of Arakan

Eight Scenes Plate of Arakan

Source: San Tha Aung (1979)

Plate 48
Buddha Images from Rakhaing

Crowned Buddha of Arakan. Bronze. Internal Varada Mudra. Right leg on left leg. Two attendants in Bhumisparsa Mudra. Two praying attendants. Two Caityas. Guardian animals and Vasumdhari.

Ten Scenes Plate of Arakan

Eight Scenes Plate of Arakan

Source: San Tha Aung (1979)

Plate 49

Miniature Bronze Zetis from Rakhaing

01

02

03

Source: San Tha Aung (1979)

Plate 50

Copper Plate Land Grant

Copper-plate Land Grant (Obverse)

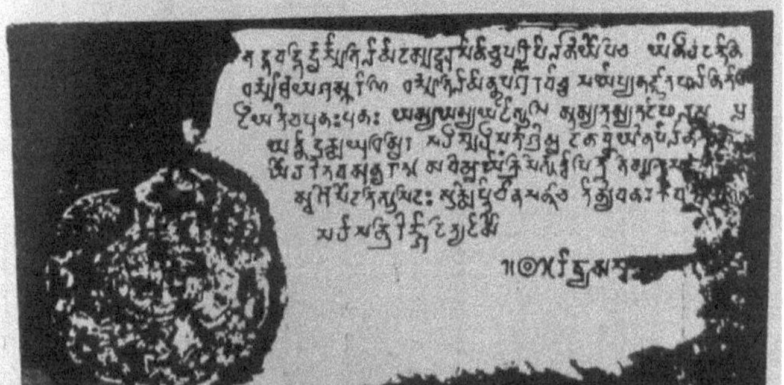

Copper-plate Land Grant (Reverse)

Source: San Tha Aung (1979)

Plate 51

Bronze Bells

Praing Daung Bell Inscription, Wethali
(c. 5th - 6th century A.D.)

01

Apaung Daw Bell Inscription, Wethali
(c. 5th - 6th century A.D.)

02

Source: San Tha Aung (1979)

Plate 52

Bronze Lamps

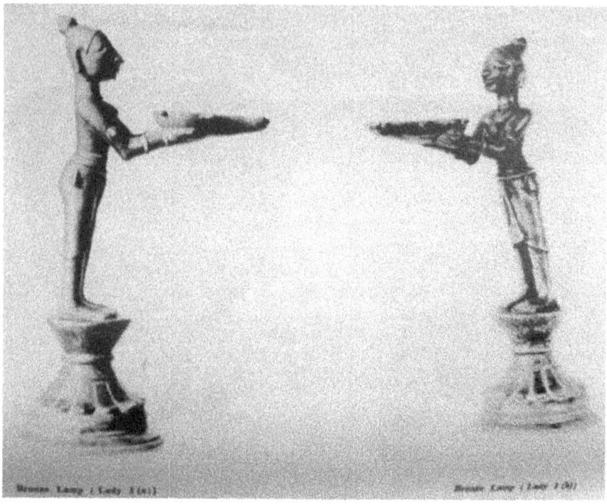

01

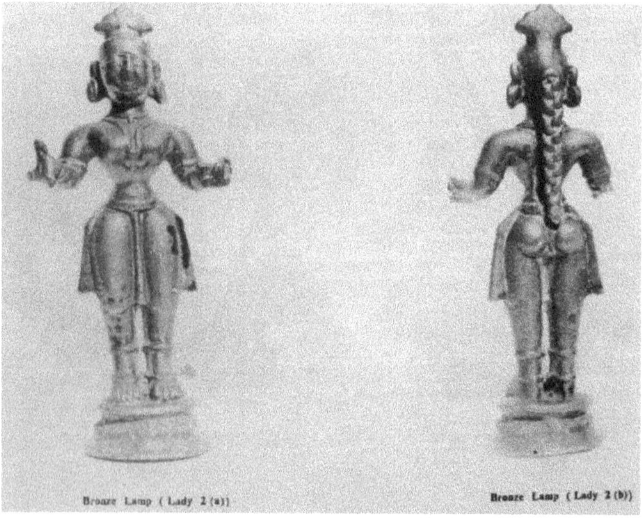

02

Source: San Tha Aung (1979)

Plate 53

Bronze Lamps

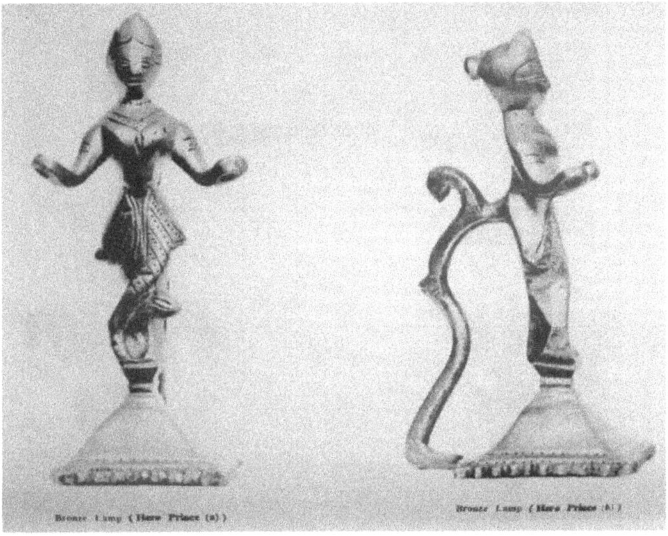

03

04

Source: San Tha Aung (1979)

Plate 54

Bronze Lamps

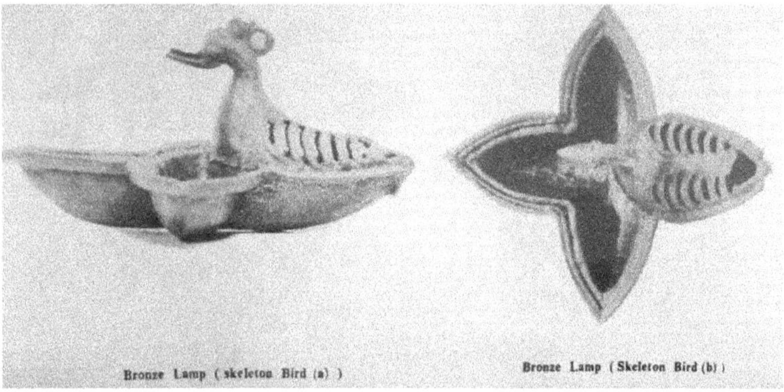

Source: San Tha Aung (1979)

Plate 55

Launggret Taung Maw Inscription

Source: Gutman (2001)

Crocodile Rock Inscription,
Lemro Period, Maha-htee.

Crocodile Rock Inscription,
Lemro Period, Maha-htee

Plate 56

Mahabodhi Inscription, Mahabodhi Temple India

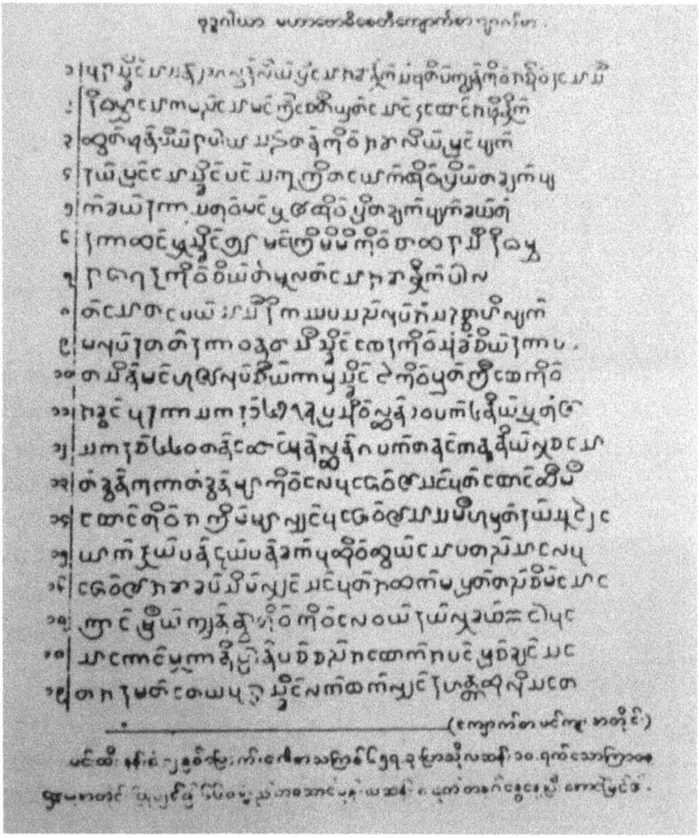

Source: Goyamray Saw Won (1994 Dec)

Plate 57

Inscribed Metal Base National Museum Bangladesh

Source: U Shwe Zan (2010)

Plate 58

Murn Run Phru
Buddha Image

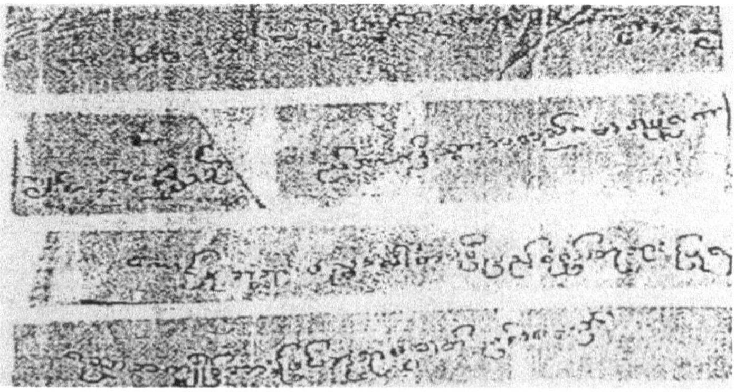

Murn Run Phru Image Inscription, Khaung Laung Kyaung, Sittway

Source: U Shwe Zan (2010)

Plate 59

Murn Hte Image]

King Nan Kya Gree

Source: State Gazetteer (1984)

Plate 60

Sangayana Hill, Vesali

Source: State Gazetteer (1984)

Plate 61

Various Inscriptions Beloging to Vesali Period Inscribed Ye Dhamma Verse

01

Surya Image Inscription
from Shin-nge-det-taung,
Vesali
(c.5th - 6th century A.D)

02

Vesali Mond Stone Slab Inscription c. 5th 6th AD

Source: U Shwe Zan (2010)

Plate 62

03

Kyitaung Phara Stone Slab Inscription, Minbra (c.5th to 6th century A.D)

04

Vesali Votive Stupa Inscription, Vesali (Face II) (c.5th -6th Century AD)

Source: U Shwe Zan (2010)

Plate 63

05

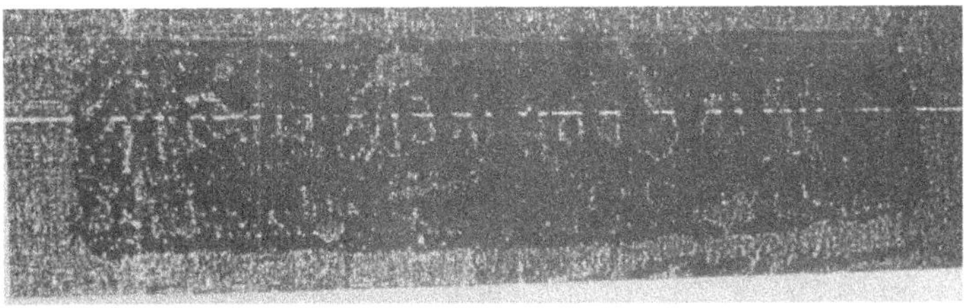

Meechaungwa Votive Stupa Inscription, Kyauk Taw A (c. 5th-6th Century AD)

06

Meechaungwa Votive Stupa Inscription, Kyauk Taw B (c. 5th-6th Century AD)

Source: U Shwe Zan (2010)

Plate 64

07

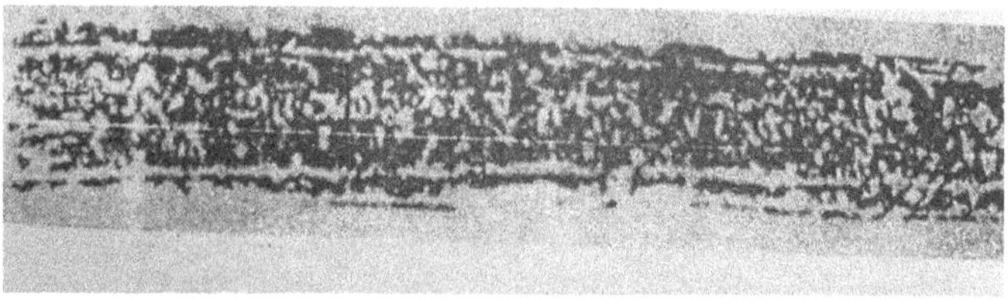

Tezarama Kyaung Votive Stupa Inscription, Mrauk Oo (c.5th-6th Century AD)

08

Selagiri Votive Stupa Inscription, Kyauk Taw (c. 5th-6th Century AD)

Source: U Shwe Zan (2010)

Plate 65

09

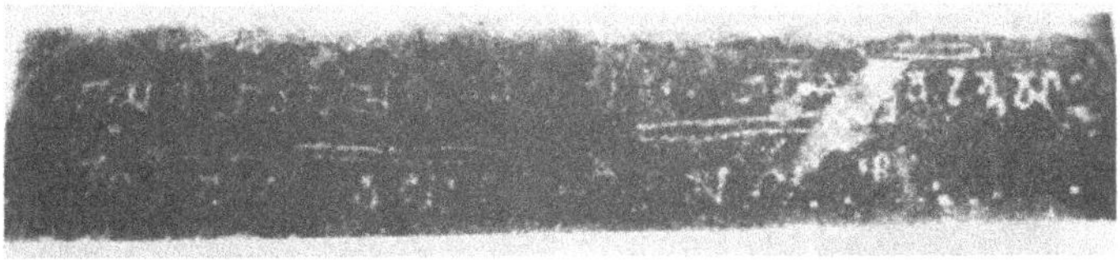

Selagiri Stone Slab Inscription, Kyauk Taw (c. 5th-6th Century AD)

10

Vesali Stne Slab Inscription of Queen of Niticandra, Vesali (c. 5th-6th Century AD)

11

Sandway Brick Slab Inscription, Sandway (c. 5th-6th Century AD)

Source: U Shwe Zan (2010)

Plate 66

12

13 Vesali Stone Slab Inscription of Viracandra, Vesali (c. 5th-6th Century AD)

Vesali Paragri Stone Slab Inscription, Vesali (c. 5th-6th Century AD)

14

Vesali Paragri Stone Slab Inscription, Vesali (c. 5th-6th Century AD)

Source: U Shwe Zan (2010)

Plate 67

15

Pataw Zeti Stone Slab Inscription, Pataw (c. 5th-6th Century AD)

16

Min Tha Chaung Stone Slab Inscription, Vesali (c. 5th-6th Century AD)

Source: U Shwe Zan (2010)

Plate 68

Some Coins Beloning to Vesali Period

01

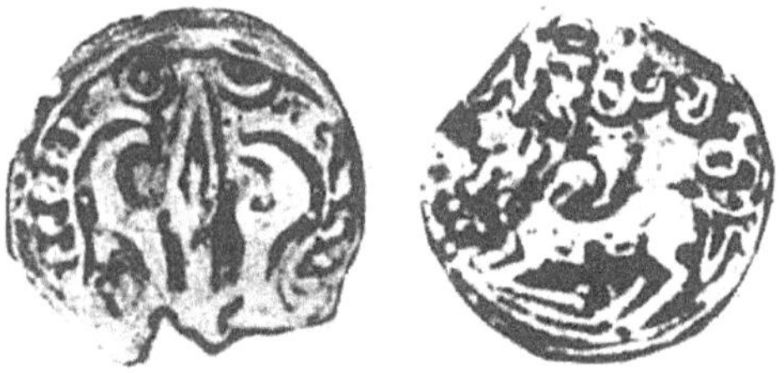

Legend on Surya Candra

02

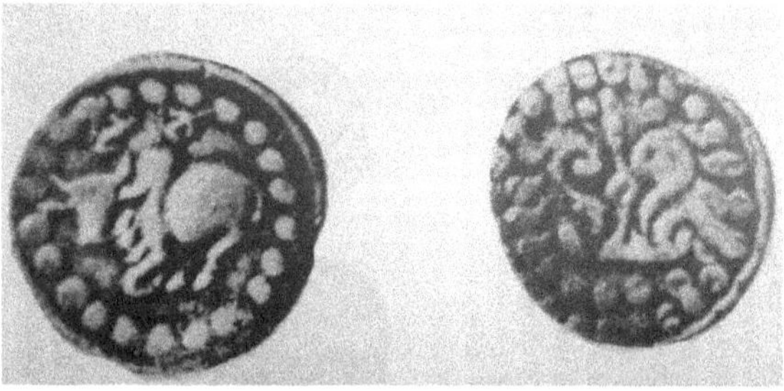

Legend on Deva Coin

03

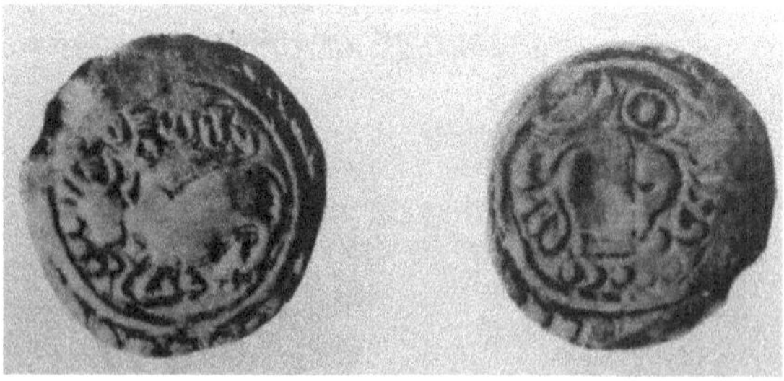

Lengend on Yajnacandra Coin

Source: U Shwe Zan (2010)

Plate 69

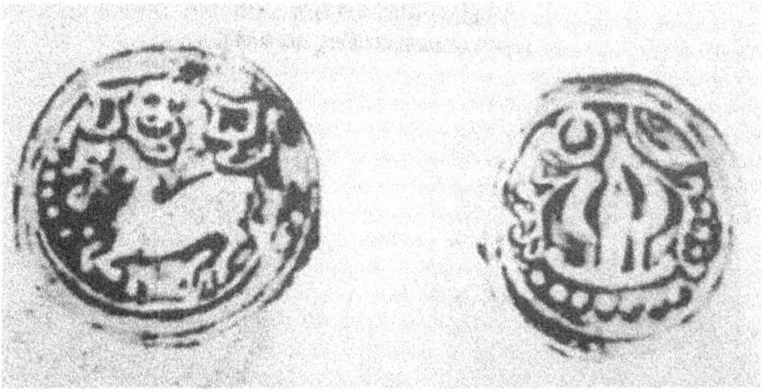

04

Legend on Candrabandhu Coin

05

Legend on Bhumicandra Coin

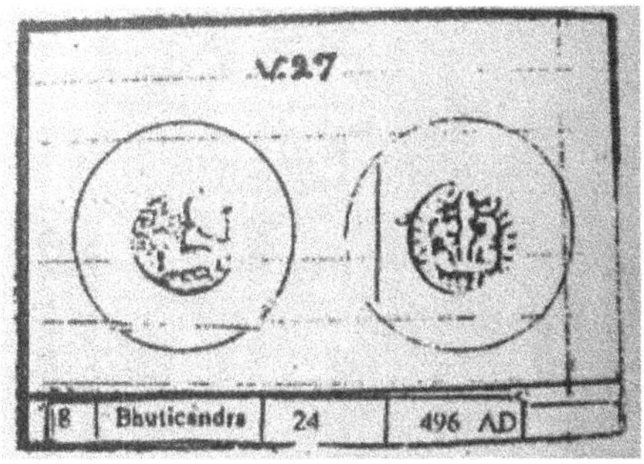

06

Bhuticandra 496 AD

Source: U Shwe Zan (2010)

Plate 70

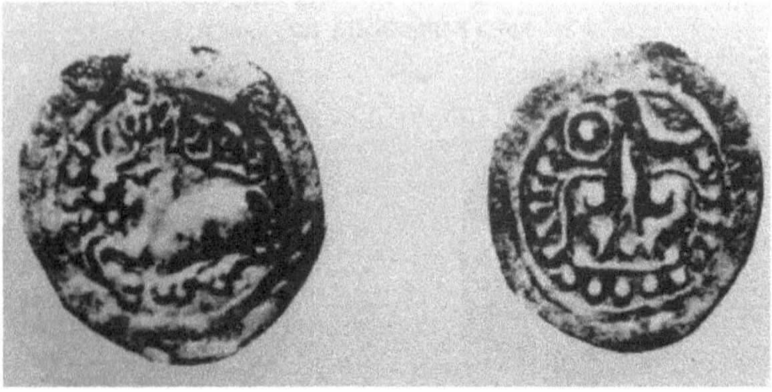

07

Legend on Niticandra Coin

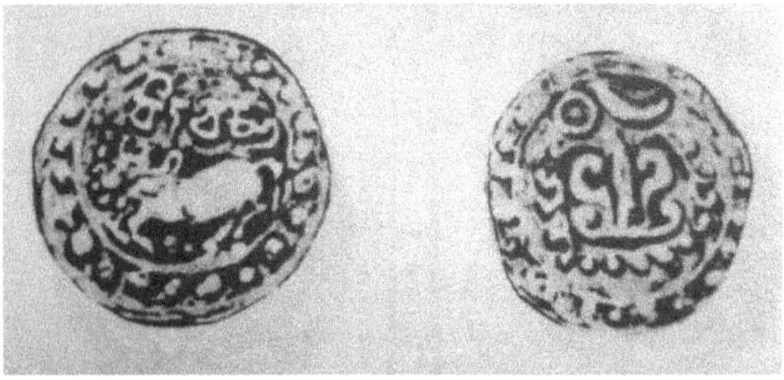

08

Legend on Viracandra Coin

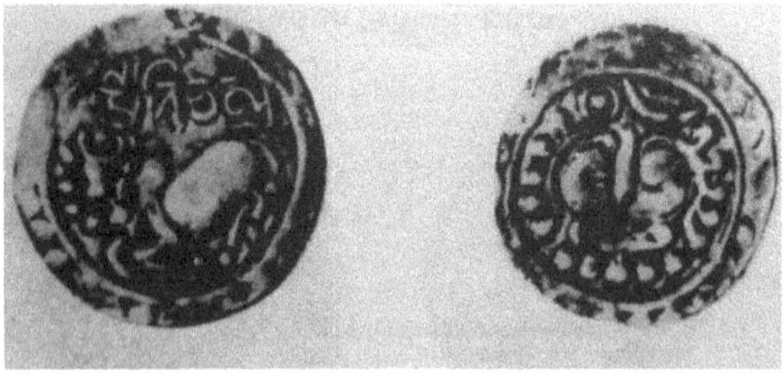

09

Legend on Priticandra Coin

Source: U Shwe Zan (2010)

Plate 71

10

Legend on Prithivicandra Coin

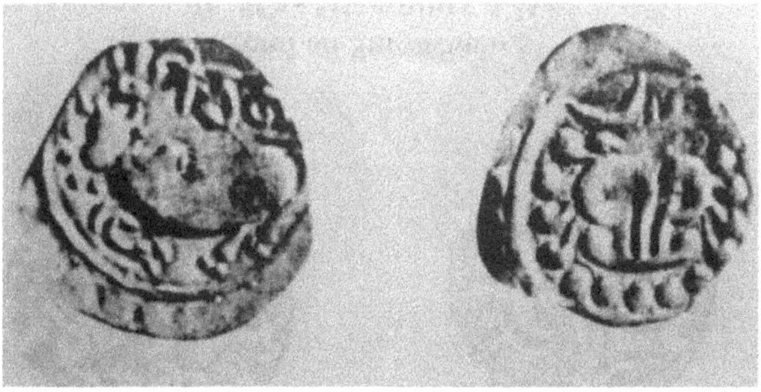

11

Legend on Dhrticandra Coin

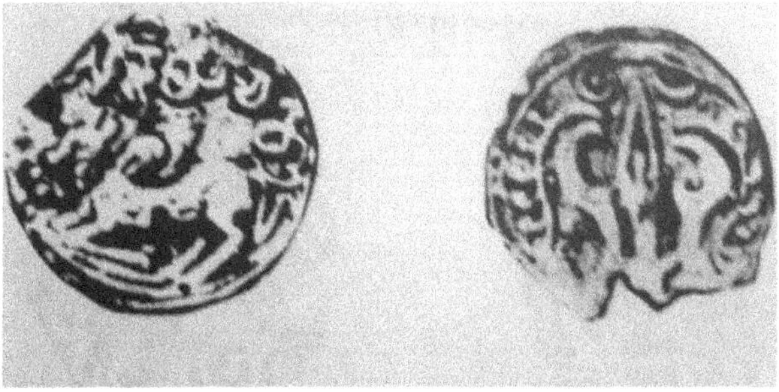

12

Legend on Suryacandra Coin

Source: U Shwe Zan (2010)

Plate 72

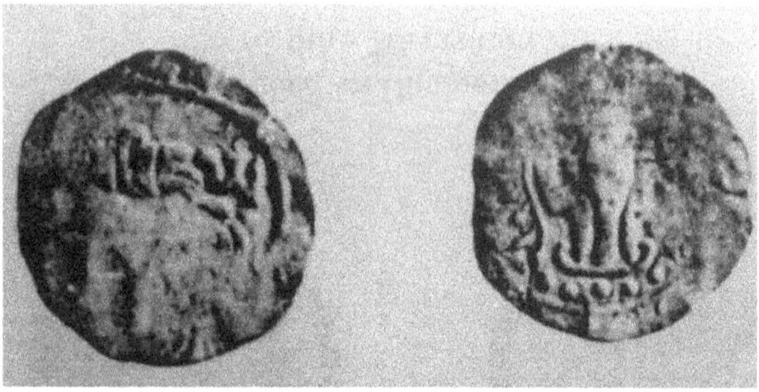

13

Legend on Dharmavijaya Coin

14

Legend on Dhammacandra Coin

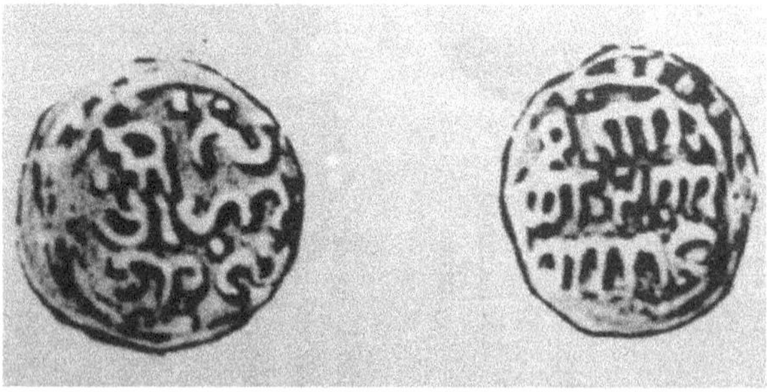

15

Legend on Culamaharaja Coin

Source: U Shwe Zan (2010)

Plate 73

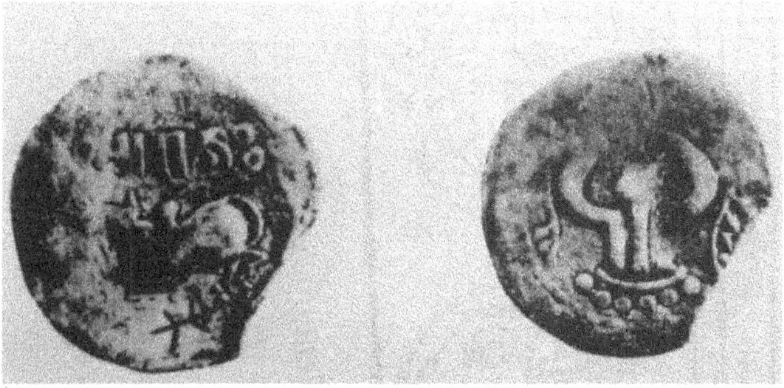

16

Legend on Dharmarajah Coin

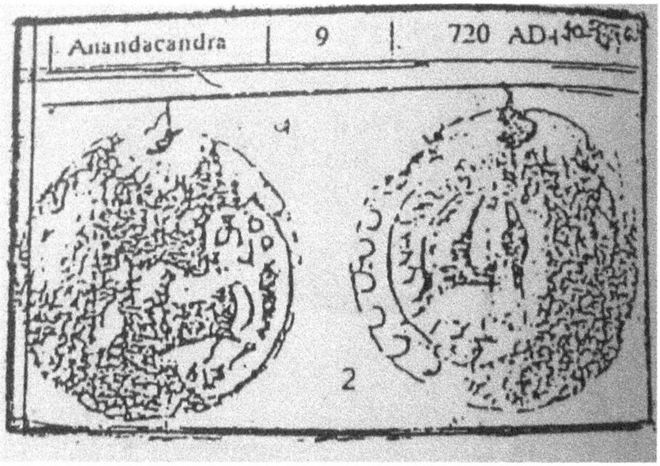

17

Anandacandra 720 AD

Source: U Shwe Zan (2010)

SELECTED BIBLIOGRAPHY

Adikarama, E. W. *Early History of Buddhism in Ceylon.* Colombo: Buddhist Cultural Centre, 1994.

Amaramoli, ed. V. *Nikayasangaraha.* Colombo: 1955. Sinhalese.

Annual Report of the Superintendent, Archaeological Survey of Burma. Rangoon: Dep. of Archaeology, Burma, 1958–1959.

Arakan Mìn Raza-krì Arei-taw Sadan [palm-leaf manuscript, number 1632] AMs, n.d. Yangon: National Library, Ministry of Culture, n.d. Arakanese/Burmese.

Arakan Ra-zawin [palm-leaf manuscript, number 95]. Calcutta: Museum of the Asiatic Society of Bengal, 1791. Arakanese/Burmese.

Arakan Ra-zawin-ngei MS Orient. 3413. London: British Library, n.d. Arakanese/Burmese.

Auboyer, Jeannine, Jean Boisselier, Michel Beurdeley, Huguette Rousset, and Chantal Massonaud. *Oriental Art: A Handbook of Styles and Forms.* Translated by Elizabeth and Richard Bartlett. New York: Rizzoli International Publications, Inc., 1980.

Aung, San Tha. *Anandacandra 8th Century Rakhaing King.* Rangoon: 1975. Arakanese/Burmese.

———. *Arakanese Coins.* Rangoon: Daw Saw Saw Sarpay, 1979. Arakanese/Burmese.

———. *Arakanese Scripts 6th Century and Before.* Rangoon: Tauk Tauk Won Press, 1974. Arakanese/Burmese.

———. *The Buddhist Art of Ancient Arakan (An Eastern Border State beyond Ancient India, east of Vanga and Samatata).* Rangoon: Daw Saw Saw Sarpay, 1979.

———. *The Early History of the Kingdom of Arakan up to 1000 AD* n.d. Arakanese/Burmese.

Berliet, Ernelle. Gèographie Historique et Urbanisation en Birmanie et ses Pays. Voisins, des origines (IIe s. av JC) a la fin du XIII siecle. PhD thesis, *Ecolè Doctorale Sciences Humaines et Sociales Université Lumière,* Lyon II, 2004. French.

Bechert, Heinz. "Some Sidelights on the Early History of Pāḷi Lexicography." In *Añjali: Papers on Indology and Buddhism: A Felicitation Volume Presented to Oliver Hector de Alwis Wijesekera.* Edited by J. Tilakasiri. Peradeniya: Felicitation Volume Editorial Committee, University of Ceylon, 1970.

Bhikkhu, U Sandamuni. *Origin and Development of Arakanese (Rakhaing) Script, Volume I.* PhD thesis, University Kolkata, Calcutta, 2003.

Bloch, Marc. *Feudal Society.* Vol. 1–2. London: 1961.

Brown, G. E. Grant. *Northern Arakan Hill Tracts.* Rangoon, Burma: Supt., Govt. Print. and Staty., 1960.

Bu, U San Shwe. *A Brief Note on the Old Capitals of Arakan.* n.d.

———. *Buywetmanyo Road.* Rangoon: ASB, 1920–21.

———. "Legend of the Early Aryan Settlement in Arakan." *JBRS* 11, no. 2 (1921): 66–69.

———. *Research Papers on Old Arakan (Collection of Articles pub. by Burmese Research Society).* Yangon: Publishers of Eminent Arakanese Literature (PEAL), 1998.

Candamalālankāra, Ven. *Arakan Razawon Theik Kyan (New Arakan Chronicle Vols. I and II).* Rangoon: 1st pub. Rangoon: Hanthavadi Press, 1931. Reprint. Publishers of Eminent Arakan Literature, November 1997. Arakanese/Burmese.

Chain, Tun Aung. *Broken Glass: Pieces of Myanmar History.* Yangon: SEAMEO Centre for History and Traditions, 2004.

Chan, Dr. Aye. "The Development of a Muslim Enclave in Arakan (Rakhine) State of Burma (Myanmar)." *SOAS Bulletin of Burma Research* 3, no. 2 (Autumn 2005): 396–420.

SELECTED BIBLIOGRAPHY

Charney, Michael W. *Buddhism in Arakan: Theories and Historiography of the Religious Basis of Ethnonyms.* Bangkok (Submitted): Arakan History Conference, 2005.

———. *Living Bibliography of Burma Studies: The Primary Sources.* London: SOAS, 2002.

———. *The Bibliography of Burma (Myanmar) Research: The Secondary Literature.* London: SOAS, 2004.

———. *Where Jambudipa and Islamdom Converged: Religious Change and the Emergence of Buddhist Communalism in Early Modern Arakan (Fifteenth to Nineteenth Centuries).* PhD thesis, The University of Michigan, 1999.

Chatterjee, Dr. S. K. *Kirat Janakriti.* Calcutta: ASB, 1951.

Chinese Test Taisho 2066 vol. LI. n.d.

Chowdhury, Vasent. *India Museum.* Town Press, n.d.

Coedes, George. *The Indianized States of Southeast Asia.* Edited by Walter F. Vella. Translated by Susan Brown Cowing. Honolulu: East-West Centre Press, 1968.

Collis, Maurice. *The Land of the Great Image—Being Experiences of Friar Manrique in Arakan,* 1st ed. London: Faber & Faber, 1943.

Collis, Maurice, and San Shwe Bu. *Arakan's Place in the Civilization of the Bay: A Study of Coinage and Foreign Relations.* Rangoon: Burma Research Society, 50th Anniversary publication's no. 2, 1960.

Chattha Sangayana CD-ROM, © copyright 1999, Version 3.0, **Vipassana Research Institute**, Dhammagiri, Igatpuri, 422 403 District Nashik, Maharashtra, India. (N.B. Unless otherwise indicated, all Pali and Pali Commentarial references mentioned in the dissertation are from the CD.)

Culavamsa, being the more recent part of the Mahāvamsa. Parts 1–2. Translated by William Geiger, and from German into English by C. Mabel Rickmers (née Duff). Colombo, 1953.

Cultural and Traditional Customs of Nationalities (Rakhaing). The Burmese Socialist Programme Party, January 1976. Burmese.

Curnika Pota, Catalog no. J-3. National Museum of Colombo, n.d. Sinhalese.

Davids, T. W. Rhys, and William Stede. *Pali-English Dictionary.* London: Pali Text Society, 1921–1925.

de Silva, K. M, ed. *History of Sri Lanka Vol. II.* Colombo: University of Ceylon Press Board, 1995.

de Silva, D. G. Bandu. "A Study on Trincomalee in the Sixteenth and Seventeenth Centuries with Special Reference to Relations with Arakan as Revealed by Portuguese Sources." *Journal of the Royal Asiatic Society of Sri Lanka (new series)* LII (2006): 175–208.

de Casparis, J. G. *Prasasti Indonesia II.* Bandung: Masa Baru, 1956.

Dias, Malini. "Historical Relations of Ancient Sri Lanka and Myanmar." *Ancient and Medieval Commercial Activities in the Indian Ocean: Testimony of Inscriptions and Ceramic-sherds, Report of the Taisho University Research Project 1997–2000.* Edited by Noboru Karashima, 2002. 170–183.

"Dipavamsa tr. BC Law." *The Historical Journal* 7, no. 4 (1958).

Duroiselle, Charles. "1924 Report of the Superintendent Archaeological Survey of Burma." *ASB, pl. Vand, Arch. Neg. 2694* (1925–6): 44–45.

Dutt, Sukumar. *Buddhist Monks and Monasteries Of India: Their History and Contribution to Indian Culture.* London: George Allen and Unwin Ltd., 1962.

Epigraphia Indica 35 (1963–1964).

Epigraphia Indica 20: 16–17, 19*ff.*, 21*ff.* (1929–1930).

Febre, Lucien. Cited in Antoine Prost. *Douze Lecons sur l'Histoire.* Paris, 1996: 239–241.

Fernando, P. E. E. "The Rakhanga—Sannas-Curnikava and the Date of the Arrival of Arakanese Monks in Ceylon." *University of Ceylon Review* 17, nos. 1–2 (1959): 41–46.

Forchhammer, Dr. E. *Report on the Antiquities of Arakan.* Rangoon: Superintendent, Government Printing and Stationary, 1892.

Fryer, G. E. "Note on an Arakanese Coin." *Journal of the Asiatic Society of Bengal* 41 (1872).

Furet, Francois. *Interpreting the French Revolution.* Cambridge, 1981.

Gangoly, O. C. *Andhara Sculptures.* Hyderabad, 1973.

Garten, Jeffrey E. "Really Old School." *The New York Times,* December 9, 2006.

Geiger, Wilhelm. *Mahavamsa: The Great Chronicle of Ceylon.* Colombo: BCC, 2003.

Godakumbara, C. E., ed. and trans. "Kadadora Grant, an Ola Leaf Manuscript from the Kadadora Vihara in the Central Province." *JCBARS (new series)* 2 (1952): 141–158.

Gombrich, Richard F. "Kosala-Bimba-Vaṇṇanā." In *Buddhism in Ceylon and Studies on Religious Syncretism in Buddhist Countries.* Edited by Heinz Bechert (Göttingen: Abhandlungen der Akademie der Wissenschaften, 1978), pp. 281–303.

Goonatilake, Hema. "Sri Lanka-Myanmar Historical Relations in Religion, Culture and Polity." *Journal of the Royal Asiatic Society of Sri Lanka (new series)* 55 (2009): 77–114.

Gunawardana, R. A. H. L. "Buddhist Nikāyas in Medeval Sri Lanka." *Sri Lanka Journal of Historical and Social Sciences* 9 (1966).

Gutman, Pamela. *Ancient Arakan: with Special Reference to Its Cultural History between the Fifth and Eleventh Centuries.* PhD Thesis, National University of Australia, 1976.

———. *Burma's Lost Kingdom—Splendours of Arakan.* Bangkok: Orchid Press, 2001.

Hall, D. G. E. *History of South East Asia.* London: Macmillan Limited, 1955.

Han, Min Nyunt. *Third Season of Excavation at Vesālī.* Yangon: Working People's Daily, Sep. 10, 1982.

———. *Third Season of Excavation at Vesālī Part II.* Working People's Daily, Sep. 10, 1982.

Han, U Nyant. "Reports on the Excavations of Old Vesālī." *Rakhaing Magazine* 17, 1995.

Harza, Kanai Lal. *History of Theravada Buddhism in Southeast Asia with special reference to India and Ceylon,* 2nd ed. New Delhi: Munshiram Manoharlal Publishers, 2002.

Havell, E. B. *The History of Aryan Rule in India.* London: George G. Harrap and Co. Ltd., 1891.

Herbert, Patricia, Anthony Milner, and Southeast Asia Library Group. *South-East Asia.* Chicago: University of Hawaii Press, 1989.

Hien, Fa. *Record of the Buddhistic Kingdoms by Fa Hien (414 AD).* Translated by Herbert A. Giles. London: Trubner & Co., 1877.

History of Ceylon Vol. 1, Part I. Colombo: Ceylon University Press, 1959.

Hla, Kyaw Zaw. *Candamuni Image.* n.d. Arakanese/Burmese.

Hla, U San. *Mahāmuni Nigone Rwa Verse Reference to Doe Wai's History.* n.d. Arakanese/Burmese.

———. *Mahāmuni Ni-gone-rwa Poem (Establishing City and Palace Section).* n.d. Arakanese/Burmese.

Hla, U Tha. *The Rakhaing Magazine* 1, no.7 (2000). Arakanese/ Burmese.

Hudson, Bob, Maung Maung Than, and Nyein Lwin. *Dhanyawadi Archaeological Plan 2005,* © Bob Hudson, Sydney (Archaeological Survey Project funded by the Australian Research Council).

Hudson, Bob. "Ancient Geography and Recent Archaeology: Dhanyawadi, Vesali and Mrauk-u." *Forgotten Kingdom of Arakan (Rakhine) Workshop: from Dhanyawadi to 1962* (a public seminar on history, identity, culture, and Asian Studies) Southeast Asian Studies Centre, Chulalongkon University, Bangkok, pp. 2–22. November 2005.

Hman-nan Mahā Yazawin-daw-gyi, 8th ed. 3 vols. Yangon: Thiha Yadana Sarpay, (2008 reprint). Burmese.

Inscription Collected in Upper Burma, Vol. II. Rangoon, 1903.

Irwin (I. C. S.), A. M. B. *The Burmese and Arakanese Calendar.* Rangoon: Hanthawaddy Press, 1909.

Jayatilaka, Sir D. B. "Sinhalese Embassies to Arakan." *Journal of the Royal Asiatic Society, Ceylon Branch* 35 (1940): 1–6.

Jayawardena, Kumari. *Nobodies to Somebody: The Rise of the Colonial Bourgeoisie in Sri Lanka.* Colombo, 2000.

Johnston, E. H. "Some Sanskrit Inscriptions of Arakan." *BSOAS* 9 (1944): 357–385.

———. "Early Coins of the Kings of Arakan (Incorporated in Some Sanskrit Inscription of Arakan)." *BSOAS* 9 (1944).

Kalà, U. *Mahā-ya-zawin-gyì.* Edited by Hsaya U Khin Soe. Rangoon: Hantha-waddy Press, 1961. Burmese.

Kavilakhanā Dipanī. Rangoon: Thudhammawadi Press, 1930. Burmese.

Kavisara, Shin. *Arakan Arei-taw-poun [palm-leaf manuscript number 136913].* Yangon: National Library, Ministry of Culture, 1839 [copy of 1787 original]. Arakanese/Burmese.

Khine, Tun Shwe. *A Study of Buddhist Sculptures Found in Rakhine Old Dhanyawaddy City Compared with in Indian Old Buddhist Arts.* Yangon: Myanmar Academy of Arts and Science the 7th Research Conference, Ministry of Education, Oct. 27, 2008.

———. *Ancient Arakanese Capitals.* Rangoon: Hla Kyaw Sein Sarpay, 1985. Arakanese/Burmese.

———. *Buddhist Art of Vesālī Period, Arakan.* Rangoon: Site-thay-daw Sarpay, 1990. Arakanese/Burmese.

———. *Rakhaing Princess E Churn.* 1990. Burmese.

———. *Rakhaing Sar-so-daw-myah (The Arakanese Poets).* Rangoon: Saik-thay-daw Sarpay, 1991. Burmese.

———. *The History of Arakan Dynasty.* Rangoon: Theik-di-myaing Press, 1985. Arakanese/Burmese.

Knox, Robert. *A Historical Relations of Sri Lanka.* London, 1958.

Kosalla, U. *Journey of Arakanese Literature.* Yangon: PEAL, n.d. Arakanese/Burmese.

Krairiksh, Piriya. *Buddhist Folk Tales Depicted at Chula Pathon Cedi.* Bangkok: Prachandra Printing Press, 1974.

Kyi, Thin. "Arakanese Capitals: A Preliminary Survey of their Geographic Siting."

Journal of the Burma Research Society 53, no. 2 (December 1970): 1–14.

Latourette, K. S. *A Short History of the Far East,* 3rd ed. New York: The Macmillan Company, 1957.

Latter, Thomas. "The Coins of Arakan: The Symbolic Coins of Arakan." *Journal of the Asiatic Society of Bengal* 15 (1846).

Leider, Jacques. "Arakan's Ascent during the Mrauk U Period." In *Recalling Local Pasts: Autonomous History in Southeast Asia.* Edited by S. Chutintaranoond and C. Baker. Chiang Mai: Silkworms Press, 2002. 53–87.

———. *Le royaume d'Arakan, Birmanie. Son histoire politique entre le début du XVe et la fin du XVIIe siècle.* PhD Thesis, Institut Nationale des Langues et Civilisations Orientales, 1998.

Liebenthal, Walter. "Sanskrit Inscriptions from Yunnan I." *Monumenta Serica* 12 (1974): 1–40.

———. "Sanskrit Inscriptions from Yunnan II." *Sino-Indian Studies* 5, nos. 3–4 (1955): 1–23.

Luce, G. H. "The Tan (AD 97–132) and the Ngai-Lao." *JBRS* 14, part 2 (1924a): 100–137.

Mae, Nga. *Arakan Ra-zawin [palm-leaf manuscript, number 3465a][circa 1840].* London: Oriental and India Office Collection, British Library, n.d. Burmese.

Majumdar, R. C., ed. *The Classical Age.* Bombay: 1998.

Malalasekera, G. P. *Dictionary of Pāli Proper Names.* Asian Educational Services, 2003 reprint.

———. *The Pali Literature of Ceylon*. Kandy, Sri Lanka: 1st pub. in 1928 by Royal Asiatic Society of Great Britain and Ireland, repub. by Buddhist Publication Society, 1994.

Marshall, Sir John. *Mohenjo-Daro and the Indus Civilization.* 3 Vols. Asian Educational Services, Facsimile of 1931 edition (March 1, 1996).

Marwick, Arthur. *The Nature of History*. The Macmillian Press Ltd, 1970.

McDowell, D. W. "Eight Coins of Arakan from Sylhet." *Numismatic Chronicle* 20 (1960).

Mirando, A. H. "Buddhism in Sri Lanka in the Seventeenth and Eighteenth Centuries with Special Reference to Sinhalese Literary Sources." *The Ceylon Historical Journal Monograph Series* 10. Colombo: Tisara Prakasakayo Ltd., 1958.

Mrat, Thu. *Mahāmuni and Remain Five Munis.* 1995. Arakanese/ Burmese.

Mudiyanse, Nandasena. "Cultural Missions to Arakan (Rakkhanga-Desa)." *Journal of the Ceylon Branch of the Royal Asiatic Society (new series)* 15 (1971): 26–35.

Ñāna, Ven. *Dhaññavatī Razawon Theik (New Dhaññavatī Chronicle).* Vols. 1–2. Rangoon: 1st pub. Hanthavadi Press, 1954, reprint. Publishers of Eminent Arakan Literature, 1996. Arakanese/Burmese.

New Light of Myanmar (English and Myanmar versions dated on Dec. 10, 1998). Yangon: Ministry of Information of the Union of Myanmar, 1998.

No, Ù. *Mahā-myat-muni Thamaing [Palm-leaf manuscript, number 40206].* Yangon: Universities Central Library, 1745. Arakanese/ Burmese.

Norman, K. R. "Pāḷi Literature: Including the Canonical Literature in Prakrit and Sanskrit of all the Hīnayāna Schools of Buddhism." *A History of Indian Literature Series*, no. 7, fasc. 2. Wiesbaden: Otto Harrassiwitz, 1983.

———. "The Pāḷi Language and Scriptures." Pp. 29–54 in *The Buddhist Heritage*. Edited by Tadeusz Skorupski. Tring: The Institute of Buddhist Studies, 1989.

Nyanaponika, Maha Thera, and Hellmuth Hecker. *Great Disciples of the Buddha: Their Lives, Their Works, Their Legacy*. Edited by Bhikkhu Bodhi. Kandy: Buddhist Publication Society, 2003.

Nyanatiloka, Ven. *Buddhist Dictionary*. Kandy, Sri Lanka: Buddhist Publication Society, 1980.

Oertel, F. O. "Excavations at Sarnath." *Annual Report of the Archaeological Survey of India 1904–5* (Calcutta: Superintendent Government Printing, 1908): 59–106.

Okkantha, Ashin Sri. *History of Buddhism in Arakan*. PhD dissertation, University of Calcutta, 1990.

Oo, Aung Tha. *Buddhasāsana and Rakhaing Land*. Rangoon: Typeset, 1974. Arakanese/Burmese.

———. "History of Arakanese Coins." *Rakhing Tan Soung Magazine*, 1972. Arakanese/Burmese.

———. *Rakhaing Culture: Vesali Period*. Rangoon: U Boe Hein, Ma Hlwa Gone, 1966. Arakanese/Burmese.

———. *Rakhaing Dynasties*. Typeset, n.d. Arakanese/Burmese.

———. *Rakhing Cultural History and Its View by Researchers*. 1978 typeset copy, reprint 1985. Arakanese/Burmese.

———. *Rakkha Mandala Rakhaing Razawon (Rakkha Mandala Arakan Chronicle)*. Rangoon: Mraratana Press, 1955. Arakanese/Burmese.

Oo, U Sein Maung. "Old Sri Kettara City." *University Paññapadesā Journal* 3, part 1 (n.d.): 202–203. Arakanese/Burmese.

Panabokke, Gunaratne. *History of the Buddhist Sangha in India and Sri Lanka*. Colombo: The Postgraduate Institute of Pali and Buddhist Studies, University of Kelaniya, 1993.

Pandi, U. *Dhannavati Razawon Theik*. Rangoon: Pyigyimandaing Press, 1910. Arakanese/Burmese.

———. *Utinnalanka Nigone (ola leaf Manuscript).* Rambree Bamboo Monastery, 1873.

Paññasāmi, Ven. *The History of the Buddha's Religion (Sāsanavamsa).* Translated by Bimala Churn Law. Delhi: Sri Satguru Publications, 1986.

Paranavitana, Senarat. "Mahāyānism in Ceylon." *Ceylon Journal of Science,* section G2, part 1 (December 1928): 35–71.

Pe, U San. "Cultural Links between Ceylon and Burma." *The New Lanka A Quarterly Review* 1, no. . (July 1950): 45–52.

Phayre, Lt. Gen. Sir Arthur P. "An Account of Arakan." *JASB* 10 (1841): 679–711.

———. "Coins of Arakan, of Pegu, and of Burma." *The International Numismata Orientalia Series* (London, 1882).

———. *History of Burma: Including Burma Proper, Pegu, Taungu, Tenasserim, and Arakan (1967 ed.).* London: Susil Gupta, 1883.

———. "On the History of Arakan." *JASB* 8 (1844): 23–52.

———. "The Coins of Arakan: The Historical Coins." *Journal of the Asiatic Society of Bengal* (1846).

Pieris, P. K. *Sri Lanka and the Portuguese.* Colombo, 1920.

Pridham, C. *Ceylon and Its Dependencies.* Vol. 1, chap. 5. London: T. and W. Boone, 1849.

Prue, Maung. *Early History of Buddhist Rakhing.* Sittway: Sittwe College Magazine, 1982–83. Arakanese/Burmese.

Questions Concerning Emergence of Theravāda Buddhasāsana in Rakhaing Land Interview to U Oo Thar Tun (Rakhaing-Myanmar Pandit) by Ven. Nyanissara of Burma, in 1984 December 26. Mae Sot, Thailand: 1st published by the Executive Committee, Arakan National League for Democracy (Exile), Bangladesh. (2002 August). Republished by Research and Recording Dept., All Arakan Students' and Youths' Congress (AASYC), 2010 August. Arakanese/Burmese.

Rahula, Ven. Walpola. *History of Buddhism in Ceylon: the Anuradhapura period, 3rd Century BC–10th Century AD*, 3rd ed. Colombo: Buddhist Cultural Centre, 1993.

Rakhaing Magazine 4. Sittway, 1977. Arakanese/Burmese.

Rakhaing State Gazetteer (Culture Section) 5. Akyab (Sittway): Rakhaing State People's Council, 1984. Burmese.

Rakhaing State Gazetteer (History Section) 1. Akyab (Sittway): Arakan People's Council, 1984. Burmese.

Raman, K. V. "Indian Influences in Southeast Asia as Reflected in the Personal Names." *Ancient and Medieval Commercial Activities in the Indian Ocean: Testimony of Inscriptions and Ceramic-sherds, Report of the Taisho University Research Project 1997–2000.* Edited by Noboru Karachiima. 2002. 184–206.

Ray, Nihar Ranjan. *An Introduction to the Study of Theravāda Buddhism in Burma.* Calcutta: University of Calcutta, 1946.

———. *Sanskrit Buddhism in Burma.* Calcutta: University of Calcutta, 1936.

Raychaudhuri, H. C. *Political History of Ancient India*, 7th ed. Calcutta: 1972.

———. *Studies in Indian Antiquities.* Calcutta: 1958.

Raymond, Catherine. "An Arakanese Perspective from the Dutch Sources: Images of the Kingdom of Arakan in the Seventeenth Century.". *The Maritime Frontier of Burma: Exploring Political, Cultural and Commercial Interaction in the Indian Ocean World, 1200–1800.* Edited by Jos Gommas and Jacques Leider. Leiden: KITLV Press, 1997.

———. "Archaeological Evidence of Buddhist Links between Sri Lanka and Arakan." *Ancient Ceylon: Journal of the Archaeological Survey Department of Sri Lanka* 6, no. 12 (1990): 9–26.

———. "Religious and Scholarly Exchanges between the Sinhalese Sangha and the Arakanese and Burmese Theravadin Communities: Historical Documantation and Physical

Evidence." Pp. 87–114 in *Commerce and Culture in the Bay of Bengal, 1500–1800.* Edited by O. Parakash and D. Lombard. Delhi: Manohar, 1999.

———. "Wathundaya: divinite de la Terre en Birmanie et en Arakan." Pichard, P. and Robinne, F. *Etudes birmanes en homage a Denise Bernot.* Paris: Ecole Franscaise d'Extreke-orient, 1998. pp. 113–127.

Rigby, G. C. *History of Operation in Northern Arakan and Yawdewin Hill. 1886–87, with a Description of the Country and Its Resources, Notes on the Tribes and Diary.* Rangoon, Burma: Superintendent, Government Print., 1897.

Rustom, C. A. *Some Coins of Arakan.* Rangoon: Nation Supplement, Nov. 11, 1962.

San, Dhañña. "Rakkhamandaing" Yangon: PEAL, 1995.

Sāsanavaṁsa. *The History of the Buddha's Religion.* Translated by B. C. Law. London: 1952.

Saunders, E. Dale. *Mudrā: A Study of Symbolic Gestures in Japanese Buddhist Sculpture.* NJ: Bollingen Series, no. 58, Princeton University Press, 1960.

Sherman, E. Lee. *A History of Far Eastern Art.* London: Thames and Hudson, 1964.

Shin, U Ba. "Old Vishnu City and Historical Outlook on It." *University Paññapadesā Journal* 3, part 3 (n.d.): 200 cont.

Shwe, Mg Tun. *Evolution of Rakhine Ancient Capitals: Geographical Appraisal.* Research paper submitted for PhD, Yangon University, 2003–2004.

Shwe, U Myint. "Anandacandra's Sanskrit Inscription." *The Union of Burma Journal of Literary and Social Sciences* 2, no. 3 (Sep. 1969).

Sircar, D. C. "Inscriptions of the Chandras of Arakan." *EI* 32 (1957): 103–109, and plates opp. 108–9.

———. "Nagarjunikonda Inscription of Virapurushadatta." *Select Inscriptions Bearing on Indian History and Civilization, Vol. I. from Sixth Century BC to Sixth Century AD.* Calcutta, 1965.

Sithugammani-thinkyan. *Arakan Ra-zawin [palm-leaf manuscript, number 2297].* Yangon: National Library, Ministry of Culture, n.d. Arakanese/Burmese.

Snellgrove, David. *Indo-Tibetan Buddhism.* Vol. 2. Boston: Shambhala, 1987.

———. *Indo-Tibetan Buddhism.* Vol. 2. Boston: Shambhala, 1987.

Snodgrass, Adrian. *Symbolism of the Stupa, Studies on Southeast Asia.* New York: Southeast Asia Program, Cornell University, 1985.

Southworth, John Van Duyn. *The Story of the World.* New York: Pocket Books Inc., 1954.

Sulurājāvaliya. Colombo: C. D. S. K. Jayawadena, 1914. Sinhalese.

Sundara, Baddanta. *Satthubimba Suttam.* Rangoon, 1993. Arakanese/Burmese.

Sway Sone Kywa Htin Kyan, First Book. Sway Sone Kyaw Htin Pitakat Press, 1927 (1289 BE). Burmese.

Tennent, J. Emerson. *Christianity in Ceylon.* London, 1850.

Tha, Kyaw Zan. "Buddhism in Arakan before Ye Dhamma." *Rakhaing Tan Saung Mazagine,* no. 16, 1980. Arakanese/Burmese.

Thaw, U Aung. *Historical Sites in Burma.* Rangoon: Ministery of Culture, 1972.

The Glass Palace Chronicle of the Kings of Burma tr. by Pe Maung Tin and G. H. Luce. Rangoon: Rangoon University Press, January 1960.

The Mahāvamsa or the Great Chronicle of Ceylon. Translated by William Geiger, assisted by Mabel Haynes Bode, with an addendum by G. Mendis. Colombo, 1950, 1st ed. 1912.

The Silver Jubilee Magazine. Rangoon: Rakhing Thahaya Association, Dec. 1987. Arakanese/Burmese.

Theobald, W. "On a Symbolic Coin of the Weithali Dynasty of Arakan." *Journal of the Asiatic Society of Bengal* 61 (1892).

Thurn-gran, Mahādhamma. *Sāsanālankāra Sadan*. Rangoon: Hansāvatī Press, 1928. Burmese.

Tilokathāra, Ashin. *Myat Mangalā Buddhist Questions and Answers*. Yangon, May 1990. Burmese.

Tosh, John. *The Pursuit of History*. Pearson Education Ltd., 2006.

Tun, Than. *Old Burma History (Kheit Haung Myanma Yazawin)*. Vol. 1. Yangon: Maha Dagon, 1964.

———. "Paya Lanma—Lord's Highway, over the Yoma—Yakhine Range." *Journal of Asian and African Studies, ILCAA, Tokyo University to Foreign Studies* 25 (1983): 223–241.

———. *Royal Orders of Burma*. Vol. 4. Kyoto: The Centre for Southeast Asian Studies, Kyoto University, 1986.

Tun, U Sein Nyo. *Review of the Most Ancient Rakhaing History*. 1966.

———. *The History of Rakhapura as Foretold by Guatama Buddha*. n.d.

van Galen, Stephan Egbert Arie. *Arakan and Bengal: The Rise and Decline of the Mrauk Oo Kingdom (Burma) from the Fifteenth to the Seventeenth Century AD*. PhD thesis, Leiden University, 2008.

Vimalakīrti (Vimalakīrtinirdeśa). Translated by Sara Boin. London: The Pali Text Society, 1976.

Vogel, J. Ph. "Prakrit Inscriptions from a Buddhist Site at Nāgarjunakonda." *Epigraphia Indica* 20, no. 1 (1929): 1–37.

Wagenaar, Lodewijk. "Looking for Monks from Arakan, a Chapter of the Kadyan-Dutch Relations in the Eighteenth Century." *Journal of the Royal Asiatic Society of Sri Lanka (new series)* 48 (2003): 91–110.

Wales, H. G. Quaritch. *Making of Greater India*. London: B. Quaritch, 1951.

Wheatley, Paul. *Golden Khersonese: Studies in the Historical Geography of the Malay Peninsula before AD 1500*. Kaula Lumpure: University of Malaya Press, 1961.

Wichramasinghe, Nira. *History Writing: New Trends and Methodologies*. Colombo: International Centre for Ethnic Studies, 2001.

Wickremasinghe, Sirima. "Ceylon's Relations with Southeast Asia with Special Reference to Burma." *The Ceylon Journal of Historical and Social Studies* 3(1960): 38–58.

Won, Goyamray Saw. *Rakhing State and Buddhasāsanā.* Yangon: Tat Lam Literature, printed by Siddhi Mying, 1994. Arakanese/Burmese.

Zan, Murn Bra Murn Thein. *Arakan Miniature Stūpas.* Rangoon: Publishers of Eminent Arakanese Literature, 2003. Arakanese/Burmese.

Zan, U Shwe. "Dilemma of Vesālī Era and the Answer." *Rakhaing Thahaya Magazine*, no. 4, 1997. Arakanese/Burmese.

———. "Mrauk Oo Period Coins or History Foretold by Coins." *Rakhing Magazine* 24, n.d. Arakanese/Burmese.

———. *Pre-Arakan Daññavadī, Myat Panthazun Magazine.* Yangon: Rakhaing Women Association, 2002. Arakanese/Burmese.

———. *Some Justifications about Vesālī: a Single Rakhine Dynasty Existing between Fourth and Ninth Century, Myat Pan Tha Zin Magazine.* Yangon: Rakhaing Women Association, n.d. Arakanese/Burmese.

———. *The Golden Mrauk Oo: An Ancient Capital of Arakan*, 2nd ed. Yangon: U Shwe Zan (Patron, Rakhaing Thahaya Association), 1997.

———. *Wethali: The Land of Historic Finds.* Rangoon: Hlaing Kyi Phyu Dhamma Vira Publishing House and e-library, November 2010.

Zan, U Shwe., and U Maung Kyaw. *Ancient History of Arakan (Daññavadī Period).* n.d. Arakanese/Burmese.

———. *Study of Ancient Arakan History—Vesālī Kyauk Hlay Gar Period.* Vol: 2, parts 1 and 2. Unpublished n.d. Arakanese/Burmese.

SELECTED BIBLIOGRAPHY

Main URLs Cited

http://www.wisdomlib.org
http://www.jstor.org
http://www.palikanon.com
http://www.rakhapura.com
http://www.aseansec.org/11834.htm
http://www.searo.who.int/en/Section898/Section1443.htm

INDEX

A

Abhayagirivihāra, 148, 205, 220, 223, 232, 257, 258
Aggabodhi IV, king, 174, 261
Ajātasattu, king, 31, 37, 44
Alo Mar Phru, king, 35, 55
Amratu, king, 34
Amāravatī, 100
Anurādhapura, 7, 22, 206, 232, 249, 250, 257
Ānandacandra, king, 16, 33, 34, 50, 93, 172-175, 226, 227, 260
Ānandodaya, 173, 184, 191
Ānandacandra Inscriptions, 2, 15, 16, 30, 33, 48, 49, 75, 118, 119, 129, 158-162, 165, 167, 171-173, 175, 176, 195, 196, 226, 227, 229, 230, 256, 259, 260
ancient Rakhaing capitals, 62, 63
ancient Rakhaing civilization, 64
Añjana, king, 31
Ārekadesa, 75
Argyre, the land of sliver, 24, 88, 89, 228
Arakan, Rakhaing, 6, 7, 10, 24, 25-27, 59-61, 74-76, 77n.119, 87-89, 97, 108, 109, 111, 115, 116, 119, 120, 150- 152, 210-214, 219, 228, 242, 247, 248, 250-264, 270-280
Arakan coastal strip, 87
Arakan history, 15, 30
Arakan littoral, 25
Arakan Mountains, Rakhaing Roma / Arakan Yoma, 59, 60, 63
Arakan State, Rakhaing State, Rakhaing Land, 18, 24-27, 59, 61, 210
Arakan people, 5n.4
Arakanese, 15, 58, 60, 76, 77n.119, 78, 126, 259, 276
Arakanese and Sinhalese literary sources, 255
Arakanese Buddhism, 280, 286
Arakanese Buddhist Council, 277n.513
Arakanese Buddhist contacts with Ceylon, 6, 251
Arakanese Buddhist hagiography, 227
Arakanese Buddhist intercourses with Sri Lanka, 280
Arakanese Buddhist monks, 264
Arakanese Buddhist society, 255
Arakanese Chronicle, 8, 259

Arakanese culture, 15, 158n.237
Arakanese contact with Sri Lanka, 259
Arakanese coins, 16, 17
Arakanese Coins, 14n.21, 17ns.26; 28, 42n.68
Arakanese Capitals, 57n.91, 60n.98, 78n.120, 85n.121, 86n.122
Arakanese Calendar, 40n.67
Arakanese calendars, 38
Arakanese capitals, 60
Arakanese history, 17, 19n.29
Arakanese historian, 13
Arakanese historical annals, 108
Arakanese inscriptions, 256
Arakanese interactions with Ceylon, 276
Arakanese king, 214, 260
Arakanese kings, 227
Arakanese literary sources, 133, 259
Arakanese Literature, 196n.351, 216n.397
Arakanese manuscript of great value, 110, 133, 135
Arakanese monarchy, 127
Arakanese missions to Sri Lanka, 264
Arakanese monks in Ceylon, 21n.35, 253n.455
Arakanese monks, 273, 275, 280, 285
Arakanese *mudrās*, 213n.389
Arakanese peasantry, 215
Arakanese people, 60, 124, 125, 251
Arakanese peoples, 247
Arakanese Poets, 12n.19, 128n.188
Arakanese race, 97
Arakanese rule, 27
Arakanese records, 278
Arakanese Saṅgha, 264
Arakanese scholar, 111, 113n.167
Arakanese scholars, 74
Arakanese Scripts, 14n.21, 48n.81, 113n.167
Arakanese sources, 255, 257
Arakanese Theravāda Buddhism, 250
Arakanese traditions, 120
Arnold, Sir Edwin, 123
Asoka, of Maurya dynasty, 7, 9; of Pātaliputta, 43, 44, 46, 100, 118, 147-149, 152, 168, 173, 223, 143, 249
Aung Tha Oo, U, 8, 110, 255

B

Bagyidaw, King, 10
Bangladesh, 33, 59, 61, 74, 86, 239
Bay of Bengal, 1, 59, 60, 61, 75, 87, 88, 94, 95, 99, 250, 260, 282, 283

INDEX

Bloch, Marc, 23
Bodaw Paya, 65, 120, 125, 128, 240, 251
Brahmanism, 3, 26, 103, 118, 120, 121, 160, 172, 203, 229, 230, 277, 281
Brahmi script, 45, 46, 115, 194-197, 200, 216, 233
Buddhism, 1-4, 16, 18, 19-22, 24-27, 76, 95, 97-100, 103-105, 107, 108, 110, 112, 115, 118-122, 132, 135, 137, 147-149, 151-154, 160, 161, 172, 195, 203, 207, 211, 214, 215, 217, 218, 220, 223, 224, 229-233, 235, 237, 242, 245, 248, 249, 256-258, 266, 267, 269, 271, 272, 274, 276, 277, 279-286
Buddhasāsana, 3, 9, 13, 43, 98, 101, 117-119, 121, 122, 237, 248, 249
Buddhaghosa, 7, 104, 249
Buddhism in Burma, 120
Buddhism in Lay-mro period, 233
Buddhism in Mrauk Oo period, 238
Buddhism in Dannavadi, 107, 115
Buddhism in Vesālī period, 3, 157, 167, 168, 230
Buddhism in Rakhaing, 4, 5, 19-24, 42, 45, 100, 108, 118, 133, 134, 158, 223, 225, 248, 278, 282,
Buddhism in Sri Lanka, 264, 272, 276,
Buddhism in India, 100
Buddhist Arakanese, 126
Buddhist traditions, 1, 21, 22, 120, 122, 173, 286
Burma, 4, 6, 10, 25, 26, 40, 59, 61, 71-73, 85, 86, 92, 93, 95, 98, 108, 115, 119, 125, 150-152, 170, 233, 234, 238-130, 250, 255, 260, 262, 273, 283
Burmans, 6, 60,
Burmese, 7, 10, 12, 24, 30, 39, 58, 61, 76, 78, 82, 239, 241, 251
Burmese conquest in 1784, 1, 4, 15
Burmese history, 10, 11
Burmese chronicles, 10
Burmese scholars, 11
Burmese/ Arakanese calendar, 38
Burmese forces, 71
Burmese rule, 39, 61
Burmese army, 240
Burmese Literature, 90

C

Cakkinda, Venerable, 13, 136, 255
Candamālālaṅkāra, Venerable, 8, 9, 30, 65, 92, 150, 235

Candamuni Buddha Image, 44, 121, 131,
Candasūriya, king, 79, 91, 100, 102, 108, 112, 115-117, 121, 122, 1240-129, 131, 133, 134, 137, 149, 151, 153, 154, 157, 159, 283, 284
Candrodaya, king, 175, 176, 188
Candrasiri of Sandway, 194
Cave Negrais, 59, 60, 89
Chittagong, 25, 59, 61, 85, 89, 150, 160, 228, 235, 239, 240
Charney, M. Walter, 19, 20, 25
Coedes, Prof. George, 87, 98, 152, 169
Commissioner of Arakan, 4n.3
Collis, M. S., 18, 98, 243,
Cūlavaṁsa, 2, 6, 37
Curnika Pota, 11, 20, 253
Cūlacandra, king, 34, 50, 55, 72, 80, 81

D

Datha Rāzā, king, 35
de Silva, D. G. Bandu, 21, 254
Dīpavaṁsa, 2, 6, 149
Dhammadūta, 249
Dhamma-zeyah, Chief Minister, 11
Dhamma Thein-gyan, Minister Scholar, 10
Dhaka, 33, 240
Dhammapāla, Anagārika, 123
Dutch, 24, 75, 240, 244, 253, 272, 274, 275
Dvencandra *a.k.a.* Maha Taicandra, king, 31, 34, 42, 49, 53, 54, 80, 91, 102, 129, 158, 159, 161, 215

E

Early Buddhism, 99, 136

F

Fa-Hien, 123, 229
Farnando, Dr. P. E., 21, 252, 253
Father Arakan, 5n.4
Forchhammer, Dr. E., 14, 46, 92, 110, 117, 118, 120, 126, 129, 131, 133, 135, 242
Fourth Buddhist Council, 223
Furet, Francois, 23

G

Geiger, William, 6, 175, 268
Goonatilake, Hema, 254
Gotama, the Buddha, 37, 42-46, 58, 59, 101, 102, 107-111, 125, 135, 154, 284
Gutman, Dr. Pamela, 16, 18-20, 24, 87, 88, 120, 126, 151, 152, 170, 174-176, 196-198, 207, 208, 216, 222, 226, 227, 251, 260, 261

Gupta, 70, 120, 158, 162, 168, 193, 194, 201, 205, 207, 210-212, 219, 278

H

Harikela Kingdom, 24, 33
Hinduism, 26, 109, 149, 159, 203, 207
Huen Tsiang, 124

I

Indus River, 67-70,
Indus Valley Civilization, 67, 69
Indian Buddhism, 95, 147, 283
Indianization, 26, of Southeast Asia, 98, 168
Irrawaddy River, 58, 72, 80, 89, 111, 228

J

Jayatilaka, Sir D. B., 21, 253
Jayawardena, Kumari, 23,
Jātakas, 244
Jetavanavihāra, 123, 148, 220, 258
Johnston, Dr. E. H., 16, 18, 93, 94, 109, 172, 175, 176, 198, 201

K

Kala, U, 10, 11,
Kandy, kings of, 253, 266; kingdom, 269, 270, 271, 276, 277
Kan Rāzā Gree, king, 31, 52, 90
Kanbā Long Nge, king, 35
Kawlia, king, 35
Khetta Thurn, king, 35, 39, 81, 235
kingdom of Arakan, 60
Kosalla, U, 198, 216
Kosala Bimbavaṇṇanā, 123
Kulacandra, king, 33

L

Law, Bimala Churn., 6
Lay-mro, 9, 27, 30; period, 33-35, 52, 53, 55, 73, 233, 238, 261, 262, 278; 39-41, 73; River, 81-84, 158, 233, 237; valley, 87, 109; 157, 233; dynasty, 233; kings, 233; 235, 245, 285
Leider, Jacques, 25
Luce, Prof. G. H., 88, 115, 152, 228

M

Magadha, 64, 65, 75, 91, 223, 229, 232
Maung-daung, Sayadaw, 10
Mahinda, Thera, 249, 275
Mahāsammata, king, 9

Mālalasekera, G. P., 6, 115, 266
Manrique, Father Sebastiao, 86, 243,
Mahādeva, Thera, 44, 149, 150, 249
Mahāyāna, 5, 107, 147, 148, 162, 203, 204, 205, 212, 223, 224, 228, 229, 230, 232, 258, 277, 278
Mahābodhi inscription, 234, 262
Mahābodhi temple, 234, 263
Mahāvaṁsa, 2, 6, 20, 37, 149
Mahāvihāra, 7, 148, 224, 250, 257, 258,
Mahāsammata, 9
Mahinsakamandala, 149, 150,
Mahāsaṅgika, 107, 147, 148, 163
Mahāparinibbāna, 116, 147
Mahāmuni, 4, 21, 37, 43, 44, 46, 48, 80, 100, 109, 117, 119, 120, 121, 126-130, 132, 133, 135, 151, 154, 207, 233, 236, 237,250, 251, 284
Mahāvastu, 163, 164, 231
Marshall, Sir John, 67
Maung Ba Thein, 208
Majjhimadesa, 9, 58, 59, 90, 111, 112, 127
Medha Paññā, 11, 37, 226, 279
Mongoloids, 63, 64, 70, 72-74, 76, 81
Mohenjo-Daro, 66-68
Moggaliputtatissa, Thera, 44, 149, 223, 249
Mirando, A. H., 252, 256, 271,
Mindon Min, king, 11, 64,
Mrauk Oo, periods, 9, 30, 39-41, 132, 157, 236, 238, 285; 27, 41; coins, 41; 45, 55, 65, 71-73, 80, 81, 83-86, 90; dynasty, 93; Museum, 115, 211, 212; 118, 119, 121, 130, 131, 158, 160, 161, 165, 167, 171, 176, 195, 201, 202, 208, 216, 235, 239-245, 251, 259, 263, 273, 275
Murn Htee (1283-1389), 35, 72, 73, 233-235, 237, 238, 262
Murn Thein Zan, 209
Mudiyanse, Nandasena, 21, 252-254
Murn Nyo, Minister Phadu, 34, 90, 128
Murn Reng Phru, king, 35
Murn Bon Than, king, 35
Murn Pati, king, 35
Murn Htee, king, 35, 72, 234, 235, 237, 238, 262
Murn Saw Mon *a.k.a.* Narameikhala, king, 35, 41, 55, 130, 131

N

Nan Kyar Nge, king, 35
Nan Kyar Gree, king, 235
Ñāṇa of Rathedaung, Venerable, 8

Nagājunakoṇḍa inscription, 99, 150-152, 207, 227, 228, 259, 260
Nālandamahāvihara, 85, 99, 100, 162, 228, 245, 277, 278, 285
Nehru, Jawahalal, 67
Nga Mae, 8, 9
Nga Murn Nga Tone, king, 34
non-Arakanese scholars, 3,
non-Arakanese scholar on Southeast Asian history, 10
non-Arakanese/Burmese scholars, 7, 30
Nikāyasaṅgāraha, 11, 264
Nīticandra, king, 48, 71, 165-168, 170, 189, 193, 195, 196
Nyanissara, of Burma, 133

O

Okkantha, Ashin Sri, 3, 175
Oo Thar Tun, U, 114, 133, 135, 136

P

Parinibbāna, 31, 36, 38, 44, 117
Paṇḍi, Venerable, 8
Pātaliputta, 9, 43, 100, 114, 154, 229, 249, 285
Pāḷi Canon, 134, 135, 137, 163, 167, 224, 232, 237, 261
Pāḷi works, 5, 133
Pāḷi scripture, 5, 6
Pāḷi commentaries, 5
Pāḷi chronicles, 6, 7
Pāḷi inscriptions, 162-164, 204, 231
Pāḷi literature, 169
Pāḷi, 6, 12, 15, 45, 74, 75, 114, 115, 133-137, 159-164, 167-169, 193, 194, 196, 198, 216, 217, 224, 225, 230-232, 235-237, 249, 255-257, 261, 276
Pāḷi Buddhism, 148, 249
Pe Phru, king, 34
Persian Gulf, 70
Persian, 75, 239
Phayre, Lt. Gen. Sir Arthur A., 4, 4n.3, 10, 19, 19n.29, 20, 32-53, 92, 109, 151, 198
Portuguese, 24, 75, 86, 239, 243, 264-272
Popa Saw Rahan of Bagan, 40, 55,
Prakrit, 76, 159, 224, 231
Ptolemy, 24, 88, 228

R

Ratnacandra, king, 33
Rālamāru, king, 31, 32, 37
Rājacandra, king, 48, 49, 159, 189
Rahula, Venerable Dr. Walpola, 22

Rakkhaṅgadesa, 11, 75, 250, 247, 248, 250, 253, 257, 270, 274, 275
Rakhaing, 1-286
Rakhaing, The Geographical Backgraound of, 58-63
Rakhaing, Flora and Fauna of, 63
Rakhaing, definitions of, 74, 75
Rakhaing, inhabitants and languages of, 75-78
Rakhaing cities, 233
Rakhaing chronicles, 6, 31, 34, 36-39, 51-54, 64, 65, 161, 236, 249, 250, 262
Rakhaing people, 1, 2, 5, 7, 64, 71, 75-78, 133
Rakhaing's location, 1
Rakhaing history, 1, 2, 4, 12, 13, 18, 63, 64, 239
Rakhaing kings, 4, 65, 74
Rakhaing studies, 2, 13, 110, 133
Rakhaing's coastal strip, 3
Rakhaing inscriptions, 14
Rakhaing language and Rakhaing scripts (*Rakkhavaṇṇa*), 12, 166, 193, 233, 236
Rakhaing culture, 4, 27, 136
Rakhaing literary sources, 19
Rakhaing vocabulary, 78
Rakhaing Empire, 95
Rāzawon, 2, 8, 9, 100, 135, 171,
Raymond, Dr. Catherine, 254, 262

S

Sammatarazā *a.k.a.* Aggo Puñña Zaw, king, 41, 50, 55
San Tha Aung, Prof., 13, 18, 108, 110, 115-118, 165, 167, 169, 196, 197, 198, 207-210, 213, 214, 216-219, 221, 222, 255
Sandamuni, U, 194,
San Shwe Bu, 13, 18, 89, 222
Sangāyanā, Buddhist council, 5, 44, 100, 149, 223-227, 230, 235, 249, 259, 261, 276-280, 286
Sandoway, 60, 61, 71, 75, 100, 198, 263
Sappadānapakāraṇa, 46, 110, 126, 129, 133, 135
Sāsanavaṁsa, 6, 252, 262, 273
Sarvāstivāda, 162, 224, 225
Satthubimba Sutta, 5, 22, 133, 136, 137, 147
Sanskrit, 3, 12, 15, 76, 130, 136, 148, 159-164, 167-169, 172, 176, 193-198, 200, 202, 204, 205, 221, 223-225, 229-232, 234, 245, 285
Saw Prai Nyo, Suvaṇṇadevi, 11, 50
Selagiri, 97, 108, 109, 115, 116, 124, 126, 170

Shwe Zan, U, 13, 194
Shit Thaung Pagoda, 15, 93, 118, 160, 165, 167, 176, 200, 201, 243
Schouten, Wouter, 243
Southeast Asia, 1, 10, 21, 25, 73, 76, 87, 95, 98, 99, 108, 133, 149, 159, 168, 172, 205, 206, 223, 241, 248, 249, 272, 276, 282-284, 286
Southeast Asian history, 4, 10,
Southeast Asian historians, 15, 169
Southeast Asian chronicles, 9
South Asia and Southeast Asia, 1, 25, 248, 286
Sri Lankan Buddhism, 148, 261
Sinhalese Theravada Pali Buddhism, 276
Singhacandra, king, 11, 33, 50, 315
Sri Lanka, 3-5, 87, 123, 126, 130, 148, 149, 174, 175, 193, 194, 204-206, 220, 223, 225-228, 230-232, 234-239, 244, 247-252, 254-259, 261-264, 272-277, 279, 280, 285, 286
Ceylon, 1, 3, 6, 11, 16, 20-22, 98, 100, 108, 129, 131, 249, 251, 259-262, 276, 277
Sricandra *a.k.a.* Sridhammavijaya, king, 11, 36, 225
Sri Lanka scholars, 20
srivatsa, 93, 159
Silamegha, king, 174, 175, 261
Sircar, Dr., 34, 47, 53, 93, 94, 109, 165, 172, 201, 208, 260
Sittway Plain, 26, 62
Sittway District, 61
Sūriyacakka, king, 9, 43, 44, 131
Sūriyacitta, king, 31
Sūriyaketu, king, 33, 52
Sūriyarenu, king, 36, 39, 40, 52

T

Taungbauk Gree Inscription, 45, 113, 114
Tun Shwe Khine, U, 13, 71, 170, 196-198, 209, 216, 222, 255
Than Tun, Dr., 59
Theravāda, 5, 9, 26, 107, 148, 162, 204, 223-225, 230, 231, 232, 244, 245, 249, 255, 256, 273, 276, 280
Theravāda Buddhism, 19, 46, 47, 135, 170, 206, 229, 245, 250, 255, 278
Thin Kyi, Dr., 57, 59
Tipiṭaka, 130, 236, 237, 244, 277, 280
Tibeto Burman peoples, 74, 76
Tosh, John, 30
Twelve provinces of Banga, 160

U

Upasaṁpadā, higher ordination, 252, 255, 256, 270, 274-276
Upasakā, 173, 211

U San Hla, 34
U Nyunt Han, 35, 109

V

Vattagamani Abaya, king, 223
Van Galen, S. E. Arie, 25
Vimaladhammasuriya I, 254, 264, 269-271, 273
Vimaladhammasuriya II, 252, 254, 257, 264, 272-276
Vīracandra, king, 165, 166, 167, 170

W

Wagenaar, Dr. Lodevijk, 21, 250, 254

www.ingramcontent.com/pod-product-compliance
Lightning Source LLC
Chambersburg PA
CBHW050848160426
43194CB00011B/2070
* 9 7 8 0 6 1 5 9 4 0 4 4 1 *